ACLS History E-Book Project

Reprint Series

The ACLS History E-Book Project (www.historyebook.org) collaborates with constituent societies of the American Council of Learned Societies, publishers, librarians and historians to create an electronic collection of works of high quality in the field of history. This volume is produced from digital images created for the Project by the Scholarly Publishing Office and the Digital Library Production Service at the University of Michigan, Ann Arbor. The digital reformatting process results in an electronic version of the text that can be both accessed online and used to create new print copies. This book and hundreds of others are available online in the History E-Book Project through subscription.

Many of the works in the History E-Book Project are available in print and can be ordered either directly from their publishers or as part of this series. For information refer to the online Title Record page for each book. Inquiries regarding this series can be directed to info@hebook.org.

ACLS
HISTORY E-BOOK

http://www.historyebook.org

UNIVERSITY OF CALIFORNIA PUBLICATIONS IN HISTORY

VOLUME XXXI

FUR TRADERS IN SIBERIA

THE RUSSIAN FUR TRADE
1550-1700

BY

RAYMOND H. FISHER

UNIVERSITY OF CALIFORNIA PRESS
BERKELEY AND LOS ANGELES
1943

University of California Publications in History
Editors (Berkeley): R. J. Kerner, G. H. Guttridge, F. L. Paxson

Volume 31, pp. xii + 1–276, frontis., 2 illus., 1 map

Submitted by editors December 11, 1940
Issued December 4, 1943
Price, Cloth $3.00
Paper $2.25

University of California Press
Berkeley and Los Angeles
California

Cambridge University Press
London, England

PRINTED IN THE UNITED STATES OF AMERICA

PREFACE

To many Americans, even in the world of scholarship, the Russian fur trade brings to mind Alaska and California. Few, apparently, realize that in Russia itself and later in Siberia the Russians carried on a traffic in furs which far exceeded their Alaskan trade and which was an intimate part of the expansion of the Russian people, an expansion which by historical accident happened to spend its momentum in North America instead of in Eurasia. From earliest times the Russians trafficked in the skins of the animals inhabiting the then forest-covered plains of Eastern Europe. For several centuries the Russians supplied Europe with most of its furs. And always, as on our own continent, their trade in furs fathered exploration. Thus both as a means of livelihood and as a vital force in the expansion of the Russian people the fur trade occupied a place of high importance in the history of Russia.

By virtue of a heightened demand for furs and of the opening of Siberia to Russian occupation the Russian fur trade attained its greatest extent during the century and a half from 1550 to 1700. It is with this period of the trade that this study is chiefly concerned. The importance of the fur trade in Russian history has long been recognized by students of that history, but so far no one, either in Russia, Europe, or America, has attempted to work out both the details of its organization and conduct and its place in the larger setting of Russia's economic development during the sixteenth and seventeenth centuries, usually referred to as the Muscovite period. That, therefore, is the twofold purpose of this investigation. It serves also to develop in detail one phase of the historical thesis set forth by Professor Robert J. Kerner, of the Department of History at the University of California, Berkeley, in his recently published essay, *The Urge to the Sea.*

The present monograph is the outgrowth of my graduate study under Professor Kerner. It was he whose vivid grasp of history first aroused in me an interest in the history of Russia and who suggested the Russian fur trade as a topic for investigation. From his historical knowledge and background I have borrowed liberally, in ways that do not lend themselves to acknowledgment through the stilted medium of footnote citations. To him I express my gratitude for those years of graduate study that have been rich in their results.

I wish to add a word of appreciation to the late Professor James Westfall Thompson, of the Department of History, and to Professors George R. Noyes, Alexander S. Kaun, and George Z. Patrick, of the Department of Slavic Languages, all at the University of California, Berkeley, for contributions to my researches, both direct and indirect.

It has been my good fortune to have carried on this research in conjunction with Dr. George V. Lantzeff, who has written an excellent study in a related field, *Siberia in the Seventeenth Century: A Study in Colonial Administration* (Berkeley, 1943). The value of his assistance in overcoming the difficulties of a language new to me and of the discussions with him of common problems of research perhaps only I can fully appreciate. I am indebted, too, to Mr. J. Gordon Spaulding, of Stockton Junior College, who has contributed much towards clarity of style and who helped me find the forest when I was lost for the trees. To Dr. Lewis W. Bealer is due appreciation for his able technical assistance in matters of bibliography. To my wife, Mary Corley Fisher, and to my father, C. E. Fisher, goes my appreciation for their help in preparing the manuscript. The task has been less arduous because of their assistance.

RAYMOND H. FISHER

Humboldt State College
Arcata, California
October, 1943

CONTENTS

ILLUSTRATIONS

MAP

ABBREVIATIONS

A.A.E.	*Akty arkheograficheskoi ekspeditsii* (16)
A.I.	*Akty istoricheskie* (39)
Chteniia	*Chteniia v imperatorskom obshchestve istorii i drevnostei rossiiskikh pri moskovskom universitete* (186)
D.A.I.	*Dopolneniia k aktam istoricheskim* (40)
P.S.Z.	*Polnoe sobranie zakonov rossiiskoi imperii s 1649 goda* (46)
R.I.B.	*Russkaia istoricheskaia biblioteka* (43)
Zh.M.N.P.	*Zhurnal ministerstva narodnago prosveshcheniia* (247)
Ogloblin	N. N. Ogloblin, *Obozrenie stolbtsov i knig sibirskago prikaza (1592–1768 gg.)* (35)

These abbreviations are used in the notes. The number in parentheses after each title indicates its place in the classified bibliography, where a full description may be found.

TRANSLITERATION AND SPELLING

The system of transliteration used herein is that followed by the Library of Congress. In the text the new and simplified system of spelling adopted by the Soviet government has been followed. In the footnotes and Bibliography the spelling used by the work cited has been kept, with this exception: *e* has been used to transliterate both *e* and ѣ.

Several Russian words have been used frequently in the textual matter. Consequently, these words, such as *promyshlennik, volost, voevoda,* and the units of currency, have been used like English words and so pluralized, that is, with *s* instead of the Russian *y, i, a,* or *ia.* Also, the soft sign has been omitted. Other Russian words, appearing but once or twice or used appositively or parenthetically, have been spelled and pluralized as Russian words. To assist the reader not familiar with the Russian language an effort has been made to suggest an approximate pronunciation of those Russian words appearing two or three times or oftener. Where the English transliteration gives the approximate pronunciation, an accent mark over the stressed syllable, upon first use of the word, has been deemed sufficient. Where the English transliteration of a word might be misleading, the pronunciation has been given parenthetically.

INDEX OF RUSSIAN TERMS

This list includes those Russian words which appear in the text twice or oftener. On the page indicated a definition or explanation of the meaning of the word is to be found.

CHAPTER I

THE EARLY RUSSIAN FUR TRADE

TRADE IN FURS is one of the oldest economic activities in Russia. In early times great forests, since then largely cut over, covered the Eastern European plains, and these forests abounded in animals with valuable fur pelts.[1] Naturally and inevitably those ancient Slavs who were the ancestors of the Russian people and who settled these forests turned to the exploitation of the pelts of these animals as a means of livelihood.[2] By the time of the coming in the ninth century of the Varangians, who gave political organization to these Slavs, the trade in furs had already become preëminent in their economic life.

THE FUR TRADE IN KIEVAN RUSSIA

The first Russian state, the Kievan Russia of the ninth to thirteenth centuries, had its basis in trade and commerce, which was carried on by its merchant-princes, who with their retinue or *druzhina* combined trading with fighting and ruling. They exchanged the raw products of their land, especially forest products, for the finished goods and luxuries of the Near East and for goods from Europe. Traveling, sometimes in boat caravans along the network of rivers of the Russian plain, sometimes overland, the Russian merchants carried their goods to Constantinople for trade with the Byzantines or to Itil at the mouth of the Volga and to "the great Bolgar town" at the juncture of the Kama and Volga rivers, trade centers which were visited by the Arabs and Khozars. They likewise pushed westward into Hungary and Bohemia and there established commercial relations with Europe.[3] In the eleventh and twelfth centuries Kiev itself flourished as a trade center visited by the merchants of Russia, the Near East, and Europe.

Of the various raw products traded by the Russians the most important single article was furs. The worth of the furs sold exceeded that of any of the other Russian wares, except possibly

[1] P. P. Mel'gunov, *Ocherki po istorii russkoi torgovli IX–XVIII v.v.*, p. 2.

[2] V. O. Kliuchevskii, *History of Russia*, I, 41, 50.

[3] S. M. Solov'ev, *Istoriia Rossii s drevneishikh vremen*, I, 248–249; M. Pogodin, "Drevniaia russkaia torgovlia," *Zh.M.N.P.*, XLVIII (1845), 95–109; P. Savel'ev, "O torgovle volzhskikh bulgar v IX i X veke," *Zh.M.N.P.*, Vol. XLIX (1846), pt. 2, pp. 33–34, 48–49.

slaves.[4] In the foreign markets where the Russians traded, their country was known as a land of furs[5]—a reputation valid even today—and Kiev was known as the storehouse of the European fur trade and the first city in Europe in that trade.[6] The high quality of the Russian furs made them an article everywhere in great demand, for even in southern countries luxurious furs were required for purposes of dress and display. Their great abundance in the more northerly regions of Russia gave to the Russians the means for acquiring the commodities and manufactures which they themselves could not, or did not, produce. From the Byzantines and Arabs they obtained wines, fruits, cloth and fine textiles, especially silk, as well as gold and silver, glassware, jewels, ship supplies, and arms.[7] From Bohemia and Hungary they brought gold and silver, glass, horses, and goods manufactured in Germany and Italy.[8] Since for the most part such goods represented the more advanced Byzantine and Arabic cultures, many of the features of which the Russians quickly adopted, the fur trade must be considered of fundamental importance to Kievan Russia.

The economic importance of furs is evident in the political significance attached to them. As a sign of submission to the princes of Kievan Russia the subject tribes annually paid tribute or *dan*. This tribute was paid oftenest in furs,[9] and was the means by which the princes, who were at the same time the merchants, obtained their furs for trade. Consequently, an assured supply of furs was so essential to the tribes that each tribe laid claim to particular hunting grounds as its own, and the entrance of other tribes into those areas was cause for war, while the individual invader risked attack and death.[10]

After an existence of more than four centuries the fur trade of Kievan Russia came to an end, and the center of the Russian fur trade shifted to the north. The decline of the fur trade in the south followed inevitably from the exhaustion of the fur resources of

---

[4] Solov'ev, *loc. cit.;* Pogodin, pp. 111–112; Savel'ev, pp. 36–38; Kliuchevskii, *op. cit.*, I, 185; *The Russian Primary Chronicle*, Harvard Studies and Notes in Philology and Literature, XII, 129; M. N. Berezhkov, *O torgovle Rusi s Gansoi do kontsa XV veka*, pp. 31–32.

[5] M. N. Pokrovskii, *History of Russia*, p. 33.

[6] Mel'gunov, p. 39.

[7] Kliuchevskii, *op. cit.*, I, 83; I. M. Kulisher, *Istoriia russkogo narodnogo khoziaistva*, I, 17–18; Savel'ev, pp. 46–47; Pogodin, *loc. cit.*

[8] Mel'gunov, p. 45.

[9] *The Russian Primary Chronicle*, pp. 147, 157, 164, 168, 180.

[10] M. N. Pokrovskii, *Ocherk istorii russkoi kultury*, I, 40–41.

the forest regions of the Dnepr River basin through several centuries of drawing upon them. This decline of the fur trade was a part of the general decline of the commercial state of Kiev and contributed greatly to the latter's collapse by depriving it of its chief article of export. In so far as they no longer possessed an abundance of furs, the Russians turned from an exchange economy to an agricultural economy—and to a concomitant feudalism—in order to gain a livelihood.[11] This transformation was in process for several decades before the final destruction of both the Kievan state and the fur trade of the south at the hands of the Mongols and Tatars between 1238 and 1240, and it tended to continue in the Suzdal region to the northeast, whither the bulk of the Russian population of the Dnepr migrated. In this upper Volga region the furs were of an inferior sort, the Russians no longer had ready access to the Black Sea markets, and the markets of the lower Volga and Dnepr rivers had been destroyed by the Mongol-Tatar invasions; thus agriculture became the basis of the economy of this new Russian center.[12] But the Russian fur trade itself did not disappear. It moved to the towns of the north and became centered at Novgorod, always an important source of furs,[13] which now became the outstanding Russian trade center.

The Fur Trade of Novgorod

The appearance of Novgorod in the thirteenth century as the preeminent commercial city of Russia was the result of both internal and external circumstances. Within Russia, Novgorod was not faced with any formidable competition, either economic or political. The Mongol-Tatar invasions had smashed the Kievan state but had left Novgorod virtually untouched. No other town of comparable importance existed in the north, and it was to be more than two centuries before the Russians of Suzdal freed themselves from the Tatar yoke. The northern trade route along the upper Volga was controlled by Novgorod, so that it was able to maintain contact with Asiatic markets. Novgorod's dominance was further consolidated by gaining access to the markets of Western Europe through the great Hanseatic League, of which it became a part in the thirteenth century. When extending their commercial

[11] Henri Pirenne, *Medieval Cities*, pp. 48–49, 54–55.

[12] Mel'gunov, pp. 23, 96; Kliuchevskii, *op. cit.*, V, 205; V. I. Ogorodnikov, *Zavoevanie russkimi Sibiri*, p. 4.

[13] A. I. Nikitskii, *Istoriia ekonomicheskago byta velikago Novgoroda*, p. 15.

power over much of the Baltic the merchants of Lübeck first established trade connections with Novgorod through Wisby on the island of Gothland late in the twelfth century.[14] Then, in 1270, direct connections with Novgorod were established when the German merchants gained the monopoly right to trade and to maintain a factory there.[15] Despite an inland location, Novgorod's geographical position was for that time favorable, since the passage to the Baltic by way of the Volkhov River and Lake Ladoga was easy, and so situated it became one of the most important Hanseatic factories.[16] The flourishing of the Hanse in the fourteenth century made Novgorod the northernmost point of a major trade route and gave to it a preëminence in northern Russia which lasted for more than two hundred years.

The role of the fur trade in Novgorod was the same as it had been in Kievan Russia: furs constituted the most important single commodity of export.[17] Since Novgorod was even less self-sufficient economically than Kiev, furs were essential to supplying its wants from abroad.[18] These were chiefly manufactured goods, and they made up the bulk of Novgorod's imports. They consisted primarily of cloth and fabrics, ready-made clothing, metals of several kinds, plate and glassware, wines and confections, arms, and many other articles. Sometimes the local supplies of grain, salt, and fish were inadequate, and they too had to be imported.[19] The trade in furs was conducted on a wholesale basis, and the furs circulated in large numbers, "in thousands, half-thousands, quarter-thousands, forties, dozens, tens, and fives, rarely in ones."[20] Big consignments of them were sent to Lübeck and Hamburg, and from there to London, Ghent, Bruges, and even Genoa.[21] Novgorod possessed virtually a monopoly of them, which assured to it its place in the system of exchange not only in the Baltic,[22] but also in Western Europe. The great number of its furs, the reputation for fine quality of Russian furs, and membership in the greatest commercial organization in Western Europe made Novgorod the world's center of the fur trade.

The exhausting exploitation of natural resources, which was the basis of Novgorod's economic life, required extensive areas upon

[14] *Ibid.*, p. 30. [15] *Ibid.*, p. 33.

[16] Emil Brass, *Aus dem Reiche der Pelze*, I, 120.

[17] Nikitskii, pp. 164–165; L. K. Goetz, *Deutsch-russische Handelsgeschichte des Mittelalters*, p. 248.

[18] Nikitskii, p. 5.

[19] Berezhkov, pp. 159–168; Nikitskii, pp. 155–164; Solov'ev, I, 710.

[20] Berezhkov, p. 174; Nikitskii, p. 164.

[21] Brass, I, 7. [22] Pokrovskii, *History of Russia*, p. 77.

which to draw. Access to such areas made possible Novgorod's greatness.[23] Great forest regions, fabulously rich in valuable furs and other raw products, lay to the northeast of Novgorod. Into these forests the Novgorodans penetrated far in quest of furs, advancing by river and portage first into the basin of the Northern Dvina River, then into the Pechora River basin, and finally into the region of the northern Ural Mountains and the Ob River.

Over this northland area Novgorod established an extensive sphere of influence or what may be designated loosely a colonial empire.[24] Novgorod's dominion over it was "vague and fluctuating, often no more than a commercial monopoly." As a free republican city, whose leaders were primarily interested in trade, it did not develop a definite colonial policy. There was, to be sure, a colonization movement from Novgorod into the Dvina River basin which brought into existence several settlements. But this colonization was undertaken by the Novgorod *boiárs* (nobles) who staked out *vótchinas* (patrimonial landed estates) that were feudal in character and often isolated from one another by stretches of dense forest.[25] Beyond the presence in some of the communities of a representative of the Novgorod town council and occasional punitive expeditions into the area Novgorod was content with having its sovereignty recognized and with being free to carry on trade there. In the Pechora country and the region of the Urals, where the colonization movement from Novgorod did not reach, the only manifestation of Novgorod's sovereignty was the imposition of tribute upon the natives, and that not even regularly.[26] Beyond this Novgorod did not interfere in the lives of the natives, who on occasions even successfully resisted the collection of tribute by the military expeditions sent to exact it.[27] Thus, although Novgorod fully exploited the fur and other resources of the Russian north, it

---

[23] Nikitskii, p. 5; Pokrovskii, *History of Russia*, pp. 76–77.

[24] The provinces over which Novgorod claimed jurisdiction are named, with its princes, in the treaties of the thirteenth to fifteenth centuries. *Sobranie gosudarstvennykh gramot i dogovorov*, I, 1, 3, 6, 13, 19; *A.A.E.*, I, 42, 63–64, 67.

[25] V. A. Popov, "Dvizhenie narodonaseleniia v vologodskoi gubernii," *Zapiski imperatorskago russkago geograficheskago obshchestva po otdeleniiu statistiki*, II (1871), 75; V. O. Kliuchevskii, *Opyty i issledovaniia*, pp. 4–5.

[26] *The Chronicle of Novgorod, 1016–1417*, pp. 6, 33, 36, 202–203; "Letopis' nikonovskaia," *Polnoe sobranie russkikh letopisei*, IX, 79; A. V. Oksenov, "Politicheskiia otnosheniia moskovskago gosudarstva k iugorskoi zemle," *Zh.M.N.P.*, CCLXXIII (1891), 247.

[27] *The Chronicle of Novgorod, loc. cit.;* E. K. Ogorodnikov, "Pribrezh'ia ledovitago i belago morei s ikh pritokami po knige bol'shago chertezha," *Zapiski imperatorskago russkago geograficheskago obshchestva po otdeleniiu etnografii*, VII (1877), 23–24.

failed to establish there a well-entrenched political organization, and the comparative ease with which Moscow later supplanted Novgorod in this region testifies to the weakness of the latter's control over it.

The easternmost part of Novgorod's colonial empire commands particular interest for the fur trade. This region was known to the Novgorodans as Iugra and embraced the territory along both sides of the northern Urals, extending eastward to the Ob River.[28] It was the northwestern corner of what later became Siberia. The chronicles indicate that the quest for furs led the Novgorodans into the trans-Ural country as early as the eleventh century;[29] they were thus the first Russians, and the first Europeans, to penetrate into Siberia and to exploit its wealth. However, the great distance of Iugra from Novgorod prevented them from more than skimming the resources there. But the knowledge of this country was never lost to the Russians; it always beckoned the more hardy adventurers with promises of rich returns, and as settlement moved eastward in the north and the fur supply dwindled, Iugra excited an increasing interest among the Russian fur traders.

The conduct of Novgorod's fur trade was in the hands of the big merchant capitalists and wealthy boiars,[30] who were also the political leaders of the city republic. This was necessarily so. The large-scale dimensions of the fur trade gave rise to practices which precluded the participation of small traders and made it a business in which only the man possessing large capital, political influence, and a strong and sizable organization could hope to succeed.[31] Great distances into the hinterland were traversed in the search for furs; a political instrument, the armed band, was one of the established means of acquiring furs; settlements were built in the wild forest regions of the Dvina for the commercial-industrial exploitation of their wealth; and it was necessary to counteract the activities of the German merchants at Novgorod, who employed shrewd agents to preserve their interests and who maintained close mutual relations.[32] Hence, wherever the fur trade was undertaken, in the in-

[28] E. K. Ogorodnikov, p. 20.

[29] "Letopis' nikonovskaia," *loc. cit.; The Russian Primary Chronicle*, p. 275; N. M. Karamzin, *Istoriia gosudarstva rossiisskago*, Vol. II, *Primechanie* No. 64; E. K. Ogorodnikov, pp. 22–23.

[30] Sigismund von Herberstein, *Notes upon Russia*, II, 25.

[31] S. F. Platonov, *Proshloe russkogo severa*, pp. 15–16.

[32] *Ibid.*, pp. 16–17. Note Popov, pp. 73–75, which relate the purchase in 1315 of a tract of land along the Vaga River by the Novgorod family, the Svoezemtsevy, who paid the native princes 20,000 squirrel skins for it.

terior or at Novgorod itself, it was the undertaking of the big businessman.

The fur merchants obtained their furs in three ways. First, there was the tribute taken from the natives. Armed bands were organized by the merchants and boiars and sent out to requisition furs as tribute.[33] This method prevailed particularly in the regions of the Pechora and Iugra, where Russian settlement only later penetrated; however, it was also used in the Dvina country. The second method was trade with the natives. Agents, supplied with knives, swords, axes, and cheap trinkets, were sent out to exchange them with the natives for squirrel, marten, sable, and other pelts.[34] The third method was one of obtaining furs directly. Those merchants with votchinas in the Dvina region maintained their own trappers and stations, obtaining furs without recourse to the natives.[35]

Smolensk: A Minor Center of the Fur Trade

Kiev dominated the Russian fur trade up to the thirteenth century; Novgorod dominated it after that; yet neither city was entirely free of competition from other Russian towns. Typical and most important of these other towns whose inhabitants engaged in the fur trade was Smolensk, strategically situated between Kiev and Novgorod on the upper Dnepr River. Entering upon the stage of Russian commerce in the twelfth century, when Kiev was beginning to decline, Smolensk duplicated the pattern of Kiev's economic life in practically all respects. It possessed its merchant-princes and their druzhinas, who imposed tribute in furs and other forest products upon the natives under their jurisdiction. These merchant-princes carried their furs and other goods to the same markets—the Volga towns, Constantinople, Hungary, and Bohemia—and exchanged them for the same kinds of goods as did the Kievans. However, where Constantinople was the biggest market for the Kievans, Itil and other Volga centers, visited by Khozar, Bulgar, and Arab merchants, were the principal markets for the Smoliane.[36]

During the Mongol-Tatar invasions Smolensk was fortunate

[33] *The Chronicle of Novgorod,* pp. 26, 33; *The Russian Primary Chronicle,* p. 275.

[34] I. V. Shcheglov, *Khronologicheskii perechen' vazhneishikh dannykh iz istorii Sibiri,* p. 5; Nikitskii, p. 98; Karamzin, Vol. II, p. 45, *Primechanie,* No. 64.

[35] Platonov, p. 18.

[36] I. M. Krasnoperov, "Ocherk promyshlennosti i torgovli smolenskago kniazhestva s drevneishikh vremen do XV veka," *Istoricheskoe obozrenie,* I (1894), 65–68, 70–78.

enough to escape the worst of their ravages, and it continued to develop its economic life. This life now became a copy, on a smaller scale, of the economy of Novgorod: that is, the town exported furs and other products of the forest and imported Western goods. The Mongol-Tatar invasions had largely destroyed the markets and trade routes to the south of Smolensk, so the Smoliane turned northward and imposed tribute upon their culturally inferior neighbors, the Lithuanians, the payment being made chiefly in furs. Meanwhile the German merchants had begun their penetration into the Baltic region, so Smolensk, like Novgorod, underwent the transformation from dependence upon the Russian market to a free and active commerce with Europe. By treaty in 1229 the Smoliane established regular trade relations with the German merchants. The Western Dvina River and the port of Riga afforded Smolensk its outlet to the Baltic. Furs constituted a principal export. They were obtained in the areas south of Novgorod's colonial domain in much the same ways that the Novgorodans obtained theirs. Relations between Smolensk and the Germans remained friendly and profitable for about a century. Then in the fifteenth century, with the attempt of the German merchants to exclude the Russian merchants from Livonia and the Baltic, those relations deteriorated. In the meantime, Lithuania arose as a political power which threatened to engulf Smolensk, and the town's fur resources began to diminish, since it did not have access to a hinterland as rich in furs as that of Novgorod. By the sixteenth century Smolensk ceased to be of importance in the fur trade.[37]

Furs as Currency

In Kievan Russia and Novgorod furs served in a special capacity which they later lost. During their early history the Russians lived under a natural economy in which much of their trade was a direct exchange of goods for goods, as against a money economy.[38] Nevertheless, the need for a medium of exchange or a standard of value existed. Silver and gold were then not yet available in sufficient amounts for them alone to be utilized for that purpose, and so the Russians had to resort to other goods of value. Furs were one of the goods most used, since they possessed permanence of value, a degree of durability, and were easily transported.[39] Thus, besides

[37] *Ibid.*, pp. 79–92, 96–97, 110–111.
[38] Nikitskii, p. 98.
[39] V. V. Sviatlovskii, *Primitivno-torgovoe gosudarstvo, kak forma byta*, pp. 64–65.

passing from hand to hand in the market as commodities, fur pelts circulated as money and, when serving in such a capacity, were called *kuný,* an early Russian word for martens.[40] Not only the whole pelt, but also parts of the fur pelt circulated as currency and represented definite values. The term *kuná,* the singular of kuny, applied to one of these units and was equivalent to the Arabic *dirgem* of the ninth and tenth centuries. The *nogáta* and the *rézana* were two other such units, although what part of the fur pelt any one of these three units represented has not been determined definitely.[41] In the course of time furs were less used as currency and were gradually supplanted by silver, which, although known to have been coined in Russia as early as the tenth century, began extensively to replace furs as currency only in the fifteenth century.[42] Still, for nearly two hundred years more, furs continued to be used as a medium of exchange.

End of Novgorod's Dominance

After two centuries of domination by Novgorod, from the middle of the thirteenth to the middle of the fifteenth century, the Russian fur trade ceased to be the virtual monopoly of the Novgorodan merchant-capitalists. The domination of the Russian fur trade by Novgorod disappeared when the city-republic lost both its colonial empire and its own political independence and when new centers of the fur trade, both domestic and export, arose to share the trade with Novgorod. As a result, although Novgorod well into the sixteenth century ranked as the foremost center where furs were traded, the Russian fur trade at the opening of that century was conducted on a new and broader basis.

Novgorod's loss of its colonial empire and of its political independence came at the hands of the Grand Prince of Moscow, Ivan III. The city itself was brought under the power of Moscow in the course of the years 1471–1478, its colonial domain during a longer period, 1465–1499.[43] Since this colonial domain was the source of Novgorod's fur supply, the loss of it meant the end of the Novgo-

[40] Nikitskii, p. 101; Krasnoperov, p. 94.

[41] Krasnoperov, p. 94; Nikitskii, pp. 101–104; Kliuchevskii, *History of Russia,* I, 137–138.

[42] Kliuchevskii, *History of Russia,* I, 138–139; cf. *The Chronicle of Novgorod,* p. 189.

[43] I. D. Beliaev, "O geograficheskikh svedeniiakh v drevnei Rossii," *Zapiski imperatorskago russkago geograficheskago obshchestva,* VI (1852), 240–241, 244–250.

rodan control of the Russian fur trade. There can be no doubt that Ivan understood the significance of this fact, understood that by seizing the regions from which Novgorod's furs came he was striking a severe blow at the economic independence, and therefore at the political independence, of Novgorod. His actions attest this. Prior to attacking Novgorod itself he seized the Dvina territory, thereby cutting Novgorod off from its eastern possessions.[44] Ivan and his predecessors knew of the animal wealth of the north, a fact confirmed by the thorough knowledge of the country which Ivan's forces displayed in conquering the territory.[45] Moreover, Ivan's first attack upon Novgorod's empire was directed against Iugra, noted for its fur and silver wealth, and in 1499 his forces established the town of Pustozersk near the mouth of the Pechora River in the heart of the fur country, while at the end of the conquest of that empire Moscow imposed tribute upon the natives.[46] All these actions assert Ivan's desire to profit from the fur resources of the northland. But he was not content with acquiring territorial control of Novgorod's colonial dominions. He went further. Following his conquest of the city in 1478, he transferred the city's most notable families to the interior of Russia, replacing them with loyal Muscovite settlers. This step smashed the political and economic power of these families and with it their domination of the fur trade. No longer would these family corporations send out military forces to requisition furs from the natives; no longer would the trading activities of the Russian world or the exclusive conduct of the commerce with the West[47] reside only in the hands of the Novgorodan merchant-capitalists.

Appearance of New Centers

Yet even before Ivan interfered, the limitation of Novgorod's preeminent position and the end of the commercial monopoly of its merchants were foreshadowed in the growth of new trade centers in Russia. Particularly in the north, towns arose which, in the fifteenth and early sixteenth centuries, developed their trade in furs to such an extent that they became new domestic centers of the fur trade. The appearance and growth of these towns were the result of

[44] *Ibid.*, p. 241.

[45] C. R. Beazley, "The Russian Expansion towards Asia and the Arctic in the Middle Ages (to 1500)," *American Historical Review*, XIII (1907–1908), 737; Beliaev, p. 245.

[46] Beliaev, p. 248.

[47] N. I. Kostomarov, *Ocherki torgovli moskovskago gosudarstva*, pp. 235–236.

the colonial expansion from Novgorod and Suzdal, of which the fur traders formed the vanguard. The origins of some of the northern towns dated as far back even as the eleventh and twelfth centuries, although little is known of their intervening history. It can only be assumed, with reason, that since the north was unsuited to the cultivation of grain,[48] trade in furs and other forest products, conducted on a small scale by hardy adventurers and by agents of the Novgorod merchants, constituted the economic life of these towns.

The foremost and oldest of the northern towns was Kholmogory, situated on the Northern Dvina River near its mouth and dating back probably to the eleventh century.[49] Here since the beginning of the fifteenth century a market had been held annually in which furs were the biggest item of trade.[50] The most important northern center of the fur trade was Ustiug, at the junction of the Iug River with the Sukhona, a tributary of the Dvina. Its origins are lost in the obscurity of the twelfth century.[51] In the fifteenth century there was carried on at Ustiug an active trade in furs, which were obtained along the Dvina and Vaga rivers or from the neighboring tribes to the east—the Voguls, Pechorans, and Permiaks—and from Russian trappers who penetrated deep into the forests of the northeast.[52] A town of earlier origin than Ustiug was Vologda, founded some time before 1147.[53] Its situation on the Vologda River, a tributary of the Sukhona, placed it on the routes from both Novgorod and Moscow to the Dvina and rendered its importance that of a transit point, though some of its furs were obtained from the surrounding regions.[54] Late in the fifteenth century or early in the sixteenth two centers of the fur trade arose in the country of the Mezen River, the basin lying between the Dvina and the Pechora and inhabited by Samoeds. One of these was Lampozhnia, where two annual fairs were held that were visited by Russians and Ta-

[48] Popov, II, 67, 96; Von Herberstein, II, 25, 31, 35–36; V. O. Kliuchevskii, *Skazaniia inostrantsev o moskovskom gosudarstve*, p. 181.

[49] E. K. Ogorodnikov, p. 118.

[50] "Anglorum navigatio ad Moscovitas," *Historiae ruthenicae scriptores exteri saeculi XVI*, I, 10; Heinrich von Staden, *Aufzeichnungen über den moskauer Staat*, p. 194.

[51] Kliuchevskii, *Skazaniia inostrantsev*, p. 255; E. K. Ogorodnikov, p. 156; Popov, p. 68.

[52] Paulus Iovius, "The History . . . of the Legation or Ambassade of Great Basilius, Prince of Moscouia, to Pope Clement VII," Hakluyt Society Works, XII, 242–243; Von Herberstein, II, 36.

[53] E. K. Ogorodnikov, pp. 178–179; Popov, p. 67.

[54] Von Herberstein, I, 115, II, 35; Popov, *loc. cit.*; Von Staden, p. 143.

tars and by the Samoeds who supplied the furs.[55] The other was the settlement of Mezen itself.[56] Still farther east on the Pechora was the previously mentioned Pustozersk, founded at the end of the fifteenth century.[57] It was frequented by Samoeds, who exchanged sables from across the Urals for linen, kettles, and foodstuffs. In fact, during a large part of the sixteenth century the whole of the sable traffic from the Ob passed through Pustozersk.[58]

Not all the fur centers of this time were found in the north. Lying in a more southerly region were two others, Viatka and Kazan. The one, Viatka, was an old Novgorod colony founded in Perm in 1174. Russian trappers and the Tatars in Perm occupied themselves with hunting beavers and squirrels for Russian merchants.[59] Viatkan enterprisers also traversed the region lying along both sides of the Urals up to the Arctic Ocean.[60] The other, Kazan, lying south of Viatka, was being visited by Russian merchants in the middle of the fifteenth century in order to obtain furs, especially squirrel skins, from the Tatars, who could penetrate into regions where the Russians dared not go.[61]

Changes in Organization

The development of towns in the north as fur centers represents a process which was basic in the Russian fur trade then and later—the eastward advance of the frontier. The depletion of fur-bearing animals in the older regions led trappers and traders to push into new and unexploited regions and left to the towns of the older regions the task of functioning less as frontier outposts and more and more as intermediaries between the sources of supply and the ultimate market. Although in the older Dvina country many kinds of fur-bearing animals still abounded at the beginning of the sixteenth century, already the most valuable sorts, such as sables, were becoming rare.[62] The increasing number of traders who pushed eastward led to the establishment of new trading centers in the less exploited regions of the Mezen and Pechora. The regions now rich-

[55] Kostomarov, p. 237; E. K. Ogorodnikov, p. 211; Richard Hakluyt, *The Principal Navigations*, I, 354.

[56] E. K. Ogorodnikov, p. 209.

[57] *Ibid.*, p. 232.

[58] Von Staden, pp. 97 n. 12, 139, 161, 194, 213.

[59] *A.A.E.*, I, 217; Popov, p. 116.

[60] Beliaev, p. 246.

[61] G. Barbaro and A. Contarini, *Travels to Tana and Persia*, p. 33; *A.I.*, I, 119.

[62] Von Herberstein, I, 114, II, 36–37.

est in furs were those of Perm, the Pechora, and the Ob.[63] Meanwhile, the Dvina towns, Kholmogory, Ustiug, and Vologda, by virtue of geographical location, became important as places where the fur merchant could establish contact with the trapper and local fur trader and where the latter could obtain grain, manufactures, and goods for exchange with the natives from whom they obtained their furs. In other words, on a smaller scale these towns duplicated the exchange economy of Novgorod.

Among themselves, these three towns were accessible to each other by rivers, the Dvina and Sukhona, while from Vologda routes led to both Novgorod and Moscow. Individually, Kholmogory and Ustiug were each the point of outlet for a hinterland area. Through Kholmogory contact with the rich fur regions of the lower Pechora and Ob country was maintained. They were reached by a route which followed the Dvina to its mouth, the coast of the White Sea to the Bay of Mezen, the Mezen and Peza rivers and a short portage to the Tsilma River, and that river to the Pechora. From there the route passed either down the river to Pustozersk near its mouth, or up it to the Shchugor River, thence by portage to the Sygva River, and down that to the Ob.[64] Through Ustiug contact was maintained with the upper Pechora territory and with Perm, both of which were accessible by way of the Vychegda, Vym, and Visherka rivers.[65] It was its access to these areas and its river connections with Kholmogory that made Ustiug the most important fur center in the north.

Besides creating intermediary centers in the fur trade once monopolized by Novgorod, the rise of the northern towns effected further change by giving opportunity for participation in the trade to others than the Novgorod merchant-capitalists. To be sure, Ivan III had smashed the power of the latter, but even before that event the growth of towns had been working to undermine their power by eliminating their direct operation in the interior. As trade centers grew, furs were obtained more through trade and less through requisition.[66] It became possible for merchants and adventurers of small capital to participate successfully in the fur trade. With the towns as headquarters they were better placed to

[63] *Ibid.*, II, 39–40.

[64] *Ibid.*, pp. 37–40; R. J. Kerner, *The Urge to the Sea*, pp. 29–30.

[65] Von Herberstein, II, 44–45.

[66] Note the unsuccessful tribute expedition from Novgorod to Iugra in 1445 which met disastrous defeat at the hands of the natives (*The Chronicle of Novgorod*, pp. 202–203).

acquire furs by trade or by trapping, and they could dispose of the pelts at the interior fur centers. Also, the way was opened for the appearance in the trade of large-scale fur traders other than Novgorodan, especially in the distant country of the Pechora and the Ob, to reach which long hazardous journeys were required.

Although the rise of new centers lessened Novgorod's dominance in the fur trade and changed the organization of it, that rise did not endanger the fur trade in Novgorod itself. Novgorod's importance rested on its position as an export center. It was the last Russian intermediary through which the furs passed on their way to the ultimate markets in Western Europe, and it continued to turn over a large number of furs, which came there through the commercial channels of the north.[67]

Danger to the fur trade of Novgorod lay, rather, in the direction of its arch political rival, Moscow. Moscow began to develop as an export center of furs on its own account; it thereby contributed to the process of diverting the fur trade away from Novgorod into new export channels, a process culminating late in the sixteenth century. As early as the middle of the fifteenth century foreign merchants—Poles, Lithuanians, and Germans—traveled to Moscow to buy furs, and the fact that many of these merchants came there solely for this purpose indicates the dimensions and importance which the trade had attained in that city.[68] In fact, furs were also its principal export.[69]

Several factors explain Moscow's rise as a competitor to Novgorod in the fur trade. As the capital of the grand princes, who were the leaders of the political consolidation of the Russian people, the city of Moscow acquired great prestige within Russia, and to it from abroad came diplomatic missions to which merchants were often attached.[70] In the process of extending their authority into the north and northeast the grand princes brought under their sovereignty various native tribes who paid tribute in furs,[71] thus bringing to Moscow a large number of furs, which constituted part of the grand princes' wealth along with gold and silver.[72] The Muscovite merchants, besides having access to the northern fur centers, obtained many of their furs in Viatka and Kazan,[73] regions which

[67] Joseph von Hamel, *England and Russia*, p. 121.
[68] Barbaro and Contarini, pp. 35, 162; Von Herberstein, I, 115.
[69] Cf. Von Herberstein, I, 112, 114; Kostomarov, p. 235.
[70] Von Herberstein, I, 111.
[71] *Ibid.*, II, 46, 109–110; Von Staden, pp. 97 n. 12, 98; Solov'ev, I, 1422.
[72] Von Staden, p. 143.
[73] Von Herberstein, I, 115; Barbaro and Contarini, p. 33.

were cut off from Novgorod when Moscow gained control of its Asiatic trade route. Moscow was the principal internal market in Russia, and it attracted fur traders from the north who exchanged furs for the grain which the northland lacked.[74]

Those disadvantages which Moscow's geographical situation in the interior of Russia entailed for it as an export center of furs tended to be offset by other circumstances. In 1503 a treaty was made with Poland which permitted the Poles the right of free trade in the Muscovite state.[75] At the end of the fifteenth century, upon being granted the imperial privilege of conducting a fair, the town of Leipzig in central Germany began to develop its trade,[76] and it quickly became a center of the European fur trade. From Leipzig eastward through Silesia and Poland into Russia the overland trade route known as *Die Hohe Landstrasse* arose and was used increasingly in the trade between Eastern and Western Europe as the Hanseatic League declined. In the later fifteenth century some attempts were made by Russian merchants to seek markets through Warsaw and the central German towns rather than through the Baltic.[77] With the development of this overland trade route, therefore, Moscow was in just as favorable a position as Novgorod, and more so later when access to the Baltic for Novgorod became restricted.

In addition to Moscow, another fur export center flourished in the late fifteenth and sixteenth centuries. This was the market at Khlopigrad, situated near the junction of the Mologa River with the upper Volga. Although late in the sixteenth century it disappeared from history, Khlopigrad maintained during its existence year-round fairs that were the most important in Russia. German, Polish, Lithuanian, Greek, Tatar, Persian, and even Italian merchants gathered there with their goods—clothes, fabrics, shoes, axes, vessels—which they exchanged chiefly for furs. The goods were usually exchanged by simple barter, since little money was used.[78]

Greatly changed as was its position in the fur trade at the opening of the sixteenth century, Novgorod remained for another half

[74] Kliuchevskii, *Skazaniia inostrantsev*, p. 253; Hakluyt, I, 255.

[75] Von Staden, p. 145 n. 2; *Sbornik imperatorskago russkago istoricheskago obshchestva*, XXXV, 401.

[76] Ernst Kroker, *Handelsgeschichte der Stadt Leipzig*, pp. 75–76, 82.

[77] A. P. Lassen, "Commerce in the Baltic from 1500 to 1700," p. 229; Gerhard Fischer, *Aus zwei Jahrhunderten leipziger Handelsgeschichte, 1470–1650*, p. 348.

[78] Von Herberstein, I, 111, II, 32–33; Von Staden, pp. 144–145.

century the principal market town in Russia where furs were bought and sold. Its situation near, and its access to, the Baltic Sea still remained in its favor. The fall of Novgorod had not served to end its commercial activity; the closing of the Hanseatic factory there in 1494 by Ivan III was intended only to break the monopoly of the Hanse as the intermediaries to Western Europe, a monopoly already undermined by the Livonian merchants and by the decline of the Hanse itself.[79] Foreign merchants still visited Novgorod; in fact, in the sixteenth century Swedish, Livonian, and German merchants ordinarily were not supposed to go to any other town than Novgorod. Only Poles and Lithuanians might go to Moscow; Turks and Tatars went to Khlopigrad.[80] Under the rule of Moscow Novgorod continued to be the center of Russia's commerce with Europe.[81] To its markets merchants from various Russian towns went to exchange furs and other raw products for goods of European manufacture, especially goods from the Flemish and Lithuanian merchants. Thus, through its active exchange of goods, Novgorod maintained its importance for several decades; it was the far-reaching control over the old Russian trade that it had lost.

During most of the sixteenth century the Russian fur trade was carried on under the conditions created by the end of the Novgorodan monopoly and the rise of new trade centers. But towards the end of the century occurred the second great shift in the trade. The first great shift had seen a transfer of the region of supply and the trading centers from Kievan Russia in the south to Novgorodan Russia in the north. The second great shift was far to the east, into Siberia, a shift, however, not of the major trading centers, but only of the source of supply of the trade. For some two hundred or more years thereafter Siberia served as the tremendously wealthy source for the Russian fur trade, which, based in this new country, was to assume its greatest proportions. As the industry first to be developed in that country, and one of its greatest, the fur trade was inextricably bound up with the earlier history of Siberia under Russian rule; indeed, the history of the Russian fur trade in Siberia is the history of the conquest and occupation of the northern half of Asia by the Russian people. This magnificent historical episode, the organization and conduct of the fur trade in Siberia and in Russia, and its importance for Russia are the theme of the following chapters.

[79] Goetz, p. 188; Berezhkov, p. 264.
[80] Von Herberstein, I, 111; but cf. Von Staden, p. 145 n. 2.
[81] "Anglorum navigatio ad Moscovitas," *Historiae ruthenicae*, p. 10.

CHAPTER II

THE FUR TRADE AND THE OPENING OF SIBERIA

THE SIXTEENTH CENTURY witnessed the growth of commerce among the European states and the beginning of their colonial expansion. The story of how the Western European nations—Portugal and Spain, then Holland, England, and France—each sought after and fought for colonies is a familiar one. But much less known is the fact that the Russians in Eastern Europe, developing their commerce, also undertook colonial expansion in the sixteenth century. Their expansion was in an eastward direction, across northern Asia to the Pacific, and ultimately into the New World. Siberia, and later Alaska, became Russia's colonies. Siberia, because geographically contiguous to European Russia, is not usually thought of as a colony, but it was just as much a colony for Russia as Mexico and Peru were for Spain, and India for England. In Siberia Russia acquired a dependency of more than four million square miles with a subject aboriginal population of many thousands; in Siberia Russia found an abundance of natural resources which it, as the mother country, exploited for its own benefit; in Siberia Russia followed the road to empire.

America filled Spain's galleons with gold and silver; India furnished England's merchants with a vast and wealthy market; Siberia offered Russia neither of these. Siberia's greatest resource was its abundant sables, among the finest furs in the world. They provided the incentive for Russia's conquest of Siberia; they also paid the costs of that conquest. In nearly every instance the presence in Siberia of the first Russian inhabitants—soldiers, traders, farmers, government officials and employees—was dictated directly or indirectly by the attractions and requirements of the sable trade.

The conquest of Siberia by the Russians marks for them the renewal of an old historical process under the stimulus of the commercial expansion of the sixteenth century. Throughout Russia's history migration and colonization have characterized the life of its people.[1] The movement to the east began early. Soon after the Russians of the Dnepr had begun their migration northeastward

[1] V. O. Kliuchevskii, *History of Russia,* I, 2.

to the Volga, the Novgorod fur traders were pushing eastward across northern Russia to Iugra. When Novgorod declined, Moscow supplanted it in Iugra. Then Moscow extended its rule over Perm and conquered Kazan, thereby bringing by the middle of the sixteenth century all of the territory up to the Ural Mountains under its control. In the meantime, freed of the burdens of Tatar rule, Russia sought to increase its commercial relations with Western Europe, and the Europeans in turn saw in Russia an opportunity to expand their trade. From this twofold development was generated the impetus for expansion into Siberia.

Russian Relations with Trans-Uralie

Though by conquest Moscow had replaced Novgorod in 1499 as overlord in Iugra, Muscovite overlordship brought no fundamental changes. During most of the sixteenth century Moscow was content, like Novgorod, to exercise only nominal sovereignty over the country by exacting fur tribute from the native inhabitants, the Voguls and Ostiaks.[2] It established no permanent agents or real authority there; nor did it try by military force to expand its overlordship beyond Iugra to other parts of Trans-Uralie (i.e., the trans-Ural country). Moscow needed all its strength and resources for internal problems and for the struggle against the neighboring Tatar states of Krym and Kazan.[3] Moreover, Iugra was accessible from Moscow only over the roundabout Pechora route and, as long as the more direct natural route to the south via the Kama River and its eastern tributaries was blocked to the Russians by the khanate of Kazan and its eastern neighbor, the khanate of Sibir,[4] it was unwise for Moscow to attempt to expand its jurisdiction in Trans-Uralie.[5] Therefore, Moscow maintained a policy of inaction along its northeastern frontier and sought only to avoid clashes with the natives living there.

Commerce, rather than conquest, provided the incentive for relations between Russia and Trans-Uralie. The trade which Novgorod had early established with Iugra was continued by Muscovite Russia and expanded into other regions of Trans-Uralie. To Russia at large the northwestern corner of Asia was terra incognita, but

[2] A. V. Oksenov, "Politicheskiia otnoshenii moskovskago gosudarstva k iugorskoi zemle," *Zh.M.N.P.*, CCLXXIII (1891), 271.

[3] V. I. Ogorodnikov, *Zavoevanie russkimi Sibiri*, p. 14.

[4] S. V. Bakhrushin, *Ocherki po istorii kolonizatsii Sibiri*, p. 147; S. M. Solov'ev, *Istoriia Rossii s drevneishikh vremen*, I, 1423.

[5] Bakhrushin, *op. cit.*, p. 67.

among the people of northern Russia its existence and fur wealth were well known.[6] The most active trade was that conducted with Iugra. In the sixteenth century the Asiatic part of Iugra, the territory between the lower Ob River and the Urals, came to be known also as Obdoriia.[7] The bolder Russian traders, usually northerners, made their way over the Urals to exchange their wares with the natives of Obdoriia for furs,[8] and the native Zyrians of Perm journeyed there to hunt and trap animals, or to trade. In turn the Samoeds, Voguls, and Ostiaks of northern Trans-Uralie brought furs to the Russian trade centers in Pechora and Perm.[9] It was from the Samoeds that the Russians acquired most of their sables.[10] Trade with Obdoriia led to trade with the next region to the east, Mangazeia, the country between the Ob river-gulf and the Taz estuary, which was noted for its fine sables.[11] Direct trade with Mangazeia by the Russians was probably already in existence by the middle of the sixteenth century;[12] after 1553, as a result of the English commercial and exploratory activities in northern maritime Russia, the trade with Mangazeia increased.[13] The Russians also extended their trading activities into the regions south of Obdoriia, to Kondoriia, the region of the middle Ob, and to the khanate of Sibir.[14] Kondoriia, though a part of the conquests of Ivan III, was less known to the Russians.[15] The Siberian khanate south of it embraced the territory east of the Irtysh River and west to the Ural Mountains south approximately of the fifty-eighth parallel of latitude.[16] From the name of this state's capital, Sibir, the name Siberia

[6] A. V. Oksenov, "Slukhi i vesti o Sibiri do Ermaka," *Sibirskii sbornik, 1886 g.*, IV, 115; Sigismund von Herberstein, *Notes upon Russia*, II, 39.

[7] P. N. Butsinskii, *Mangazeia i mangazeiskii uezd*, p. 1.

[8] G. F. Müller, *Opisanie sibirskago tsarstva*, pp. 47, 161; A. V. Oksenov, "Torgovye snosheniia russkikh s obitateliami severo-zapadnoi Azii do epokhi Ermaka," *Tomskiia gubernskiia vedomosti*, 1888, No. 11, pp. 14–15; I. I. Tyzhnov, "Obzor inostrannykh izvestii o Sibiri 2-i poloviny XVI veka," *Sibirskii sbornik, 1887*, pp. 105–106; cf. below, p. 25 n. 42.

[9] Müller, *op. cit.*, p. 156; A. N. Pypin, "Pervyia izvestiia o Sibiri i russkoe eia zaselenie," *Vestnik Evropy*, Vol. XXVI (1891), No. 8, p. 764.

[10] Heinrich von Staden, *Aufzeichnungen über den moskauer Staat*, pp. 98, 139, 143, 213.

[11] Pypin, pp. 746–747; S. F. Platonov, *Proshloe russkogo severa*, p. 72; Anthony Jenkinson, *Early Voyages and Travels to Russia and Persia*, I, 105–106; Bakhrushin, *op. cit.*, p. 84.

[12] Bakhrushin, *op. cit.*, p. 84; Von Staden, p. 252; cf. Butsinskii, *op. cit.*, pp. 5–8.

[13] Bakhrushin, *op. cit.*, p. 147; Giles Fletcher, *Russia at the Close of the Sixteenth Century*, p. 9; Von Staden, *loc. cit.*

[14] Von Herberstein, I, 115, II, 47.

[15] Butsinskii, *op. cit.*, p. 1.

[16] V. I. Ogorodnikov, *op. cit.*, pp. 15–16.

is derived. Trade with this part of Trans-Uralie had begun in the second half of the fifteenth century,[17] but because of certain impediments it was not as active as that with the north. The direct route to Sibir passed through the hostile khanate of Kazan. The merchants of Kazan, who obtained furs from Sibir and sold them to the Russians, opposed the efforts of the latter to establish direct relations with the Siberian khanate, and on one occasion the Siberian khan himself stopped the trade of the Russians.[18]

Growth of the Fur Trade in the Sixteenth Century

The trade with Trans-Uralie represented only a small part of the economic activity of Russia and by itself was not of much importance. But it does represent the first step in the expansion of the Russians into Siberia. It served to make them aware of the great fur resources of the country and to acquaint them with the routes across the Urals. Alone, however, it could not precipitate a large-scale movement eastward. Such a movement required the growth of forces in Russia which were strong enough to impel men into Siberia, to push aside the obstacle presented by the independent khanate of Sibir, and to demand the active assistance of the government. During the sixteenth century such forces were forming, and by the beginning of the 'eighties they had gained momentum enough to sweep aside all barriers and to set in motion the Russian eastward advance. The most effective of these forces, the one which provided the initial impulse for this advance and supplied the sustaining power behind it, was the fur trade. Because of certain developments in Europe and in Russia which affected Russia's fur trade, that trade expanded tremendously. This expansion caused men to turn their attention increasingly towards Siberia and led finally to a definite step to open the region for Russian exploitation.

The first development to manifest itself clearly was a great rise throughout Western Europe in the demand for furs, particularly Russian furs.[19] This increase in demand became apparent in Russia in the first quarter of the sixteenth century[20] and maintained itself

[17] Oksenov, "Torgovye snosheniia," No. 10, pp. 8–9; *idem,* "Slukhi i vesti," p. 109; A. P. Shchapov, *Sochineniia,* II, 284.

[18] Oksenov, "Torgovye snosheniia," *loc. cit.; Sobranie gosudarstvennykh gramot i dogovorov,* II, 52.

[19] Joseph von Hamel, *England and Russia,* pp. 115–116; William Camden, *The History of . . . Elizabeth, Late Queen of England,* pp. 102–103.

[20] Paulus Iovius, "The History . . . of the Legation or Ambassade of the Great Basilius Prince of Moscouia, to Pope Clement VII," Hakluyt Society Works, XII, 249.

for a century and a half thereafter. It was so strong that it was a major cause of the transfer at the middle of the century of the European center of the fur trade from Novgorod to Leipzig,[21] which, though it was dependent upon the Russian fur supply, was more centrally situated in relation to the European markets. This demand was general throughout Europe. The Russian "Trade Book" for 1575 reveals fur exports to Germany, Holland, France, Spain, Portugal, and Italy, reporting that "expensive sables, unripped and with bellies and feet, are valued in all countries."[22] In Moscow in the 'seventies it had become almost impossible to buy "salable sables"; one had to send to the north and intercept them en route to the foreign markets.[23] In the meantime English agents moved about the northern maritime country buying up furs and by the 'eighties had pushed across the Urals.[24] High fur prices were the natural result, and more than one observer has left testimony to the excessive prices commanded by Russian furs.[25]

The fact of an increased demand for furs can readily be established, but the cause is not so easily determined. The explanation, however, seems to lie in the quickening economic development and expansion of sixteenth-century Western Europe. Through the newly discovered commercial channels from India and the Orient came the luxuries and fineries of the East. A taste for the material refinements of living became widespread in Western Europe.[26] The influx of gold and silver from the New World created a period of rising prices and gave momentum to a greater commercial activity. The prosperity of the time enabled more people to indulge the human desire for luxuries. Furs, which were long the possession chiefly of a small landed aristocracy and of the very wealthy, were now being acquired by the new and larger commercial aristocracy, and even by the lower classes, which sought to imitate them. For several decades the wearing of furs was the fashion for both men and women.[27] Furs were everywhere worn for purposes of ostenta-

[21] A. P. Lassen, "Commerce in the Baltic from 1500 to 1700," pp. 231–232.

[22] *Torgovaia kniga,* Zapiski otdeleniia russkoi i slavianskoi arkheologii russkago arkheologicheskago obshchestva, I (1851), 133.

[23] A. A. Vvedenskii, *Torgovyi dom, XVI–XVII vekov,* pp. 93–94; Bakhrushin, *op. cit.,* p. 148.

[24] Von Hamel, p. 303; Bakhrushin, *op. cit.,* p. 147; Platonov, p. 70.

[25] Paulus Iovius, *loc. cit.;* Jenkinson, II, 208; Richard Hakluyt, *The Principal Navigations,* I, 383.

[26] J. M. Vincent, *Costume and Conduct in the Laws of Basel, Bern, and Zurich, 1370–1800,* pp. 46–47.

[27] Hakluyt, I, 283, 286, II, 78; N. I. Kostomarov, *Ocherki torgovli moskovskago gosudarstva,* p. 240; Vincent, pp. 46–47, 57, 58, 60, 61.

tion, not merely for warmth; the collars, cuffs, and edges of garments were trimmed with fur; the official robes of government officers were often adorned with it.[28] The mode became extreme enough to evoke criticism for effeminacy and the desire for "superfluous pleasures."[29] Russia, since it possessed fine furs in greater numbers than any other country, benefited greatly from this mode; and chiefly through its fur trade Russia, though distant from the new trade centers of Europe and the maritime routes of the Atlantic, experienced the commercial renascence and expansion of the sixteenth century.

The impact of the rising demand for furs would not have made itself so sharply felt in Russia, had there not begun the breaking-down of certain barriers which stood across the path of its fuller participation in the world's trade.[30] Politically, the grand princes of Moscow had rid themselves of Tatar overlordship and had consolidated the Russian people sufficiently to permit them to turn to problems of commercial development. Geographically, the Russians were brought by conquest and discovery into closer and more direct contact with the centers of trade in both the East and the West. In 1514 they captured Smolensk from the Poles, and its possession placed them in a more favorable position for trade with Poland-Lithuania and with the German towns, especially Leipzig. Later the Russians gained a temporary foothold (1558–1581) on a strip of the Baltic coast, which provided them with a direct outlet on the sea at Rugodiv, a port which they established alongside Narva. At the middle of the century, in 1553, the English discovered the northern route to Russia around the North Cape and through the White Sea to the mouth of the Northern Dvina River. This was a direct sea route to Russia, unencumbered by troublesome Sound dues and free of danger from jealous Baltic powers, a route which was immediately and extensively utilized by the English, and later by the Dutch and Germans.[31] When Russia lost its Baltic territory in 1581, the northern route acquired even greater importance, and the increasing traffic over it led to the establishment in 1585 of a new port, Arkhangelsk, at the mouth of the Dvina River. To the east and southeast commercial relations were facilitated for the Russians by Ivan IV's conquests of the khanates of Kazan (1552)

[28] *Torgovaia kniga, loc. cit.*
[29] Paulus Iovius, *loc. cit.*
[30] Bakhrushin, *op. cit.*, p. 147.
[31] Fletcher, pp. x–xi.

and Astrakhan (1555). These conquests gave the Russians control of the entire Volga River to the Caspian Sea by adding the middle and lower Volga to their possession and opened to them the markets of Central Asia. Furthermore, the overthrow of Kazan placed the Russians also in control of the Kama River and its tributaries and thus opened and secured the direct southern route to Siberia, the only feasible route along which an advance into Siberia could be made.[32]

There remained one more development to complete the setting for the Russian advance into Siberia. That was the extermination of fur-bearing animals in Russia under the steady and heavy export of their pelts abroad.[33] Just when the fur resources of Russia proper became exhausted cannot be stated exactly. The difficulties experienced in the 'sixties by the English merchants in the north, who found sables and other rich furs expensive beyond profit and good grades of the less expensive furs sometimes hard to get, indicate that at that time the depletion of the fur supply was assuming serious proportions.[34] Complete exhaustion of the supply in Russia, however, did not occur until the seventeenth century, or even later.[35] Even at the beginning of the seventeenth century, Perm and Pechora, the regions which since the beginning of the sixteenth century had produced the most and best pelts, were still yielding good furs.[36] But the exhaustion did not have to be complete to be an effective factor in impelling the Russians into Siberia. It needed only to be great enough to set a sufficient number of men, or in the present instance, the right men, in motion, and that point was reached in the decade of the 'seventies.

The Stroganovs

For the opening of, and first conquest in, Siberia Russia is indebted to the famous Stroganov family.[37] This family rather than the cau-

[32] Bakhrushin, *op. cit.*, p. 88.

[33] *Ibid.*, p. 148; P. P. Mel'gunov, *Ocherki po istorii torgovli IX–XVIII v.v.*, p. 209.

[34] Hakluyt, I, 383, 400; Jenkinson, II, 208.

[35] Mel'gunov, pp. 180, 210; V. I. Ogorodnikov, *op. cit.*, p. 4; S. M. Seredonin, *Sochinenie Dzil'sa Fletchera "Of the Russe Common Wealth" kak istoricheskii istochnik*, pp. 121–122; N. Ianitskii, "Torgovlia pushnym tovarom v XVII v.," *Kievskiia universitetskiia izvestiia*, LII (No. 9, 1912), 1–2; G. F. Müller, "Nachricht von dreien im Gebiete der Stadt Casan, wohnhaften heidnischen Völkern, den Tscheremissen, Tschuwaschen, und Wotiacken," *Sammlung russischer Geschichte*, III, 327.

[36] Fletcher, p. 9; Vvedenskii, *op. cit.*, pp. 93–94.

[37] V. I. Ogorodnikov, *op. cit.*, pp. 26–27; Bakhrushin, *op. cit.*, p. 99; cf. *Sibirskiia letopisi*, pp. 10–11, 59.

tious Muscovite government took the initiative in opening the resources of Trans-Uralie to Russian exploitation. In their position as wealthy merchant-capitalists and fur traders the Stroganovs possessed the resources and influence which enabled them to organize an undertaking towards that specific objective. Through them the forces of expansion contained in the rise in demand for furs, the increased commercial relations between Russia and the rest of the world, and the exhaustion of fur-bearing animals in Russia were first translated into action.

The Stroganovs possessed large tracts of land in the region of the Vychegda River and in Perm along the Kama and Chusovaia rivers. These lands had been acquired by purchase or as votchinal grants. The creator of this private empire and quasi-frontier march, Anika Stroganov (1498–1570), had developed extensive industrial and commercial enterprises, which included salt making, iron and silver mining, and wholesale and retail trade, particularly in furs, in the Volga markets and towns of the Muscovite state.[38] At Solvychegodsk on the Vychegda River he built up a large and very profitable trade in furs. Many of his furs he obtained from Trans-Uralie. Originally the natives brought the pelts to Solvychegodsk, where they exchanged them for wares of Russian and European manufacture, especially iron goods. But their fine quality and high value soon induced Anika to send his own agents across the Urals into Obdoriia and Mangazeia, where they acquired the valuable furs at low prices, exchanging them for trinkets and cheap manufactured goods. With the acquisition of the family's Kama or Perm holdings after the conquest of Kazan in 1552, their fur trade probably expanded, for they procured furs now not only from the north through Vychegda and Ust Vym, but also over the more direct southern route through Perm, in whose towns and outposts fur storehouses were established.[39] The fur trade of the Stroganovs was not confined to the domestic markets. At Murmansk and Kola they sold large numbers of furs to the English, and several times in the decade of the 'seventies they sent their agent, the Dutchman Oliver Brunel, to Holland and Paris to dispose of shipments there.[40] One indication of the importance of their fur trade

[38] A. A. Vvedenskii, "Anika Stroganov v svoem sol'vychegodskom khoziaistve," *Sbornik statei po russkoi istorii posviashchennykh S. F. Platonovu,* p. 96.

[39] *Ibid.*, pp. 103–104.

[40] V. A. Kordt, *Ocherk snoshenii moskovskago gosudarstva s respublikoiu soedinennykh Niderlandov do 1631 g.*, p. xxxi; Platonov, *op. cit.*, pp. 66, 78.

is the fact that Tsar Ivan himself sent to them for sables.[41] The wealth which they accumulated from this trade was tremendous: the churches they built in their villages attest its size, the one at Solvychegodsk being built entirely of hewn stone instead of the customary wood.[42]

Great as the holdings of the Stroganovs were, conditions were not such as to leave them content with their Solvychegodsk and Perm votchinas. Although they were still making great profits from their fur trade, the decreasing supply of fur-bearing animals in Russia and the incompletely satisfied demand experienced in the 'seventies pointed clearly to the advantage and desirability of exploiting more extensively the fur resources of Trans-Uralie. This could best be done by gaining the right to occupy and possess the country across the Urals on the same basis as they held their Perm votchina, and through their friend at court, Boris Godunov, the tsar's son-in-law, they applied for that right.[43] It must be added, though, that at the same time other incentives urged them to this step. In undertaking to mine iron and silver in the trans-Ural region, in the Tura River basin, the Stroganovs found it essential to possess all the territory along the Tura and Tobol rivers.[44] Possession of this territory would likewise enable them to put an end to the periodical raids on their Kama holdings by the natives from Siberia.[45] Their application received favorable consideration, and in 1574 Ivan issued a charter which conveyed to them the territory along the rivers Losva, Tavda, and Tobol.[46]

The territory conveyed to them by the charter constituted approximately the northern half of the khanate of Sibir, then ruled by Kuchum Khan. Ivan regarded Kuchum as his tributary vassal, but Kuchum had repudiated the relationship; hence to take pos-

[41] Vvedenskii, *Torgovyi dom*, p. 92.

[42] The principal source for this account of the Stroganovs' fur trade with Trans-Uralie, and the source for such accounts as Vvedenskii, "Anika Stroganov," pp. 102–103, Müller, *Opisanie*, pp. 54–55, Pypin, pp. 764–765, is the description written in 1609 by Isaac Massa, the Dutch visitor to Russia (1600–1608, 1614–1620), who knew the Stroganovs. It was first published in 1612 at Amsterdam by Hessel Geritz and later was included by Witsen in his *Noord und oost Tartarye* (1692 ed.), II, 509–518 (G. Henning, "Die Reiseberichte über Sibirien von Herberstein bis Ides" *Mitteilungen des Vereins für Erdkunde zu Leipzig*, 1905, pp. 266–267). An English version appears in Samuel Purchas, *His Pilgrimes*, XIII, 171–179; a Russian translation is in Tyzhnov, pp. 105–110.

[43] Purchas, XIII, 173–174.

[44] V. I. Ogorodnikov, *op. cit.*, p. 22.

[45] *Sibirskiia letopisi*, pp. 5–8, 52–55; cf. *D.A.I.*, I, 175–176, 182–183, 184–185.

[46] Müller, *Opisanie*, pp. 70–73.

session of this territory the Stroganovs would have to use armed force. For that purpose they organized an expedition and employed to command it the famous Volga Cossack leader (*atamán*) and brigand, Ermak Timofeevich.[47] At the head of a band of about eight hundred men Ermak set out in September, 1579, and two years later, in October, 1581, captured Sibir, the capital of the Siberian khanate, at the juncture of the Tobol and Irtysh rivers.[48] Ermak's victory broke the power of the khanate, but the Russians found themselves in such a precarious position that no private means, not even those of the Stroganovs, could cope with it.[49] Therefore, Ermak dispatched a group of his men to Moscow, who were to offer his services to the tsar and to ask for reinforcements. They took with them the furs collected as tribute.

Up to the time when the men sent by Ermak arrived in Moscow, the policy of the tsar remained unchanged. He was opposed to the expedition sent into Siberia by the Stroganovs. In 1582 a band of natives, set in motion by Ermak's advance into Siberia, raided certain towns in Perm. This evoked a sharp reprimand from the tsar, who severely criticized the expedition on the ground that it had aroused the natives and at the same time left the frontier open to attack.[50] But shortly thereafter Ermak's envoys arrived in Moscow, bringing with them a large number of valuable furs—2,400 sable, 800 black fox, and 2,000 beaver pelts—and the information that Ermak had taken Sibir and placed the natives under tribute to the tsar.[51] This put a new complexion on the matter. The destruction of the khanate was an accomplished fact, and there was valuable booty as evidence. Instead of disavowing Ermak's unauthorized act, the tsar decided to support him. Reinforcements were sent, and when in the summer of 1584 Ermak met his death, the conquest came under the aegis of Moscow.[52]

[47] Of the three schools of opinion which seek to explain the origin of Ermak's expedition the one adopted here is that of Professor V. I. Ogorodnikov (*op. cit.*, pp. 23–25). The school represented by Müller (*Opisanie*, pp. 76–81) and Bakhrushin (*op. cit.*, p. 153) presents Ermak's expedition simply as a raid for rich fur booty, a raid backed by the Stroganovs to rid themselves of the Cossacks, who were troublesome and unwelcome guests in Perm. The third group interprets the expedition as a raid by Ermak and his men for fur booty, without any relation to the Stroganovs (*Sibirskiia letopisi*, p. 208). However, in all three interpretations the role of furs as the incentive is equally prominent.

[48] *Sibirskiia letopisi*, pp. 25, 59, 71.

[49] *Ibid.*, pp. 30, 75–76.

[50] *D.A.I.*, I, 185–187; Müller, *Opisanie*, pp. 117–118; J. F. Baddeley, *Russia, Mongolia, China*, I, lxx.

[51] *Sibirskiia letopisi*, pp. 30, 75–76, 137–138, 207–208, 249–250; Müller, *Opisanie*, pp. 106, 112–113, 119.

[52] *Sibirskiia letopisi*, *loc. cit.*

The decision of the tsar to support Ermak meant, of course, that Moscow had abandoned the hands-off policy in relation to the Ural frontier which it had maintained since the days of Ivan III. Although there is no documentary evidence of the considerations which led Moscow to reverse its policy, the long history of fur tribute as an objective in Russian conquests and the prominent place which furs occupied in Moscow's subsequent activities in Siberia clearly reveal that the fur trade was the primary reason for the change. The conquest of the country beyond the Urals promised huge returns in the form of tribute from the natives. Indeed, the tribute sent by Ermak was five times that which Ivan IV had ten years before imposed upon Kuchum, with only temporary success.[53] At the same time, the ease with which the comparatively small band of Ermak had defeated Kuchum's forces (the expedition of Ivan III to Iugra in 1499 had numbered four thousand men)[54] revealed the weakness of the khanate and the exaggeration of its power in the minds of the Russians. The risks of expansion were not great, whereas the opportunities for profit were. The Stroganovs had precipitated the conquest; Moscow could hardly do other than continue it.

---

[53] *Sobranie gosudarstvennykh gramot i dogovorov*, II, 63–65; *A.I.*, I, 341; Solov'ev, II, 306; V. I. Ogorodnikov, *op. cit.*, p. 20; *Sibirskiia letopisi*, pp. 6–8, 53–55.

[54] I. D. Beliaev, "O geograficheskikh svedeniiakh v drevnei Rossii," *Zapiski imperatorskago russkago geograficheskago obshchestva*, VI (1852), 247.

CHAPTER III

THE FUR TRADE AND THE CONQUEST OF SIBERIA

THE CONQUEST and occupation of Siberia were accomplished by two waves of invaders.[1] The first consisted of a variety of adventurers and enterprisers—not the least of whom was the state itself—who entered Siberia principally to exploit its fur wealth. These men explored and conquered unknown regions, opening them to Russian settlement; they constituted the vanguard of the Russian advance. The second wave was composed of agriculturalists and settlers of various sorts, who in the real sense occupied the country and thus gave permanence to the Russian conquest. Our concern will be with the first wave of invasion, since its motivating force was the Siberian fur trade.

The conquest of Siberia reveals a familiar historical pattern, the subjugation of backward peoples by a more advanced people seeking to exploit the natural wealth of the country. The natives who inhabited Siberia were no match for the Russians. They lacked almost completely any political organization; they had developed only a low level of material culture; they were of diverse racial origins; and the social ties among them were weak.[2] In addition, strife existed among and within the various tribes, and many of them lived a nomadic life, which did not lend itself to sustained opposition to the Russians. On the other hand, the Russians, though fewer in numbers, were a united and strong force. Socially and racially they were a homogeneous people, and behind them stood a strong centralized government, which commanded considerable material resources. The Russians carried firearms, and so, despite their numerical inferiority, they possessed military superiority.[3] They were able, consequently, to impose their rule upon the native population and to exploit it as an agency for gaining the great fur wealth of Siberia. What the Russians did in Siberia for furs, Spain had already undertaken in Mexico and Peru for gold and silver.

[1] George Vernadskii, "Gosudarevy sluzhilye i promyshlennye liudi vostochnoi Sibiri XVII veka," *Zh.M.N.P.*, n.s., LVI (1915), 332.

[2] V. I. Ogorodnikov, "Russkaia gosudarstvennaia vlast' i sibirskie inorodtsy v XVI–XVIII vv.," *Sbornik trudov professorov i prepodavatelei gosudarstvennogo irkutskogo universiteta*, I, 70–71.

[3] P. N. Butsinskii, *Zaselenie Sibiri*, p. 298.

THE CONQUERORS OF SIBERIA

The defeat of Kuchum was not long in becoming known in Russia, particularly in the north, through which the surviving members of Ermak's band passed on their way home.[4] These men had acquired a large number of valuable furs in the course of their expedition.[5] Almost immediately there began a movement of fortune-seekers across the Urals in search of furs. Most of them came from the north, where many of the inhabitants were fur traders and enterprisers in forest products and therefore cognizant of the opportunities opened to them by the fall of Sibir.[6] The Russians were seized with a fur-fever, much like the gold-fever which possessed the American "forty-niners" of a later century. In Siberia sables worth from 10 to 20 rubles, black foxes worth from 100 to 300 rubles, were to be found. Could a man but obtain a few of them, a single trip would then suffice to enable him to settle down in comfort for the rest of his life. A pauper could become a rich man in one season. To illustrate, in 1623 a Siberian official reported that one Ivan Afanasiev had stolen two black fox skins, one valued at 30 r., the other at 80 r. With these 110 rubles, it has been calculated, Ivan could have purchased more than fifty acres of land, erected a good cabin, bought five good horses, ten head of cattle, twenty sheep, several dozen fowl, and still have had almost half of his capital left over.[7] Some did indeed acquire a plot of land and settle down in Siberia. Others remained there too, either to continue the adventurous and wild life of a hunter and trapper or to carry on trade in one of the several towns which arose in this new country.[8]

Two groups of immigrants first appeared in Siberia, drawn there by the fur trade. They were the private enterprisers and the state employees. It was by means of their activities that Siberia was conquered and brought under Russian rule. In the first group, the private enterprisers, two types are distinguishable, traders and

[4] I. V. Shcheglov, *Khronologicheskii perechen' vazhneishikh dannykh iz istorii Sibiri, 1032–1882 gg.*, p. 46.

[5] *Sibirskiia letopisi*, pp. 32–33.

[6] P. N. Butsinskii, *Mangazeia i mangazeiskii uezd*, pp. 50–51; Ogloblin, III, 96; N. N. Ogloblin, "Semen Dezhnev (1638–1671 gg.)," *Zh.M.N.P.*, CCLXXII (1890), 284.

[7] Butsinskii, *Mangazeia*, pp. 1–2. As this illustration suggests, the purchasing power of the Russian ruble in the seventeenth century was considerably higher than in later centuries. Its value then was twelve to fifteen times greater than in prerevolutionary days, when it was fifty-one cents. V. O. Kliuchevskii, *Opyty i issledovaniia*, pp. 160, 164, 171.

[8] G. F. Müller, *Opisanie sibirskago tsarstva*, p. 247.

promýshlenniks. The former included merchants or their agents and small traders, who sought to avail themselves of the new sources of furs. These traders (*torgovye liudi*), more particularly those who became resident in Siberia, sometimes joined the expeditions which went out to conquer new territory.[9] However, their participation in the conquest was perhaps not as extensive as that of the second type, since their business was to acquire furs for sale in the Russian and foreign markets mainly by exchanging or purchasing them from the promyshlenniks. It was the latter who obtained the furs at the source, and for that reason participated actively and extensively in the conquest. The term promyshlenniks ordinarily referred to men who worked for themselves, exploiting natural resources.[10] It may also be understood here to include the so-called *pokrúchenniks*, men who worked for an employer, but who in all other respects conducted themselves as promyshlenniks.[11] The role of the promyshlenniks is akin to that of the *coureurs de bois* in Canada. They hunted and trapped fur-bearing animals, or got them from the natives by trade, extortion, or as tribute. So active were they in the fur trade in Siberia that in that country the term "promyshlennik" became synonymous with fur hunter or trapper.[12] By the very nature of their occupation they became explorers and conquerors.

The second group drawn to Siberia by the fur trade, the state employees, was sent there to further and protect the interests of the state. Because the exploitation of the fur wealth of the country was the principal interest of the state, the fur trade became the chief activity of the state employees; and because conquest was a means of establishing regular sources of furs, the state employees participated actively in the conquest. In fact, the tribute exacted from the natives—*iasak* (pronounced yah-sáhk)—always attended conquest and constituted the objective of Moscow's conquest of Siberia.

Of the state employees the highest in rank and authority were the *voevodas* (pronounced vaw-yeh-vóe-das). They were the military and administrative heads of the towns and forts and the adjacent territories, and were appointed for a short term, usually

---

[9] *D.A.I.*, II, 175, 263, IV, 13; Vernadskii, *op. cit.*, pp. 336, 342; Ogloblin, "Semen Dezhnev," p. 265.

[10] Müller, *op. cit.*, p. 247; J. E. Fischer, *Sibirische Geschichte*, I, 14 n. 5, 290–291; J. F. Baddeley, *Russia, Mongolia, China*, II, 13 n. 2.

[11] Vernadskii, *op. cit.*, pp. 339–340. Also see below, p. 150.

[12] Vladimir Dal', *Tolkovyi slovar' zhivogo velikorusskago iazyka*, III, 1302.

from two to four years.[13] Upon them rested the responsibility of seeing that Moscow's orders were carried out and of preserving the interests of the state.

The rank and file of state employees were the "serving men" (*sluzhilye liudi*).[14] The ranks of the serving men who performed military service included cossacks, *streltsý*, boiar-sons (*deti boiarskie*), and foreigners—Poles, Lithuanians, and Swedes sent to Siberia as prisoners of war for military service.[15] The cossacks were the most numerous and active of the serving men.[16] A social caste, not a national or racial group, they were a kind of irregular troops stationed on the frontier, whose duties were to maintain order and to guard the frontier, to impose and collect iasak. They were selected from freemen in Russia and Siberia, and in return for their military service, which was compulsory, they received a salary and were granted the use of a plot of land for cultivation.[17] They were organized into detachments (*sotni,* originally "hundreds"), each of which elected its own leaders, or atamans. When their services were not in demand by the local authorities, they were free to explore and conquer on their own account.[18] During the earlier stages of the conquest streltsy were sent to Siberia to supplement the cossacks.[19] They were fewer than the latter and by the middle of the seventeenth century there were enough Russians in Siberia from which to fill the ranks of the cossacks. The streltsy were ordinarily infantrymen, commanded by regularly appointed officers.[20] The boiar-sons belonged to a rank higher than that of the cossacks and streltsy, a rank sometimes granted to individual serving men in return for a special service. Their numbers were much smaller and they served usually as military leaders, both of cossacks and streltsy.[21] The foreigners composed a small element among the serving men and, quickly adapting themselves to their new environment, they soon became barely distinguishable from

[13] Ogloblin, III, 89.

[14] In its wider meaning the term *sluzhilye liudi* included also the voevodas and their military assistants. *Ibid.*

[15] *Ibid.*, pp. 101, 103–104, 109; Butsinskii, *Zaselenie Sibiri,* p. 248.

[16] Ogloblin, III, 104.

[17] *A.I.*, II, 58; *D.A.I.*, IV, 179, 182, 247; Butsinskii, *Zaselenie Sibiri,* p. 185; G. V. Lantzeff, *Siberia in the Seventeenth Century,* pp. 67–68.

[18] "Istoricheskie akty o podvigakh Erofeia Khabarova na Amure v 1649–1651 gg.," *Zhurnal dlia chteniia vospitannikam voenno-uchebnykh zavedenii,* 1840, No. 105, pp. 60, 62.

[19] V. K. Andrievich, *Istoriia Sibiri,* I, 147.

[20] Lantzeff, pp. 66–67.

[21] J. E. Fischer, I, 179 n. 3; Lantzeff, pp. 63–65.

their Russian companions.[22] Ultimately all of these military serving men came to be known by the one name, cossacks.[23] They and the promyshlenniks were the conquerors of Siberia.

At first glance the state employees and promyshlenniks seem to constitute two different types of invaders: the one an official representative or servant of the state, the other a private profiteer who entered Siberia at his own expense and risk. Actually, they differed but little; their psychology and interests, their duties, and their organization and mode of life were the same.[24]

As individuals they displayed like qualities of character—boldness, courage, great persistence and endurance. They both possessed a passion for adventure and a greed for booty—to such an extent that they often disregarded the means they employed.[25] The fur trade occupied them both, and the serving man was almost as much a fur trader as the promyshlennik; in fact, many serving men were erstwhile promyshlenniks, for the new serving men were recruited principally from the ranks of the latter.[26] The official duties of the serving men brought them into a direct contact with the natives which offered them excellent opportunities for acquiring furs.[27] Up to 1625 they participated freely in the fur trade, and though the reforms of Suleshev in that year forbade further participation by them, they commonly disregarded the prohibition.[28] In turn, the promyshlenniks were almost as much state employees as private enterprisers.[29] Frequently the numbers of the serving men were inadequate, and promyshlenniks had to be utilized for state service. They assisted as volunteers (*okhotniki*) in the collection of iasak and in the conquering expeditions.[30] Or sometimes the promyshlenniks were commissioned by the voevodas themselves to collect iasak and to conquer new lands in the name of the tsar.[31]

---

[22] Andrievich, *loc. cit.*

[23] J. E. Fischer, I, 97–98; P. A. Slovtsov, *Istoricheskoe obozrenie Sibiri*, pp. 6–7 and 7 n. This coalescing of the several ranks of serving men into one general type, the cossack, probably arose from the facts that amidst frontier conditions the original distinctions of rank broke down and that the cossacks were the most numerous and active of the serving men.

[24] Vernadskii, *op. cit.*, pp. 333, 346.

[25] V. I. Ogorodnikov, *Zavoevanie russkimi Sibiri*, p. 43.

[26] *D.A.I.*, IV, 247; Ogloblin, III, 151.

[27] *D.A.I.*, II, 270–271.

[28] *A.I.*, IV, 443; *D.A.I.*, III, 340; *R.I.B.*, II, 964; Butsinskii, *Zaselenie Sibiri*, pp. 248–249; Andrievich, I, 149.

[29] Vernadskii, *op. cit.*, p. 337.

[30] *D.A.I.*, II, 240, III, 21, 58, 258, IV, 13, 320, V, 335; Vernadskii, *op. cit.*, pp. 336–338, 342.

[31] "Istoricheskie akty o podvigakh Erofeia Khabarova," pp. 54–55.

Likewise in their organization and mode of life the serving men and promyshlenniks resembled each other. Under an acknowledged leader (*peredovshchík*), the promyshlenniks joined together in armed bands, or *vatágas,* which were no different from the cossack bands organized by the serving men, since the military service of the serving men was not the disciplined routine associated with a settled society. Considerable freedom existed for the play of initiative and enterprise; their instructions "to collect iasak and seek new lands" amounted to a roving commission. In a country where they were the force of the law, the bands of serving men acted as independently of authority and of each other as did the vatagas of the promyshlenniks.[32] Like the promyshlenniks, too, the serving men shared the booty among the members of the band.[33]

Thus promyshlennik bands and cossack bands alike, or frequently parties composed of both promyshlenniks and serving men, roamed the wilds of Siberia, hunting wild animals and seeking new lands and natives from whom iasak could be taken. Differing originally in function, the one a fur trader, the other the agent of the state, promyshlennik and serving man became hardly distinguishable from one another. The merging of the interests of one and the duties of the other fashioned the conquerors of Siberia, adventurous undisciplined freebooters in pursuit of valuable furs.

The Character of the Conquest

The fur trade and conquest proceeded hand in hand in Siberia. For reasons to be discussed in a subsequent chapter the entrance of the Russians into Siberia brought a steady decrease in the number of fur-bearing animals there. As hunting grounds became exhausted, of necessity others had to be found, so that beyond the frontier of Russian occupation there were always some promyshlenniks, more adventurous than the rest, who sought to escape the more crowded areas or to find some unexploited region, which, preferably, they might keep to themselves.[34] Sooner or later the discoveries of a few men became the knowledge of many, and hunters began to push into the new regions. Conquest of these regions almost invariably followed because it was the most direct and profitable means of obtaining furs, both for the state, which collected

[32] *D.A.I.*, II, 231–232, III, 340, IV, 382–383, VIII, 264–265, 268–269; Vernadskii, *op. cit.*, pp. 348–349; Andrievich, I, 154; F. A. Golder, *Russian Expansion on the Pacific, 1641–1850*, p. 74.

[33] Vernadskii, *op. cit.*, pp. 350–352.

[34] *D.A.I.*, III, 102, VII, 150; Andrievich, I, 63, 148.

them as tribute, and for the serving men, who obtained them either as gifts or by threat of force.[35] Frequently, in fact, the Siberian authorities and serving men did not wait upon the exploratory activities of the promyshlenniks but set out themselves to find and conquer new regions in order that furs might be collected from their inhabitants. Exhaustion of hunting grounds, discovery of new ones, and their subjection to Russian authority—that is the process by which Siberia came under Muscovite control; and since the demand for furs was tremendous, the exhaustion of hunting grounds proceeded quickly. It is this rapid exhaustion, more than any other factor, which explains the rapidity of the conquest of Siberia. It is also the basic factor in the eastward advance of the Russians across Siberia.

The process by which Siberia was conquered is not peculiar to it. It repeats for the most part that by which a large part of the United States and most of Canada were explored and were subjected to European rule. The major difference lies in the practice by the Russian state of exacting formal tribute in furs from the Siberian natives. This had the effect of bringing about the political subjugation of a given area more quickly in Siberia than in North America. But otherwise both regions owe their opening and first exploitation to the fur trade.

The search of the Russian invader for valuable furs and his passion to learn what lay beyond the frontier knew no limits. No land was too distant, no risk too great for him if it promised the chance for gain and adventure.[36] Siberia was a vast land, almost every part of which yielded the precious sable and other prized fur-bearing animals. Beckoning promyshlenniks and serving men alike, they drew these restless conquerors always eastward, until nearly all of Siberia was brought under the sovereignty of the Russian tsar.

Although the nature of the Russian advance changed in its progress across Siberia, its strategy remained essentially the same. This strategy was based on the river, the portage, and the *ostróg*, or fort.[37] Four large river systems and several smaller ones spread themselves over Siberia and form natural lines of communication.

---

[35] Müller, *op. cit.*, p. 249; Andrievich, I, 149. It was a widespread custom among the natives of Siberia to bestow gifts, especially furs, upon those who visited them. This custom served the more to invite exploration by the state employees.

[36] Butsinskii, *Mangazeia*, p. 60.

[37] The strategy and methods of Russian expansion in Siberia have been worked out in detail in R. J. Kerner, *The Urge to the Sea*.

Along these rivers the Russians advanced. With the boats then in use most of the rivers in Siberia were navigable for long distances, and in flat-bottomed boats the Russian invaders moved up and down these waterways, pulling their boats when wind or current was against them.[38] Separating three of the four great river systems of Siberia are only low rolling mountains, and the Russians were enabled, thereby, to establish short portages between them. Joined by these portages, the rivers formed an extensive system of natural highways and afforded the basis for effective control of the country. Although the Russians used overland routes as well, traveling in sledges in the winter when the rivers froze over and in horse-drawn carts in the summer,[39] the rivers were their main lines of communication, and their strategy of conquest was essentially a river strategy.

As the means of controlling the rivers the Russians set up forts, the ostrogs. The ostrog was constructed in the form of a rectangular wooden stockade, ten to twenty feet high, along which a parapet was built. Bastions housing artillery stood in each corner, over the gateway, and sometimes along the sides.[40] Within the stockade were contained various buildings, the voevoda's office (*s'ezzhaia izba*), the customhouse, living quarters, granary, church, and other buildings.[41] Around the main stockade was a second stockade, and a moat.[42] The Russians located their ostrogs so as to command strategic points, such as the confluence of rivers, the ends of portages, or tenable points along the rivers. With these ostrogs they secured their conquests and provided themselves with bases for advancing into unconquered areas. The ostrogs served also as centers of the state's fur trade. A supplementary agency of control was the *zimovie,* or blockhouse (literally, "winter quarters"). Blockhouses were built in the forests, on the tundras, along the rivers, on the shores of lakes and the ocean, at portages—in general,

[38] *D.A.I.*, II, 255, III, 104, 233, 346, 391, VIII, 263; Baddeley, II, 6, 16, 18. When available, horses were used in towing boats; otherwise man power had to be used.

[39] *D.A.I.*, III, 103, 344, IV, 88; Baddeley, II, 7; Slovtsov, p. 6.

[40] *D.A.I.*, II, 255; *R.I.B.*, II, 138, 428; P. N. Butsinskii, *K istorii Sibiri,* p. 26; *idem, Mangazeia,* p. 16.

[41] Butsinskii, *Zaselenie Sibiri,* pp. 63, 163; *idem, K istorii Sibiri,* p. 26; Müller, *op. cit.,* pp. 184–185. The Russian outpost at Fort Ross in California was such a structure. For a description of it see E. O. Essig, "The Russian Settlement at Ross," *California Historical Society Quarterly* (San Francisco), XII (No. 3, September, 1933), 191–217.

[42] *D.A.I.*, II, 255; *R.I.B.*, II, 428.

in places where there were no other habitations.[43] Built for defending the Russians against the natives, these blockhouses, quartering as many as fifty men, served equally as winter quarters, outposts for the collection of iasak, and headquarters for the serving men and promyshlenniks who roamed the outlying and distant regions of Siberia.[44] It was not unusual for a blockhouse to be enlarged into an ostrog,[45] for the steady influx of Russians into Siberia made additional administrative centers necessary.

Within eighty years after the fall of Sibir the Russians overran almost all of Siberia. Only the Amur Valley, the peninsula of Kamchatka, the Kirghiz steppes, and the uppermost part of the Enisei did not come under Russian rule during that period.[46] The conquest, by virtue of its river strategy, assumed the geographical pattern of a series of advances in which the river systems were successively explored and brought under Russian control. The westernmost river system, the Ob-Irtysh, was the first to be conquered, during the two decades 1585–1605.[47] The conquest of the Enisei and its principal tributaries, the Lower Tunguska, the Stony Tunguska, and the Angara (or Upper Tunguska) followed, control being effectively established by 1628.[48] The conquest of the next great river system, the Lena, began in 1620. The lower and middle Lena were conquered by 1640; the upper Lena, inhabited by the Buriats, was not subjugated until the early 'fifties.[49] Between 1636 and 1651 the Russians occupied successively the river basins in northeastern Siberia between the lower Lena and the Bering Sea.[50] In 1638 they entered the country east of Lake Baikal, that is, Trans-Baikalie, and by the 'fifties had gained control of it.[51] They also entered the Amur Valley, in 1643, but there they encountered the Chinese, a people with a culture more advanced than their own, who prevented them from gaining a firm hold and compelled them ultimately to yield control, in 1689, by the Treaty of Nerchinsk.[52]

---

[43] *D.A.I.*, III, 320, 331, IV, 88; *Entsiklopedicheskii slovar'*, Vol. XII:2, p. 590.

[44] *D.A.I.*, III, 40, 276.

[45] Butsinskii, *Mangazeia*, pp. 52, 57; *idem, K istorii Sibiri*, p. 19.

[46] V. I. Ogorodnikov, *Zavoevanie russkimi Sibiri*, pp. 37, 45, 104, 107; S. V. Bakhrushin, *Ocherki po istorii kolonizatsii Sibiri v XVI i XVII vv.*, pp. 159, 160.

[47] Ogorodnikov, *Zavoevanie russkimi Sibiri*, p. 40; Bakhrushin, *op. cit.*, p. 110.

[48] Ogorodnikov, *Zavoevanie russkimi Sibiri*, pp. 45–47.

[49] *Ibid.*, pp. 48, 50, 66–67.

[50] *Ibid.*, pp. 54–61.

[51] *Ibid.*, pp. 67, 73.

[52] *Ibid.*, pp. 68–69, 74–75, 102.

The Conquest in Western Siberia

In its earlier stages the conquest of Siberia was a venture initiated and directed by the state. The state, like any private enterpriser, sought to profit from the fur resources of Siberia, and since it possessed political authority and great resources, it was in a position to dominate the conquest. It dispatched its officials and serving men to Siberia, and there, under its direction, these men systematically carried out the conquest and collected tribute.

The conquest in Western Siberia proceeded according to a plan. At intervals Moscow instructed its voevodas to send detachments of serving men to build ostrogs at advantageous points.[53] Then, with these ostrogs as bases, the serving men went out into the surrounding regions to subject the natives, by force or persuasion, and to impose iasak upon them, which was paid annually thereafter. From these ostrogs expeditions also went to find new lands, the inhabitants of which could be placed under tribute to the tsar. By these means the territory subject to a given ostrog increased and often became too large for effective administration and control. The more distant a region was from an ostrog, the less possible its complete subjugation and the more difficult and uncertain the collection of iasak, so that it became necessary to build new ostrogs in the outlying regions.[54] By this process of establishing, consolidating, and then expanding its control Moscow conquered the territory between the Ural Mountains and the Enisei River.

The systematic conquest of the basin of the Ob and Irtysh rivers, that is, Western Siberia, began with the establishment of Tiumen (1586) on the lower Tura River and Tobolsk (1587) at the confluence of the Tobol and Irtysh rivers. These towns secured the route from Russia and formed the basis for extending the conquest over the whole river system. Losva (1590) and Pelym (1593) were founded to ensure more prompt and easier collection of tribute from the Voguls of the upper Tavda area, who formerly paid their tribute to Tobolsk, and to bring other natives under tribute.[55] A few years later (1600), for the more adequate defense of the iasak-paying natives against the maraudings of the Nogai Tatars from the south, Turinsk was built on the Tura River midway between Verkhoturie and Tiumen.[56] Tara (1594) was built on the

[53] Bakhrushin, *op. cit.*, p. 153.
[54] Müller, *op. cit.*, pp. 247–248.
[55] *Ibid.*, pp. 175, 183, 193; Butsinskii, *Zaselenie Sibiri*, pp. 160–162.
[56] Butsinskii, *Zaselenie Sibiri*, pp. 62–63.

upper Irtysh to protect Tobolsk from the south and to end the raids by the remnants of Kuchum's forces upon the tribute-paying natives, who thereafter paid their tribute to Tara rather than to Tobolsk as before.[57] Surgut (1594) was established on the Ob River to subdue the native ruler Vonia, head of the Narym Ostiaks, and to obviate sending serving men from Tobolsk up the Ob to collect iasak from them.[58] Narym, farther up the Ob, began as a blockhouse occupied by serving men from Surgut;[59] and in turn, serving men from Narym advanced up the Ket River, a tributary of the Ob, and imposed tribute upon the Ostiaks there. They proved difficult to hold in submission, so Ketsk ostog was built (about 1602).[60] Tomsk (1604) was established in the country of the upper Ob at the invitation of the local native chieftain, who agreed to pay iasak. Iasak formerly collected from Surgut was now more easily collected from Tomsk.[61] From Tomsk cossacks moved into the Kuznetsk region to collect iasak from the local Tatars, and eventually (1618) Kuznetsk ostog was built there.[62] From Tomsk cossacks also were sent eastward towards the Enisei to explore and to place the natives under tribute.[63] In the north the Russians established Berezov (1593) to enable better iasak collection and to bring the Samoeds under tribute.[64] Mangazeia (1600) was built so that the state could collect tribute from the Samoeds in the rich fur regions of the Taz. Thus, taking up the original conquest where Ermak had left it, Moscow proceeded to create a network of ostrogs in the Ob-Irtysh region by which it maintained its control and through which passed a profitable revenue in furs.

The Conquest in Eastern Siberia

A conquest planned and supervised by Moscow was possible in Western Siberia. In the basin of the Ob-Irtysh river system the natural conditions were everywhere similar to the northern districts of Muscovite Russia. But beyond the Enisei a new country began, distant from Moscow and with very different physiographic characteristics and a more diversified native population. As the Russians penetrated deeper into Siberia, the administration found

[57] Müller, *op. cit.*, pp. 206–207, 223; Butsinskii, *Zaselenie Sibiri*, pp. 143–148.
[58] Butsinskii, *K istorii Sibiri*, pp. 1–3.
[59] *Ibid.*, p. 19.
[60] *Ibid.*, p. 24.
[61] Müller, *op. cit.*, pp. 315–317, 321–322.
[62] *Ibid.*, pp. 335–348.
[63] *Ibid.*, p. 354.
[64] *Ibid.*, p. 198; Butsinskii, *Zaselenie Sibiri*, p. 173.

it more difficult to orient itself in the new regions, and gradually the initiative in conquest passed to the local authorities and to individual groups of Russian people. Moscow ceased playing the leading role, and in the place of its coördinated conquest there developed an orderless elementary movement of the Russian peoples always farther to the east.[65]

Freer than in Western Siberia to give rein to their own initiative and interests, the serving men and promyshlenniks themselves assumed the dominant role in the subjugation of Eastern Siberia. That did not mean, however, that Moscow became less interested in obtaining for itself the profitable fur revenue from iasak. The state still insisted upon its share from all conquests, and all conquering was done in the name of the tsar and for his "profit." But since at a distance Moscow could only loosely organize and control the conquest of the country beyond the Enisei, it had to make use of the instruments at hand, the serving men and promyshlenniks drawn to the frontier by the hope of personal gain, who, in turn, utilized their position as state agents to their own advantage. It was in Eastern Siberia that the serving men adopted many of the characteristics of the fur trader, and the promyshlenniks those of the state employee. The conquest was neither entirely a state enterprise, nor wholly a series of private undertakings; it was the combination of two interests, which sought to exploit Siberia's fur wealth.

In the occupation of Western Siberia the promyshlenniks had been overshadowed by Moscow. Yet even there theirs had been an essential part of the conquest. They had explored unknown regions, found new sources of furs, and brought back information important for the building of new ostrogs.[66] They had first exploited the rich Mangazeia region; they, along with serving men, had first pushed up the Ob River from Surgut to impose iasak upon the natives.[67] With their penetration into Eastern Siberia, they emerged from the dominance of Moscow, and their activities became increasingly conspicuous.

Here the promyshlenniks not merely explored, but shared in the conquest as well.[68] Found in the outermost regions of the Rus-

[65] Ogorodnikov, *Zavoevanie russkimi Sibiri*, pp. 40–41; Bakhrushin, *op. cit.*, p. 159.

[66] Müller, *op. cit.*, p. 247; Andrievich, I, 34.

[67] Müller, *op. cit.*, pp. 248, 299; Butsinskii, *Mangazeia*, pp. 11, 40.

[68] K. P. Zagoskin, *Russkie vodnye puti i sudovoe delo do-petrovskoi Rossii*, p. 324, cited by N. Ianitskii in "Torgovlia pushnym tovarom v XVII v.," *Kievskiia universitetskiia izvestiia*, LII (No. 9, 1912), 3.

sian occupation and more numerous than the serving men, they were usually the first to enter a new region.[69] The activities of the state, the building of ostrogs, the collection of iasak, and the restrictions placed upon their trading with the natives, interfered with their fur trade, so that these independent souls sought regions not yet subject to iasak in the free unsettled wilds of the north and east.[70] After establishing themselves in blockhouses as their living quarters and centers of defense, these men, in armed bands, searched out new fur regions, which they exploited by hunting or by trade with the natives.[71] They visited the native villages and ascertained the number of inhabitants and the extent of the fur resources. If the forces of the promyshlenniks were strong enough, they sometimes exacted iasak from the natives; otherwise they might join forces with serving men and return to place the natives under the sovereignty of the tsar and to collect iasak.[72] It was not at all uncommon for the leaders of the bands of serving men to draft promyshlenniks to assist in their conquering expeditions, as they were customarily instructed to do.[73]

The official conquest and annexation of new territory were the work of the serving men. Where the promyshlenniks had opened the way, the serving men followed, often to protect the promyshlenniks from the natives, "to bring the unsubjugated natives under the exalted hand of the sovereign," and to collect iasak.[74] Expeditions for this purpose were organized in the principal towns and sent out to conquer the new regions and explore them further.[75] These expeditions commonly remained out in the wilds a year or more, often two or three, and sometimes as long as seven, years. The band of serving men might move over a considerable expanse of territory, placing natives under oath to the tsar and collecting iasak; or it might secure itself in a particular region, build blockhouses, and then divide into small parties, which were assigned to conquer different regions.[76] If the expedition saw fit to remain out

[69] Bakhrushin, *op. cit.*, p. 160; *D.A.I.*, III, 99–100, 276, IV, 88, VII, 150.

[70] Andrievich, I, 63–64; V. I. Ogorodnikov, *Zavoevanie russkimi Sibiri*, pp. 81–82; *D.A.I.*, III, 259.

[71] *D.A.I.*, III, 100, 276, IV, 88; *R.I.B.*, II, 374, 968–970; J. E. Fischer, I, 501.

[72] *D.A.I.*, III, 102, 173–174, IV, 404; Slovtsov, p. 6; Butsinskii, *Mangazeia*, p. 60.

[73] *D.A.I.*, II, 175, 240, III, 21, 24, 58, 258, 276, 351, IV, 13, 72, 320, VII, 150.

[74] *D.A.I.*, III, 276, IV, 88; *R.I.B.*, II, 851–856.

[75] *D.A.I.*, II, 256, III, 320, 322, 343–344, 350, IV, 82, 242.

[76] *D.A.I.*, IV, 16–27, 267–268.

for some time, the iasak collected was sent with a few serving men to the town from which the expedition originated.[77] Losses in man power were made good from the promyshlenniks and traders found in the region. Upon returning from regions in which an expedition had succeeded in establishing Russian authority, some of the serving men were left in blockhouses to continue the search for and conquest of new lands and to make the annual iasak collections.[78] In time these serving men were relieved by a new shift, whom the voevodas dispatched to continue the work of conquest and iasak collection.[79] By such a process Russian control was extended over Eastern Siberia.

A common practice by which new lands were opened and conquered combined the activities of both promyshlenniks and serving men.[80] A so-called *opýtovshchik*[81] applied to the authorities of an ostrog for permission to explore unknown lands.[82] The local authorities willingly granted such permission, since it offered them opportunities for personal gain and increased "the tsar's profit." The opytovshchik then gathered together a band of hunters and representatives of wealthy Moscow and north-Russian merchants. The voevoda added a detachment of serving men, and sometimes a "sworn man" (a deputized townsman)[83] to look after the interests of the state.[84] He instructed the opytovshchik to collect iasak from the natives of the discovered lands and to build ostrogs and blockhouses, which served as bases of operations for the Russians. After erecting such fortifications, the band divided itself into small groups and dispersed in various directions, some to explore and collect iasak, others to catch fish and hunt and trap wild animals. At times of temporary failure or when compelled to retreat, the Russians repaired to these fortifications; here, too, they defended themselves against sieges by aroused natives.[85] These expeditions

[77] *D.A.I.*, II, 240.

[78] *D.A.I.*, III, 56, 100, 242.

[79] *D.A.I.*, II, 243, III, 21, 333, 338, IV, 71, 201, 267.

[80] Ogloblin, III, 94–97.

[81] This term, now obsolete in the Russian language, referred to a type of enterpriser on the frontier who embodied the characteristics of both the promoter and prospector.

[82] *D.A.I.*, II, 231, 263, III, 258, IV, 88–89, 95–96, VII, 150; "Istoricheskie akty o podvigakh Erofeia Khabarova," p. 62.

[83] In Russian, *tseloval'nik*, "one who has kissed the cross," i.e., taken an oath.

[84] *D.A.I.*, II, 175, 263, IV, 50, 72, 73, VII, 149–150.

[85] *D.A.I.*, III, 322, IV, 88–89; "Istoricheskie akty o podvigakh Erofeia Khabarova," pp. 54–56, 84–91; V. I. Ogorodnikov, "Russkaia gosudarstvennaia vlast' i sibirskie inorodtsy v XVI–XVIII vv.," p. 72; *idem*, *Zavoevanie russkimi Sibiri*, pp. 43–44.

best exemplify the merging of private and state interests in the conquest of Eastern Siberia.

The Russian occupation in the Ob-Irtysh basin had hardly been secured before the advance into the Enisei began. The initiative and forces for this advance came chiefly from two of the easternmost outposts, Mangazeia and Ketsk. In 1607 promyshlenniks and traders from Mangazeia entered the Enisei at Turukhansk (founded in 1607) and pushed up the Lower Tunguska to levy iasak on the Ostiaks there. In 1610 another detachment went up the Enisei to the Sym River and there collected iasak for the first time. The same year a band of promyshlenniks and merchants sailed down the Enisei to its mouth, the first Russians to do so.[86] Subsequent expeditions of serving men and promyshlenniks extended the area of iasak collection about the lower Enisei, and by 1626, 28 cossacks and 189 promyshlenniks were known to be operating on the Lower Tunguska, while 44 cossacks and 312 promyshlenniks were established on the Stony Tunguska.[87] The upper Enisei was opened in the same manner. Ketsk serving men reached the Sym River in 1605 and collected iasak. Two years later more Ketsk serving men advanced to the Enisei and up the Angara, collecting iasak. In 1608 a third expedition of serving men moved up the Enisei to the region of the later Krasnoiarsk. To crush the resistance of hostile natives and to facilitate iasak collection Moscow ordered an ostrog built on the Enisei, and thereupon Eniseisk was founded in 1619.[88] For similar reasons Krasnoiarsk on the upper Enisei was built in 1628.[89] From Eniseisk and Mangazeia new expeditions were undertaken, which resulted in the conquest of the Lena, the third great river basin.

The Russians who first penetrated into the Lena basin found it to be rich in fur-bearing animals. Since the yield in Western Siberia was beginning to diminish, it was only a matter of time before the Russians began to overrun this new region.[90] Serving men and promyshlenniks from Mangazeia opened the lower Lena. By 1619 the jurisdiction of Mangazeia had been extended to the Lena. In 1620 serving men reached the Viliui River, and from the local Tungus learned of the Lena Iakuts, whereupon they descended the

[86] Müller, "Sibirskaia istoriia," pp. 42–43, 99–101; *R.I.B.*, II, 849–851.
[87] Andrievich, I, 64.
[88] Müller, "Sibirskaia istoriia," pp. 197–211.
[89] *Ibid.*, pp. 228, 235.
[90] *R.I.B.*, II, 961–964.

Viliui to the Lena. In 1630 thirty men from Mangazeia were sent to the Lena under Martyn Vasiliev, who collected the first iasak from the northern Iakuts.[91] The upper Lena, meanwhile, was opened by promyshlenniks and serving men from Eniseisk. As early as 1619 promyshlenniks and serving men advanced from Eniseisk up the Angara River, where they were told by the Tungus of the "great river" to the east.[92] Vasilii Bugor, at the head of a cossack band of ten men, reached the Lena in 1628 and took iasak from the local Iakuts. Thereafter serving men were sent yearly from Eniseisk to collect iasak from the previously subjected natives and to conquer more of them. Seeing the need of an ostrog on the Lena River for defense against hostile natives and collection of iasak, the Eniseisk voevoda sent a detachment of twenty men under Petr Beketov in 1631 to build one there.[93] The new ostrog was Iakutsk, on the middle Lena. With its establishment the Eniseisk serving men, assisted by promyshlenniks, began to act more aggressively, and in the following years parties of them subjected the natives of the Olekma, Aldan, lower Lena, and Olenek rivers.[94] The wealth of furs in the Lena region attracted Russians from all parts of Siberia, especially Tomsk, and by the 'forties they had reached the Okhotsk Sea, dotting their course with blockhouses for iasak collection.[95]

The unceasing advance of the Russians "against the sun" moved by the same process to the Bering Sea and into the rest of Siberia. Northeastern Siberia was conquered by detachments from Eniseisk and Iakutsk. Those led by Elisei Buza (1636–1639), Ivanov Postnik (1638–1639), Mikhail Stadukhin (1643–1645), and Fedot Alekseev and Semen Dezhnev comprise the better-known expeditions.[96] Typical of the merging of private and state enterprise is the most famous of them, the one headed by Alekseev and Dezhnev. It was organized in 1647 by Alekseev, the agent of a rich Moscow merchant, for the purpose of obtaining furs and walrus tusks and of opening the Anadyr country. He requested that Dezhnev, a Iakutsk cossack, head a detachment of serving men to look after the interests of the state. Composed of traders, promyshlenniks, and serving men, this

[91] J. E. Fischer, I, 502–503; V. I. Ogorodnikov, *Zavoevanie russkimi Sibiri*, p. 48.

[92] *R.I.B.*, II, 374.

[93] *R.I.B.*, II, 970–971.

[94] J. E. Fischer, I, 506–507; Andrievich, I, 66–68; *D.A.I.*, II, 240.

[95] V. I. Ogorodnikov, *Zavoevanie russkimi Sibiri*, pp. 47–50; Andrievich, I, 70–71.

[96] *D.A.I.*, II, 241–242, 243, III, 99–100; J. E. Fischer, I, 518–519, 531–533; Andrievich, I, 68–69.

expedition in the years 1648–1656 journeyed to the Kolyma River and thence by land or by sea around the East Cape to the Anadyr River.[97] In this region Dezhnev—Alekseev was lost early in the journey—remained seven years, exploring and collecting iasak, which he forwarded to Iakutsk.[98]

The conquest in the northeast was accompanied by the entrance of promyshlenniks and serving men into the southern part of Eastern Siberia, the territory inhabited by Buriats, between the Uda River (a tributary of the Selenga) and the Iablonovoi Mountains, and the Amur Valley. Expeditions under Petr Beketov (1628), Ivan Galkin (1630), Martyn Vasiliev (1641), and Kurbat Ivanov (1643) conquered the Buriat territory west of Lake Baikal, in which region they erected several blockhouses and placed the Buriats under iasak.[99] Rumors of gold, silver, and valuable furs drew the Russians into the country east of Lake Baikal, or Trans-Baikalie, where they established themselves in the 'forties. Of furs they found plenty, but the gold and silver among the Buriats proved to have been obtained from Mongolia in exchange for valuable furs. In Trans-Baikalie the Russians heard reports of the Amur as a region of fertile lands, as well as of gold, silver, and furs.[100] These reports prompted the Iakutsk voevoda to organize in 1643 under Vasilii Poiarkov a party of serving men and promyshlenniks, who proceeded by way of the Lena, Aldan, and Zeia rivers to the Amur.[101] There Poiarkov and his men sailed down the river to its mouth, and thence by way of the Okhotsk Sea, Ula, Maia, and Aldan rivers back to Iakutsk. Poiarkov brought back nearly five hundred sable pelts as iasak and reported a great abundance of fur-bearing animals, much grain, but no indigenous gold and silver.[102] The shorter and better route into the Amur Valley, the Olekma and Shilka rivers, was opened by promyshlenniks in the course of their hunting and trading.[103] Their activities and those

[97] Dezhnev's purported sea voyage is a disputed question. Cf. G. F. Müller, "Nachrichten von Seereisen, und zur See gemachten Entdeckungen," *Sammlung russischer Geschichte*, III, 7–20, and Ogloblin, "Semen Dezhnev," pp. 249–306, with Golder, pp. 67–95.

[98] Ogloblin, "Semen Dezhnev," pp. 253–254, 259, 265, 267–268; Dezhnev's report is in *D.A.I.*, IV, 16–27.

[99] *D.A.I.*, II, 254–255, 261, III, 21; Andrievich, I, 72–76; V. I. Ogorodnikov, *Zavoevanie russkimi Sibiri*, pp. 62–65.

[100] *D.A.I.*, II, 248; P. P. Golovin, "Instruktsiia pis'mianomu golove Poiarkovu," *Chteniia*, 1861, No. 1, pt. 5, pp. 1–4, 8–9.

[101] Golovin, pp. 1–44.

[102] *D.A.I.*, III, 50–56.

[103] *D.A.I.*, III, pp. 102–104, 173.

of the serving men in the Amur inspired the famous Khabarov expeditions, which constituted the first attempt at occupation of the Amur by the Russians.

Like the Dezhnev expedition, Khabarov's expeditions combined private enterprise with state interest. Khabarov was an established promyshlennik and noted opytovshchik, who had migrated from Solvychegodsk to the Enisei and thence to the Lena, where he had grown wealthy in the fur trade. Seeking to exploit the fur wealth of the Amur, he petitioned and received from the Iakutsk voevoda, Frantsbekov, permission to form an expedition of volunteers, which was intended both as a business venture to benefit Khabarov and as an effort to extend the tsar's rule to the natives of the Amur.[104] Khabarov invested 3,500 rubles (about 50,000 r. today) and Frantsbekov himself lent an equal amount. Khabarov made two expeditions into the Amur. The first (1649–1650), which numbered one hundred and fifty volunteer serving men and promyshlenniks, failed to collect any iasak, but made the important discovery that the natives of the Amur were tributary to the Chinese emperor.[105] The second expedition (1651–1653), of about three hundred and thirty men, proceeded down the Amur to a point below the Ussuri River, collecting much iasak, destroying the towns of those natives who refused submission, and even defeating an overwhelmingly large force of Manchus. But in spite of the successes of Khabarov and his men the significance of Chinese overlordship in the Amur became increasingly evident to the Russians: a force of two or three hundred men engaged in a raiding expedition could not hope to acquire control of territory claimed by such a powerful state as the Chinese empire. To conquer the Amur would require a strong military force of several thousand men; to hold the territory would entail a considerable movement of agricultural settlers, who would provide food for such a force. The Russians met neither of these requirements. Moscow tried to send a large force into the Amur, but failed. Numerous Russians in Siberia flocked into the Amur Valley, drawn there by reports of its great natural wealth, but such men were interested in booty, not agriculture, and the natives, under the direction of the Chinese, reduced their grain output. The Russians thus failed to gain a firm hold in the Amur and were evicted from the region by the Chinese in 1689.

The failure of the Russians in the Amur reveals by contrast the

[104] "Istoricheskie akty o podvigakh Erofeia Khabarova," pp. 54–56, 62–63.
[105] *D.A.I.*, III, 260; V. I. Ogorodnikov, *Zavoevanie russkimi Sibiri*, p. 85.

essential character of the conquest of Siberia in the course of the seventeenth century. Facing primitive, politically unorganized peoples, the Russians could conduct a conquest successfully by means of small bands of freebooters in pursuit of furs. But this method could bring no other result than failure when employed against a strong advanced state with a large disciplined military force, like the Chinese empire. The seriousness of the failure to keep the Amur Valley with its fertile lands was not lost upon the Russians, and the significance of the loss became greater as the fur-bearing animals, which were Siberia's greatest single resource, decreased in number.

In describing the relation of the fur trade to the conquest of Siberia, there is the danger of explaining that conquest only in terms of the fur trade. The fur trade alone did not give rise to the conquest, for other incentives and attractions urged men to Siberia. Social and economic conditions in Russia, especially the spread and tightening of the bonds of serfdom, drove many to seek the greater freedom of Siberia.[106] The love of adventure contributed greatly to extending the conquest—that is, the love of adventure together with the hope of personal enrichment, for it is doubtful whether the love of adventure by itself urged many to subject themselves to the hardships and dangers of life on the frontier. Once in Siberia, the Russians learned of other sources of wealth, which drew them into the unknown—valuable walrus ivory along the Arctic shores, rare birds, gold and silver in Trans-Baikalie and the Amur, the fertile lands of the Amur.[107] Yet none of these forms of wealth was common to the whole of Siberia; each was confined to some one or two particular regions. The importance of furs in the conquest thus becomes clear: they were found in abundance, as was no other form of wealth, in virtually all parts of Siberia, and they gave rise to the hope and expectation of gain which set aflame the spark of adventure in those hardy souls who were ever pushing farther into the unknown.

It is not a usual concept to think of the love of adventure as motivating the actions of a state. If we seek to explain the active participation of the Muscovite state in the conquest of Siberia in something more than material terms, we may adduce the motive of imperial prestige. But Muscovite rulers were often practical men

[106] Butsinskii, *Zaselenie Sibiri,* pp. 220–221; Bakhrushin, *op. cit.,* p. 73; V. I. Ogorodnikov, *Zavoevanie russkimi Sibiri,* p. 6.

[107] *D.A.I.,* II, 258, III, 51, 68–69, 100, 109–110, IV, 51, 70–71.

who spoke in proud terms but acted according to their material interests. Though the conquest of Siberia enhanced their prestige and more than doubled their imperial domains, it was the revenue in furs which particularly engaged their attention and made possible the conquest.[108] Other sources of wealth existed in Siberia and the tsars did not ignore them, but furs, by virtue of their abundance, stood first and foremost as the practical purpose of conquest, paying not only the costs of conquest, but yielding a profit as well.

[108] *R.I.B.*, II, 962: "If the sovereign ordered the excess of Siberian people sent to this great river Lena and towns or ostrogs built wherever suitable, and ordered the peoples of the new lands along this great river Lena and other rivers brought under the exalted hand of the tsar, and iasak collected, there would be a great increase for the sovereign's treasury, and the Lena river would be another Mangazeia." From instructions to *stol'nik* Petr Golovin and *d'iak* Efim Filatov, sent to Siberia to the river Lena for the building of an ostrog and the subjection of the Siberian natives to Russian rule, August 6, 1638.

CHAPTER IV

THE ACQUISITION OF FURS BY THE MUSCOVITE STATE

Russia was an exception among the colonial powers of the sixteenth and seventeenth centuries. Whereas the other colonial powers left the economic exploitation of their colonies to private enterprisers of one sort or another, the Muscovite state participated actively in the exploitation of the resources of Siberia. Not content with benefiting from Siberia's fur resources indirectly through the trade of its subjects, the state was determined to profit directly by trading in Siberian furs itself. This was the natural consequence of the fact that the tsar was himself an enterpriser, indeed the greatest in Russia, and that the fur trade was one of his most important enterprises.[1] No distinction existed between the tsar as ruler and the tsar as merchant; full use was made of his political authority and resources to carry on the state's trade in furs, even to the point of establishing a monopoly over certain parts of it. Hence, the state not only participated in the fur trade, but was also the biggest operator in the trade, for no private enterpriser, or group of enterprisers, could hope to equal the scale on which the state was able to conduct its business.

It is the participation of the state which sets the Russian fur trade apart from that of other countries. For that reason, an account of the conduct and organization of this trade may well begin with the description of the activities of the state. These activities were widespread. On the one hand, they extended throughout Siberia, whence nearly all the furs acquired by the state came, and related there to the acquisition of furs and to the protection of the state's trade against encroachment from competitors. On the other hand, they reached into many parts of Russia, to the various markets in which furs were sold, and even across the border into a few markets outside Russia. Since a full treatment of the state's fur trade should take account of these widespread activities, and of the size of the trade as well, we shall devote several chapters to that trade, under these topics: the acquisition by the state of furs in Siberia, the protection of its fur trade there, the volume of its

[1] Richard Hakluyt, *The Principal Navigations*, I, 298; Samuel Collins, "Nyneshnee sostoianie Rossii," *Chteniia*, 1846, No. 1, pt. 3, p. 18. Cf. pp. 142–145 below.

fur receipts, and the disposal of its furs at home and to the merchants from abroad.

The acquisition of furs by the state in Siberia was administered by the agency in Moscow which had charge of Siberian affairs. This agency was at first the Department of Ambassadors (the equivalent of the modern ministry of foreign affairs). Subsequently, about 1596, Siberia came under the supervision of the Novgorod Quarter (*Novgorodskii Chet*), only to be transferred, two or three years later, to the jurisdiction of the Kazan Palace. In another fifteen years or so a special division for Siberian affairs, the Siberian Department (*Sibirskii Prikaz*) arose in the Kazan Palace, and by 1637 this division had become an independent department with separate quarters, its head deciding all matters relating to Siberia, except the most important, which were referred to the tsar.[2] In Siberia itself the conduct of the fur trade of the state was one of the most important tasks of the officials and serving men whom the Siberian Department employed to carry on the conquest and administration of the country. The voevodas, guided by detailed instructions from the Siberian Department, supervised and were responsible for the several activities necessary to the obtaining of furs for the state; the serving men, often assisted by the promyshlenniks, carried them out. Thus it was by means of a political rather than a commercial organization that the state acquired its furs.

The state obtained its furs in three distinct ways, in the form of tribute or iasak from the natives, as a tithe imposed on the Russian promyshlenniks and traders, and by purchase. Each of these sources and the technique of acquisition pertaining to each will be described in some detail.

Iasak

Iasak, which was the term given to the fur tribute collected by the Russians from the natives of Siberia during the late sixteenth and the seventeenth centuries, was a combination of Siberian with Russian practice. The word itself, Old-Turkish in origin, took on several meanings; but among the Siberian natives it meant a compulsory tax imposed by law, in distinction from voluntary contributions, or *pominki.* It was tribute paid by the conquered to their conquerors, and as a sign of subjection it carried with it the

[2] P. N. Butsinskii, *Zaselenie Sibiri,* pp. 231–232; Ogloblin, I, 7, III, 209, 210, IV, 116–117, 123, 125–127; N. P. Likhachev, *Razriadnye d'iaki XVI veka,* "K str. 15–17," pp. 97–98.

implication of degradation.[3] The practice of imposing iasak had been in existence in Siberia long before the advent of the Russians, having been taken over by the peoples of Siberia from the Mongol-Tatar conquerors who penetrated to the Urals. The petty Mongol, Tatar, and Kalmyk states which followed the disintegration of the

FUR TRIBUTE TO THE CONQUEROR

Mongol-Tatar empire levied iasak upon the Siberian tribesmen and were still doing so when the Russians conquered Siberia. At the same time, certain tribes like the Ostiaks, Buriats, Kirghizes, and Tungus had succeeded in exacting iasak from neighboring tribes.[4]

[3] S. V. Bakhrushin, "Iasak v Sibiri v XVII veke," *Sibirskie ogni*, 1927, No. 3, p. 96; Joseph Klein, *Der sibirische Pelzhandel*, p. 40 n. 14.

[4] S. V. Bakhrushin, *Ocherki po istorii kolonizatsii Sibiri*, pp. 96–97; *Sibirskiia letopisi*, pp. 319, 321; G. F. Müller, *Opisanie sibirskago tsarstva*, pp. 216, 354; *idem*, "Sibirskaia istoriia," p. 204; *R.I.B.*, II, 159–160, 204, 446, Vol. XV, pt. 2, p. 5.

The Russians first encountered iasak in the thirteenth century among the natives of the Volga, who paid it to the Tatars, and in the sixteenth century the word found its way into frequent usage by the Russians.[5] Iasak was not, therefore, a Russian importation into Siberia, but an institution which had developed independently there. Nevertheless, it was in all essentials the equivalent of the Russian dan of Kiev, Novgorod, and Moscow, so when the Russians conquered the Siberian natives and exacted iasak from them, no fundamental change was involved on either side: the Russians continued a familiar practice, while for most of the Siberian inhabitants there occurred merely a change of masters.[6] The Russians carried this tribute system with them as they advanced across Siberia, modifying it to accord with the local conditions which they encountered and in some instances altering it radically.

The iasak exacted by the Russians was paid almost always in unfinished furs. There were occasions when it was accepted in such mediums as reindeer skins, grain, walrus ivory, money, jewelry, and horses,[7] but at such times the different medium was specified, so that by itself the term iasak referred to the tribute in furs. Because sables were plentiful and in most demand, the state made them the standard and insisted they be used whenever possible.[8] Sometimes sable coats (*shuby*) and caps (*shapki*) were taken in place of pelts.[9] If the natives could not find enough sables, they were allowed to pay their iasak in other pelts—in foxes, beavers, otters, martens, ermines, lynxes, wolves, or squirrels—but when these furs were used as iasak, the number of pelts required was determined according to their value in terms of sables.[10] Only pelts of good quality were acceptable, and they had to be in good condition, that is, not ripped, torn, or in any way damaged, and with the tails, paws, and belly intact. Young sables (*nedosoboli*)[11] were not wanted; pelts that were rotten, worn, or otherwise inferior

[5] Bakhrushin, "Iasak v Sibiri," p. 96; Müller, *Opisanie*, p. 71; *D.A.I.*, I, 168, 170.

[6] Bakhrushin, "Iasak v Sibiri," p. 98; Müller, *Opisanie*, pp. 354–355.

[7] *A.I.*, IV, 69; *D.A.I.*, II, 226, III, 350, VII, 151, VIII, 14; Müller, *Opisanie*, pp. 185, 332; Bakhrushin, "Iasak v Sibiri," p. 103; Ogloblin, I, 102.

[8] *A.I.*, II, 101, III, 325, IV, 69; *D.A.I.*, II, 176, 268, III, 335, 336, IV, 179–180, 202, 267; *R.I.B.*, II, 101–102, Vol. XV, pt. 5, p. 10; Müller, *Opisanie*, pp. 225, 279, 304.

[9] *D.A.I.*, IV, 72; Müller, *Opisanie*, pp. 195–196.

[10] *A.I.*, IV, 53; *D.A.I.*, III, 377, IV, 364, VI, 355–359; Müller, *Opisanie*, pp. 195–196; Bakhrushin, "Iasak v Sibiri," p. 104 n. 2; Ogloblin, I, 93.

[11] I.e., summer or autumn sables. N. Ianitskii, "Torgovlia pushnym tovarom v XVII v.," *Kievskiia universitetskiia izvestiia*, LII (No. 9, 1912), 2 n. Cf. below, p. 155.

were refused.[12] Inferior sables varied in value from those worth 1½ r. apiece to those worth 15 r. and less per forty pelts.[13] In the later years of the seventeenth century, when the supply of good sables was diminishing, the state demanded that the natives turn over to it as iasak any pelts of the best grade of other animals, particularly foxes, which they caught.[14] The furs which the natives paid to the state had to be of their own hunting, although there were exceptions.[15] However, these instructions with respect to the nature of the iasak were not too rigidly adhered to.[16]

The system of iasak which the Russians established in Siberia was not everywhere the same. The diversity of native peoples, their different modes of life and capacity to resist gave rise to important differences, the greatest of which derived from the dissimilarities between settled and nomadic natives: the system adopted for the former would not work for the latter. Other differences grew out of the rule, prior to the Russian period, of various parts of Siberia by Tatar peoples, who introduced and accustomed some of the Siberian tribes to a system of tribute. The Russians had also to take into account the fact that some Siberian peoples were overlords of other native peoples. The methods of exacting and collecting iasak which the Russians first developed on a large scale were those established in Western Siberia, where the native population for the most part was sedentary and accustomed to a tribute system. These methods the Russians extended to other parts of Siberia where the same or similar conditions prevailed, but they were not able to establish them in all Siberia.

By the beginning of the seventeenth century the Russians had laid the foundations of their system for the collection of fur tribute from the natives. In part it represented a borrowing from the former khanate of Sibir; the rest was of Russian devising. As the means to a systematic collection of iasak the country was divided into districts or *vólosts,* each volost comprising the area occupied by a given tribe. These volosts were the domains, taken over by the Russians and converted into iasak districts, of the princelings and petty chieftains, once the vassals of Kuchum Khan, who were now required by the Russians to assist them in the collection of

[12] *D.A.I.,* II, 162, 176–177, 268, III, 377, IV, 72–73, 202, 347; *R.I.B.,* II, 746; Müller, *Opisanie,* pp. 279, 304; *P.S.Z.,* III, 216.

[13] *D.A.I.,* III, 377; Ogloblin, IV, 123.

[14] *D.A.I.,* IV, 49, 325, 364, VIII, 28.

[15] *D.A.I.,* III, 377, IV, 360, 362, 407.

[16] *D.A.I.,* III, 335; see below, chap. v.

iasak.[17] Within the volosts the natives lived in village communities known as *iurts*. The volosts themselves were grouped into larger units called *uezds* (pronounced oo-yézds), each uezd having a Russian town as its administrative center and being governed by a voevoda from that center. Its boundaries were not, however, always clearly defined. By this division of the natives into volosts, and within the volosts into iurts, the Russians were better able to keep a year-to-year record in the iasak books—which were both a census of the natives and a tax list—of the payments made by each native.

The collection of iasak was carried out under the direction of the voevodas, and it constituted perhaps their chief duty. The first step towards collection was, of course, to bring the natives under agreement to pay it. Military force had to be resorted to frequently, but just as often the natives offered no resistance, particularly if they were already tributary to some other people.[18] Occasionally native tribes voluntarily sought Russian sovereignty.[19] To assure regular payment, the serving men were instructed to obtain an oath of allegiance to the tsar and to procure hostages in the persons of the "best" men, that is, princelings, chieftains, shamans, and the like.[20] These hostages were kept under guard a month, half-year, year, or more, according to local circumstances, and then exchanged for other hostages.[21] After the first payment to the conquering serving men the natives were required to pay the iasak annually.

Iasak was collected in two ways: (1) the natives themselves brought it to the town or ostrog where the Russian officials were stationed, or (2) the voevoda sent out collectors to the native villages and volosts. It rested with the natives which method was used. The first was customary when they lived near the administrative center.[22] The iasak was brought in by the native princelings and "best" men, who turned it over to the voevoda and inspected the hostages or exchanged them for new ones.[23] The voevoda, who had personally to receive the iasak, recorded it and gave the na-

[17] Bakhrushin, "Iasak v Sibiri," pp. 98–101.

[18] Müller, *Opisanie*, pp. 225, 305, 331, 343–344, 354–355; *D.A.I.*, III, 21, 322, 334, 338, IV, 267; S. Okun', "K istorii Buriatii v XVII v.," *Krasnyi arkhiv*, LXXVI (No. 3, 1936), 180, 183.

[19] Müller, *Opisanie*, p. 106.

[20] *Ibid.*, pp. 225, 236, 304; *D.A.I.*, II, 269, 270, III, 276, 278, IV, 205, 267, VII, 149.

[21] *A.I.*, IV, 443; *D.A.I.*, II, 270, 273, IV, 21, 107; *R.I.B.*, VIII, 475.

[22] Müller, *Opisanie*, p. 280; *A.I.*, II, 78, 102; *D.A.I.*, II, 243–246, III, 351, IV, 72, 104, 202; *R.I.B.*, Vol. XV, pt. 5, p. 18.

[23] Müller, *Opisanie*, p. 236; *D.A.I.*, II, 273.

tives receipts. He was not supposed to detain or molest the native representatives in any way or to impose extra exactions upon them.[24]

The second method of collection was used when the natives lived at some distance from a town or ostrog. The collectors were serving

FUR TRIBUTE (IASAK) PAID AT A SIBERIAN OSTROG

men selected by the voevodas, who were expected to appoint literate serving men, the "best" men—boiar-sons, atamans, detachment leaders, and the like—when possible. Often a sworn man or two accompanied the serving men. Taking the native hostages with them for inspection by their fellow tribesmen, the collectors proceeded to the villages of the iasak men and appeared at the specified

[24] Müller, *Opisanie*, p. 212; *D.A.I.*, II, 269, IV, 362.

collection places (*suglany*), where the natives came with their iasak.[25] The collectors gave the natives receipts for the iasak and recorded each native's payment in the iasak book.[26]

In those regions which were so distant from an ostrog as to make a round trip difficult within a season, serving men under a boiar-son, ataman, or other high-ranking serving man, sometimes accompanied by a sworn man or two, were sent into these outlying regions to conduct the annual collection of iasak.[27] At favorable spots in the wilds blockhouses were erected, which served as local administrative centers. In them the hostages were kept, and to them the natives brought their iasak. Though this method of collection through subsidiary centers began in Western Siberia, it attained its widest use in Eastern Siberia. In Western Siberia *godoval'shchiki,* or "year men," were sent out from Tobolsk and other important towns for periods of a year to collect iasak.[28] Surgut and Narym originated as blockhouses erected by year men.[29] But in Eastern Siberia the greater distances and the absence of any sizable Russian agricultural population which would develop towns, necessitated the widespread use of these blockhouse centers. In these centers the serving men remained on tours of duty for two, three, and four years, performing on a smaller scale many of the functions of the voevoda in the town. They were instructed to remain until relieved by a new detachment of serving men.[30] Because of the sparseness of the Russian population they often drew upon the local promyshlenniks and traders to assist them in the collection of iasak.[31]

The iasak was ordinarily collected in the late fall and early winter, after the hunting season. October, November, and December were the usual months for the iasak men to appear in the towns with the iasak and for the collectors to make their rounds of the volosts.[32]

At the outset of the conquest of Siberia by the Russians, Moscow

[25] Müller, *Opisanie*, pp. 194, 195, 279; *D.A.I.*, II, 268, 269, IV, 103–104, 363; V. I. Ogorodnikov, "Russkaia gosudarstvennaia vlast' i sibirskie inorodtsy v XVI–XVIII v.v.," *Sbornik trudov professorov i prepodavatelei gosudarstvennogo irkutskogo universiteta*, I, 74.

[26] *D.A.I.*, II, 269, IV, 104, 202; *R.I.B.*, Vol. XV, pt. 5, p. 19; Ogorodnikov, *loc. cit.*

[27] *D.A.I.*, II, 161, 175, 241, III, 332–333, IV, 71.

[28] *D.A.I.*, II, 77; Ogloblin, I, 181.

[29] P. N. Butsinskii, *K istorii Sibiri*, pp. 1, 19.

[30] *D.A.I.*, IV, 72.

[31] *D.A.I.*, III, 284, 337, IV, 72, 201, 403–404.

[32] *D.A.I.*, II, 175, 255, III, 220, 276, 277, 284, IV, 205; *A.I.*, IV, 49; Müller, *Opisanie*, pp. 323, 335, 354–355.

instructed its voevodas to collect iasak yearly according to the ability of the natives to pay—enough to make a profit for the sovereign, but not so much as to work hardship upon the natives.[33] But within a few years Moscow began to systematize the collection of iasak, placing it upon a definite basis. Iasak books were introduced in which were recorded the iasak paid and any existing arrears.[34] The iasak was levied as an established annual tax either directly upon the individual native or upon the volost as a whole.[35] The rate of the iasak when levied as a tax on the individual varied with the district and time. At the beginning of the century it was high, 10 to 12 sables per man,[36] and there are records of its being as high as 18 or 22 sables per man; but more often the rate was from 5 to 7 sables.[37] In some volosts married men paid more than unmarried men, 10 sables for the married, 5 for the unmarried man.[38] By the middle of the century, however, the quota had dropped to about 3 sables per man in Western Siberia.[39] The iasak rate when applied to the volost was set at a total of so many furs from each man, but within the volost the individual native's share would be greater or less than the average, according to his ability to pay. Thus in Pelym volost the average was set at 7 sables per man.[40] About 1626 a new basis was introduced in parts of Siberia, e.g., Berezov, Obdorsk, Surgut, Verkhoturie. Because fur prices fluctuated from one year to the next, and because the natives got rid of the poor sable pelts—those worth 13, 20, and 50 kopeks—as iasak, and sold or traded the good pelts for 7 or 8 rubles or more, the administration established the iasak in Western Siberia on a basis of value rather than quantity. Poor men paid in some places furs to the value of 1 r. or 1½ r., and rich men furs worth 2½ r. to 3 r. The rate varied between 1 and 4 rubles, with single men paying in some regions

[33] Müller, *Opisanie*, pp. 161–162; *R.I.B.*, II. 838; V. I. Ogorodnikov, *op. cit.*, pp. 74–75.

[34] V. I. Ogorodnikov, *op. cit.*, p. 75; Müller, *Opisanie*, pp. 194, 224–225; *R.I.B.*, II, 123. Few iasak books prior to 1626 are preserved, since in that year most of the records of the Siberian Department were destroyed by fire (*R.I.B.*, VIII, 350; Ogloblin, I, 90).

[35] *R.I.B.*, II, 125, 200–202; V. I. Ogorodnikov, *op. cit.*, p. 74.

[36] Müller, *Opisanie*, pp. 195, 261; Müller, "Sibirskaia istoriia," p. 42; P. N. Butsinskii, *Mangazeia i mangazeiskii uezd*, p. 22; *idem, K istorii Sibiri*, pp. 11, 27.

[37] A. Gnevushev, "Akty vremeni pravleniia tsaria Vasiliia Shuiskago," *Chteniia*, Vol. CCLIII (1915), No. 2, pt. 1, pp. 73–74; *A.I.*, I, 77, 101, 111, III, 325.

[38] Müller, *Opisanie*, pp. 291, 296–297; Bakhrushin, "Iasak v Sibiri," p. 104.

[39] V. I. Ogorodnikov, *op. cit.*, p. 75.

[40] Bakhrushin, "Iasak v Sibiri," pp. 104–105.

half that paid by married men.[41] This change met with protest from the natives, because the voevodas tended to undervalue the furs. At the end of the century the old basis was restored.[42]

The liability for iasak extended to all healthy men from eighteen to fifty years of age.[43] Slaves owned by the natives were occasionally held liable.[44] Although at first exempted from paying iasak, dependents (*zakhrebetniki*) and adolescents (*podrostki*) were later called upon to pay, not at the adult rate but whatever amount they could.[45] On the other hand, the poor, the aged, crippled, maimed, sick, and blind were exempted, as were the natives who were baptized or who entered some state service—for instance, farming, fishing, or the post service.[46] Sometimes the princelings of tribes which formerly exacted iasak from others (e.g., Enisei Kirghizes) were exempted, together with their immediate kinsmen, but Moscow sought to hold down the number of these exemptions.[47]

The system of iasak just described worked well enough as long as the native tribes remained within a given and limited area, but when the Russians came into contact with the nomadic tribesmen of Siberia, they found that the frequency and ease with which these tribesmen moved about the country presented a different set of problems. Possessing a mobility not allowed to the Russians, the nomadic natives could resist or avoid payment simply by disappearing.[48] Much as the Russians may have preferred, and attempted, to apply a regular system of iasak collection, the life of these tribes would not permit it, and the Russians had to make important modifications.

The principal nomadic tribes with which the Russians dealt were

---

[41] *R.I.B.*, VIII, 429–434, 493, 517, 590; Bakhrushin, "Iasak v Sibiri," p. 104; Butsinskii, *Zaselenie Sibiri*, pp. 313, 315, 317; P. A. Slovtsov, *Istoricheskoe obozrenie Sibiri*, I, 19. This does not mean that money was acceptable as iasak; with exceptions, it was not, for reasons explained below, p. 69.

[42] V. I. Ogorodnikov, *op. cit.*, p. 75; Butsinskii, *Zaselenie Sibiri*, pp. 313–314.

[43] *D.A.I.*, IV, 361; V. I. Ogorodnikov, *op. cit.*, p. 74; Butsinskii, *Zaselenie Sibiri*, p. 312.

[44] Müller, *Opisanie*, p. 261.

[45] *A.I.*, IV, 522; *D.A.I.*, III, 377, IV, 72–73, 202; *R.I.B.*, VIII, 484, 590; Ogloblin, I, 92; I. P. Kuznetsov-Krasnoiarskii, *Istoricheskie akty XVII stoletiia (1633–1699)*, I, 56. Moscow ordinarily considered as adolescents those natives between eighteen and twenty-one years of age (*D.A.I.*, II, 227).

[46] *A.I.*, II, 10–11; *D.A.I.*, IV, 361; *R.I.B.*, II, 173, 175–176, 202, 838, VIII, 493; Müller, *Opisanie*, pp. 185, 262, 279, 281, 292; Butsinskii, *K istorii Sibiri*, p. 23; S. V. Bakhrushin, "Sibirskie sluzhilye tatary v XVII v.," *Istoricheskie zapiski*, I (1937), 71–72.

[47] Bakhrushin, "Iasak v Sibiri," p. 102.

[48] *D.A.I.*, II, 226, III, 338, IV, 199; Ogloblin, III, 54; Kuznetsov-Krasnoiarskii, p. 8.

the Samoeds of the tundra region of the Ob and Enisei, many of the Tungus of Eastern Siberia, and the Kirghizes and Buriats in southern Siberia.[49] Some of them, especially the Kirghizes and Buriats, led a semisedentary life, and for such natives it was possible for the Russians to establish an administrative unit, the *ulus*. This corresponded to the volost among the sedentary tribes in other parts of Siberia and seems to have comprised a family or clan, headed by an elder who was customarily dignified by the title of prince or princeling.[50] But even the natives with this sort of tribal organization would move away and disappear if the Russians dealt too severely with them.

In dealing with wandering peoples the Russians had to content themselves with an irregular collection of iasak, irregular both in amount and time of collection. The Russians were never very successful in getting the nomadic natives to submit to iasak paid annually and in a specified amount; rather, these natives paid what it suited them to pay.[51] They resisted with general success all efforts of the Russians to record their names in iasak books for the purpose of collecting iasak from them on the basis of either the volost or individual. For that reason the volost was not established in those parts of Siberia where they lived.[52] Although iasak books were in time introduced among these nomads, they were never widely used or complete. The iasak was paid sometimes by the individual, at other times by the family or clan (*rod*), some payments in fixed amounts, others annually in varying amounts.[53] The Samoeds of Mangazeia paid an average of two sables per family, as did certain Tungus clans on the Toui River.[54] It is evident that the rate imposed upon these natives was on the average lower than that set for their settled brethren. The paying of the iasak was itself equally uncertain. There was no assurance that the natives would come annually to the blockhouses in the regions where they nomadized. In fact, they often failed to appear; or it sometimes happened that one year they paid at one blockhouse and the next year at another

[49] V. I. Ogorodnikov, *op. cit.*, p. 74.
[50] *D.A.I.*, II, 161, 270; Bakhrushin, *loc. cit.*
[51] *R.I.B.*, Vol. XV, pt. 5, p. 27; I. M. Trotskii, *Kolonial'naia politika moskovskogo gosudarstva v Iakutii XVII v.*, pp. 9, 53–54.
[52] Butsinskii, *Mangazeia*, p. 19.
[53] *D.A.I.*, III, 335–336.
[54] *D.A.I.*, IV, 267; Müller, "Sibirskaia istoriia," p. 99; Trotskii, *loc. cit.*; Ogloblin, I, 92–93; V. I. Ogorodnikov, *op. cit.*, p. 74; Butsinskii, *Mangazeia*, p. 21.

far from the first.[55] This irregularity in payment was an important departure from the system of iasak found elsewhere in Siberia.

Because of the mobility of the nomadic tribesmen, it was futile for the Russians to send collectors to find them and make the collections. The best the Russians could do was to build blockhouses and seek to attract the natives to them. The resorting of the Russians to a technique of this kind in the region of the nomad tribes constituted the second important departure from the system of iasak used elsewhere. However, it must be recognized that the Russians found it to their advantage to use variously parts of this technique among the settled natives under their rule.

The means used by the Russians to attract the natives to the iasak blockhouses were the oath, the hostage system, and gifts. At the time of conquering the native tribes they took pains to exact from the natives an oath (*shert'*) to be loyal to the tsar and to pay iasak.[56] The form of the oath varied, depending upon the belief of the natives, whether the Mohammedan or some primitive faith, and the Russians kept a sharp eye for those religious forms which were most effective in holding the natives to their obligations.[57] The hostage system, though the Russians used it like the oath throughout Siberia, was utilized particularly in connection with the nomadic tribesmen. Its effectiveness arose from the strong family solidarity and loyalty and the weak interclan ties which existed among many of the natives.[58] In spite of the difficulties of capturing and holding hostages, the Russians always attempted to obtain two or three of them from a tribe or clan at the time of conquering it.[59] These hostages they kept in the blockhouse or in some sort of prison, under constant surveillance. The hostages had, of course, to be treated well, or the natives would refuse iasak. By holding hostages the Russians succeeded in drawing the natives to the blockhouses, there to assure themselves of the well-being of their kinsmen; at the same time the Russians guaranteed the security of their collectors under conditions where there was real danger of attack by the natives.[60] The third means of attraction, the bestowal of gifts

[55] Bakhrushin, "Iasak v Sibiri," pp. 108–110; Butsinskii, *Mangazeia,* p. 23; Ogloblin, III, 54.

[56] *R.I.B.*, VIII, 475; Okun', p. 183; Trotskii, p. 9.

[57] Bakhrushin, "Iasak v Sibiri," p. 111; Trotskii (pp. 10–11), contains an oath administered to the Buriats in the years 1642–1645.

[58] Müller, "Sibirskaia istoriia," p. 218.

[59] *D.A.I.*, III, 56, 279–280, VII, 149; Okun', pp. 181, 183.

[60] Butsinskii, *Mangazeia,* pp. 20, 22; *D.A.I.*, II, 257, IV, 21–22; Bakhrushin, "Iasak v Sibiri," pp. 112–116.

(*podarki*), was widely used and very effectively, as evidenced by the fact that, when the Russians offered no gifts, no iasak was forthcoming.[61] The gifts were articles in great demand by the natives—grain, beads, trinkets, inexpensive jewelry, iron goods such as knives and axes, copper goods, tin, grain, and cloth.[62] This practice became well established, to such an extent that even natives long pacified were presented with gifts when they brought in their iasak; it was used also among the settled natives as a means of keeping their good will. For the same purposes the Russians feted the natives with food and drink when they brought in their tribute.[63]

One supplementary source of fur revenue, closely connected with iasak, should be mentioned—the pominki. In its true form it was a voluntary contribution which the natives offered in honor of the tsar.[64] In practice, however, it assumed several forms, which ranged from that of a gift made by the natives to that of a fixed requisition exacted from them; it was also given in return for goods.[65] Originally presented by the volost as a whole, in many instances it was changed and made the gift of the individual natives. Often, too, by virtue of repeated payment and the insistence of Moscow, the pominki was transformed from a voluntary into a required contribution, first in unfixed, then fixed, amounts. Whenever pominki was paid on the latter basis, it differed from iasak in name only.[66] The natives paid pominki also to the voevoda and his assistants.[67] And just as Moscow took the tsar's pominki and made it a required contribution, so it did with the voevoda's pominki.[68] That did not prevent the voevodas, however, from collecting additional pominki for themselves. By certain native peoples iasak was paid as pominki, since, as erstwhile exacters of tribute themselves, they objected to the implication of inferiority attached to iasak, and insisted upon terming their tribute to the Russians "pominki."[69]

Iasak, then, represented the fur revenue which the state obtained from the natives of Siberia. In form, it was an outright requisition

[61] Bakhrushin, "Iasak v Sibiri," pp. 116–119; *D.A.I.*, IV, 73; *R.I.B.*, II, 850, 1127; Müller, *Opisanie*, p. 213; *idem*, "Sibirskaia istoriia," p. 227.

[62] *A.I.*, IV, 523; *D.A.I.*, II, 163, 167, 242, 256, III, 336, 338, IV, 202; Ogloblin, II, 69, III, 81.

[63] *D.A.I.*, II, 268, IV, 107, 205; *R.I.B.*, Vol. XV, pt. 5, p. 17; Müller, "Sibirskaia istoriia," p. 227.

[64] *D.A.I.*, II, 271, IV, 75.

[65] *D.A.I.*, II, 268, IV, 73, 202; *R.I.B.*, Vol. XV, pt. 5, p. 18.

[66] Bakhrushin, "Iasak v Sibiri," pp. 105–106; Butsinskii, *Zaselenie Sibiri*, p. 317.

[67] Butsinskii, *Zaselenie Sibiri*, p. 317; Ogloblin, I, 101–102, 104.

[68] *A.I.*, IV, 53–54; *D.A.I.*, II, 268, 272, III, 376–377, IV, 109, 204, VIII, 11.

[69] Bakhrushin, "Iasak v Sibiri," p. 96.

made upon a conquered people by a conquering people, with little given in return except protection.[70] In practice, however, the Russians were often forced, as we have seen, to make concessions to the natives by awarding gifts in return for iasak. Even so, it remained a direct and profitable means by which the Russian state tapped the fur resources of Siberia, and iasak constituted the principal reason for the presence and activity of the state in Siberia.

The Tithe

Iasak was only one means of tapping the fur wealth of Siberia. Private enterprisers brought large numbers of furs out of its forests and sent or carried them westward to Russian and foreign markets. By making a levy upon these furs the state secured to itself a generous part of them and provided itself with a second source of furs.

The tax by which the state diverted to itself a part of the furs which entered into the trade through the channels of the promyshlenniks and fur traders was a tithe (*desiataia poshlina*). The state sought to arrogate to itself one-tenth of all the furs which the Russian enterprisers, whether promyshlenniks, traders, or serving men, brought from the hunting grounds.[71] This tithe was exacted in the form of every tenth pelt from each kind of fur-bearing animal, "with the best from the best and with the medium grade from the medium . . . without choice as they come." From those lots of furs that were less than ten pelts the state collected 10 per cent of their value in money.[72] For the purpose of collecting this tithe Moscow employed a system which was separate, though not divorced, from the collection of iasak.

In the earlier years of the conquest of Siberia the voevodas, their assistants, and the serving men carried out the collection of the tithe.[73] But they contrived so many abuses in collecting it that Moscow was led in the early decades of the seventeenth century to take the collection itself out of their hands and turn it over to

[70] *D.A.I.*, II, 161, IV, 205; *R.I.B.*, II, 204–205, Vol. XV, pt. 5, p. 9.

[71] *P.S.Z.*, III, 507. Although in most cases the serving men were not allowed to hunt and trade in furs, there were a few exceptions to that prohibition. The furs which they thus legitimately acquired were subject to the tithe (see below, n. 83 and p. 67).

[72] *A.I.*, II, 27; *D.A.I.*, II, 154, III, 50, IV, 209; *P.S.Z.*, III, 239, 495, 499; Müller, *Opisanie*, p. 311. The tithe was sometimes collected in money from lots that were larger than ten (Ogloblin, II, 27, 38). The taking of a tithe by the state was not applied to furs alone, but to all raw goods produced in Siberia.

[73] *A.I.*, II, 57–58, 77–78, III, 88; *R.I.B.*, II, 140; Müller, *Opisanie*, pp. 274, 311.

a different set of employees, the customs heads and sworn men. The voevodas were left without any responsibilities in the collection of the tithe and served only as checks upon the customs head, receiving periodically, as custodians of the local treasuries, the customs receipts.[74] The customs head, along with the voevoda, maintained his headquarters in the town or ostrog, and had charge of the customs and tithe collection there and in the area under the settlement's jurisdiction.[75] These officials were sent from Russian, usually northern, towns, having been elected by the local citizenry and appointed by the Siberian Department; or they were elected by the local Siberian merchantry. They served ordinarily one or two years, though not in their home towns.[76] Their assistants in collecting the tithe and other customs duties were the sworn men. Moscow required these sworn men to be elected for a specified period of time from the best of the local promyshlenniks and traders or other settlers, to perform any one of several services for the state, particularly the collection of the tithe.[77] The serving men were never wholly eliminated from the customs service, especially those in Eastern Siberia who served in the distant blockhouses, where they were empowered to collect the tithe as well as iasak.[78] Serving men were also called upon to serve as guards at the customs stations, though they did not actually participate in the collection of the tithe itself.[79]

The collection of the tithe was undertaken wherever the authority of Moscow extended. The principal collection points were towns, since they were situated on the main river and land routes, along which the promyshlenniks and fur traders traveled with their furs, and to them people came to buy and sell furs.[80] They were also the first centers of collection. Subsidiary customs stations or barriers were established in the outlying settlements (*slobody*) in the area under the jurisdiction of the towns, and in the ostrogs and blockhouses controlling those regions distant from the towns.[81] This was

[74] *A.A.E.*, IV, 440; *A.I.*, III, 338, 340, IV, 33–34, 447; *D.A.I.*, III, 44, 340, IV, 110–111, 350–351; *R.I.B.*, Vol. XV, pt. 5, p. 26.

[75] *D.A.I.*, II, 159, IV, 110–112; *P.S.Z.*, III, 494, 513.

[76] *A.I.*, III, 339–340, IV, 39–42, 47; *D.A.I.*, IV, 111; *R.I.B.*, Vol. XV, pt. 5, p. 26; Ogloblin, III, 48–49.

[77] *D.A.I.*, II, 154, 159, IV, 33–34, 40, 49, 110, 211, 404; *R.I.B.*, Vol. XV, pt. 5, p. 25.

[78] *D.A.I.*, III, 75, 335–336, IV, 208.

[79] *A.I.*, III, 336; *P.S.Z.*, III, 497.

[80] *A.I.*, II, 58, III, 88; *D.A.I.*, IV, 109–110, 210.

[81] *A.I.*, III, 336, IV, 284, 287; *D.A.I.*, II, 154, III, 39–40, IV, 208–210; *P.S.Z.*, III, 497, 513; Bakhrushin, *Ocherki*, pp. 101, 104, 107, 113, 114.

particularly true of more sparsely populated Eastern Siberia, where there were only a few towns, like Eniseisk, Krasnoiarsk, Iakutsk, Ilimsk, and later Nerchinsk, in which a customs head was stationed.

The objective of the state was to collect its fur tithe from the promyshlenniks and fur traders as they came from the hunting grounds, before they sold or exchanged their newly acquired furs.[82] The state, therefore, ordered that no trading in furs should be conducted until the tithe had been paid[83] and, further, that all trading should be done where there was a customs agent stationed or present.[84] Since nearly all Siberia's furs—until the latter part of the seventeenth century—were sent out of Siberia to the Russian and European markets, the state could expect to exact its tithe in the first town through which the furs passed on their way westward. This was indeed the procedure followed by Moscow in Western Siberia during the earlier years of the conquest. From anyone who arrived in a town with furs for which he had not paid the tithe the customs official collected the tithe. This worked reasonably well until the increasing traffic and the building of new roads, many of them around the towns, compelled the establishment of subsidiary customs barriers near and between the towns for more effective collection of the tithe and other duties. At such barriers, however, the tithe was collected only from those furs which were to be sold locally. It was not ordinarily collected from those travelers who were carrying furs to some Siberian or Russian town; these were sent to the customhouse in the near-by town to pay their tithe.[85]

As Moscow extended its authority into Eastern Siberia, it used essentially the same technique of collecting the tithe.[86] In the more important ostrogs, which later became towns, it placed customs stations in charge of a customs head, who himself established subsidiary customs barriers in the territory under his jurisdiction. In those regions within reasonable distance of a town or ostrog that were without any customs barriers, the head relied upon the

[82] *D.A.I.*, III, 40, 42, IV, 210, VIII, 263; *R.I.B.*, Vol. XV, pt. 5, pp. 24–25.

[83] *A.I.*, II, 70, 78, IV, 524; *D.A.I.*, II, 156, 162, IV, 110, 211. This regulation varied. Promyshlenniks in Eastern Siberia were allowed to trade furs among themselves, and when they reached the first customs station, the tithe was collected from all furs in their possession, whether acquired by hunting or trade (*R.I.B.*, Vol. XV, pt. 5, p. 25).

[84] See p. 75 n. 23.

[85] *A.I.*, III, 336–337, IV, 284; *P.S.Z.*, III, 497.

[86] *A.I.*, I, 446; *D.A.I.*, II, 155, 158, IV, 109–110, 210.

serving men in the area to send anyone with furs in his possession to the town or ostrog to pay the tithe.[87] But in the distant and outlying regions the promyshlenniks and fur traders remained for long periods of time, conducting their business and trade, and the administration found it necessary to send its agents to these men if it hoped to collect the tithe. For this task it utilized sworn men and the serving men sent out to the blockhouses to collect iasak. They were required to travel from one blockhouse to another, collecting the tithe and other duties.[88] In their presence, the promyshlenniks and fur traders were then free to carry on their trade. Promyshlenniks who participated in conquering expeditions paid the tithe to the leader of the expedition.[89]

In collecting the tithe the state used a system of receipts in order to avoid duplicate collection and to prevent evasion of payment. To promyshlenniks and traders who expected to remain in the place where they paid the tithe and to sell their furs, the customs agent simply issued a receipt of payment (*otpis'*), which contained a description of the furs from which the tithe had been taken.[90] But to those who were taking their furs to a Russian market or to some Siberian town the customs agent gave a travel document or passport (*proezzhaia gramota*), recording in detail the furs from which the tithe had been taken as well as the date of payment and the name of the payer. A passport was valid only for the person to whom it was issued and only for the particular goods specified in it, which were sealed at the time of its issue. This passport a traveler had to show along with his furs at each customs barrier he came to; otherwise he risked having his furs confiscated or having to pay a second tithe.[91] If he sold a part of his furs in the town in which he paid his tithe and then wished to go to another, he was required to exchange the customs receipts for the unsold part of his furs for a passport. In fact, any time that a person sold a part of his furs in one place and then moved to another, he was required to obtain a new passport from the customs head or other agent.[92] Any furs found in the possession of a person which were in

[87] *A.I.*, IV, 70; *D.A.I.*, II, 102, 103, VIII, 4.

[88] *D.A.I.*, III, 40, 336, IV, 208, 210; Ogloblin, I, 104, II, 43–44.

[89] Ogloblin, I, 96.

[90] *D.A.I.*, III, 40.

[91] *A.I.*, III, 337–338, IV, 33, 446; *D.A.I.*, II, 155, 158, III, 42, 43, IV, 49, 110, 209; *R.I.B.*, Vol. XV, pt. 5, p. 25; Müller, *Opisanie*, p. 274.

[92] *A.I.*, III, 88, 337–338, V, 6; *D.A.I.*, III, 45.

excess of those listed in the passport were subject to confiscation.[93] By use of the passport Moscow sought to make certain that it received its tithe from all furs brought from the forests of Siberia.

Purchase

The tithe was a requisition from the Russians just as iasak was a requisition from the natives. Together these two sources accounted for most of the furs obtained by the state. Supplementing them was a third method of acquiring furs, which, as undertaken in Siberia by the state, took on also the character of a requisition, though not entirely so. This method was that of purchase. It has considerable significance for the fur trade of the state, not because of the number of furs acquired in this way, for the number was small, but because its use marks that part of the fur trade in Siberia which the state wished to make a monopoly of the tsar.

The state never attempted to monopolize the entire trade in furs, as it did for some commodities. The most extensive monopoly that the state attempted came at the end of the seventeenth century, when it endeavored to monopolize the export trade in all furs and the domestic trade in sables and black foxes.[94] Yet it did decree for itself a preëminent position in the fur trade, which, had its decrees been fully enforced, would have left that trade pretty much to the state because few private enterprisers would have found it profitable enough to risk the dangers and uncertainties. This position constituted a monopoly of the sale of the best furs, which were the furs most in demand abroad and those which brought the most profit.[95] The insistence by the state that the iasak be paid only in the good and the best furs was one manifestation of this monopoly; the order that the tithe be taken from the medium and best grades of pelts, but not from the inferior grades, was another.[96] The logical extension of these practices was the purchase by the state of the fine furs which it did not receive as either iasak or the tithe, and this it attempted to do.[97]

The state's purchasing of the best furs affected both the Russian private enterprisers and the Siberian natives. It did not occur,

---

[93] *D.A.I.*, IV, 209.

[94] *A.I.*, V, 470, 471; *P.S.Z.*, III, 282–283, 405–406, 501, 507.

[95] Butsinskii, *Mangazeia*, p. 45.

[96] Cf. *D.A.I.*, III, 377, in which iasak collectors sent to a tribe of Iakuts were instructed to search out and take as iasak an exceptionally fine sable reported to be in the possession of one of the tribe.

[97] Ogloblin, II, 39, 45.

however, under conditions of the open competitive market, but as an adjunct to the collection of the tithe and iasak, since the state endeavored to assure itself that it secured all the best furs by reserving first choice for itself.[98] When the private enterprisers presented themselves at the customs barriers to declare their goods and pay the tithe, the state bought those furs of a specified value which did not fall to it as the tithe. Thus the customs officials at Mangazeia, by an order of 1621, were required to buy all sables valued at 100 r. or more per forty, though later, in 1635, the order was changed, and traders were required to sacrifice only those sables worth 10 r., 15 r., and 20 r. a pelt.[99] In the Iakutsk jurisdiction in the 'thirties and 'forties the voevodas were instructed to buy black and dark brown fox pelts valued locally at 10 r. to 50 r. or more, as well as good black beavers, and single sables worth 5 r. to 10 r. or more.[100] The voevoda of Verkhoturie was ordered in 1675, and the voevoda of Mangazeia in 1678, to see that blue or black arctic fox pelts were bought from any merchant who passed through with such furs in his possession.[101] To buy such furs the state used the moneys and goods received as customs duties, taxes, fees, and fines, and those from other government monopolies like tobacco and wine.[102] In fairness to the state, however, it must be noted that the customs agents were instructed to pay the prevailing local prices for the furs purchased for the tsar.

The purchase from the natives of the best furs, that is, the best ones remaining after the iasak requirements had been met, took place in connection with the payment of iasak. The collectors who went out to the volosts and native villages were supposed to buy the remaining best furs—sables, black foxes, and beavers—and they carried with them goods from the sovereign's treasury for that purpose.[103] Those natives who themselves brought their iasak to the collection centers were ordered to bring with them their best furs for sale to the state and not to sell them to private traders.[104] This purchasing of furs from the natives might seem at first sight to be no different from the granting of gifts in exchange for iasak (de-

[98] *A.I.*, IV, 539; *D.A.I.*, II, 158, III, 40, IV, 49–50.

[99] Butsinskii, *Mangazeia*, pp. 44–45.

[100] *D.A.I.*, II, 158, III, 40.

[101] *A.I.*, IV, 539; *D.A.I.*, VIII, 28.

[102] *A.I.*, II, 102; *D.A.I.*, III, 42, 140, IV, 209; Ogloblin, I, 243–245, III, 79, IV, 138.

[103] *A.I.*, II, 102–103; *D.A.I.*, II, 136, 176, 242, IV, 202, VII, 151; Ogloblin, IV, 138.

[104] Butsinskii, *K istorii Sibiri*, p. 6.

scribed above), but there was an important distinction. The gifts, which were a device to promote the payment of iasak, by no means equaled in value the market value of the furs taken as iasak, and the furs so received were looked upon as iasak, whereas in the state's purchase there was involved the buying at the locally prevailing prices of the fine furs remaining after the iasak specified had been paid.[105]

The state purchased furs in Siberia from one other group, the serving men. The serving men were ordinarily forbidden to hunt fur-bearing animals or to trade furs, but those who were sent out to conquer new lands were allowed the privilege of hunting and trading furs on a small scale after they had succeeded in exacting iasak from the natives. The fine furs thus acquired by these men the state bought according to the local prices.[106] The state also bought the fine furs given by the natives to collectors as the collectors' own pominki.[107]

Aside from the furs obtained as iasak, the tithe, and by purchase, the state acquired a residual number of them from a few miscellaneous sources. One was confiscation. To maintain the integrity of its fur trade the state laid down many regulations governing the conduct of its employees and of the private enterprisers. Those who acquired furs in violation of these regulations were subject to the seizure of their furs by the state.[108] Another source was the receipt of furs in payment for drink bought from the state's liquor shops and for occasional goods of the state sold to private purchasers.[109] Also, there is record of sables acquired in exchange for the property of a serving man dying in Siberian service, who had willed his effects to the sovereign.[110] No source of furs was too petty to be scorned by the state.

The Dispatch of Furs to Moscow

By means of iasak, tithe, and purchase an immense volume of furs was drawn annually into the local state treasuries in the voevodal towns and ostrogs in Siberia. These towns and ostrogs functioned as collection depots from which the furs were sent yearly to the

---

[105] Bakhrushin, "Iasak v Sibiri," pp. 120–126.
[106] *A.I.*, IV, 444, 522; *D.A.I.*, II, 271, IV, 74, 203–204, 354; *R.I.B.*, Vol. XV, pt. 5, p. 22; *P.S.Z.*, III, 510.
[107] *D.A.I.*, II, 271, IV, 74.
[108] Ogloblin, I, 243–245, II, 42, 45, 59–60, III, 16.
[109] *D.A.I.*, IV, 210–211, VI, 31, 33, 359; Ogloblin, IV, 158.
[110] *D.A.I.*, IV, 23.

Siberian Department at Moscow. The treasury in any town or ostrog was the responsibility of the voevoda there, and in it were deposited all furs taken for the state within the territory under its jurisdiction, whatever their source—iasak, pominki, and purchased furs from the natives; tithe and purchased furs taken by the customs heads; or furs from petty sources.

When it came time for the fur treasury, or sable treasury as it was called, to be dispatched to Moscow, the voevoda called in reliable promyshlenniks and fur traders to sort the furs into the best, medium, and inferior grades (the state received inferior furs despite its orders to the contrary) and to appraise them according to the local prices.[111] If there were no appraisers available, the voevodas had instructions to send the furs to Tobolsk, where they would be evaluated and whence they would be forwarded to Moscow.[112] The voevodas were warned not to permit too high an appraisal of the furs, for the otherwise higher Moscow price would not then represent a profit; to discourage this practice the state undertook to recover from the voevodas any losses from excessive evaluation.[113] Because of this stipulation most of the voevodas saw to it that the furs were undervalued in order that the great difference between their estimated Siberian value and the Moscow value would reflect their concern for the "profit of the tsar."[114] No furs were to be sent to Moscow without evaluation.[115] After the furs had been appraised, the voevoda drew up lists of them and their values, which he signed and sealed and had countersigned by the appraisers.[116] These lists had to describe each pelt and specify its source, as well as state whether it was with or without the tail, lest the tail be cut off en route to Moscow.[117] The pelts were then sewn together in pairs and packed in bundles, usually of forty, flat between two boards; foxes, however, were customarily packed in tens, and small pelts like minks and squirrels in sixties, eighties, and hundreds.[118] The bundles were then put in sacks, leather pouches, or

[111] *D.A.I.*, II, 230, III, 109, 304, IV, 106, 365; *R.I.B.*, Vol. XV, pt. 5, p. 20.

[112] *D.A.I.*, IV, 367.

[113] *A.I.*, IV, 453; *D.A.I.*, IV, 117, 316; Ogloblin, IV, 156; *P.S.Z.*, III, 211.

[114] *D.A.I.*, IV, 118, VIII, 11–12, 14; Ogloblin, IV, 129; Butsinskii, *Zaselenie Sibiri*, p. 316.

[115] *D.A.I.*, IV, 161, 365; *R.I.B.*, Vol. XV, pt. 5, p. 23.

[116] *D.A.I.*, II, 230, IV, 106; Ogloblin, I, 91. For examples of such lists see *D.A.I.*, VIII, 12–13; Trotskii, pp. 62–63.

[117] *D.A.I.*, III, 109, IV, 161; Trotskii, *loc. cit.* The tail was as valuable as any part of the pelt.

[118] *D.A.I.*, VIII, 12; Ogloblin, IV, 80, 129; J. E. Fischer, *Sibirische Geschichte*, I, 213 n. 221; P. J. Stralenberg, *An Historico-Geographical Description of the North and Eastern Parts of Europe and Asia*, p. 428.

wooden boxes, to which the voevoda affixed his seal, and these containers, together with the iasak and customs books, were sent to Moscow in the care of picked men.[119] Spring or early summer was the customary season for forwarding the sable treasury, but the time of year was by no means fixed.[120]

When the furs reached the Siberian Department, they were sorted again, checked against the lists, and appraised according to Moscow prices.[121] The increase in value of furs in Moscow over their value in Siberia varied, often reaching 100, and sometimes 500, per cent.[122] Normally it averaged around 20 per cent, except towards the end of the century, when a growing scarcity of the finer furs probably made for a greater increase.[123] For example, the iasak from Tobolsk in 1628 was appraised there at 608 r., and in Moscow at 725 r., the Moscow value being 19 per cent higher than the Siberian value. Furs sent from Berezov in the same year and worth there 38 r. were worth 53 r. in Moscow (28 per cent higher). The iasak from Ketsk in 1627 was appraised in Tobolsk at 866 r. and in Moscow at 1,298 r. (49 per cent higher). The tithe collections at Mangazeia in 1628 were valued there at 15,354 r. and in Moscow at 17,285 r. (12.5 per cent higher); the tithe collections for 1635 were appraised at 10,749 r. and 12,952 r. respectively (an increase of 20.5 per cent).[124] This difference in value explains why the state would not accept money in place of iasak.[125] It also explains why the salaries to the state employees in Siberia were not paid in furs, despite the fact that they were the main source of income there for the state. The state measured its profit on the basis of this difference between the Moscow and Siberian values of furs, but, except for the furs which were bought, that difference did not measure the actual profit. The actual profit, of course, should have been figured as the difference between what it cost the state to acquire the furs in Siberia—which was not the market

[119] *A.I.*, II, 111–112; *D.A.I.*, II, 230, VIII, 15, 324; *R.I.B.*, II, 141–142, Vol. XV, pt. 5, p. 23; Ogloblin, IV, 156, 158; Müller, *Opisanie*, p. 281.

[120] Ogloblin, I, 318; Müller, *Opisanie*, p. 273; cf. Bakhrushin, *Ocherki*, pp. 76, 78.

[121] Ianitskii, pp. 21–22; *D.A.I.*, IV, 365; Ogloblin, IV, 83, 156–157.

[122] S. V. Bakhrushin, "Torgi gostia Nikitina v Sibiri i Kitae," *Sbornik statei: Pamiati Aleksandra Nikolaevicha Savina, 1873–1923*, Trudy instituta istorii rossiiskoi assotsiatsii nauchno-issledovatel'skikh institutov obshchestvennykh nauk, I (1926), 374.

[123] *D.A.I.*, VIII, 12–13.

[124] Ogloblin, IV, 156–157; Butsinskii, *K istorii Sibiri*, p. 28 n. 1; *idem*, *Mangazeia*, p. 49; *idem*, *Zaselenie Sibiri*, p. 316.

[125] *D.A.I.*, IV, 362. See above, p. 57.

price of them there—and the value of the furs in Moscow, or more accurately, what it actually sold them for. But Muscovite accounting theory, if any, had not advanced that far.

Before passing to the next phase of the fur trade of the state, we may pause to note here that the means adopted by the state for obtaining its furs derived almost entirely from the political authority of the state. Iasak and pominki were an explicit and overt recognition of the sovereignty of the tsar over the conquered natives of Siberia. The tithe was a clear manifestation of the power of the state to tax. And the political power of the state was present in the purchasing of furs to the extent that the obligation of the private enterprisers and natives to sell those furs which the state wanted was made compulsory. The political character of its methods stands in greater relief when attention is directed to the fact that the state did not itself undertake the hunting and trapping of the animals. It depended upon the natives and promyshlenniks to do that. However, iasak, tithe, and purchase comprised a system of acquisition of such comprehensiveness that the state could afford to leave the trapping of the animals to others.

CHAPTER V

THE PRESERVATION OF THE STATE'S FUR TRADE

So profitable a system of obtaining furs, one which would take all the best ones for the state, could not go unchallenged. The natives and the Russian enterprisers, who supplied the state with its furs, did not assume their roles voluntarily. And it was not to be expected that the state employees, surrounded by opportunities for acquiring furs readily, would not take advantage of these opportunities. The state was thus confronted with certain dangers to its fur trade, against which it was compelled to adopt protective measures. These related to the three types of operators in the fur trade of the state: namely, the natives, the private enterprisers, and the state employees. Accordingly, three sets of measures were developed: (1) those concerning the treatment and conduct of the natives, (2) those pertaining to the conduct and treatment of the private enterprisers, and (3) those relating to the conduct of the state employees. From an examination of these measures and of their enforcement a clearer picture may be gained of the conduct of the state's trade in Siberia and of the extent to which, as well as the means by which, the state reserved the fur trade to itself.

The Policy of the State towards the Natives

In the light of Russian practice and Siberian custom the imposition of tribute upon the native population was the natural method for the Muscovite state to use in exploiting the fur resources of Siberia. But it was a method which could easily give rise to much harm to the native population, with consequent injury to the fur trade of the state. If the Russians imposed too heavy exactions upon the natives or treated them too harshly, they created the possibility of a native revolt or of the state's loss of fur revenue through the impairment of the capacity of the natives to pay. The possibility of revolt was the lesser danger, since the natives were either docile or unable to resist the Russians for long. The greater danger arose from the temptation to exploit and abuse the natives because of their weakness. Carried too far, oppression at the hands of the Russians would make it difficult or impossible for the natives to pay the tribute desired by the state. Since Moscow had undertaken the conquest chiefly for the sake of furs, it was anxious, naturally, to avoid these contingencies. As the occasion arose, therefore, it specified in detail how the natives should be treated and what its employees should do to prevent discontent on the part of the natives and any impairment of their capacity to pay.

The subject of many of the regulations issued by the Siberian Department was the iasak itself—the amount to be collected, those liable for its payment, the manner in which it should be collected, and so forth. The intention behind the regulations was to collect from each native, family, or volost a number of pelts which should accord with the ability of the natives to pay and yet not be a burden upon them.[1] If the quota became too burdensome, it was reduced and the arrears were canceled.[2] The old, the sick, the crippled, the blind, and the poor—all those who in some way became incapacitated for hunting—were released from the payment of iasak.[3] If the numbers of the natives were reduced by death, captivity, or migration, the remaining natives were not held responsible for the iasak of the absent ones, and such arrears as the latter might have accumulated were canceled.[4] The children of the natives were not required to pay iasak, and adolescents reaching eighteen years, as well as newly subjected natives, were sometimes allowed to start their payments at a lower rate.[5] When the natives had difficulty in meeting the annual payment on time, they were allowed extra time.[6]

At the same time Moscow laid down very clearly the manner in which its servants in Siberia should conduct themselves towards the natives. They were strictly forbidden to collect any exactions over and above the iasak and pominki, and they were not to collect iasak oftener than the stipulated annual payment.[7] Once the natives had agreed to pay iasak, they were to be treated kindly, without cruelty, extortion, or oppression of any sort, and allowed to live in

[1] *D.A.I.*, II, 161–162, 270, IV, 355; *R.I.B.*, II, 838, VIII, 508; G. F. Müller, *Opisanie sibirskago tsarstva*, pp. 194–195; P. N. Butsinskii, *Zaselenie Sibiri*, p. 319.

[2] Müller, *op. cit.*, pp. 194–195, 195–196, 261–262; Butsinskii, *op. cit.*, pp. 319–320.

[3] *R.I.B.*, II, 175–176, 202, VIII, 490–493, 668–669; Ogloblin, III, 159–160.

[4] There were some exceptions to this regulation. Sometimes the voevodas were instructed to collect iasak for a deceased native from his relatives. *D.A.I.*, III, 377; Müller, *op. cit.*, pp. 195, 196; Butsinskii, *op. cit.*, p. 314.

[5] *D.A.I.*, II, 227; Müller, *op. cit.*, p. 296; Butsinskii, *op. cit.*, p. 314.

[6] *D.A.I.*, IV, 363; Müller, *op. cit.*, p. 280; Ogloblin, I, 98–99.

[7] *D.A.I.*, II, 272, IV, 111–112; *R.I.B.*, VIII, 508–509, Vol. XV, pt. 5, p. 27.

peace.[8] The hostages which the serving men took from the natives were to be adequately sheltered and fed during the period of the captivity and were not to be abused in any way.[9] Force was to be employed against the natives only after all other means of persuasion had failed, and then only in a measure sufficient to bring them to terms without serious injury to their capacity to pay iasak.[10] For example, Moscow advocated seizing the women and children of the natives and holding them until the first iasak payment had been made and the customary hostages given.[11]

Besides these stipulations, Moscow instructed the Siberian officials, as occasion arose, to do certain other things to maintain the capacity of the natives to pay and to prevent their discontent. Sometimes it developed that the place to which the natives brought their iasak was located at a greater distance than some other collection center, or that the collectors proved abusive. Upon the petition of the natives, Moscow allowed them to send their iasak to a more conveniently located place or to have it collected by other and more friendly serving men or to bring it in themselves.[12] Occasionally the natives complained that no merchants were visiting their villages, whereupon Moscow ordered the voevoda to send merchants to trade grain and cloth with them.[13] Private enterprisers were not to be allowed to encroach upon the hunting grounds of the natives.[14] The natives were given protection from other natives hostile to them, since some natives were more successful in resisting the Russians and attacked the iasak-paying natives because they rendered tribute to the conquerors.[15] The voevodas were instructed not to allow forceful baptism of the natives, lest their hostility be aroused, nor to permit the seizure of the wives and children of the natives. The voevodas were also to be on guard against the sale of native women and children to the merchants and serving men.[16] This was a practice in which the natives often took the initiative;

[8] *A.I.*, II, 102, III, 325, IV, 448; *D.A.I.*, II, 176, 268, 270, 272, IV, 114, 201, 360; *R.I.B.*, II, 832, 840, VIII, 575, Vol. XV, pt. 5, p. 27.

[9] *A.I.*, IV, 527; *D.A.I.*, II, 175, 270, 273, III, 333, IV, 107, 112; *R.I.B.*, II, 856.

[10] *A.I.*, IV, 449; *D.A.I.*, II, 272; *R.I.B.*, Vol. XV, pt. 5, p. 28.

[11] *D.A.I.*, III, 334, IV, 406; *R.I.B.*, II, 842.

[12] *A.I.*, II, 78, 102, III, 195–196; A. Gnevushev, "Akty vremeni pravleniia tsaria Vasiliia Shuiskago," *Chteniia*, Vol. CCLIII (1915), No. 2, pt. 1, p. 71; Butsinskii, *op. cit.*, pp. 248–249.

[13] *A.I.*, III, 234–235.

[14] *A.I.*, pp. 165–166, V, 204, 346–347; *D.A.I.*, VIII, 262; *R.I.B.*, II, 765–766.

[15] Gnevushev, pp. 73–74; *R.I.B.*, VIII, 567.

[16] *A.I.*, IV, 519–520, 523, 526; *D.A.I.*, II, 273, III, 223, IV, 78, 206, 359; *R.I.B.*, Vol. XV, pt. 5, p. 29; *P.S.Z.*, II, 662.

if allowed to go very far, it would in time reduce the number of natives who could provide furs.[17] Gambling was likewise a practice indulged in too much by the natives, to the detriment of the state's fur revenue, so the Russians were forbidden to gamble with them.[18]

The natives, on their part, were expected to do nothing which would prejudice the iasak of the state. They were not to carry on trade with the Russians prior to the collection of iasak.[19] Their best furs they were required to save for the state, either contributing them as iasak or selling them after fulfilling their iasak obligations.[20] Trade in furs with other natives not subject to the Russians or the export of furs to any neighboring foreign lands were forbidden them.[21] In general, Moscow demanded that they satisfy its iasak requirements in full, without arrears, and in good, complete pelts, reserving their trading activities until after the state's demands had been met.[22]

On the whole, the policy which Moscow laid down with respect to the Siberian natives exhibited a leniency and restraint that was remarkable for a state exploiting weaker and backward peoples. It was guided in its stipulations by enlightened self-interest. However, the enlightened policy promulgated by the tsar's officials at the top depended for its execution upon the servants of the tsar at the bottom, and the beneficent intent of this policy was not always or everywhere realized. The extent to which it fell short in execution will become evident as the chapter proceeds.

Regulations Relating to the Private Enterprisers

The Russian private enterprisers and the natives constituted the two original sources for the furs of the state. In its attitude towards the private enterprisers, however, the state was concerned primarily not with the preservation of their usefulness as a source of furs, but with their actions as competitors. Although it sought to protect its Russian subjects in Siberia, it found itself oftener engaged in protecting its own fur trade against their encroachments. To this end it laid down several regulations intended to confine their activities within definite limits.

Most of the regulations pertaining to the private enterprisers

[17] P. N. Butsinskii, *K istorii Sibiri,* p. 13.
[18] *A.I.,* III, 348; Butsinskii, *Zaselenie Sibiri,* p. 322.
[19] *D.A.I.,* II, 177.
[20] See above, pp. 51, 66.
[21] *D.A.I.,* II, 177, IV, 76, 205.
[22] *D.A.I.,* II, 268, IV, 365.

concerned their trading activities. Two ever-present and important regulations related to trade with the natives. The first prohibited trade of any kind by the Russians with the natives prior to the annual collection of iasak. The second forbade trade in the native volosts and villages between Russians and natives; all trade had to be carried on in the towns, ostrogs, or blockhouses.[23] The explanation of these regulations lay in the desire of the state to assure to itself the best furs of the natives. Because, in contrast with the usual practice of the state, the Russian traders offered goods in exchange for furs, they had little difficulty in acquiring the best ones from the natives, with the result that the natives passed off inferior pelts as iasak or paid none at all.[24] By limiting trade with the natives to the period after the collection of iasak the state gained first choice of the best furs for itself; by insisting that all trade be conducted under the immediate supervision of its officials it was enabled to obtain any fine pelts which the natives had concealed from the collectors or which they held over and above their iasak quota. Also, the state thereby assured to itself the tithe from the furs sold by the natives to the Russians.[25] Violation of these regulations brought, for the Russians, confiscation of their furs and severe punishment by beating.[26] For the natives, there seems to have been no penalty.

Trade between Russians was subject to similar restrictions. This trade had also to be conducted at the established centers of the tsar's authority—the towns, their suburbs (*slobody*),[27] the ostrogs, blockhouses, and customs barriers.[28] In the towns and ostrogs the state built official market places (*gostinnyia dvory*), where customs agents were stationed, and required that all trade be transacted in them.[29] Trade outside these specified centers, so-called "secret" trade, was illegal; anyone caught with furs so obtained or for which there was no receipt of declaration was subject to the con-

---

[23] *A.I.*, II, 58, IV, 287–288, 523, 524; *D.A.I.*, II, 156, 177, IV, 73, 110, 353, 365; *R.I.B.*, Vol. XV, pt. 5, p. 25; Müller, *op. cit.*, p. 304; Butsinskii, *K istorii Sibiri*, p. 6; Ogloblin, IV, 128, 130, 132.

[24] *A.I.*, IV, 327; *D.A.I.*, IV, 104, 353; *R.I.B.*, II, 167; Ogloblin, IV, 132; Butsinskii, *K istorii Sibiri*, p. 6; *idem*, *Mangazeia i mangazeiskii uezd*, pp. 46–47.

[25] *A.I.*, IV, 524.

[26] *D.A.I.*, II, 156, 162, 177, 274, IV, 50, 73, 202, 210; Ogloblin, IV, 128, 132.

[27] *Sloboda* (pl., *slobody*) is translated herein usually as "suburb," sometimes as "outlying settlement." It was a suburb in a jurisdictional rather than geographical sense.

[28] *A.I.*, II, 58, 102, III, 88; *D.A.I.*, II, 156, IV, 110, 210, 353–354; *R.I.B.*, II, 844, Vol. XV, pt. 5, pp. 24–25.

[29] *D.A.I.*, II, 160; *R.I.B.*, II, 844; Müller, *op. cit.*, pp. 274, 275–277.

fiscation of his furs and to corporal punishment.[30] Secret trade between Russians had, of course, the object of evading the tithe and other duties incidental to sales transactions and of escaping the sale of the best furs to the state. In the sparsely settled areas like Eastern Siberia the opportunities for such evasion were great. To check it, the state ordered that the serving men sent out to the state blockhouses should visit the blockhouses of the promyshlenniks and collect the tithe and other duties from them.[31] Also, to make evasion difficult, the state required that all traders, promyshlenniks, and serving men in any outlying regions who proposed to leave for some particular ostrog should report to the nearest blockhouse of the state, where the serving man in charge was to make out lists of their furs, seal the furs, and send the lists to the ostrog. Serving men on the march were to do the same with those merchants they encountered en route.[32] To prevent the smuggling of furs past towns and ostrogs, the state established customs barriers on the side roads passing around a town or ostrog, and any side road constructed without official authorization was ordered dug up.[33] The customs heads and voevodas were also instructed to be on watch lest traveling merchants leave their furs with friends in or near the town until ready to depart; they were required to search thoroughly the carts and sledges of any merchants who presented themselves at the customhouses, as well as their persons and the persons of those with them. Merchants might be quite willing to declare their ordinary furs but be loath to do so with their best ones for fear of having to sell them, and might therefore seek to conceal them. Any concealed furs that were uncovered were, of course, confiscated.[34]

A second group of regulations forbade trading in certain goods. Firearms, swords, pikes, suits of armor, knives, and axes were not to be sold to the natives for furs. Because the possession of such goods gave to the Russians their superior power, the natives were eager to acquire them, and the private trader, considering only his own interests, was quite willing to supply them in exchange for the highly prized furs. But the state, seeing the problem in its larger aspects and realizing the greater difficulty of holding under control natives equipped with the white man's weapons and tools,

[30] *A.I.*, II, 58; *D.A.I.*, III, 40, 42, 339, IV, 354; Ogloblin, II, 42.
[31] *D.A.I.*, IV, 210.
[32] *A.I.*, IV, 69; *D.A.I.*, III, 42, IV, 205, 337.
[33] *A.I.*, III, 336–337; *D.A.I.*, IV, 110; *P.S.Z.*, III, 508.
[34] *A.I.*, III, 337.

could look only with alarm upon their sale to the natives. Therefore, it not only forbade their sale to the natives, but prohibited any traffic or transporting of them by private individuals.[35] Those who carried these prohibited goods ran the risk of having them confiscated, as well as all other goods and furs in their possession. The sale of intoxicating liquors to the natives was also prohibited, not primarily, however, because of their demoralizing effects upon the natives, but because their sale was a government monopoly.[36] Although the state did not make a practice of selling liquor to the natives, it did regale them with strong drink as an inducement to submit to iasak or as a reward for bringing in their annual payments.[37] The sale of tobacco to the natives was likewise forbidden. Its use was banned not only in Siberia, but all over Russia, since the state considered smoking dangerous and contrary to Russian law and custom. Its use also increased the fire hazard among the wooden buildings everywhere prevalent in those days.[38] In 1662 Moscow ordered the voevodas of Verkhoturie and Berezov to see that merchants entering Siberia did not bring with them copper coins rather than Russian goods for purchasing furs, and to seize the goods and furs of those merchants who did. These copper coins were legal tender, to be sure, Moscow having issued them in 1656, but they had been issued at a forced ratio to silver, so that they quickly depreciated. Merchants could afford, therefore, to pay twice or more the usual prices for furs. By not bringing with them goods of food and clothing, upon the importation of which Siberia was dependent, these merchants created a scarcity of supplies that increased prices and worked hardship upon the serving men and natives, to the consequent detriment of the state's fur trade.[39]

[35] *A.I.*, II, 28, 102, III, 87–88, IV, 559–560, VII, 331; *R.I.B.*, III, 830; Müller, *op. cit.*, p. 311. In later years the state evidently considered this practice no longer dangerous, or sought to keep to itself the benefits of trading goods so much desired by the natives, for it used itself iron goods and implements, such as axes, for gifts to the natives in return for iasak. See above, p. 60.

[36] *D.A.I.*, III, 41, IV, 364; *R.I.B.*, Vol. XV, pt. 5, p. 21; Ogloblin, III, 158; Butsinskii, *Mangazeia*, pp. 27–28.

[37] G. F. Müller, "Sibirskaia istoriia," p. 227; Ogloblin, III, 158.

[38] *D.A.I.*, III, 41, 44, IV, 73; *P.S.Z.*, III, 329; Adam Olearius, *The Voyages and Travels of the Ambassadors Sent by Frederick, Duke of Holstein, to the Great Duke of Muscovy*, p. 62; P. P. Mel'gunov, *Ocherki po istorii russkoi torgovli IX–XVIII vv.*, p. 181.

[39] *A.I.*, IV, 327–329; *D.A.I.*, IV, 276–277; V. O. Kliuchevskii, *History of Russia*, III, 231–232; N. I. Kostomarov, *Ocherki torgovli moskovskago gosudarstva*, p. 343. Butsinskii (*Mangazeia*, p. 36) states that in 1644 the Mangazeia voevoda wrote that the lack of grain prevented the sending of serving men to the blockhouses to collect iasak.

The participation in the Siberian fur trade of one group of merchants was entirely prohibited. These were the foreign merchants from the West. From the time when Chancellor opened the northern sea route to Russia, English, and subsequently Dutch and German, navigators had endeavored to sail eastward from Kholmogory and Arkhangelsk in search of a northeast passage. They also traded aggressively in the north, and at the time that Siberia was first opened had reached Pustozersk and the Urals.[40] With the opening of the rich fur regions of the Taz, some of the foreigners at Arkhangelsk began employing Russians to show them the sea route to the Ob gulf and Mangazeia, and a few foreigners, according to one report, did succeed in reaching Mangazeia over this route, whence they sought to proceed farther east to the Enisei.[41] Moscow took alarm at such activity, fearing that the foreign merchants might trade directly with the natives and thus deprive the state of its tithe. It even entertained apprehensions of an armed invasion by foreign merchants. These fears caused Moscow in 1619 to order the ocean route to Mangazeia closed, to Russians as well as foreigners, lest the Russians, inadvertently or otherwise, direct the foreigners along this route; and an ostrog was ordered built on the portage on Ial-mal Peninsula to enforce this edict. This extreme measure for preventing the possibility of losing Siberia is one of the strongest indications of the value which Moscow attached to its new dominions. Thereafter, Mangazeia had to be reached from Russia over the longer inland routes, a circumstance which effectively barred the foreigners of the West from Siberia.[42]

Aside from its restriction on their trading activities the state sought to limit the private enterprisers in another direction. This was the restriction against their operating in the hunting grounds of the natives. The promyshlenniks hunted naturally wherever the animals were plentiful or easily accessible and, unless carefully watched, ignored the right of the natives to their traditional hunting grounds. Invasion of these grounds by the Russians with their ruthless hunting methods soon exterminated the animals and made difficult or impossible the payment of iasak by the natives. Therefore, the state prohibited such invasion and threatened with con-

[40] Cf. Samuel Purchas, *His Pilgrimes,* XIII, 193–293, which contains accounts of the activities of the English on the north coast.

[41] *R.I.B.*, II, 1051.

[42] S. V. Bakhrushin, *Ocherki po istorii kolonizatsii Sibiri,* pp. 85–87; Butsinskii, *Mangazeia,* pp. 37–40; G. V. Vernadskii, "Protiv solntsa," *Russkaia mysl',* XXXV (No. 1, 1914), 60–62.

fiscation of his furs and with corporal punishment any promyshlennik caught trespassing in the natives' hunting grounds, and instructed its voevodas to direct the promyshlenniks to hunt in the grounds of those natives not paying iasak.[43] Though enterprisers of a different sort, the peasants in Siberia also endangered the hunting grounds of the natives by their frequent selection of these grounds for farming. The peasants were therefore forbidden to settle in these areas, on pain of whipping; or if they found it necessary to settle on hunting grounds, they were required to limit their clearing to the acreage actually to be plowed.[44] Neither promyshlenniks nor peasants were to abuse the natives in any way.

Not all the state's orders were restrictive of the business pursuits of the traders and promyshlenniks. Since the state depended upon them for an appreciable part of its fur revenue, it encouraged and tried to aid them in those activities which did not conflict with its own interests. Because the promyshlenniks were valuable to it both as payers of the tithe and as discoverers of new regions of fur-bearing animals, Moscow required its voevodas and serving men to extend protection to them, and to defend them during their hunting from attacks and plundering by the natives,[45] such attacks being not infrequent.[46] The traders it endeavored to assist by building shelters at suitable points, by protecting them from avaricious officials, and by other means.[47] The state was jealous of its fur trade, but it was not rapacious.

Regulations Relating to the State Employees

The third group in Siberia with which the state had to deal was its own employees. They represented a very important element in its fur trade, since the degree of its success depended upon them. In their hands rested the collection of iasak and the tithe, the purchase of furs, and the administration of the provisions and regulations designed to protect the sources of its fur income. It was essential, on the one hand, that they execute the orders of the tsar faithfully; on the other, that they should not exceed their authority and instructions. Yet even more than for the private enterprisers the

[43] *A.I.*, III, 165–166; *D.A.I.*, III, 214, VIII, 3, 8, 263, 267.

[44] *A.I.*, V, 108, 346–347; *R.I.B.*, II, 765; Ogloblin, III, 276; Butsinskii, *Zaselenie Sibiri*, p. 331; *idem*, *K istorii Sibiri*, p. 28.

[45] *D.A.I.*, II, 162, 231, IV, 77; *R.I.B.*, II, 851–856.

[46] *D.A.I.*, II, 262, III, 279, 284, IV, 120; *R.I.B.*, II, 850, VIII, 536–538; Ogloblin, I, 196–197, III, 79.

[47] *A.I.*, IV, 32–35; *D.A.I.*, II, 160, III, 43–47.

state found it necessary to circumscribe the actions of its employees with regulations that were aimed at preserving the integrity of its fur trade.

Many of these regulations pertained to the performance by the state employees of their official duties, that is, the collection of iasak and the tithe, and the purchase of furs for the government. Moscow specified that the voevodas, serving men, customs heads, and sworn men were not to steal fur receipts or to tamper with them in any way. They were not to accept bribes or gifts from anybody or to act in collusion with either the Russian enterprisers or the natives. Neither were the employees to abuse or oppress the iasak men and the promyshlenniks and traders, nor to force from them any extra exactions. The state employees were to work zealously and honestly for the tsar, to increase his fur revenue by every legitimate means.[48]

Regulations such as these, which are directed against malfeasance in office, are, of course, common to all governments. Of a more particular sort were certain regulations adopted by Moscow to safeguard its fur income and to afford some protection for the natives against rapacious state employees. It required that one or two sworn men accompany the iasak-collecting expeditions of serving men, to keep watch on the latter and to act as receivers for the furs collected.[49] Or, if the natives lived not too far from the administration center, the serving men were ordered to bring back with them a few of the natives' "best" men to report on the conduct of the collectors while making their rounds in the volosts.[50] If the collectors proved too abusive and oppressive, the natives were directed to bring in the iasak themselves.[51] As an additional safeguard, Moscow instructed the voevodas to have the returning iasak collectors met outside the towns and ostrogs by other serving men, who were to take over all furs in the possession of the former and to carry them to the voevodas for checking. Should any discrepancies from the iasak books appear, the voevodas were to inquire into them.[52] If the collectors left any illegally acquired furs with near-by natives to be claimed later for their own purposes, the natives were to bring them in to the voevodas.[53] Serving men caught in any of these illegal

[48] *D.A.I.*, II, 159, 163, III, 40, 41, IV, 110, 115–117, 369; *R.I.B.*, II, 832.

[49] *D.A.I.*, II, 163, 177, 268, III, 334–335, 342, IV, 73.

[50] *D.A.I.*, II, 268; Müller, *Opisanie*, p. 280.

[51] *A.I.*, II, 78, 102; Butsinskii, *Zaselenie Sibiri*, pp. 248–249.

[52] *D.A.I.*, II, 271, IV, 107–108, 203, 355; *R.I.B.*, II, 847–848, Vol. XV, pt. 5, p. 21; Müller, *Opisanie*, p. 281; *P.S.Z.*, III, 240.

[53] *A.I.*, IV, 445, 522; *D.A.I.*, II, 272, IV, 75, 109, 204, 355.

practices were to have their furs confiscated and were to be beaten and then imprisoned for a week or two.[54] With respect to the voevodas, Moscow made stipulations by which it hoped to deter them from irregularities in connection with the iasak. It required of some voevodas that, when the natives brought in the iasak to them, a sworn man must be present at the time of delivery.[55] Although the detailed records kept in the iasak books made tampering with the tsar's fur income difficult, Moscow established an additional check by having the incoming voevoda go over the accounts of the outgoing one.[56] The same method of checking the outgoing official by the incoming one was applied to the customs heads.[57] The account books of both voevodas and customs heads were, of course, checked upon receipt at the Siberian Department, and any deficiencies which were thus revealed the retiring official had to make good out of his own pocket.

A second group of regulations concerned the participation of the state employees in the fur trade. In the early decades of the occupation of Siberia their duties and rights were not clearly defined, and the first employees sent to Siberia were quick to take advantage of the lack of definitive regulations and to engage extensively in the fur trade for themselves. But abuses arose in connection with their trade; they neglected their official duties, and so the state forbade them to engage in it.[58] This prohibition was in effect by the beginning of the seventeenth century with respect to the voevodas and their assistants, and Suleshev, while voevoda at Tobolsk from 1623 to 1625, extended it to all the serving men.[59] It was applied also to the customs heads and sworn men, who had to forego all participation in business during their terms of service, as well as any association with their friends.[60]

With respect to the voevodas and their assistants the state endeavored to make the prohibition complete by forbidding them to participate even indirectly in the trade. They were not to act through any agent or member of their families, who were also for-

[54] Ogloblin, IV, 125.
[55] Müller, *Opisanie*, p. 280.
[56] *D.A.I.*, IV, 101, 346; Ogloblin, IV, 140, 141.
[57] *D.A.I.*, IV, 111, 351; Ogloblin, III, 177, 178, 321, IV, 156; Butsinskii, *Mangazeia*, p. 43.
[58] *D.A.I.*, II, 159, 274, IV, 111, 116–117, 354; *R.I.B.*, II, 832, Vol. XV, pt. 5, p. 26.
[59] Butsinskii, *Zaselenie Sibiri*, pp. 235, 248; Müller, *Opisanie*, p. 312; cf. *R.I.B.*, VIII, 350.
[60] *D.A.I.*, II, 159, III, 41, IV, 351.

bidden to engage in trade.[61] Furs carried by anyone for a voevoda, voevoda's assistant, or member of his family were subject to confiscation.[62] To deter the voevodas from engaging in the fur trade through the use of agents, Moscow refused to recognize the validity of any promissory note given to a voevoda, since the voevodas utilized this device as a guarantee against embezzlement by their agents.[63] In order further to prevent trade by its Siberian officials the state limited the amount of goods which they might transport with them into Siberia.[64] Such goods were to be used only for their personal needs, not for trade; if in Siberia they found themselves in need of more supplies, they were to purchase them in the official market place or through the customs head.[65]

The serving men, on the other hand, aside from the prohibition against trading in furs and the confiscation of furs acquired by trade, appear to have been subject to few supplementary regulations. An order to the voevodas of the westernmost towns of Siberia instructing them not to allow any serving man on his way to Russia to take with him more than fifty rubles' worth of goods and furs is the only such regulation to come to light.[66] As a matter of fact, Moscow permitted its serving men in certain parts of Siberia, chiefly the part of Eastern Siberia under the jurisdiction of Iakutsk, to trade in furs on a small scale. They were permitted to trade their excess supplies with the natives for furs and to trap animals after they had collected iasak. The furs acquired by serving men under the specified circumstances were to be declared upon arrival at Iakutsk or the blockhouse where the serving men were stationed, and the tithe was to be paid from them. Any good furs or furs given to them by the natives the state bought; the rest the serving men were allowed to dispose of for their own needs.[67] Such small-scale traffic in furs was looked upon by the state less as trade

[61] *A.I.*, III, 338; *D.A.I.*, IV, 116–117, 354, 359–361, 364, VIII, 262; Butsinskii, *Zaselenie Sibiri*, p. 236; *P.S.Z.*, III, 349.

[62] *A.I.*, III, 336–338, V, 43–46; *D.A.I.*, IV, 359; I. P. Kuznetsov-Krasnoiarskii, *Istoricheskie akty XVII stoletiia (1633–1699)*, I, 10–14.

[63] Butsinskii, *Zaselenie Sibiri*, p. 244.

[64] *D.A.I.*, II, 274, IV, 111.

[65] *A.I.*, III, 340, 341; *D.A.I.*, IV, 111, 361; *R.I.B.*, Vol. XV, pt. 5, p. 26; Butsinskii, *Zaselenie Sibiri*, 236.

[66] *D.A.I.*, III, 46. This restriction was later lifted (1693), the state even going so far as to allow serving men to bring into Siberia 50 rubles' worth of goods duty-free (*P.S.Z.*, III, 161).

[67] *A.I.*, IV, 444–445, 522; *D.A.I.*, II, 151, 178, 271, III, 210, IV, 74–75, 108, 203, 209; *R.I.B.*, Vol. XV, pt. 5, p. 22; I. M. Trotskii, *Kolonial'naia politika moskovskogo gosudarstva v Iakutii XVII v.*, p. 7.

than as a form of additional compensation and as an encouragement to conquest.[68]

With these regulations forbidding trade in furs by the state employees we complete our list of measures adopted by the state to protect its fur trade and monopoly. Moscow issued other regulations, but they concerned situations which were unique or of so infrequent occurrence that they need not be considered. From the regulations which we have examined it becomes clear that each of the three groups involved in the state's fur trade presented to the state a particular problem bearing on the conduct of its trade and on the enforcement of its monopoly. The natives, the state's main source of furs, had to be treated equitably so that their capacity for paying tribute might be preserved and their disaffection from Russian rule prevented. The private enterprisers—also a source, but to an equal degree competitors—had to be restricted to a residual trade with the natives; they had to be confined to their own hunting grounds and held to the payment of the tithe and to the sale of their best furs to the state. The state employees, the executors of the state's orders, had to be held to the proper performance of their duties by a system of checks and by keeping them from participation in the fur trade. To meet these situations, the state resorted largely to measures of prohibition, confiscation, and corporal punishment. With what success, we shall see.

Our recounting of the protective regulations of the state shows more sharply how much of the fur trade in Siberia the state aimed to keep for itself. It did not, and could not, monopolize all that trade, but it did seek to monopolize the trade in the best furs. It tried to do this by taking from the natives all their furs of the good and best grades, preferably as iasak and pominki, otherwise by purchase. From the Russian enterprisers—whom it wished also to exploit, but not so extensively—it purposed to take a tenth of their furs and to buy all their best ones. The furs of those who opposed the monopoly it would confiscate. This monopoly the officials of the tsar never clearly or comprehensively expressed in writing, but it was in fact the monopoly contained in their instructions to the Siberian voevodas.

The monopoly which the state sought and the monopoly which it effected were not, however, one and the same thing. It was an ambitious task which the state had set for itself in attempting to hold a large, and the choicest, part of the Siberian fur trade in its

[68] *P.S.Z.*, III, 510; Trotskii, p. 79.

own hands, and in executing this task it was not wholly successful. The protective regulations of the state often proved unavailing, and the private enterprisers and the state employees by their illegal activities encroached considerably upon its monopoly, causing noticeable harm to its trade. We come, therefore, to a consideration of the inroads made in the state's trade by these two groups.

Infringement of the Private Enterprisers on the State's Monopoly

The means by which the private enterprisers made inroads on the monopoly of the state have already become evident from our description of the regulations opposing the activities of this group: namely, they drained off the best of the natives' furs before the state could obtain them; they used prohibited goods in trading with the natives; they managed to evade the tithe and the sale of their own best furs to the state; and they invaded the hunting grounds of the natives. Our interest here, consequently, is in the extent and prevalence of these activities.

The facts, unfortunately, are hard to ascertain; those who evade government regulations are not wont to leave records of their evasion. From the complaints registered by Moscow and by the Siberian authorities it appears that secret trading and trade in prohibited goods were common enough to be regarded as a usual rather than unusual condition.[69] A not uncommon practice of the promyshlenniks and traders for avoiding the authorities while engaged in illegal trade was to live among the natives.[70] The invasion of the hunting grounds of the natives was of such extent as to be an important factor in reducing the quota of iasak which the natives found they could pay.[71] Although both hunters and peasants were equally guilty, the invasion of the peasants seems to have been the more serious in that their destruction of the forest drove the animals out permanently.[72] Evasion of the tithe and of the compulsory sale of best furs was probably as common as illegal trade. However, for those who transported furs from one part of Siberia

[69] *R.I.B.*, II, 167; Ogloblin, IV, 132; Müller, "Sibirskaia istoriia," p. 35; Butsinskii, *K istorii Sibiri*, pp. 6, 12; S. Okun', "K istorii Buriatii v XVII v.," *Krasnyi arkhiv*, LXXVI (No. 3, 1936), 185; *D.A.I.*, II, 234–235, where seizure of furs obtained by illegal trade is reported.

[70] Butsinskii, *Zaselenie Sibiri*, p. 332.

[71] *A.I.*, III, 165–166, V, 346; *D.A.I.*, III, 214, VIII, 3, 267; *R.I.B.*, II, 765–766; Butsinskii, *Zaselenie Sibiri*, pp. 317, 330; *idem, K istorii Sibiri*, pp. 12, 23, 28.

[72] Cf. *R.I.B.*, II, 961.

to another, or out of Siberia to Russia, avoidance of the customs officials themselves was difficult. Towns, ostrogs, and customs barriers were located on the highways which a traveling merchant had to follow, and side roads existed only in connection with the large settlements, so, though he might avoid one barrier, he could not avoid them all.[73] Eventually he would meet an official who would collect the tithe, if it were not already collected. But for those who hunted and traded furs locally in a given region evasion was probably easier.[74] The familiarity which comes from living in a place would suggest various means of avoiding the eye of the customs official. Evasion of this sort was easiest in the little-settled areas of Eastern Siberia, especially in those areas where the state had to depend upon its serving men stationed in blockhouses to collect its tithe and buy up the best furs. The promyshlenniks, called upon by the serving men to declare their furs, would declare only their inferior pelts and conceal their best ones.[75] Nevertheless, usually the state ultimately received its tithe, for though the hunter might escape it, the trader who bought from him and carried the furs to Russia would have to pay it somewhere along the line. That left one other method of evasion, at least of full payment, and it was the one most used, especially in connection with the regulation concerning the best furs. This was the bribing of the customs officials.[76] It was much the safest means of evasion and, in the long run, the cheapest, because it reduced the dangers of confiscation. This practice seems to have been common, if we are to believe the complaint found in the customs decree of 1698,[77] and very likely the state lost as much fur revenue from this evil as from any other illegal practice.

There is nothing surprising in the fact that the state was not able fully to enforce its monopoly against the private enterprisers. It was sheer impossibility for it to attempt to exclude the traders and promyshlenniks from a large part—and that the choicest—of the fur wealth of an area as vast as Siberia. Even under the most favorable conditions the enforcement of such a monopoly was impossible.

[73] *R.I.B.*, II, 143; *D.A.I.*, III, 110; Butsinskii, *Mangazeia*, p. 42.

[74] *D.A.I.*, VIII, 3.

[75] *D.A.I.*, IV, 404.

[76] Butsinskii, *Mangazeia*, pp. 45–46; S. V. Bakhrushin, "Torgi gostia Nikitina v Sibiri i Kitae," *Sbornik statei: Pamiati Aleksandra Nikolaevicha Savina, 1873–1923*, Trudy instituta istorii rossiiskoi assotsiatsii nauchno-issledovatel'skikh institutov obshchestvennykh nauk, I (1926), 385–386; cf. *D.A.I.*, II, 159.

[77] *P.S.Z.*, III, 495.

The great profits of the fur trade attracted many who were willing to risk its dangers. The policing of so large a country required far more men than Moscow could assemble there. But most of all, the state could not rely upon its own enforcement agents to enforce its protective regulations, for these agents likewise engaged in the fur trade; they themselves encroached upon the monopoly of the state.

Encroachment of the State Employees on the State's Monopoly

The continued participation of the state employees in the fur trade, despite the prohibitions against it, was the greatest source of injury to the fur trade of the state. Because they occupied places of authority, of which they did not hesitate to take advantage, the state employees were in a position to inflict considerably more damage upon the state's fur trade than could the private enterprisers. They not only cut into the monopoly of the state by themselves engaging in the trade, but caused serious losses through irresponsible methods of acquiring furs. Numerous petitions from the natives, private enterprisers, lesser Siberian officials, and serving men alike bear eloquent witness to their abuses.[78] The extent of their encroachment and the injuries they inflicted upon the state's fur trade will become evident from a description of their illegal trade.

The participation of the state employees in the fur trade extended from the voevoda at the top to the ordinary serving man at the bottom. The high officials, the voevodas and their subordinates, carried on the most extensive trade. They were usually men of high social rank in Russia—many of them were of princely or boiar families—and of some wealth.[79] They possessed the means, therefore, to undertake trade in furs on a large scale.

These men acquired their furs in a number of ways. They might themselves buy them or exchange goods for them like any merchant, and they sometimes did. But after they were barred from the fur trade, they most commonly acted through agents. These agents might be members of their families, for nepotism was rampant in the administration of Siberia; private traders, whom they provided with money or goods with which to obtain furs from other traders and the natives; serving men, whom they also supplied with goods to be exchanged, during the collection of iasak, for furs from the

[78] E.g., Trotskii, pp. 1–2, 20–47, 56–62, 98–99, 109–111, 111–112, 119–120, 125; *A.I.*, II, 166–167, 195–196.

[79] Ogloblin, I, 181.

natives; or pokruchenniks, whom they commissioned to hunt fur-bearing animals.[80] The iasak collectors were the ones most frequently used as agents, and in acting for the voevodas, as well as for themselves, they carried on the very practices which they were expected to prevent on the part of the private traders, that is, trading with prohibited goods and taking the best furs of the natives.[81] Moreover, the serving men often forced the goods on the natives. In 1626 the Eniseisk voevoda sent 600 rubles' worth of goods with the iasak collectors to be traded, by force if necessary, for the natives' best furs.[82] The voevodas at Mangazeia, prior to 1685, had customarily provided the collectors with cheap and bad goods, which the collectors exchanged for the best furs of the natives, acquiring in a year as many as 12,000 sables and other furs, while collecting only 3,600 pelts as iasak.[83]

There were yet other means which the voevodas in their positions of authority found for obtaining furs with little cost to themselves. Extortion in various forms was practiced upon the natives, traders, promyshlenniks, and serving men, such as imprisoning them and then compelling them to buy their freedom.[84] Even though not supposed to interfere in the collection of customs, the voevodas forced extra customs collections from the promyshlenniks and traders.[85] From the natives they obtained furs by threatening the hostages or those who brought in the iasak, by having the collectors collect extra furs from the natives in the volosts, by robbing or otherwise oppressing them en route to their voevodal posts, and in other ways.[86] Collusion with the serving men was another means of acquiring furs;[87] so was peculation. The voevodas exchanged their poor furs for the good furs in the state treasury, or stole them outright; they also appropriated the voluntary pominki brought in by the natives for the sovereign.[88] The documents refer oftener

[80] *A.I.*, III, 336; *D.A.I.*, III, 41, 209, 210; Ogloblin, I, 181, II, 31, III, 165, 183, 188; Butsinskii, *Mangazeia*, pp. 46–47.

[81] Ogloblin, III, 188, IV, 130; Butsinskii, *Zaselenie Sibiri*, pp. 236, 247.

[82] Ogloblin, I, 165.

[83] *D.A.I.*, XI, 69.

[84] *D.A.I.*, II, 267, III, 209–211; Müller, *Opisanie*, p. 326; Ogloblin, III, 154, 155, 181, 333, IV, 115–116; *P.S.Z.*, III, 211.

[85] *A.I.*, IV, 33, 288; *D.A.I.*, III, 43, IV, 117–118, 346.

[86] *A.I.*, II, 77, 101, III, 321; *D.A.I.*, IV, 11, Müller, *Opisanie*, pp. 326–327; Ogloblin, III, 165, 182, 183; Butsinskii, *Zaselenie Sibiri*, pp. 321–322; Okun', p. 185; *P.S.Z.*, III, 349.

[87] *D.A.I.*, II, 270.

[88] *D.A.I.*, III, 210, IV, 118, VIII, 264–265, XI, 69; Müller, *Opisanie*, pp. 281, 327; Ogloblin, IV, 134, 156; *P.S.Z.*, III, 211; Trotskii, p. 10.

to this abuse than to any other perpetrated by the voevodas. The furs which they thus acquired they disposed of in the Russian markets. Since their term of office was short, from two to four years, some took their accumulation of furs with them back to Russia, paying the tithe if necessary; but usually they sent their furs with agents to be sold in Russia.[89] "The report has reached the sovereign tsar" that "many furs received as bribes" are sent by Siberian voevodas, heads, and others to their estates in Russia—so states one document.[90] Other documents corroborate this impression of widespread corruption.[91]

What the voevoda and his assistants did on a large scale, the serving man did on a smaller one. Opportunities for profiting from the fur trade and for obtaining furs easily were likewise open to him. The serving man ordinarily did not possess the means for carrying on an export trade to Russia, but he could, and did, carry on a good business locally, or he could act as agent for the voevoda or for private merchants.[92] The best opportunities for the serving men to acquire furs easily came from the iasak-collecting expeditions, over which there could be little effective supervision. When on tours of collection, they trapped the animals, or they carried with them goods which they exchanged for furs from the natives—the good furs, of course.[93] But a cheaper means was to get the furs from the natives at no personal cost—as more or less voluntary gifts, as bribes, by theft, or by various forms of extortion and outright violence.[94] The collection of iasak a second or third time within the same year and the forced sale of goods seem to have been common means of extortion. With iasak of a fixed amount it was difficult to tamper, but where the amount was not fixed, stealing without detection was relatively easy. Also, it was possible to extort furs from the natives who paid iasak on a money-value basis simply by undervaluing the furs presented. Like the voevodas, the serving men exchanged their poor furs for the good ones taken as iasak,[95] or

---

[89] *D.A.I.*, II, 160, III, 210, IV, 118; Ogloblin, IV, 87, cf. I, 183.
[90] Ogloblin, IV, 137.
[91] *P.S.Z.*, III, 282, 350.
[92] Butsinskii, *Mangazeia*, pp. 46–47; cf. *P.S.Z.*, III, 357, and *D.A.I.*, VII, 150.
[93] *D.A.I.*, II, 270, III, 339–340, IV, 115, VIII, 11; Ogloblin, III, 174.
[94] *A.I.*, II, 77–78, 101, III, 166–167, 312, IV, 347, 382–383; *D.A.I.*, II, 267, VIII, 264, 266, 267, XI, 66; *R.I.B.*, II, 182, 967, VIII, 507–508; Ogloblin, III, 173–174; Butsinskii, *Zaselenie Sibiri*, p. 321.
[95] *A.I.*, IV, 523; *D.A.I.*, II, 163, 267, IV, 75, 204, VIII, 264, 268–269; *R.I.B.*, II, 183; Müller, *Opisanie*, p. 280; Ogloblin, I, 187; Butsinskii, *Zaselenie Sibiri*, p. 321; Okun', p. 184; Kh. Trusevich, *Posol'skiia i torgovyia snosheniia Rossii s Kitaem (do XIX v.)*, pp. 86–87.

stole outright furs received as iasak. So profitable to the serving men was the collection of iasak that they clung to the right of collection tenaciously, resisting any changes which took a part of their territory away from them and allocated it to another jurisdiction. This right was at the bottom of many disputes and much open warfare between rival bands of serving men in certain parts of the Enisei and Lena regions.[96] Some serving men even paid the voevoda for the privilege of collecting iasak.[97] This right was also one of the principal attractions of exploring and conquering new lands; as the returns from the natives of conquered regions diminished, new regions of unexploited natives became necessary to offset the decline.[98] The promyshlenniks and traders were likewise fair prey. Furs could be obtained from them either by extortion or in collusion for overlooking illegal hunting or illegal trade with the natives.[99] Coöperating with the voevodas in their several forms of graft and tampering with the sable treasury en route to Moscow were additional ways to get furs.[100] For the disposal of their furs the serving men resorted to the local Siberian markets, which were visited by merchants or their agents from Russia. Sometimes, however, they dispatched the furs to Russia in the care of agents or else took them themselves when accompanying the sable treasury to Moscow.[101]

In so far as can be determined, the temporary state employees, the customs heads and sworn men, to whom the state turned as a means of checking the abuses and corruption of the regular employees, participated in the fur trade too. Considering the fact that they were called from their regular pursuits as traders and

[96] *R.I.B.*, II, 966–967; V. K. Andrievich, *Istoriia Sibiri*, I, 149–152; Butsinskii, *Mangazeia*, pp. 18, 24.

[97] *P.S.Z.*, III, 239, 403.

[98] Cf. Bakhrushin, *Ocherki*, p. 162.

[99] *D.A.I.*, II, 162, IV, 364, 404, VIII, 6–7, 263; Ogloblin, III, 173, IV, 13.

[100] *D.A.I.*, II, 267, III, 209–210, VIII, 264–265; Ogloblin, III, 176, IV, 157.

[101] *D.A.I.*, II, 158, 160, VIII, 11; G. Potanin, "Privoz i vyvoz tovarov goroda Tomska v polovine XVII stoletiia," *Vestnik imperatorskago russkago geograficheskago obshchestva*, Vol. XXVII (1859), pt. 2, pp. 125, 127, 139.

The extent to which the state intended to exclude the serving men from the fur trade is not entirely clear from the documents. It is not unusual to find customs records from the seventeenth century showing the payment of the tithe by serving men, with no attempt at concealment of their trading operations (Potanin, p. 125; Ogloblin, II, 42. In fact, serving men who trapped their pelts themselves were in some places exempted from the tithe (Ogloblin, II, 42). Possibly these serving men did not participate in the collection of iasak. The participation of serving men in the fur trade in Siberia was certainly extensive enough to make efforts to conceal it superfluous. This probably explains the appearance of the names of serving men in the customs records.

promyshlenniks, forbidden to associate with their friends, and paid a low salary, there is no reason to believe that they foreswore their commercial connections and did not take advantage of their temporary state service. Their participation appears, however, not to have brought as much abuse in its wake as did that of the voevodas and serving men.[102] The fact that the traders and promyshlenniks preferred the administration of the customs collection by the customs heads and sworn men to that by the voevodas and serving men points to that assumption.[103] This circumstance and the increasing use which the state made of the sworn men indicate that their employment brought some improvement in the administration of the fur trade.

The principal form of malfeasance of which the temporary employees were guilty was the acceptance of bribes.[104] The success of the state's efforts to eliminate the abuses and losses to its trade arising from the voevodas' trade by making it difficult and unprofitable was centered in the enforcement by the customs heads of the provisions prohibiting the shipping of furs out of Siberia by the voevodas and their agents. Yet, in spite of these provisions, the voevodas' trade in furs continued to flourish. The conclusion is, therefore, that the customs heads and sworn men, in return for bribes, allowed the voevodas to carry more than 500 rubles' worth of goods into Russia and required the agents carrying their furs to pay only the tithe and ordinary duties.[105] The customs heads were open to bribery in another connection, the order to buy the best furs of the private enterprisers. This ruling worked a great hardship on the latter's trade, and, to avoid sacrificing their good furs, they had to turn to bribing the customs officials to undervalue the furs. Merchants sometimes tried to get around the provision by making coats of their valuable furs, "for their own needs," but the customs officials, unless bribed, were prone to look upon this practice as evasion.[106]

The consequences to the state of the participation of its employees in the fur trade are apparent. The immediate result was the loss of revenue through such offenses, whether of commission or omission. First, the oppressive exploitation of the natives impaired the ability of the latter to pay iasak and resulted not infrequently in native

[102] It did exist among them, however. See *A.I.*, III, 195; *D.A.I.*, IV, 111; Ogloblin, I, 126, 187, 190–191, III, 150, 171, 177–178, 190, 320–321.

[103] Butsinskii, *Zaselenie Sibiri*, p. 235.

[104] Bakhrushin, "Torgi gostia Nikitina," pp. 385–386.

[105] Butsinskii, *Zaselenie Sibiri*, pp. 245–248.

[106] Butsinskii, *Mangazeia*, pp. 45–46.

outbreaks and in attacks upon Russian settlements or on bands of serving men or promyshlenniks.[107] The extra exactions imposed upon the natives, as often as not, were as great or greater than the iasak itself. The burden of such extra exactions often brought impoverishment of the natives, sometimes death, and certainly a reduction in the number of pelts they could pay to the state.[108] These exactions probably were the principal cause for the decline of the iasak rate, which by itself was not excessive.[109] The less docile natives expressed their resentment by moving away or by revolting from Russian authority, the result in either case being a loss of iasak. Second, the state employees, through their readiness to accept bribes from the promyshlenniks and traders, reduced the state's fur income by failing to collect the tithe in full, to confiscate furs illegally obtained, or to purchase the best furs. And third, they caused serious losses to the state by stealing from the sable treasuries, by exchanging their poor pelts for the state's good ones, and by competing themselves with the state, carrying on all the practices which the state depended upon them to prevent on the part of private enterprisers. Indeed, too frequently, when the voevodas and serving men did enforce the regulations against illegal trade, it was only to prevent the private traders from acquiring from the natives the valuable furs which they themselves wished to obtain. How great was this immediate loss of revenue cannot be said; it must have been considerable.

But the failure of the state employees to enforce the revenue and preservative measures of the state had more far-reaching consequences. Their maladministration reduced the total possible fur income of the state. The diversion of a large number of furs received from the natives and private enterprisers into the hands of the state employees meant that, if the natives paid their quota of iasak and the private enterprisers made the profit they desired, both groups had to draw more heavily upon the supply of fur-bearing animals in Siberia. The ultimate exhaustion of that supply was thereby hastened, and this in turn was reflected in the decline

[107] *A.I.*, II, 101–102, III, 312–313; *D.A.I.*, II, 270–271, XI, 66, 67; *R.I.B.*, VIII, 615–616; Ogloblin, III, 165, 314, IV, 134; Butsinskii, *K istorii Sibiri*, p. 12. Some of the outbreaks, especially those during the Troublous Times (1605–1613), were political in character. But in Western Siberia all revolts after 1613 were protests against the abuses of the voevodas and serving men (Butsinskii, *Zaselenie Sibiri*, p. 304).

[108] *A.I.*, III, 312, V, 108; *D.A.I.*, III, 214.

[109] Butsinskii, *Zaselenie Sibiri*, p. 320; Okun', p. 184.

of fur revenue for the state in the several parts of Siberia. Furthermore, this diversion of furs from legitimate to illegitimate channels was a hindrance to the healthy economic development of Siberia and hence indirectly injurious to the state. In view of these circumstances, therefore, it must be concluded that the state was unable to effect its monopoly of the fur trade to the extent which it desired.

To attempt at this point an analysis of the basic causes of the maladministration of the fur trade of the state would carry us too far afield. They relate to the much larger problem of corruption and inefficiency in the Siberian administration as a whole. Yet, since the state suffered a loss of revenue through maladministration, a few observations concerning its deeper causes are not out of place. First of all, it must be noted that abuse and corruption in local administration were not confined to Siberia; they were all too prevalent throughout the Muscovite state,[110] the result of trying to administer according to a feudal notion of government what was in process of becoming politically a modern state. However, in Siberia these evils were probably worse, because the greater distance from Moscow rendered supervision of the local authorities more difficult and because the tremendous geographical extent of Siberia made centralized administration within it impossible.[111]

Second, conditions in Siberia encouraged and invited abuse and corruption. Life on the frontier was hard and dangerous; sufficient food was often lacking, its cost sometimes so high as to force men into debt; the state paid its employees low salaries and those never in full. Such circumstances bred strong temptations for corruption. At the same time, such men as went to Siberia were not overscrupulous about the means employed in seeking their own gain. Like the old Roman provincial governors, many voevodas sought their Siberian appointments deliberately because of the great opportunities for personal wealth, especially for recouping personal fortunes. Those voevodas sent against their wishes sought to compensate themselves generously for the rigors of Siberian service. The serving men were hardy and adventurous souls, many of whom preferred the hardships and dangers of the frontier to increasing bondage in Russia just because the frontier did offer chances for quickly gained riches. The inability of many natives

[110] Kliuchevskii, *op. cit.*, III, 153, 156; Kostomarov, pp. 333–334.
[111] Butsinskii, *Zaselenie Sibiri*, p. 237.

to defend themselves against the depredations of the Russians was a further attraction for such men. How, then, could men of this sort be held under control? In a newly conquered country, inhabited by weaker and inferior peoples, it was easy for the Russians to revert often to a sort of robber trade. Under such conditions the attempts of an administratively inefficient state to preserve and enforce even a near-monopoly were bound to fall short of the goal.

CHAPTER VI

THE DEPLETION OF THE SUPPLY OF FUR-BEARING ANIMALS

WHENEVER THE FUR TRADE has been conducted under pioneer conditions, where conservative regulation is difficult or impossible, the depletion of the supply of fur-bearing animals has always resulted. In this respect the Siberian fur trade was no exception. We have seen, on the one hand, that the Russians went into Siberia with the specific intention of acquiring its sables and other fur-bearing animals, and on the other, that Moscow had great difficulty in securing its own fur trade against the intrusion of the private enterprisers and state employees, let alone trying to set up and enforce a geographically extensive program of conserving the animal resources of Siberia against the depredative activities of these men. Under these circumstances, the animals were killed off at a rate with which their reproductive powers could not keep pace, and inevitably their numbers decreased.

CAUSES OF THE DEPLETION

Prior to the advent of the Russians in Siberia the natives, with their primitive mode of life and limited trade relations, had not drawn excessively upon the supply of fur-bearing animals. But the appearance of the Russians created new conditions which served to reduce that supply very markedly. Altogether four new factors were introduced to cause this reduction.

The first factor was the increase in the number of hunters. How many Russians went into Siberia in pursuit of furs we do not know, but a few examples may give some notion of their numbers. In 1626 there were 189 promyshlenniks known to be operating along the Lower Tunguska River and 312 promyshlenniks along the Stony Tunguska.[1] Butsinskii estimates that from 500 to 1,000 promyshlenniks and traders passed through Mangazeia yearly en route to hunting grounds farther east.[2] In 1642 at Iakutsk 839 men passed through customs eastward to hunt sables.[3] Khabarov, for his first expedition into the Amur in 1649 and 1650, had little

[1] J. E. Fischer, *Sibirische Geschichte,* I, 502.

[2] P. N. Butsinskii, *Mangazeia i mangazeiskii uezd,* p. 51.

[3] S. V. Bakhrushin, "Istoricheskie sud'by Iakutii," *Iakutiia: sbornik statei,* p. 295.

difficulty in assembling 150 volunteers from the ranks of the promyshlenniks and serving men, and his second expedition contained 330 of them.[4] In 1680, the Iakutsk voevoda wrote that prior to his arrival one hundred or more promyshlenniks and traders hunted and traded along the Olekma.[5] A rough estimate would set the increase in number of hunters represented by the Russians at between one-fifth and one-quarter.

More devastating in its exhaustive effect upon the number of fur-bearing animals in Siberia was the second factor, the far more effective hunting technique introduced by the Russians. The natives hunted simply with bow and arrow, whereas the Russians hunted systematically with traps (*kulemki*) and nets (*obmety*) and used dogs to run the animals down.[6] In some parts of Siberia the Russians also made use of the crossbow, especially among the islands of the Amur.[7] With their hunting methods the Russians caught many more sables than did the natives, as many as ten times the number killed by the natives in the same locality.[8] Thus, prior to the advent of the Russians, the killing of the animals with bow and arrow was not so destructive of the supply; the natural increase could keep pace with the kill, until the Russians introduced more efficient hunting methods.

The third factor—and the most devastating of all in its effect—was the tremendous demand of the Russians for furs. It is this which explains the two preceding factors, the presence of Russian hunters in Siberia and their more efficient methods of hunting. But it went beyond that. To satisfy the tribute requirements, to meet the demands of the Russian merchants and traders, and to satisfy the greed of serving men and officials, the natives drew

[4] *D.A.I.*, III, 360.

[5] *D.A.I.*, VIII, 3.

[6] *D.A.I.*, III, 57, 214; Bakhrushin, *op. cit.*, p. 295; P. N. Tret'iakov, "Pervobytnaia okhota v severnoi Azii," *Iz istorii rodovogo obshchestva na territorii SSSR*, pp. 222–223. Poiarkov, reporting (1646) his observations of the Daurs living along the Amur River, wrote: "they obtain . . . these sables also like the other Siberian and Lena natives: they shoot with a bow, and any other form of hunting, such as the Russians use to catch sables, with nets and traps, they do not know" (*D.A.I.*, III, 57).

[7] Jodocus Crull, *The Ancient and Present State of Muscovy*, I, 62. There seems to have been little use of firearms in hunting fur-bearing animals.

[8] P. N. Butsinskii, *K istorii Sibiri*, p. 12; G. Vernadskii, "Gosudarevy sluzhilye i promyshlennye liudi vostochnoi Sibiri XVII veka," *Zh.M.N.P.*, n.s., LVI (1915), 353. Some of the natives, especially those in the regions longer occupied by the Russians, adopted the more efficient hunting methods of the Russians (*D.A.I.*, VII, 17; cf. Tret'iakov, *loc. cit.*). A description of the Russian hunting methods is given on pp. 155–157 below.

much more heavily upon the supply of fur-bearing animals than they had done previously. Under the natives' economy the inroads upon this supply were extremely moderate, but under the impact of European commercial demands hunting grounds were cleaned out in a very short time.

The fourth, and least harmful, factor was the advance of settlement. A number of peasants came to Siberia and established farms, and serving men also settled on the land. The state encouraged agricultural settlement, for the food problem in Siberia was a serious one.[9] Preparing the land for agriculture necessitated cutting down or burning the forests; as a result some animals were killed and the rest driven away, to distances as great as a hundred miles or more.[10] Although this destruction of the forests drove away more animals than it killed, it nevertheless depleted the supply in the localities concerned and reduced the areas in which they could live and thrive. Agricultural settlement was intended as permanent and was therefore final in its effect, since it left small opportunity for restoring the depleted animal resources through natural processes. The settled agriculturist's mode of life and the hunter's way of living were not compatible, and when the farmer appeared, the hunter had to give way.

Rapidity of the Depletion

We turn now to the question of how rapidly this depletion took place. Despite the fact that Siberia first gained prominence as a country of practically untouched fur resources, nothing which approaches exact information has come down to us about the original abundance of animals found in the various parts of Siberia at the time they came under Russian control. However, a few reports have survived which indicate that it must have been great.

The first conqueror of Siberia, Ermak, along with his men, acquired enough furs to send 5,200 pelts to the tsar, besides those retained for himself and his followers.[11] After the Russians had established themselves on the Irtysh and its tributaries, the Konda

[9] G. V. Lantzeff, *Siberia in the Seventeenth Century,* pp. 162 ff.

[10] *A.I.*, V, 108, 346; *R.I.B.*, II, 765–766; Ogloblin, III, 274; P. N. Butsinskii, *Zaselenie Sibiri,* pp. 317, 330; *idem, K istorii Sibiri,* p. 28; S. V. Bakhrushin, "Sibirskie sluzhilye tatary v XVII v.," *Istoricheskie zapiski,* I (1937), 64–65; Kh. Trusevich, *Posol'skiia i torgovyia snosheniia Rossii s Kitaem (do XIX v.),* p. 183 n. 19; S. R. Krasheninnikov, *A History of Kamtschatka and the Kurilski Islands,* p. 109.

[11] See above, p. 26.

region paid iasak annually of several thousand pelts; and from a native prince in that region the Russians, in 1594, took 426 sable, 300 fox, 61 beaver, and 1,000 squirrel skins.[12] When the Russians first came into contact with the Enisei Tungus, in 1620 and 1621, the native chieftains each bestowed gifts of 40 and 45 sables on the Russians, and the ordinary natives brought iasak and pominki of 8, 9, or 10 sables apiece. But what particularly impressed the Russians was the fact that these natives lined their snowshoes with sable skins.[13] The region around the mouth of the Olekma, in the Lena basin, was reported to be so rich in fur-bearing animals that hunting parties of thirty, forty, and fifty men caught as many as 280 sables apiece.[14] Vasilii Poiarkov, reporting in 1646 his journey down the Amur to the Pacific, stated that among the Daurs sables, as well as lynxes and foxes, were so plentiful that a native, using only bow and arrow, could catch ten sables within a day's journey of his village.[15] Besides finding a great plenty of fur-bearing animals, the Russians discovered that the natives, yet unfamiliar with European goods and demands, placed a low value on them. For a copper kettle certain natives of the Lena are supposed to have given as many sables as would fill the kettle itself.[16] From this and other reports one gains the impression that large numbers of fur-bearing animals were to be found in the several parts of Siberia at the time of the first appearance of the Russians in them.

But within a comparatively short time the influx of Russian hunters and traders began to make itself felt, and reports were heard of the difficulty of finding animals with good pelts in the regions in which they had once been so abundant. In 1627, promyshlenniks from Mangazeia reported to officials in Moscow that in the areas around Mangazeia and Turukhansk and in those along the lower Enisei and the Lower Tunguska rivers the sables and beavers were "hunted out" (*opromyshlialis'*), that in those places where they had been accustomed to hunt in the past the animals were becoming scarce.[17] In fact, the depletion around Mangazeia reached such a point that, when the town was destroyed by fire

[12] Butsinskii, *Zaselenie Sibiri*, p. 320; G. F. Müller, *Opisanie sibirskago tsarstva*, p. 201.

[13] G. F. Müller, "Sibirskaia istoriia," pp. 217–220.

[14] K. G. von Baer, "Uebersicht des Jagd-Erwerbes in Sibirien besonders im Östlichen," *Beiträge zur Kenntniss des russischen Reiches*, VII (1845), 128.

[15] *D.A.I.*, III, 57.

[16] Baer, *loc. cit.*; *R.I.B.*, II, 964.

[17] *R.I.B.*, II, 849, 851.

in 1643, it was not thought worth while to rebuild it; instead, the government offices and officials were transferred to Turukhansk, which became New Mangazeia.[18]

The natives, too, complained of difficulty in finding enough sables for trade and iasak, and they abandoned some of their volosts because of the extermination of the fur-bearing animals.[19] These complaints were followed by a reduction in the iasak quotas of the natives. By 1608 the iasak rate in Tobolsk and Pelym uezds had been lowered from 10 and 12 sables per man to 7.[20] Two years later, some of the Ostiaks in Surgut uezd were granted a decrease from 11 to 9 sables as the individual quota.[21] For Western Siberia in general the rate of 10 to 12 sables per man, which prevailed at the turn of the century, had dropped to an average of 3 at the middle of the century, and by the end of the century the authorities were having to accept cheaper furs and money in place of the usual furs.[22]

These figures reflect as well as anything the decrease in the number of fur-bearing animals in Western Siberia; they suggest that by the middle of the century the richer part of the sable resources there had been exhausted. Thereafter, the best sables were to be found in Eastern Siberia, where the story was repeated. Promyshlenniks in the Lena region complained as early as 1649 that districts which in previous years had yielded from 120 to 260 sables for each member of a hunting party now yielded only 15 or 20 sables for the whole party.[23] In 1677 the natives around Barguzin reported that no more sables were to be found.[24] Reports from several parts of Eastern Siberia within the next few years indicate that the scarcity was widespread. Ilimsk and Kirensk uezds had been "hunted out" and were being abandoned by many promyshlenniks.[25] This was also true along a number of the tributaries of the Lena, even in their upper reaches.[26] The lower Amgun (Argun?) River and the Amur likewise were nearly stripped of sables;

[18] Butsinskii, *Mangazeia*, pp. 56–57.

[19] *R.I.B.*, II, 765–766; Ogloblin, I, 98, III, 157; Butsinskii, *Zaselenie Sibiri*, pp. 317–318, 320; Butsinskii, *K istorii Sibiri*, pp. 11, 23.

[20] Müller, "Sibirskaia istoriia," p. 26.

[21] *Idem*, *Opisanie*, p. 261.

[22] V. I. Ogorodnikov, "Russkaia gosudarstvennaia vlast' i sibirskie inorodtsy v XVI–XVIII v.v.," *Sbornik trudov professorov i prepodavatelei gosudarstvennogo irkutskogo universiteta*, I, 75; *D.A.I.*, VIII, 11–14.

[23] *D.A.I.*, III, 214.

[24] *D.A.I.*, VII, 193.

[25] *D.A.I.*, VII, 365, VIII, 183.

[26] *D.A.I.*, VIII, 19.

only brown and red foxes remained.[27] In several outlying regions a scarcity of serving men forced the authorities to abandon the state's blockhouses.[28] At the same time the natives were experiencing difficulty in meeting their iasak payments.[29] By 1690 the country around Iakutsk had been virtually denuded of sables, and many promyshlenniks were turning to other occupations.[30] Indeed, it was by then being recognized that Eastern Siberia was in the same condition, at the end of the century, that Western Siberia had reached at the middle of the century.[31] That being so, one would conclude that the exhaustion of fur-bearing animals in Siberia was rapid, a reduction of about 75 per cent in half a century. There is other evidence, however, which points to a less rapid reduction in the number of animals.

The best evidence for judging the rapidity of the depletion would be, of course, the number of furs taken annually out of the several parts of Siberia. But our chief difficulty in arriving at any certain conclusions about the fur revenue of Siberia is the limited information available. Except for Western Siberia, information about the fur returns from the various parts of Siberia is little more than fragmentary. With respect to Western Siberia, however, the information is sufficient for making a reasonably accurate estimate of the rate of depletion there. Considering the meagerness of data about the fur returns of Siberia, it is fortunate that what information we do possess applies largely to Western Siberia. The Ob-Irtysh basin was the first major part of Siberia to be conquered by the Russians, and almost all of it was overrun by them within twenty years' time, two circumstances which give it a unity and distinctness of experience that permit a fairly clear definition of the decline in the number of fur-bearing animals there. With the rate of depletion in the Ob-Irtysh basin ascertained, we may use that rate as a measure for determining the probable experience of the other major parts of Siberia, the Enisei basin, the Lena basin, Baikalie, and the Amur Valley.

The information to be considered consists of iasak returns from

[27] *D.A.I.*, VIII, 184.

[28] *D.A.I.*, VII, 364–365.

[29] *D.A.I.*, VIII, 16, 19.

[30] *A.I.*, V, 347; A. P. Shchapov, *Sochineniia*, III, 646; Bakhrushin, "Istoricheskie sud'by Iakutii," p. 296.

[31] *P.S.Z.*, III, 211, 283; S. V. Bakhrushin, "Torgi gostia Nikitina v Sibiri i Kitae," *Sbornik statei: Pamiati Aleksandra Nikolaevicha Savina, 1873–1923*, Trudy instituta istorii rossiiskoi assotsiatsii nauchno-issledovatel'skikh institutov obshchestvennykh nauk, I (1926), 374.

eleven of the thirteen uezd administrative centers in Western Siberia for various years between 1624 and 1647 and for the years 1698 and 1699. The tithe receipts, admittedly, are left out of consideration, chiefly because there are few data, but also because in Western Siberia more and more the tithe was collected in a few large commercial centers like Tobolsk, Tomsk, and Verkhoturie rather than in the local centers, like Ketsk, Surgut, and Tara, of the uezds where the furs were acquired.[32] The iasak, on the other hand, was collected in such centers and thus is a more reliable index for each area involved. The table opposite shows the returns.[33]

Examination of this table discloses that the fur-bearing animals were not exterminated so rapidly in Western Siberia as the reports cited above would indicate. To be sure, six of the towns, Tiumen, Berezov, Turinsk, Narym, Mangazeia, and Ketsk, show a marked decline in iasak receipts, more than half within three-quarters of a century, Ketsk showing the most marked decline. However, Pelym, Tara, and Surgut experienced a decrease noticeably less than half, whereas Verkhoturie maintained a fairly even level of iasak returns. Tobolsk, strangely, shows a decided increase, the explanation of which is obscure, unless the number of iasak-paying natives in its jurisdiction increased, for one cause or another. If we take the year 1628, the year between 1624 and 1647 for which the figures are most complete, and supply estimates for the four towns for which there are no figures, we will obtain a result that can be compared with the total returns for the years 1698 and 1699. For these towns the following estimates seem warrantable: Surgut, 2,700 r., Turinsk, 400 r., Narym, 1,600 r., and Mangazeia, 5,000 r. The total therewith becomes 18,686 r. For 1698 the total is 13,285 r., and for

[32] Butsinskii, *Zaselenie Sibiri*, p. 159.

[33] The figures in this table are drawn from several sources. All those for the years 1698 and 1699 are taken from a survey of the state's income and expenditures in Siberia which was ordered drawn up in 1702 in the Siberian Department by the tsar, Peter the Great, from the estimate lists (*smetnyia spiski*) sent to Moscow by the Siberian voevodas of the nineteen administrative centers. This survey is published in *R.I.B.*, VIII, 689–892. Since only the total value of the furs collected in each center is given, the value of the iasak for these years had, in most instances, to be approximated from the number of furs received as iasak. The sources of the figures for the other years are as follows: TIUMEN, Butsinskii, *Zaselenie Sibiri*, p. 101; TOBOLSK, *ibid.*, pp. 141–142, Ogloblin, IV, 156; PELYM, *Zaselenie Sibiri*, p. 170; BEREZOV, *ibid.*, p. 183; TARA, *ibid.*, pp. 159, 320; TURINSK, *ibid*, p. 79; VERKHOTURIE, *R.I.B.*, II, 537, *Zaselenie Sibiri*, p. 61, *D.A.I.*, VIII, 13; SURGUT, NARYM, and KETSK, Butsinskii, *K istorii Sibiri*, pp. 11, 22, 27–28; MANGAZEIA, Butsinskii, *Mangazeia*, pp. 21, 25, 49–50. All these figures are taken from the archives of the Siberian Department. It is not certain that some of the figures cited as iasak do not include tithes.

Annual Iasak Collections[33]

(Values in rubles at Siberian prices)

Year	Tiumen	Tobolsk	Pelym	Berezov	Tara	Surgut	Turinsk	Narym	Verkhoturie	Mangazeia	Ketsk
1624........	...	.....	...	.....	1,631	.....	↑	.....	...	.....	.....
1625........	...	.....	...	.....	.....	3,000		1,600	711	.....	1,200
1626........	...	.....	...	.....	.....	.....		.....	713	.....	.....
1627........	...	915	...	.....	1,408	.....		.....	682	.....	.....
1628........	500	663	645	3,887	1,014	.....		.....	709	.....	.....
1629........	535	786	.....	3,654	.....	.....		1,600	684	5,000	1,012
1630........	...	.....	...	.....	.....	.....		.....	670	.....	.....
1631........	...	.....	...	.....	.....	.....		.....	591	.....	.....
1632........	...	.....	...	.....	.....	.....	between	.....	445	.....	.....
1633........	356	.....	...	.....	.....	.....	500 and	.....	546	.....	.....
1635........	...	.....	872	.....	1,231	.....	300	.....	671	.....	.....
1636........	...	.....	...	.....	.....	.....		.....	...	7,143	.....
1638........	...	.....	...	.....	.....	.....		.....	...	9,376	.....
1640........	...	1,997	...	.....	.....	.....		.....	...	.....	.....
1642........	...	.....	...	.....	.....	.....		.....	...	6,458	.....
1643........	...	.....	850	.....	.....	.....		.....	...	4,100	.....
1644........	...	2,233	...	.....	.....	.....		.....	814	.....	.....
1646........	...	.....	...	.....	.....	.....		.....	...	7,234	.....
1647........	...	.....	...	.....	.....	.....	↓	.....	...	.....	.....
1671........	...	.....	...	.....	.....	.....	...	....	632	.....	.....
1698........	101	3,600	566	1,500	1,280	1,938	170	690	700	2,700	40
1699........	106	2,700	534	1,320	1,300	1,687	154	660	530	1,600	35

1699, 10,626 r. Thus, for the eleven towns concerned the figures show a decline of less than half, about 45 per cent, over a period of seventy years. On the basis of 45 per cent in seventy years, the decline in a hundred years would be about 65 per cent, a hundred years being the period during which the whole of Western Siberia had been under Russian authority by 1699. Whether this was in fact the extent of the decline we cannot be sure. There is reason to believe, however, on the basis of calculations given in the following chapter, that in 1605 more than 50,000 sable skins were sent to Moscow from the eleven towns.[34] In 1698 9,000-odd sable skins were sent to Moscow; in 1699 the number was slightly above 8,400. By these figures a decline of more than 80 per cent is shown. Probably the actual decline over the century was somewhere between the two figures, roughly 75 per cent. This, it is to be observed, is only half the rate of 75 per cent within fifty years or so which was originally suggested above.

Because of the want of data concerning the decline of fur-bearing animals in the other parts of Siberia, for those regions we are compelled to resort to the method of approximating the extent of the decline by applying to them data concerning the experience of Western Siberia. At the end of the seventeenth century the basin of the Enisei had been under Russian occupation between eighty and ninety years. On the basis of the 75-per cent decline in a hundred years computed for Western Siberia, the decline in the Enisei must have amounted to between 60 and 70 per cent. On the same basis, the decline in that part of Eastern Siberia under the jurisdiction of Iakutsk, namely, the Lena basin north of the Stanovoi Mountains and northeastern Siberia, must have reached 50 per cent, since that region was occupied by the Russians in the 'thirties and 'forties. This estimate is seemingly corroborated by the fact that in 1640 the value of the iasak collected at Iakutsk amounted to 26,000 r. and that of the iasaks in 1698 and 1699 to 14,000 r. and 17,000 r. respectively.[35] Yet such corroboration is uncertain at best, for in the course of the intervening sixty years changes occurred in the territory under the jurisdiction of Iakutsk. The Baikal region at the end of the century had been subject to Russian control since the 'forties and 'fifties, so the decrease there

[34] See below, pp. 110–111.

[35] P. N. Miliukov, "Gosudarstvennoe khoziaistvo Rossii v sviazi s reformoi Petra velikago," *Zh.M.N.P.*, CCLXXI (1890), 346 n. 1. The figures for 1698 and 1699 are approximations based on *R.I.B.*, VIII, 793–796.

must have been less than half. The Amur remained under Russian control only until 1689, but in the forty years that it was subject to Moscow the depletion of its supply of fur-bearing animals probably amounted to about 30 per cent.

Qualifying Factors in the Depletion

If the statistical evidence does not confirm the impression of rapid decline conveyed by the reports of the original abundance of fur-bearing animals and of its subsequent exhaustion, what, then, is the explanation? The explanation is threefold. In the first place, although undoubtedly in a given hunting area the hunters quickly exhausted the original abundance of animals, they did not necessarily exterminate them. Many hunters, when entering a new region, were interested only in its best sables, and once the region had been stripped of them, they moved on to other grounds. The sables with inferior pelts were permitted to survive, and with fewer hunters visiting the area the subsequent decline was much slower, so that complete exhaustion did not occur for several years, or even decades. Also, areas that had been worked out and abandoned were probably revisited by the animals, which are known to have migrated.[36] It is not unlikely, on the other hand, that the reports of early abundance were exaggerated. One writer refuses to believe that thirty to fifty promyshlenniks each obtained as many as 280 sables in one season along the Olekma River, when nearly a century later the first hunters to enter Kamchatka—where the sables, though of inferior quality, were almost as numerous as those in the Lena region—counted themselves fortunate if they caught 60, 80, or 100 in a year. A few hunters along the Olekma, so this writer argues, probably obtained as many as 280, a number which, with the passage of time, came to be considered as the fortune of each of the hunters in a group.[37] Although authentic contemporary records give credibility to so high a return for the early years[38] this writer is probably right. Such returns were the exception rather than the rule. The traders who obtained their furs from the natives probably experienced also a short-lived abundance following their first contacts with new tribes of natives. The first large numbers of sables obtained at ridiculously low prices were the result of several years' accumulation and of the natives' ignorance

[36] Baer, p. 120.
[37] *Ibid.*, pp. 128–129.
[38] E.g., *D.A.I.*, III, 214.

of what the Russians were willing to offer for them.[39] Soon the natives learned not to sell their furs so cheaply.

The second point in explanation is the fact that the accounts of exhaustion refer usually to sables. The pelts of other kinds of animals were considerably less in demand and therefore the supply was not so rapidly depleted.[40] As the number of sables decreased, the exploitation of these other animals increased. In the second half of the seventeenth century there appear increasingly in the instructions to the voevodas and customs heads orders to buy other valuable pelts such as polar foxes, and at the end of the century the state attempted a complete monopoly of black fox pelts as well as sable pelts.[41] The iasak and tithe returns for 1698 and 1699 show large numbers of beavers and ermines, kinds of furs only occasionally encountered in the records of the first half of the century. Huge numbers of squirrels, sometimes in the tens of thousands, likewise appear in the records for 1698 and 1699.[42] The greater exploitation of these animals tended to offset the decline of sables.

The third, and most important, point in explanation is that the two kinds of evidence refer to areas of different compass, to the relatively small locality, like the country around a blockhouse, on the one hand, and on the other, to the considerably larger region, like the uezd. The most striking examples of depletion refer to particular localities, which, teeming with fur-bearing animals, were visited by a swarm of promyshlenniks, who hunted with an intensity that soon exterminated at least the better sables. Whereupon the promyshlenniks moved to other localities, often in the same region. The large region was not worked all at once; rather, it was worked locality by locality, so that the extermination of the animals in the whole region required much more time. That is why the rapid exhaustion recounted of certain hunting grounds was not experienced by the whole uezd in which these grounds were situated. Naturally, the larger the area involved, the longer the time required to exhaust its animal resources. In the same way an area like Western Siberia, which comprised several uezds, required an even longer time.

---

[39] Baer, p. 139; cf. above, p. 97, where the furs accumulated by one of the native princes in the Konda region are enumerated.

[40] *D.A.I.*, VIII, 184; *P.S.Z.*, II, 176; J. F. Baddeley, *Russia, Mongolia, China*, II, 252.

[41] *A.I.*, IV, 539; *D.A.I.*, IV, 365, VIII, 29; *P.S.Z.*, III, 498, 505, 507.

[42] *R.I.B.*, VIII, 693–694, 737–738, 767–768, 783–784, 795–796, *et al.*

Absence of Conservation Measures

Although in the longer-occupied regions the depletion of fur-bearing animals was great enough in time to prompt Moscow to establish new centers of authority farther east, the problem of the depletion itself the state never tackled seriously. It did make some feeble attempts at solution in those areas threatened with exhaustion. For example, it instructed the voevoda of Perm in 1635 to prohibit the use of traps to catch beavers and otters—a commentary, incidentally, on the greater effectiveness of the Russian hunting methods.[43] There is also this odd instruction to the Tobolsk voevoda in 1664: no one was to be allowed to buy or raise live fox cubs, lest they become extinct.[44] The prohibition against invasion of the natives' hunting grounds by the Russians may be looked upon as a partial conservation measure of the state; yet even had it been observed generally, it would have served largely to transfer the exhaustive hunting of the Russians to other regions and would not have constituted any basic solution. Any conserving effects which the various regulations of the state may have had were incidental. The state was concerned only with its immediate income and made no attempts to conserve the animal resources of Siberia through restricting the killing of the animals, or other measures. Even if it had tried seriously to check the depletion, there is no reason to believe that it could have succeeded. The problem of enforcement would have been too great.

The Bearing of the Depletion on the Eastward Advance

The effect of the depletion of fur-bearing animals as a prime causal force in the Russian advance across Siberia has already been pointed out in a previous chapter. Nevertheless, having examined the depletion in detail, we are warranted in returning briefly to this phase of the subject in order to present a clearer picture of how the depletion affected the course of the advance. It is recalled that most of Siberia was overrun in about eighty years, a period of time which had not yet served to exhaust the fur resources of the first major section to be conquered, namely, Western Siberia. This disparity would appear to minimize the importance of the exhaustion of fur resources as the principal factor

[43] *A.A.E.*, III, 393–394.
[44] *D.A.I.*, IV, 365–366.

in the eastward advance. However, it does not, and for the following reason.

It was not the exhaustion of the region as a whole, of an uezd or a river basin, which drove the promyshlenniks and traders farther and farther east at so rapid a pace. Rather, it was the exhaustion of the most accessible localities in it which did this. When a given locality became depleted or exhausted, the promyshlenniks found it easier, in searching for new regions abounding in fur-bearing animals, to move long distances along the major rivers and across portages than to push into the more isolated upper parts of tributaries or to leave the river routes and seek hunting grounds less distant but harder to reach. This tendency is seen in the fact that often, when the supply of animals in the lower part of a river valley was exhausted, the less accessible upper parts still yielded adequate numbers.[45] It is also reflected in a report of Mangazeia promyshlenniks in 1627. Encountering a growing scarcity of sables in the hunting grounds in the country around Mangazeia, the promyshlenniks had begun to hunt sables in the districts farther up the Lower Tunguska River, which was the natural water route and therefore the easiest route, eastward from Mangazeia.[46] Similarly, other promyshlenniks sailed down the Einsei to its mouth, along the coast, and then back up the rivers emptying into the Arctic in search of new hunting grounds.[47] Again, there is record of an order by the Iakutsk voevoda in 1680 to promyshlenniks instructing them not to hunt in the iasak areas near such rivers as the Olekma, Vitim, Aldan, Viliui, Maia, and others tributary to the Lena, but to hunt in the non-iasak areas of the Indigirka and Kolyma rivers.[48] In other words, the Russians preferred to hunt illegally in the hunting grounds of the iasak-paying natives along the rivers easily reached from Iakutsk than in the unrestricted areas of the distant Kolyma and Indigirka rivers, which were accessible only by an overland route or dangerous sea voyage. In consequence, the eastward advance pushed rapidly over the easier routes, the water routes, and the Russians brought these under control first, leaving the large areas between them for later occupation.

As the depletion of fur-bearing animals impelled the first rapid

[45] *D.A.I.*, VIII, 184; Krasheninnikov, pp. 109, 110; M. B. Shatilov, *Vakhovskie ostiaki*, p. 133; A. Titov, *Sibir' v XVII v.*, p. 35.
[46] *R.I.B.*, II, 851.
[47] Müller, "Sibirskaia istoriia," pp. 101–102.
[48] *D.A.I.*, VIII, 267.

conquest, so it also led in time to the exploration and conquest of many of the intervening areas. Then, too, the advance of settlement followed the lines of easiest advance and thus hastened the depletion of animals already begun there by the first invading promyshlenniks. Those men who were unable to push far to the east—settled natives and local traders and promyshlenniks of small capital—had to resort to the hunting areas which were nearer but were at the same time more difficult of access. Thus, gradually, the unexplored and unconquered intervening areas were filled in. Illustration of this is found in a report of the Iakutsk voevoda in 1690. Having stated that in the country around Iakutsk sables had disappeared, the voevoda adds that the natives living there have to go by horse for a month and a half or so to hunt sables.[49] It is significant that they went on horseback. They had to find their sables in localities which could not be reached by the more easily traveled rivers, localities which, consequently, had not hitherto been exploited. It is this filling-in process which helps to explain why the depletion of fur-bearing animals was less rapid than it at first seems.

[49] *A.I.*, V, 347; cf. also *D.A.I.*, VIII, 19–20.

CHAPTER VII

THE FUR INCOME OF THE STATE

Although it is possible to describe in detail how the state acquired its furs, it is rather difficult to ascertain the number and value of the furs which it took out of Siberia. The existing information about the Siberian fur yield from the beginning of the conquest to the end of the seventeenth century is far from complete; most of it lies unused in the archives of the Siberian Department, and the scholars who have had access to these archives have evidenced only a passing interest in this subject. Yet, some notion of the size of the state's income from furs is essential to a full understanding of the importance of its fur trade. Therefore, even though our information is far from complete, an estimate of the size and fluctuations of the trade during the period under study will be attempted here.

Four questions come to mind concerning the state's fur income from Siberia. The first is, naturally, what was the annual revenue received from this source? The second, what proportion did each source of furs contribute to this revenue? The third, what percentage of the entire income of the state did the fur revenue represent? And the fourth, after deducting the cost of conquering and administering Siberia, did the state's fur trade show a profit, and if so, how much? These questions cover the principal aspects of the financial importance of the fur trade to the state.

Annual Fur Revenue from Siberia

For determining the annual fur income from Siberia specific data exist for certain years at the beginning, middle, and end of our period, 1585–1700. These years may be grouped in three subperiods, 1589–1605, 1635–1644, and 1680–1701. To determine the annual income for the intervening years we must resort to estimates based on the known data and on our knowledge of the course of conquest during those years.

The first year for which there are data which may be considered reliable is 1589. The Englishman, Giles Fletcher, who resided in Russia almost continuously from 1574 to 1590, says in his account of the Muscovite state that in 1589 there "was gathered . . . out of

Siberia for the emperours' customs, viz., 466 timber[1] of sables, 5 timber of martrones, 180 black foxes."[2] Although he designates these furs as customs receipts, it is more than probable that only a small part of them was taken as the tithe and that, on the contrary, most of them were collected as iasak from the natives, for Fletcher did not always have an accurate understanding of Russian terms.[3] It is open to question how effectively Moscow had been able to establish its customs collection in Siberia within three years after it had resumed the conquest begun by Ermak; besides, most of the Russian traders and promyshlenniks in Siberia were then operating in the Iugra and Mangazeia regions, to which Moscow had yet to extend its authority. According to calculations made by Butsinskii, approximately 3,750 natives in the seven uezds of Verkhoturie, Tiumen, Tobolsk, Tara, Turinsk, Pelym, and Berezov were paying iasak to the Russians in the first decade of the seventeenth century.[4] But in 1589 Moscow had not yet penetrated into the Tara and Berezov uezds, and it was not until 1598 that it had completed its subjugation of the other five uzeds. Hence, probably less than half the 3,750 natives had been subjected to iasak in 1589. If we take Fletcher's figures, we get a sum of 19,020 pelts (18,640 sables, 200 martens, 180 black foxes), and that figure divided by the then prevailing iasak rate, namely, from 10 to 12 sables per man, gives a result between 1,500 and 1,900, presumably the number of individuals paying iasak in 1589. This result bears out our contention that about half of the 3,750 natives mentioned by Butsinskii was the number of iasak-payers in 1589 and justifies the conclusions that Fletcher's figures refer chiefly to the revenue from iasak and that they are an accurate statement of the Siberian fur income for the year 1589.

Although the value of this fur revenue is not stated, it may be deduced from the content and value of a subsidy composed entirely of furs, which was sent to the Holy Roman Emperor, Rudolf II, at Prague in 1595.[5] This subsidy was made up as follows:

[1] A timber comprised forty pelts; probably so called because the pelts were bound between two boards. The Oxford English Dictionary (1933), Vol. XI, sec. 2, p. 36.

[2] *Russia at the Close of the Sixteenth Century*, p. 53.

[3] Cf. S. M. Seredonin, *Sochinenie Dzhil'sa Fletchera "Of the Russe Common Wealth" kak istoricheskii istochnik*, pp. 320, 322.

[4] P. N. Butsinskii, *Zaselenie Sibiri*, pp. 14, 324.

[5] *Pamiatniki diplomaticheskikh snoshenii drevnei Rossii s derzhavami inostrannymi*, II, 236–237; N. M. Karamzin, *Istoriia gosudarstva rossiiskago*, Vol. X, *Primechanie*, No. 309, p. 100.

	Value in rubles
1,009 forties (40,360) sables	28,907
519 forties (20,760) martens	5,190
120 black foxes	565
337,235 squirrels	6,744½
3,000 beavers	2,708½
1,000 wolves	530
Total	44,645

According to the values of the furs given here, which are in terms of the prices for furs in Moscow, the average value of the sables was 28.7 r. per forty, of martens 10.4 r. per forty, and of black foxes 4.7 r. each. Applied to the returns of 1589, these values give results of 13,374 r., 50 r., and 846 r. respectively, a total of 14,270 r. Besides sables, martens, and black foxes, a small number of pelts of other animals—beavers, red foxes, squirrels—must also have been sent to Moscow from Siberia, so that the round figure of 15,000 r. (Moscow value) fairly represents the value of the Siberian fur revenue of the state for 1589.

If 15,000 r. was the value of the fur income of the state in the fourth year of the conquest of Siberia, what was it in 1605, when Russian authority had been established in almost all of Western Siberia? No such specific information as that left by Fletcher exists for the year 1605, but the probable income in that year may be estimated. By 1605, twelve uezds had been established in Western Siberia. In addition to the seven already mentioned, there were those of Surgut, Narym, Ketsk, Mangazeia, and Tomsk. In Surgut uezd, more than 600 natives were paying iasak at the beginning of the seventeenth century.[6] In Mangazeia uezd, which was created some time after 1600, the number of iasak-payers varied from year to year, but in the early years their number must have been between 300 and 500. Tomsk uezd was marked out only in 1604, so that in 1605 the number of iasak-paying natives was probably not more than 300.[7] These figures, added to the 3,750 already cited, make a total of around 5,000, if we set 400 as the number of iasak-payers for Mangazeia. This number multiplied by 11 (the middle figure of the iasak rate of 10 to 12), gives 55,000, the number of sable pelts, or their equivalent, taken that year in ten of the twelve towns. For Narym and Ketsk, the number of pelts collected as iasak in

[6] P. N. Butsinskii, *K istorii Sibiri*, p. 7.

[7] G. F. Müller, *Opisanie sibirskago tsarstva*, p. 271.

1605 is known: namely, 4,400 and 3,000 respectively.[8] Thus the final total is 62,400 pelts. This total represents 1,560 forties, and in terms of the 1595 Moscow value of sables their value was 44,772 r. or, in round figures, 45,000 r., which may be taken as the approximate value of the state's fur income in 1605. Admittedly, the tithe receipts have not been taken specifically into account, for the good reason that they are not known and there is no reasonably accurate way of estimating them. On the other hand, allowance in the foregoing figure may be considered to have been made for them, since the rate of 11 sables per native was applied to the whole of Western Siberia, whereas it is definitely known that in the longer-occupied parts the rate had dropped and that almost from the beginning of the conquest the natives fell into arrears in their payments.[9]

For the period 1589–1605 it has been necessary to depend in part upon indirect evidence in order to ascertain the annual income in furs. For the other two periods, 1635–1644 and 1680–1701, this, fortunately, is not necessary. The exact value of the fur income for certain years within these periods is known from official records. The fur receipts in these years are tabulated in terms of Siberian value as follows:[10]

Year	Value in rubles
1635	63,518
1640	81,648
1644	102,021
1680	102,026
1681	113,042
1690	58,762
1691	77,365
1698	103,467
1699	74,982
1701	*ca.* 75,000

The striking feature of the earlier period is the rapid increase in the annual income, a two-thirds increase in nine years. This increase is explained by the fact that during these years the Russians were consolidating their power in the rich Lena country and were beginning their penetration into country almost as rich, along

[8] *Ibid.*, p. 261; G. F. Müller, "Sibirskaia istoriia," p. 38; Butsinskii, *K istorii Sibiri*, pp. 16, 25.

[9] *R.I.B.*, II, 123–125; Müller, *Opisanie*, pp. 194–195, 195–196.

[10] P. N. Miliukov, "Gosudarstvennoe khoziaistvo Rossii v sviazi s reformoi Petra velikago," *Zh.M.N.P.*, CCLXXI (1890), October, p. 345 (for the years 1635, 1640, and 1644), p. 346 (for 1680), p. 346 n. 4 (for 1701); Ogloblin, IV, 113 (for 1690 and 1691), 161 (for 1681); *R.I.B.*, VIII, 887–888 (for 1698 and 1699).

the Indigirka and Kolyma rivers and into the upper Angara region. That they were reaping the usual high returns of first advance into a new region is shown by the rise in the iasak revenue of Iakutsk from 10,735 r. in 1637 to 26,999 r. in 1640.[11] The most noticeable feature of the fur revenue in the later period is the fluctuation in value between 75,000 and 100,000 rubles. The highest figure, that for 1681, and the lowest, that for 1690, appear to be exceptional.[12] The absence of any definite trend in these figures reflects the static condition of the Russian occupation of Siberia: during this period no conquests of any new areas were made.

For the years intervening between the three periods, that is, for the years 1606–1634 and 1645–1679, we must resort to approximation. In making our approximations we should bear in mind these considerations: For those years during which the Russians were pushing eastward and conquering new regions in Siberia a rising fur income may be expected. The penetration of the Russians was so rapid that it carried them into new areas of fur-bearing animals faster by far than was required to offset the exhaustion of animals in regions already occupied. This fact is pointedly demonstrated by the rising fur income in the period 1636–1644. Conversely, for those years when the rapid penetration ceased and when all of Siberia that was conquered by the Russians in the seventeenth century had been brought under their dominion, the rise in the fur income may be expected to have ended and after a few years to have begun to decline, since there was no longer the compensating factor of unexploited regions to offset the inevitable depletion of the supply of fur-bearing animals.

The annual fur revenue during the first two decades of the intervening years, the decades from 1606 to 1624, is the more difficult to approximate. The natives of Siberia became aware of the internal disorders in Russia which broke out after the death of Tsar Boris Godunov in 1605. Many native tribes attempted to throw off Muscovite sovereignty, and others failed to pay the stipulated amount of iasak, so huge arrears accumulated during these years.[13] Whereas formerly several thousand pelts were sent yearly from the Big Konda country, between 1615 and 1617 only eighty sables were

[11] Miliukov, p. 346 n. 1.

[12] Ogloblin, IV, 113.

[13] A. Gnevushev, "Akty vremeni pravleniia tsaria Vasilia Shuiskago," *Chteniia*, Vol. CCLIII (1915), No. 2, pt. 1, pp. 65, 66, 68–69, 70–71, 72–73; Butsinskii, *Zaselenie Sibiri*, p. 320.

collected there as iasak.[14] Also, the value of the ruble declined very markedly in the Troublous Times.[15] During these years, however, the eastward advance of the Russians continued unabated; the invaders pushed into the Enisei basin, building Turukhansk blockhouse in 1607 and Eniseisk in 1618. The political disaffection of the natives in the Ob-Irtysh basin does not seem to have spread here. In 1625, the Tobolsk voevoda, Iurii Suleshev, restored order in the disorganized condition of the collection of iasak, and considerable increases in the iasak revenue were effected through his reforms. How great an increase was made is not related, beyond the statement that it was "much."[16] While these reforms were increasing the fur receipts in Western Siberia, in Eastern Siberia, during the decade 1625–1634, the Russians penetrated into the Lena basin along the western tributary rivers, building Iakutsk in 1631, and at the end of the decade were opening many new lands. Such were the major developments which must guide our approximations for the years 1606–1634.

If 63,000 rubles' worth of furs were sent to Moscow in 1635, then, considering the expansion of the preceding ten years and the iasak reforms of Suleshev, the fur revenue probably rose from about 45,000 r. to 60,000 r. in that decade. For the years preceding it, 1606–1624, marked as they were by native uprisings and disorganization in the collection of iasak, the fur income probably fluctuated between 25,000 r. and 45,000 r., the lowest returns being those of the last years of the Troublous Times and the first years of the new Romanov dynasty, elected in 1613. What the actual returns were in these years must remain unknown, since most of the iasak and tithe records for that time were destroyed by fire.[17]

In estimating the returns for the second intervening period, 1645–1679, it is to be remembered that during this time the remaining unconquered parts of Siberia (except Kamchatka) were overrun by the Russians. The rapid expansion of the early 'forties continued into the late 'fifties; Trans-Baikalie was entered and occupied, as was the Amur River valley, and the occupation of the Aldan, Maia, Indigirka, Olekma, and Anadyr river regions was consolidated. These years must have marked the high point in the annual fur revenue of the state, for during them virtually all

[14] Butsinskii, *Zaselenie Sibiri,* p. 320.
[15] V. O. Kliuchevskii, *Opyty i issledovaniia,* pp. 158–161.
[16] *R.I.B.*, VIII, 350–351.
[17] *R.I.B.*, VIII, 350; Ogloblin, I, 90.

Siberia east of the Lena River and Lake Baikal was brought under Russian control.[18] Thus, the 102,000 ruble revenue of 1644 must have risen by virtue of these conquests to around 125,000 r., perhaps to 130,000 r., in the middle 'fifties. During the years that followed, in the 'sixties and 'seventies and the remainder of the century, no new regions were conquered. The process of occupation became then chiefly one of consolidating the territorial gains. Hence, from this time on, with no major regions of untouched fur resources to swell the total, the annual returns undoubtedly began to drop off, and the yearly income declined in the 'sixties and 'seventies to the level of an income of 75,000 to 100,000 rubles in the last two decades of the century. The approximations for this second intervening period, it is to be hoped, will be replaced by authentic figures based on data which must be in the archives of the Siberian Department.

The discussion of the annual fur revenue for the whole period, 1585–1700, has been broken into five shorter periods, presented in not wholly chronological order. We recapitulate our findings, therefore, both the known and estimated, by tabulating them in chronological order:[19]

Years	Income of the state (in rubles)
1589	15,000 (12,000)
1605	45,000 (36,000)
1606–1624	25,000–45,000
1625–1634	45,000–60,000
1635	63,518
1640	81,648
1644	102,021
1645–1655	100,000–125,000
1656–1679	125,000–100,000
1680	102,026
1681	113,042
1690	58,762
1691	77,365
1698	103,467
1699	74,982
1701	*ca.* 75,000

[18] Cf. Juraj Križanić, *Russkoe gosudarstvo v polovine XVII veka,* chap. (*razdel*) 51, p. 122 (in Supplement to No. 5, "Russkoi Beseda," 1859).

[19] The figures for 1589 and 1605 are Moscow values, about 20 per cent higher than Siberian values, in which the revenue for all the other years is given. For purposes of comparison the Siberian value equivalent is given in parentheses,

The poverty of data concerning the state's Siberian fur income has led several writers to depend upon statements by the historian Karamzin and the seventeenth-century writer Kotoshikhin, for their information on this subject. The statements of both men, however, must be rejected on the basis of the foregoing findings; each erred in the direction of too high a figure. Karamzin wrote that about 1586 Siberia furnished (*dostavliala*) the tsar's treasury with 200,000 sables, 10,000 black foxes, and 500,000 squirrels.[20] Kotoshikhin asserted in his account of the Muscovite state, written in 1666 and 1667, that the Siberian fur revenue amounted at that time to 600,000 r. or more a year.[21] That the enormous returns represented by Karamzin's figures were possible a year or two after Moscow had resumed the conquest initiated by Ermak is, of course, incredible. In fact, we do not even need our findings to dispose of this statement, for examination of the excerpt which Karamzin quoted in support of his statement reveals that he misread its meaning. He mistook the numbers give above of sables, black foxes, and squirrels, which some Russian official predicted would be received from Siberia, for pelts already received.[22] Kotoshikhin's figure is so far above even the highest possible actual returns at that time that not even the higher Moscow value of furs can be advanced to

---

but it should be remembered in comparing the figures for 1589 and 1605 with the rest that the ruble declined greatly in value during the Troublous Times.

[20] Karamzin, X, 26.

[21] Grigorii Kotoshikhin, *O Rossii v tsarstvovanie Aleksiia Mikhailovicha,* p. 104.

[22] Karamzin, Vol. X, *Primechanie,* No. 44. Translated, the excerpt which Karamzin cited and quoted reads thus:

"[The sovereign] assessed (*polozhil*) iasak on the Siberian kingdom, the Big Konda, the Little Konda, the Pelym kingdom, the Tura, the Irtysh, the [K]Irghiz kingdom, the Pegaia Orda, and the Great Ob, on all the towns, on ninety-four of them, to take (*imat'*) from year to year 5,000 forties of sables, 10,000 black foxes, and 500,000 great Siberian and Ilimetskie squirrels."

It is to be noted that in 1586 the Russians were established only in the Siberian kingdom.

Even the expectation of collecting this number of furs was gross exaggeration, an exaggeration best explained by Baer, the scholar first to dispute Karamzin's statement. The excerpt quoted was taken from the archival collection, "Polish Affairs," and thus pertains to Polish-Muscovite diplomatic relations. Shortly before his own death in 1587, Stefan Batory, king of Poland, on the ground that with the end of the dynasty at the death of the childless tsar, Fedor Ivanovich, the Muscovite state would be thrown into confusion, proposed to the Russians that after Fedor's death Russia should be united with Poland. This the Russians refused to listen to and, in order to refute Batory's unhappy prediction, advanced the just beginning conquest of Siberia as evidence of their prosperity, enlarging upon the expected fruits of conquest in typical Russian fashion. K. V. von Baer, "Uebersicht des Jagd-Erwerbes in Sibirien, besonders im Östlichen," *Beiträge zur Kenntniss des russischen Reiches,* VII (1845), 135–136; S. M. Solov'ev, *Istoriia Rossii s drevneishikh vremen,* II, 557.

account for it. His erroneous figure can be accounted for only by the fact that, as he himself tells us, it was based not on official records, but on unsubstantiated recollection.[23]

Relative Importance of the Sources of Fur Revenue

The second question pertaining to the Siberian fur income of the state concerns the proportion which each source of furs contributed to that income. The information on this question is, as in the preceding instance, insufficient for always exact conclusions, but it is extensive enough to show the relative importance of each source.

The most complete item of assembled data is the survey of the income and expenditures of the state in Siberia for the years 1698 and 1699.[24] From it may be calculated the number of pelts received as iasak and the tithe, as well as from the other sources of furs in each of the nineteen administrative towns. The importance of each source would be shown more accurately if the value of the furs rather than the number of furs could be given. However, the value of only the total number of furs received in each town is specified, and to approximate the value of the furs from each source would give a result no more accurate than the number of pelts themselves. The number of pelts from all nineteen towns is given by sources in the following table:

Source	1698	1699
Iasak	100,392	106,289
Pominki	4,298	2,455
Arrears collected	1,147	1,156
	105,837	109,900
Tithe	16,864	42,283
Confiscated because of concealment	3,072	3,124
Taken on inspection[25]	40	219
Purchased	1,753	562
Presented by Russians	11	247
	127,577	162,335

It was common practice in Siberia to cut from the sable pelts the tails and paws, as well as strips about two inches wide from the belly of the pelt (the cheapest part), called *pupki,* and to trade

[23] Kotoshikhin, *loc. cit.* Miliukov (p. 346 n. 3) appears to have been the first to disprove Kotoshikhin's statement.

[24] See above, p. 100 n. 33.

[25] Not clear whether taken as confiscated or purchased pelts.

them separately from the pelts. Many of these tails, paws, and belly-strips, especially the latter, were taken into the Siberian treasuries. Therefore, a supplementary table concerning them is added:

Source	1698	1699
Iasak	17,908	13,827
Pominki	293	339
Arrears collected	10	575
	18,211	14,741
Tithe	97	739
Confiscated because of concealment	239	252
Taken on inspection[26]	...	161
Purchased	850	271
	19,397	16,164

From these tables it appears that the furs taken from the natives far exceeded in number those taken from the Russians. In 1698, iasak and pominki accounted for 83 per cent of the total and in 1699 for 67 per cent, whereas the tithe accounted for 13 per cent and 29 per cent respectively, and the other sources for only 4 per cent in each year. The question then follows—especially since, towards the end of the seventeenth century, the tithe was paid increasingly in money rather than furs[27]—whether these proportions were true in general throughout the period under study. Since we possess no other body of data comparable to the financial survey used above, one can only cite those random cases where for a given place and year the receipts in both iasak and tithe are given. They are tabulated thus:[28]

Town	Year	Iasak	Tithe	Other sources	Ratio (per cent)
Pelym.....	1598	2,783 pelts	221 pelts	....	92 : 8
Surgut.....	1625	1,827 pelts	858 pelts 1,230 strips	....	65 : 35
Mangazeia.	1636	7,143 r.	17,267 r.	....	30 : 70
	1638	9,376 r.	11,443 r.	....	45 : 55
	1642	6,458 r.	12,594 r.	....	34 : 66
	1646	7,234 r.	5,111 r.	....	59 : 41
Viliui River	1640	908 pelts	2 pelts	79 pelts	100*
Kuznetsk..	1647	4,000 pelts 7,500 strips	7 pelts	....	100*
Eniseisk...	1674	11,685 r.	6,221 r.	68 r.	65 : 3.46 : 0.04

* Receipts from tithe negligible.

[26] Not clear whether taken as confiscated or purchased pelts.
[27] Ogloblin, II, 38–39.
[28] The data for this table are found in *A.I.*, IV, 53; *D.A.I.*, II, 234–235, VI,

Except for Mangazeia, these figures show a preponderance of iasak revenue, varying from 65 per cent at Eniseisk to virtually 100 per cent at Kuznetsk. Moreover, it must be borne in mind that the tithe was collected mainly in a few large towns like Tobolsk, Eniseisk, Tomsk, Iakutsk, Mangazeia (and Mangazeia's tithe income dropped markedly after the middle of the century), and later Nerchinsk, whereas many small ostrogs and the blockhouses served almost exclusively as centers for collecting iasak and returned only iasak revenue.[29] Consequently, one comes to the conclusion that the figures for 1698 and 1699 fairly represent the proportions of revenue contributed by each source: namely, 65 to 80 per cent for iasak, 15 to 30 per cent for the tithe, and a residual 5 per cent or less for the other sources.

Proportion of State's Fur Income to Its Total Income

The third question to be considered is the proportion which the annual gross fur revenue from Siberia bore to the total income of the state. The data are few, but because they are well distributed over the period under study, the question can be answered to a reasonable degree of satisfaction. The total annual income of the state is known for the end of the sixteenth century, for the middle of the seventeenth century, and for the years 1680 and 1701; in other words, the total annual income for the first two and last five decades of our period is represented. The annual income for the second quarter of the seventeenth century may be estimated; hence the first quarter of the century is the only part of our period not represented.

The total annual income of the state in the late sixteenth century was, according to Seredonin, about 400,000 r.[30] This figure is based upon a critical study of the figures left by Fletcher and represents a marked downward revision of the total reached by him.[31] Fletcher's figures apply particularly to the late 'eighties, but there is no reason to believe that the annual income of the state did not remain around 400,000 r. until after the death of Boris Godunov.

359; *R.I.B.*, II, 140–141; Ogloblin, I, 97–98; P. N. Butsinskii, *Mangazeia i mangazeiskii uezd*, pp. 21, 25, 49–50.

[29] For instance, there is no record (up to 1645) of any merchant's having lived in Ketsk (Butsinskii, *K istorii Sibiri*, p. 26).

[30] Seredonin, p. 335.

[31] I.e., 1,413,000 r. net income.

Thus, the estimated 15,000 r. of fur revenue for 1589 was approximately 3.75 per cent of the total revenue of the state for that year, and the 45,000 r. of 1605 approximately 11 per cent.

After the middle of the seventeenth century—more exactly, during the early 'sixties—the total annual income of the state was, on the authority of Kotoshikhin, 1,311,000 r., exclusive of the Siberian fur and money revenue.[32] In view of the fact that the annual income increased but little in the late 'sixties and the 'seventies, after Kotoshikhin's time, one may assume that the income had not increased much in the 'fifties, prior to his time, and that during that decade it was slightly below his figure. Thus the estimated peak of 125,000 r. in annual fur receipts in the 'fifties was nearly 10 per cent of the total annual income of the state, and the lower figure of 100,000 r. was above 7 per cent. For the year 1680 the total income has been calculated by Miliukov as about 1,500,000 r., including the Siberian revenue.[33] The fur income of that year, 102,026 r., was therefore 6.8 per cent of the total. Miliukov calculated also the income for the year 1701 and arrived at the figure 2,955,765 r.[34] The doubling of the budget in the two decades after 1680 resulted from the reforms instituted by Peter the Great. Of this new figure of nearly 3,000,000 the 75,000 r. in furs received in 1701 was 2.5 per cent.

What the state's annual income was in the two or three decades after 1605 is largely conjectural. The disturbances of the Troublous Times and the difficulties of reëstablishing order in the Muscovite administration afterwards make even an approximation difficult. By the second quarter of the century, however, the country had quieted down, and the state's finances were restored to a more stable basis. Hence, it is possible to assume that, if the total income of the state increased by 200,000 r. between the early 'sixties and 1680, then it probably reached and passed the one million ruble mark during the 'thirties and 'forties. If so, the 63,000 r. in furs of 1635, the 81,000 r. of 1640, and the 102,000 r. of 1644 represented 8 per cent, 9 per cent, and 10 per cent respectively of the total revenue.

Like that of most modern states, the income of the Muscovite state, under the pressure of increasing financial need, tended al-

---

[32] Kotoshikhin, pp. 104, 138.

[33] Miliukov, pp. 104–105. His calculations result in minimum and maximum possible totals, 1,410,766 r. and 1,561,667 r.

[34] *Ibid.*, p. 351.

ways to rise. With this rising income the fur revenue from Siberia kept pace as long as new lands were opened there. When new lands ceased to be available, then the fur revenue leveled off and began a gradual decline, so that, whereas up to the 'sixties of the seventeenth century it had constituted between 7 and 10 per cent of the total annual income, thereafter it came to constitute a decreasing percentage of the total, from less than 7 per cent in 1680 to a little more than 2 per cent in 1701. In other words, during the period of pre-Petrine Romanovs, up to 1680 and 1690, when the state's budget was comparatively small, the fur income, even when declining in the later years, was a considerable part of the state's revenue. But with the onset of Peter's reforms at the turn of the century, the budget doubled, new sources of income were found, and furs became of minor consequence in the state's financial economy.

Profitableness of the State's Fur Trade

The fourth and last question to engage our attention refers to the profitableness of the fur trade of the state, that is, how much in excess of the cost of conquering and administering Siberia the fur trade returned to the state. The cost of administering Siberia as a whole is known at present only for the last decade of the seventeenth century; for the rest of our period there is known only the cost of administering a few towns, and that but for a few years. However, although the degree of profitableness can be gauged only at the end of our period, the fact of profitableness can be taken as certain.

The total income from Siberia and the state's expenditures there in the years 1691, 1698, and 1699[35] are tabulated below:

	1691	1698	1699
Income			
Fur receipts	77,365 r.	103,467 r.	74,982 r.
Money receipts	18,000 r.	40,208 r.	56,538 r.
	95,365 r.	143,675 r.	131,520 r.
Expenditures			
Salary to serving men	53,995 r.	54,445 r.	54,086 r.
Various expenses	15,208 r.	6,282 r.	5,853 r.
	69,203 r.	60,727 r.	59,939 r.
Excess of fur receipts over expenses			
Without money revenue	8,162 r.	42,740 r.	15,043 r.
With money revenue	26,162 r.	82,948 r.	71,581 r.

[35] The figures for 1691 are in Ogloblin, IV, 113; those for 1698 and 1699 in *R.I.B.*, VIII, 887–888.

From the data of this table it is seen that the fur revenue alone was sufficient to cover the costs of administration and still return a comfortable profit to the state. But its income from Siberia was not confined to furs; from the promyshlenniks, traders, and local inhabitants it took in a variety of money receipts, receipts which, in view of the excess of fur income over expenditures, may well be looked upon as pure profit. However the money revenue may be viewed, the fur revenue and it together represented a large margin of profit in proportion to the annual cost of administering Siberia.

Due regard for strict accuracy demands, however, the indication of two qualifying circumstances. On the one hand, the value of the fur income tabulated above is its Siberian value, and since the furs were sold in Moscow and the export markets, the return was even higher. On the other hand, the salaries of the Siberian serving men were rarely paid in full, despite the great surplus of revenue.[36] This incongruous circumstance is explained by the fact that none of the furs themselves was used in Siberia to pay administrative expenses, for the state wished to realize on the higher prices for them in Moscow and abroad. Salaries were paid, rather, in money, grain, and commodities.[37] Since the local resources were usually not enough, money, grain, and commodities had to be shipped in, and often the state's resources were insufficient to pay its obligations in full. Whether the unscientific accounting methods of the Russians took complete account of the costs of shipping in money and supplies is uncertain. If they did not, the added expense may be considered offset by the higher Moscow value of furs. And if the above figures do not give a strictly accurate result, they do give a close approximation of the margin of profit yielded the state by its fur trade for the three years involved.

The fact that in the last decade of our period the fur trade of the state was returning a handsome profit above the cost of administering Siberia may be taken as basis for assuming that it had always returned a large profit. By the 'nineties most of Siberia had been conquered, and the longer the Russians occupied a region, the higher the cost of administration tended to go; hence one may conclude that for this decade administrative expenses were on an average higher than for any previous decade of our period. Yet

[36] *D.A.I.*, III, 276, IV, 362; Ogloblin, *loc. cit.; R.I.B.*, VIII, 697–890, *passim;* Butsinskii, *Zaselenie Sibiri*, p. 246. The financial survey for 1698 and 1699 shows what salaries should have been paid and what salaries actually were paid.

[37] *D.A.I.*, IV, 348; *P.S.Z.*, III, 257.

the fur income of the decade, though still fairly high, was not increasing; the fur income had been higher, and at such time as it had been lower, that is, prior to 1640, the administrative costs had also been lower. Thus one may assume that the state's fur income had always yielded a profit. This assumption is corroborated by the experience of such towns as Tobolsk, Verkhoturie, Mangazeia, Surgut, Narym, and other towns in Western Siberia during the reign of Mikhail Fedorovich (1613–1645). In some of these towns the fur revenue was pure profit, since the money income was sufficient for local expenses. In the others, except one, the fur revenue made up the deficit of expenses over money receipts and returned a profit besides. Tara was the only exception.[38]

Because in the past the statements of Karamzin and Kotoshikhin about the volume of furs taken out of Siberia by the state have gained greater circulation than the authentic figures by Ogloblin and Miliukov, the impression has been created of a huge and unprecedented stream of fur wealth flowing into the state treasury. This exaggerated impression our findings greatly reduce; the one-fourth of the total income of the state—the proportion represented by the fur revenue, according to Kotoshikhin—is found to have been actually one-tenth at most. Nevertheless, one-tenth of the state's income is not an inconsiderable part, and the fur trade must stand as an important source of revenue for Russia during the late sixteenth and the seventeenth centuries. The state certainly considered this revenue important, for it put forth much effort to protect its trade. Moreover, the fur income was a particularly useful form of wealth, as we shall see. But equally significant is the fact that much of this income was clear profit to the state. The conquest and occupation was thus a highly profitable business venture for Moscow, and the statement of a German writer that "the sable provoked the opening and conquest of Siberia and also paid a great part of the costs with its pelt" must be amended to "it paid *all* of the costs with its pelt."[39]

[38] Butsinskii, *Zaselenie Sibiri*, pp. 61, 79, 101, 142, 159, 170, 182–183; *idem, Mangazeia*, p. 29; *idem, K istorii Sibiri*, p. 7.

[39] F. Berg, *Baltische Wochenschrift* (Dorpat), 1905, No. 28, p. 262, cited by J. Klein in *Der sibirische Pelzhandel*, p. 5.

CHAPTER VIII

THE DISPOSAL OF FURS BY THE STATE

NOT UNTIL LATE in the seventeenth century did the state dispose of any of its furs in Siberia. Until then, the great quantities of them which it acquired there were all sent to Moscow, which as the seat of government of the tsar was the center of his fur business. Here the furs from Siberia, as well as those few obtained in European Russia, were disposed of in two ways. First, they were sold or exchanged for other goods. The larger number of the furs disposed of in this way was sent to the Russian export markets, since the big demand for furs came from abroad; the lesser number was sold or exchanged in Moscow itself. The second way of disposal of furs was their use for various purposes other than commercial; they served often in the place of money. In this chapter we shall discuss the state's disposal of its furs within Russia, the agencies of disposal, the sale and exchange of furs by the state in Moscow, and the noncommercial uses to which it put them. The export trade of the state, or rather, the sale of its furs in the export markets, will be considered in subsequent chapters.

THE STATE TREASURIES

The tsar sold his furs chiefly through three agencies, the Sable Treasury, the Treasury Court, and the treasury merchants. The first two, situated in Moscow, were more than sales agencies; they served as fur storehouses for the state, and from them furs were disbursed for other than sales purposes. The merchants, on the other hand, were simply sales agents for the government. In the Sable Treasury and Treasury Court a considerable duplication of functions existed, and the two might just as well have been merged into one governmental agency. However, an absence of definite spheres of jurisdiction and an overlapping of functions characterized the central administrative institutions of seventeenth-century Russia, and in this respect the two treasuries were no different from many other governmental departments.

The Sable Treasury (*Sobolinaia Kazna*) was a division of the Siberian Department. Into it came all the furs sent from Siberia; here the furs were sorted a second time, evaluated at Moscow prices, and then stored to await sale or other disposal.[1] Like the Siberian Department, the Sable Treasury arose during the first half of the seventeenth century. During the period when the Kazan Palace handled the administration of Siberia, the receipt and disbursement of furs warranted no special administration beyond that of a few "elected" heads and sworn men, who were given no authority and acted only as fur experts or appraisers (*tsenovshchiki*).[2] But soon a small division was created, which took over these functions. It was known under the general name of "the sovereign's treasury." Gradually this treasury was transformed into the Sable Treasury, a special division allocated to the Siberian Department and possessing its own personnel of heads, sworn men, and "masters," the heads enjoying a good deal of responsibility and authority. Beyond that, further specialization took place within the Sable Treasury itself, and separate sections came into existence, the "appraisers' chamber" (*rostsennaia palata*), "merchants' chamber" (*kupetskaia palata*), "money receipts" (*denezhnyi priem*), the "furriers' chamber" (*skorniashnaia palata*), and others, in charge of which were heads, under whom worked sworn men and craftsmen. The heads and sworn men were merchants of the upper ranks, elected (*vybornyia*) from Moscow and north-Russian towns by their fellow merchants for service in the Sable Treasury. They served ordinarily for one year. This administration of the Sable Treasury by merchants rather than by the customary serving men gave to it a character unique among Muscovite administrative institutions.[3] It attained this mature form of organization only by the middle of the seventeenth century. However, for the sake of convenience, we shall use the term "Sable Treasury" to include its predecessor departments and divisions.

The Treasury Court (*Kazennyi Dvor* or *Kazennyi Prikaz*) was a department by itself. It was the tsar's own treasury, the treasury for his household, a fact which distinguished it from the other treasuries and departments which took in revenue of one sort or another. It was literally the "court of chests" which the Russian name signifies.[4] As the "business office" of the household of the tsar

[1] Grigorii Kotoshikhin, *O Rossii v tsarstvovanie Aleksiia Mikhailovicha*, p. 105; Ogloblin, IV, 83–85.

[2] Ogloblin, IV, 84.

[3] *Ibid.*, III, 154, IV, 76–78; Kotoshikhin, p. 104.

[4] I. E. Zabelin, *Dopolneniia k dvortsovym razriadam . . . sobrannyia iz knig i stolbtsov prezhdebyvshikh dvortsovykh prikazov arkhiv oruzheinoi palaty*, p. iii.

it performed the closely connected services of providing for the wardrobe of the tsar, his family, and his retinue, of supplying a variety of articles and utensils for the household, and of conducting the business enterprises of the tsar in various textiles and cloths—satins, velvets, taffetas, silks, and others. Thus furs, both as an article of domestic use and an object of the tsar's trade, came under the purview of the Treasury Court. Almost all its furs it received from the Sable Treasury,[5] although not infrequently it bought furs in small quantities in the open market, either because it needed them for some special purpose or because of the high quality of the particular furs bought.[6] It also received a few of its furs as gifts to the tsar from individuals, as goods confiscated for attempted smuggling, and even as iasak from the native peoples in Perm.[7] It maintained its own appraisers and its own corps of furriers, who made the pelts into garments for the royal household and for donation to Russian and foreign notables. It also hired workers from among the local furriers in Moscow.[8]

The Treasury Merchants

The Sable Treasury and the Treasury Court sold and disbursed furs only in Moscow. For the sale and exchange of its furs in markets other than Moscow, in the Russian export markets and abroad, the state depended upon the third agency, the treasury merchants. These men were private merchants who acted as commercial agents for the tsar. Because the trade and customs collection of the state called for men of a training and experience not possessed by the ordinary serving men or state servitors, the state turned to the wealthy merchants for the performance of these services, giving them certain privileges in return.[9] They formed what was in fact, if not in name, a special serving class.

These wealthy merchants, upon whose services the tsars drew, belonged to three groups, which comprised the uppermost ranks

[5] *R.I.B.*, IX, 20, 21, 25, 26, 27, 32–33, 34–35, 35–36, 36–38, 39–40; A. G. Viktorov, *Opisanie zapisnykh knig i bumag starinnykh dvortsovykh prikazov, 1584–1725*, I, 87, 90, 91, 93, 95; Ogloblin, IV, 88–89, 163.

[6] *R.I.B.*, IX, 4, 11, 13, 24; Viktorov, I, 76, 94; G. D. Khilkov, *Sbornik kniazia Khilkova*, p. 182; Kotoshikhin, p. 5.

[7] *R.I.B.*, IX, 23, 25, 34; Viktorov, I, 86, 90; Zabelin, pp. 5, 8, 22, 26, 47, 48, 49, 339, 418, 564, 568–569, 613.

[8] Kotoshikhin, p. 80; *R.I.B.*, IX, 1–14, 44–148, *passim*, in which are recorded wage payments by the treasury to its own furriers and to others hired by it.

[9] M. A. D'iakonov, *Ocherki obshchestvennago i gosudarstvennago stroia drevnei Rusi*, p. 290.

of the commercial class of Russia: the *gosts*, the *gostínaia sótnia*, and the *sukónnaia sótnia.* The gosts, the highest-ranking merchants, constituted a small select group limited to thirty members.[10] As individual merchants they did a business varying from twenty thousand to a hundred thousand rubles a year, a large sum for those times. Attainment to this select group came only through appointment by the tsar, who granted the chosen merchant a charter conferring upon him certain privileges, such as the right to trade abroad, the right to buy a votchina of his own, exemption from certain taxes and fees, and others.[11] The gosts were drawn from all parts of Russia and were chosen from the other two groups, which constituted the two highest merchant guilds in Russia.[12] After appointment, the gosts usually moved to Moscow, if they did not already reside there, since the tsar's service demanded their presence in the capital for long periods of time. The merchants of the gostinaia sotnia comprised a larger group of wealthy merchants, which varied in numbers from more than one hundred to three hundred and fifty. New members were selected by the old members from the lower ranks of merchants. The merchants of the sukonnaia sotnia represented a similar group; its real differences, if any, from the gostinaia sotnia are not clear. The members of both guilds enjoyed nearly all the privileges enjoyed by the gosts, except that they were not allowed of their own initiative to trade abroad or to buy votchinas of their own, and were socially inferior in rank.[13]

The services which the merchants of all three groups were called upon to perform were several. Members of all three groups acted as heads and sworn men in the Sable Treasury. The gosts, and sometimes the merchants of the gostinaia sotnia, supervised the sovereign's salt and fishing enterprises; they were entrusted with the buying of goods and supplies for him and carried on his trading operations.[14] In the trading operations of the tsar merchants

[10] Kotoshikhin, p. 166.

[11] N. I. Kostomarov, *Ocherki torgovli moskovskago gosudarstva*, pp. 318–321; *Sobranie gosudarstvennykh gramot i dogovorov*, IV, 196; S. V. Bakhrushin, "Torgi gostia Nikitina v Sibiri i Kitae," *Sbornik statei: Pamiati Aleksandra Nikolaevicha Savina, 1873–1923*, Trudy instituta istorii rossiiskoi assotsiatsii nauchno-issledovatel'skikh institutov obshchestvennykh nauk, I (1926), 387.

[12] Although the term "guild" has been applied to these two lower groups of merchants, not enough is yet known of their membership, organization, and functioning to be certain that they were guilds in the medieval European use of the word.

[13] Kostomarov, *loc. cit.; A.A.E.*, IV, 354–355.

[14] Kotoshikhin, pp. 157–159; Kostomarov, p. 320; D'iakonov, pp. 290–291.

of the two lower guilds usually served in the capacity of assistants to the gosts. These trading operations included, of course, the sale and exchange of furs. The gosts were commissioned by the Sable Treasury and Treasury Court to dispose of large amounts of furs in Russian and foreign markets. Ordinarily they took the furs on consignment, paying over to the treasuries upon returning to Moscow goods or money equivalent to the value of the furs sold, and also any unsold furs.[15] For each trip a gost received a grant or "salary" (*zhalovanie*) from the tsar.[16] In addition, because of his official connections, he was able to make a good profit by trading on his own account.[17] The great wealth of the gosts, which could be seized by the state, was presumably the state's assurance of faithful performance of their commissions, though they were also required to swear an oath by kissing the cross.[18] It is probably true, although the fact cannot be ascertained with certainty, that the bulk of the furs of the state were disposed of by the gosts, since they sold and exchanged them in wholesale lots and carried on the export trade.

Other Disbursement Agencies

The Sable Treasury, the Treasury Court, and treasury merchants constituted the usual and regular channels for the sale and exchange of furs by the state. They were not, however, the only channels. Less regular and occasional outlets were provided by other government departments. The Artillery Department sometimes took furs from the Sable Treasury to buy iron and artillery supplies. Thus, in 1624 it sent a shipment of furs through Novgorod to be sold abroad probably in German towns, whence much of its equipment came.[19]

The Department of Ambassadors was another outlet. The tsar included gosts in the retinue of the envoys sent on diplomatic missions to other countries, just as the foreign envoys who came to Russia were often accompanied by merchants. As members of the ambassadorial retinue the merchants enjoyed exemption from customs payments. The gosts carried with them on such trips chiefly furs. The retinue which went with the boiar Streshnev to Poland in 1646 took with it a large consignment of furs for sale and ex-

[15] Ogloblin, IV, 64, 69, 81, 82, 155, 164, 165.
[16] *Ibid.*, p. 164; P. N. Butsinskii, *Mangazeia i mangazeiskii uezd*, p. 50 n.
[17] A. S. Lappo-Danilevskii, *Russkiia promyshlennyia i torgovyia kompanii v pervoi polovine XVIII stoletiia*, pp. 11–12.
[18] D'iakonov, p. 290.
[19] Ogloblin, IV, 56.

change.[20] The Russian envoys of the mission to France in 1688 took many furs with them and appeared to be more anxious to sell furs than to negotiate concerning Polish and Turkish affairs.[21]

A third subsidiary outlet was the Department of Secret Affairs. Created under Mikhail Fedorovich (1613–1645) to manage the field sports of the tsar, especially falconry, it became also a bureau of secret police and an office for administering matters pertaining to the household of the tsar. As the personal and favored office of Tsar Aleksei Mikhailovich (1645–1676) this department managed the silk trade with Persia, another state monopoly. It was in this connection that the department handled furs. Under its direction gosts took large numbers of them, chiefly sables, from the Sable Treasury and Treasury Court and exchanged them for raw and boiled silk.[22] Unlike the first two departments, for which the sale of furs was incidental or secondary to their regular functions, the Department of Secret Affairs carried on the exchange of sables for silk as a regularly assigned function. However, its operation of this enterprise continued only for a few decades; with the death of Aleksei in 1676 the department was abandoned.

The Sale of Furs in Moscow

The sale of furs in Moscow—and it was in Moscow that the state made most of its domestic sales of furs—was carried on by the Sable Treasury and the Treasury Court. These two agencies sold furs both wholesale and retail. To such persons as boiars, serving men, churchmen, even peasants, it retailed them for personal consumption, usually in small lots.[23] Money rather than goods was used to pay for the furs, though frequently the purchasers were extended credit for as long as a year or two; but failure to pay brought drastic action by the state.[24] To merchants, both Russian and foreign, and to the traders and furriers in Furriers' Row in Moscow the Sable Treasury and Treasury Court sold and exchanged furs in wholesale lots, varying from a dozen rubles or so to a thousand and ten thousand rubles in value.[25]

[20] *Ibid.*, p. 160.

[21] *Sbornik imperatorskago russkago istoricheskago obshchestva*, XXXIV, iii, 17.

[22] *R.I.B.*, XXIII, ii, 1413–1582, *passim;* cf. A. I. Zaozerskii, *Tsar' Aleksei Mikhailovich v svoem khoziaistve*, p. 254 n. 4, and Viktorov, I, 96.

[23] Ogloblin, IV, 64, 66, 74, 86, 87, 166; Viktorov, I, 54 ff.; *P.S.Z.*, II, 233.

[24] Ogloblin, III, 152, 155, IV, 64–65, 71, 72, 155, 159; Viktorov, I, 56.

[25] Ogloblin, III, 152, IV, 65, 71, 90; *R.I.B.*, IX, 15, 17, 19; cf. Viktorov, I, 52–59.

Such transactions, since the amount of money in Russia was insufficient and a direct exchange of goods was a normal procedure in trade, usually involved the exchange of furs for other goods rather than for money, and in these transactions the state appeared both as seller and buyer, according to the occasion. For example, on June 16, 1627, the Sable Treasury sent to the Treasury Court 9 forties of sables worth 475 r. with which to buy Turkish satin from Moscow merchants, and in the same year, at the request of the Department of Gold Affairs, the Sable Treasury paid out for gold on four separate occasions to the merchant Andrei Semenov sables worth 663 r., 672 r., 907½ r., and 907 r. respectively.[26] In fact, furs were the customary means by which the tsar acquired gold, of which the Muscovite state never had enough.

The foreign merchants, when they came to Moscow with goods, had first to present themselves at the Treasury Court, where the agents of the tsar selected the best goods or whatever goods were required by the treasury and gave in return furs and other goods, but chiefly furs.[27] Foreign envoys who brought goods with them for trade followed the same procedure.[28] Sometimes the sale of furs fell off, and too many of them accumulated in the treasuries, whereupon the treasury officials distributed them among the gosts, compelling them to take the furs, for which they were given about a year to pay.[29] The evidence is not specific, but in so far as can be determined, all such sales and exchanges of furs for goods appear to have been transacted on the premises of the Sable Treasury and Treasury Court or through other departments. Despite the fact that another of the tsar's departments owned and rented the shops in the rows of the market places, the two treasuries do not seem to have utilized them in selling furs.

Furs as Salary Grants

The great stores of furs which came into the Sable Treasury represented a source of wealth which the tsar could utilize for other purposes than trade. Because it lacked gold and silver in quantities sufficient for a complete money economy—Russia produced prac-

[26] Butsinskii, *op. cit.*, p. 50 n.

[27] *R.I.B.*, IX, 33; Zabelin, p. 328; Richard Hakluyt, *The Principal Navigations*, II, 87; P. P. Mel'gunov, *Ocherki po istorii russkoi torgovli IX–XVIII v.v.*, p. 179; Viktorov, I, 84–89.

[28] Viktorov, *loc. cit.*

[29] Kotoshikhin, p. 105; Giles Fletcher, *Russia at the Close of the Sixteenth Century*, p. 57.

tically no gold or silver itself—Russia still possessed in the seventeenth century a half-barter, half-money economy in which goods were given in exchange for services and were otherwise utilized where today money would be employed. In this capacity furs served extensively, perhaps more than any other good. The Sable Treasury and Treasury Court functioned as bursar's offices and paid out furs to specified individuals upon authorization (*pamiat'*) of the tsar, his officials, or the departments, or they delivered furs over to the other departments, which in turn paid them out.[30] The occasions for such payments were various, but most of them are comprehended within three general uses: they were awarded as grants by the tsar in payment of services; they were presented as gifts or donations to notables of one sort or another; and they were used for purposes of diplomacy.

The tsar's grants for service were usually in the nature of a reward for a particular service rather than of a stipulated salary over a given period of time. The regular salary paid to the serving men of the state was taken care of by other means, whereas the payment of furs was reserved ordinarily for noteworthy service or for members of the upper ranks of Russian society. These grants varied considerably in their content and were by no means restricted to furs. Grants of furs alone were not uncommon, but oftener furs were but one of several commodities and articles making up the award; textiles of various kinds, domestic utensils of gold, silver, copper, and tin frequently accompanied them.

The occasions for awarding these grants were numerous, yet distinctive military service appears as the most frequent reason. The disbursement books of the Treasury Court show these typical payments:

December 25, 1613. By order of the sovereign . . . the sovereign's grant, 40 martens worth 40 r. a forty, was given to [each of] Smolensk residents, Fedor Elizar'ev, son of Lyzlov, and Pavl Odintsov, son of Samarin, for service and prisoners.

January 2, 1614. By order of the sovereign . . . the sovereign's grant, 10 *arshins* [7.7 yds.] of green damask worth 26 *altyns* 4 *dengas* per arshin . . . and 40 sables worth 15 r. . . . and a ladle worth 2 r. 29 a. 4 d., was given to courtier (*striapchii*) Dmitrii Vainov, son of Volikov, for [military] service at Tikhvinskii. . . .

March 10, 1614. By order of the sovereign . . . the sovereign's grant, 10 arshins of . . . damask worth 26 a. 4 d. per arshin . . . , 40 sables worth 15 r.,

[30] Ogloblin, IV, 53–54, 89, 92; Zabelin, p. 158.

and a silver ladle weighing 30 *zolotniks* [4.5 ounces] worth 2 r. 4 a...., was given to Andrei Vasil'ev, son of Usov, for service and for besieging and taking Gdovsk.[31]

An exception to the reserving of furs for particularly meritorious service was the regular payment of furs and other goods to the cossacks of the Russian Ukraine, which came under Muscovite sovereignty after 1654. By agreement with Moscow the cossacks maintained a force of 60,000 men to defend the southern frontier. In recognition of their services the tsar sent each year large amounts of sables, woolen cloth, damasks, and taffeta to the cossack leaders, and upon discharge from this force each man received a grant from the tsar which included sables. A colonel was awarded woolen cloth and satin, or damask, for clothes, 40 sables worth 100 r., a pair of sables worth 20 r. for a cap, and 50 r. in money; to a *sotnik,* ataman, or captain (*iasaul*) woolens and taffeta, 40 sables worth 50 r., a pair of sables worth 10 r. for a cap, and 20 r. in money were given; and to a cossack of the ranks woolen cloth, a pair of sables worth 5 r. and 5 r. in money were given.[32] The military commanders of the tsar's regular troops were also sometimes awarded grants of furs.[33]

But the tsar also rewarded nonmilitary services. One which was frequently singled out for the tsar's salary was the customs service of the gosts and guild merchants, especially for increasing the customs revenue over the previous year.[34] Thus, on February 27, 1617, the gosts Mikhail Smyvalov and Ivan Sverchkov each received a silver ladle worth 6 r. 25 a. as well as 10 arshins of damask worth 10 r. and 40 sables worth 24 r.; Dmitrii Larionov, a silver ladle (no value given), 10 arshins of damask worth 10 r., and 40 martens worth 10 r. These men during the year 1616 had increased the customs revenue at Arkhangelsk by 3,197 r.[35] Other services were similarly rewarded. On February 26, 1664, a pair of sables worth 2 r. a pair was issued from the Sable Treasury to Stepan Petrov and Andrei Pavlov "for drawing up a map of Devichie field."[36]

[31] *R.I.B.*, IX, 212, 217, 253; see also, *ibid.*, pp. 213, 244, 254, 328, and Zabelin, p. 93.
The denga and altyn are two units of currency which ceased to circulate in Russia after the seventeenth century. One ruble equaled two hundred dengas; one altyn equaled six dengas. The kopek, which replaced the denga and altyn, equaled two dengas.

[32] Kotoshikhin, pp. 82, 126; Ogloblin, IV, 14, 54, 89–90.

[33] Ogloblin, IV, 89.

[34] *Ibid.*, III, 154, IV, 164, 168; Kotoshikhin, p. 159.

[35] Zabelin, pp. 90–91.

[36] Ogloblin, IV, 66.

Sables worth 225 r. were awarded in February, 1628, to certain merchants of Moscow, Kazan, Iazh, and Iaroslavl "who were sent with the sovereign's treasury in 1621 to Persia for trade."[37]

The service of the foreigners from the West was usually remunerated by grants which included furs. Upon arrival and departure from Russia the foreigners received goods from the tsar's treasuries to defray their traveling expenses. For example, in March, 1614, a forty of sables worth 23 r., 4 forties worth 88 r., a forty of martens worth 12 r., 15 pairs of sables worth 45 r., 6 pairs worth 12 r., and seven pairs worth 10½ r. were sent to Kholmogory to the Englishman Arthur Aston and his retinue.[38] In 1635, Doctor Arthur Dee, after fifteen years of service to the tsar, was given among other things upon departure 300 rubles' worth of sables.[39] A Dutch organ-master, returning to Holland in 1639, received 100 r. in money and forty sables valued at 40 r.[40] It was not unusual also for the tsar to award grants in furs and other goods to these foreigners during the course of their service in Russia.[41] These grants in October, 1615, paid to the Englishman Aston and certain of the men with him are illustrative:

To Prince Arthur Aston: a gold goblet, a ladle, 40 sables worth 30 r., a silver ladle worth 2 *grivenkas* [*ca.* 20 kopeks], a cup, two pieces of velvet . . . , two pieces of damask . . . , 40 martens worth 12 r., two pieces of fine woolen cloth . . . , a black fox worth 10 r., 100 rubles in money, a gelding horse.

To cavalry captain Jacob Shaw: 40 sables worth 20 r., a ladle worth 2 grivenkas, figured velvet, fine damask, fine woolen cloth, 35 rubles in money, a horse.

To Jacob's kinsman, John Carr: 40 sables worth 17 r., a ladle worth 1½ grivenkas, fine damask and taffeta, fine woolen cloth, 25 rubles in money.

To ensign John Griffin: 40 sables worth 16 r., a ladle worth 1½ grivenkas, damask and fine woolen cloth, 20 rubles in money.

To William Griffin: 40 sables worth 16 r., a ladle worth 1 grivenka, damask and fine woolen cloth, 15 rubles in money.

To Thomas Hearn: 40 sables worth 16 r., a ladle worth 1 grivenka, damask and fine woolen cloth, 15 rubles in money.

To George Dromont, David Farsay: the same as to Thomas Hearn.

To Henry Hendrickson: 40 martens worth 12 r., damask and fine woolen cloth, a cup worth 2 r., 12 rubles in money.

To Thomas Matthews: 40 martens worth 12 r., fine damask, fine woolen cloth, a cup worth 2 r., 12 rubles in money.[42]

[37] *Ibid.*, p. 164.
[38] Zabelin, pp. 19–20.
[39] *R.I.B.*, VIII, 270.
[40] *R.I.B.*, VIII, 285.
[41] *R.I.B.*, VIII, 125, 182–184, 193, 265, 302, 322.
[42] *R.I.B.*, VIII, 115–116.

The payments to foreigners were ordinarily made through the Department of Apothecaries, which employed many foreigners as doctors and chemists, the Department of Foreigners, and the Department of Ambassadors,[43] though some received their grants at an audience with the tsar.[44]

Furs as Gifts

Grants, which were of the same content as those awarded for service, were made as gifts or donations to various individuals, chiefly churchmen of the Orthodox faith and members of the tsar's family. Both the Sable Treasury and Treasury Court were often called upon by the tsar to send furs and other goods to Russian churchmen.[45] For example, these gifts are recorded in the disbursement books of the Treasury Court for 1613–1614:

> November 29. The sovereign . . . bestowed a gift upon the Krutitskii metropolitan, John, and to him were given as the sovereign's grant 6¾ arshins of taffeta . . . , silk . . . worth 23 a. 2 d. an arshin . . . , and blankets (*tski*) containing 70 sables worth 24 r. 26 a. 4 d. . . . in addition there were given to him eleven martens, ten worth 8 a. 2 d. apiece and one worth 10 a. . . . , a pair of sables worth 1 r. . . . , and beaver trimmings worth 6 a. 4 d. . . .
>
> July 3. By order of the sovereign . . . the sovereign's grant of 40 sables worth 40 r. . . . and 15 arshins of damask . . . worth 23 a. an arshin . . . were given to Blagoveshchensk priest Kiril.[46]

But to an even greater extent the tsar was called upon to make grants, which included sables and other furs, to Orthodox churchmen outside of Russia. When Constantinople fell to the Turks and the Byzantine empire made its exit from history, the role of supporter and protector of the Orthodox East passed from the Byzantine emperor to the Russian tsar. Throughout the sixteenth and seventeenth centuries the tsars dared not antagonize the Turkish sultans to the point of war, so their support of the Orthodox East remained largely moral and financial. During the seventeenth century in particular a steady stream of churchmen visited Russia to petition for "charity" (*milostynia*) from the tsar. All ranks, both secular and regular, from patriarchs and metropolitans on down, came from every part of the Orthodox East—Syria, Palestine, Egypt, Greece, Serbia, Bulgaria, and the Danubian principali-

[43] Ogloblin, IV, 89, 90, 94, 165, 174; *R.I.B.*, IX, 260, 332; Viktorov, I, 128; *A.I.*, III, 395–396.

[44] *R.I.B.*, VIII, 301–302, 320–322; Viktorov, *loc. cit.*

[45] Ogloblin, IV, 90, 165; Zabelin, pp. 506, 581.

[46] *R.I.B.*, IX, 194–195, 331.

ties—seeking financial support by which to maintain their cathedrals or monasteries, pay off debts, or replace possessions stolen by brigands. And these clerics rarely departed from Moscow or Putivl[47] empty-handed. Furthermore, the tsars quite frequently dispatched charity with their envoys to Constantinople or with visitors returning home from Russia to be delivered to the patriarchs and other high-ranking church dignitaries, for the support and coöperation of these hierarchs were of much assistance to the tsar in his dealings with the Turks.[48]

In giving this financial assistance the tsars drew generously upon the Sable Treasury. It was customary to grant charity to suppliants both upon arrival in and departure from Moscow; and it was also customary to present a personal gift to each suppliant in addition to the subsidy or charity proper. The four non-Russian patriarchs, whenever they or their representatives visited Moscow, collected tremendous sums. The personal gift ordinarily was 2,000 r. in sables and the subsidy varied from 2,000 or 3,000 r. to as much as 9,000 r. in sables. The amounts presented to the lesser churchmen were much lower. The personal gifts in sables to metropolitans, archbishops, and bishops varied between 30 and 40 rubles, and to archimandrites between 20 and 25 rubles, with occasional outstanding exceptions, like the sables worth 1,100 r. granted to the bishop of Gaza in 1669. Archdeacons and cellarers received martens rather than sables, in amounts of 20 and 15 rubles respectively. The charity awards ran much higher, from 50 to 300 or 400 rubles, sometimes entirely in sables, more often in various articles, among which sables were included.[49] On those occasions when the tsar sent gifts and charity with his envoys or distinguished visitors to the higher Orthodox dignitaries, the amounts were usually much less than those presented in Moscow.[50] The Russian envoys to Constantinople in 1624 carried with them 9 forties of sables worth 330 r. for the patriarch of Constantinople, 2 forties worth 120 r. for the patriarch of Jerusalem, and 26 forties worth 600 r. for various monasteries.[51] Four years later, sables in about the same

[47] Putivl, on the southwestern frontier of the Muscovite state, was the usual point of entrance from the Orthodox East. Payments to suppliants were sometimes made there.

[48] N. E. Kapterev, *Kharakter otnoshenii Rossii k pravoslavnomu vostoku v XVI i XVII stoletiiakh*, pp. 103–113, 119, 276–277.

[49] *Ibid.*, pp. 115–116, 130–133; Paul of Aleppo, *The Travels of Macarius, Patriarch of Antioch*, II, 276, 277, 303; Zabelin, p. 197; Ogloblin, IV, 91.

[50] Zabelin, pp. 196, 491, 494; Ogloblin, IV, 93, 164.

[51] Zabelin, pp. 379–380.

amounts for the same recipients were sent with the Russian ambassadors to the Porte.[52] In June, 1626, the archimandrite of Jerusalem departed from Moscow with sables worth 440 r. for the patriarch of Jerusalem and sables worth 160 r. for the patriarch of Alexandria.[53] In October of the next year the tsar and his father, the patriarch Filaret, sent 28 rubles' worth of sables to the bishop of Salonica, 20 rubles' worth to the archimandrite of Sinai, and 180 rubles' worth to the inmates of the monastery at Mt. Athos. The following month the patriarchs of Constantinople and Alexandria each received sables valued at 400 pieces of gold.[54]

Payments involving sables to churchmen did not stop here. A number of prelates, ousted from their ecclesiastical offices by the Turks, came to Moscow to settle, there to live off the charity of the tsar. The customary gift of sables was made to them upon arrival, and since most of them came to find the Russian environment uncongenial, there was usually occasion for presenting them with a gift of sables upon departure. The value of the sables or other furs awarded on these occasions varied, again according to the recipient's rank, from 15 or 20 rubles to 400 r. or more.[55] Since the Muscovite state did not maintain in the seventeenth century permanent diplomatic representatives in the Ottoman empire, the tsars long depended upon high church officials residing in the empire to render advice in diplomatic matters and to participate in negotiations with the Porte. Such services always merited gifts of sables, like, for instance, the two hundred rubles' worth of sables given to the metropolitan of Adrianople in 1667.[56] Not uncommonly suppliants who came to Moscow brought with them Russian prisoners whom they had ransomed from the Turks. They were reimbursed by the tsar's treasury, half in sables and half in money : one hundred to one hundred and twenty rubles for a nobleman, fifty to sixty rubles for a man in the ranks.[57]

How much the tsars paid out in furs and goods of all kinds to the various Orthodox churchmen in the course of the sixteenth and seventeenth centuries cannot be calculated, but from the evidence in the archives it must have been enormous. One fact seems certain, however, and that is that the Sable Treasury bore a large part

[52] *Ibid.*, pp. 511, 513.
[53] *Ibid.*, p. 448.
[54] Butsinskii, *op. cit.*, p. 50 n.
[55] Kapterev, pp. 146, 152–153, 162–163.
[56] *Ibid.*, pp. 310–311, 318, 322.
[57] *Ibid.*, p. 139.

of the financial burden which the tsar's position as supporter and protector of the Orthodox East imposed upon him.[58]

Furs were presented as gifts by the tsar to others besides churchmen, particularly on special occasions or for special purposes. Whenever it was necessary for the tsar's physician to bleed or purge him, he presented the physician with a forty of sables.[59] Members of the tsar's family were frequent recipients of sables from him. For instance, on September 7, 1627, the Sable Treasury sent to the Treasury Court at the order of the tsar Mikhail Fedorovich 40 sables valued at 65 r. so that he might give them to his father on the Day of the Birth of the Virgin Mary.[60] Holy days in general were occasion for this tsar to present furs to his father.[61] Upon his mother, the abbess Marfa Ivanovna, he also bestowed gifts. On January 2, 1614, the official in charge of the Treasury Court took 40 sables of 60 r. Siberian value to the sovereign's household for presentation to the abbess for a dwelling.[62] Holy days were occasion for sable gifts to her, too, as was her birthday.[63] The birth of the tsarevich Dimitrii Alekseivich to the tsar Aleksei Mikhailovich evoked an order to send 3 forties of sables, worth 165 r., 115 r., and 100 r., into the royal household.[64] Gifts to persons outside the tsar's own family were by no means uncommon. The weddings of his court servitors, the christening of the children of boiars and princes, the baptism of foreigners into the Orthodox faith all prompted gifts of furs by the tsar.[65]

Furs in Diplomacy

Beyond selling and trading, the tsar drew most heavily upon his great store of furs in the course of his diplomatic relations with other states. Furs helped to make the wheels of diplomacy turn more smoothly. They were given as gifts to foreign rulers and their envoys in the exchange of ambassadorial courtesies. At certain critical moments in the foreign relations, when it could ill afford armed conflict, Moscow employed furs as subsidies or bribes and thereby obviated the need of fighting. They were utilized, further,

[58] *Ibid.*, pp. 118, 120, 144–146.

[59] Adam Olearius, *The Voyages and Travels of the Ambassadors sent by Frederick, Duke of Holstein*, p. 89.

[60] Butsinskii, *op. cit.*, p. 50; Ogloblin, IV, 163.

[61] Ogloblin, IV, 165; Zabelin, pp. 316, 325, 415.

[62] *R.I.B.*, IX, 216.

[63] Zabelin, p. 432.

[64] Ogloblin, IV, 67.

[65] Zabelin, pp. 109, 146; *R.I.B.*, VIII, 205–207, 210, 214, 217, 223–225, 232; *P.S.Z.*, I, 513–514.

to encourage the friendliness of those states whose hostility would endanger Moscow.

During the seventeenth century the relations of the West with Russia increased; visits to Moscow of envoys from Western states occurred more frequently. Sometimes when these envoys arrived in Moscow and customarily when they departed, the tsar presented them with gifts of furs.[66] Thus the ambassador from the Holy Roman Emperor in 1597 received a gift of sables when leaving Moscow, as did the English ambassador, John Merrick, who was presented in 1615 with 2 forties of sables and a black fox skin, besides 40 more sables to be taken to the courtiers of the king.[67] On July 15, 1618, at an audience with the tsar three Swedish envoys received 320 sables valued at 345 r. and 3 black foxes valued at 36 r., while six of the courtiers in their entourage received 240 sables worth 134 r.; three secretaries each received 40 martens worth 12 r. and the clergyman with the suite a pair of sables worth 5 r.[68] In the same fashion the Holstein ambassador in 1634 was given, upon leaving Moscow, 11 forties of the best sables, while the rest of his suite were presented with a forty of martens apiece, and the menials with one or two pairs of martens.[69] Gifts of furs were sent outside Russia to foreign rulers. In 1614 the tsar dispatched 5 forties of sables worth 140 r. to the Persian shah, who shared with him a mutual but more overt hostility to the power of the Turkish empire.[70] In response to gifts from the Danish king in 1622 the tsar sent 1,459 rubles' worth of sables to him.[71] The Russian ambassadors who went to foreign courts customarily carried with them furs to be bestowed upon the sovereigns they visited.[72] The Russian embassy that visited King Sigismund of Poland in 1610 presented him with 532 sables and 7 black foxes.[73]

More important, however, was the role which furs played in assisting the Muscovite state to hold in check the Turkish power to the south. Upon one occasion the great wealth of furs of the tsars enabled Russia to strike indirectly at the Ottoman empire,

[66] Olearius, pp. 41, 73; Zabelin, pp. 163–164, 189.
[67] N. M. Karamzin, *Istoriia gosudarstva rossiiskago,* Vol. X, p. 188, and *Primechanie,* No. 319; Viktorov, I, 128; also Zabelin, 41.
[68] Zabelin, pp. 132–133.
[69] Olearius, p. 19.
[70] *R.I.B.*, IX, 192; also Zabelin, p. 10.
[71] *Ibid.*, pp. 305–308.
[72] Olearius, p. 73; Khilkov, pp. 401, 466, 506, 523, 532, 537; Hakluyt, I, 365.
[73] V. N. Berkh, *Tsarstvovanie tsaria Mikhaila Fedorovicha i vzgliad na mezhdutsarstve,* p. 44, and *Primechanie,* No. 29.

when to have engaged openly with that power would have been dangerous. The tsar, Fedor Ivanovich, and his adviser, Boris Godunov, sympathetic to the request of the Holy Roman Emperor, Rudolf II, for assistance against the infidel Turks, were not willing to jeopardize Russian commerce with the Turks by siding openly with the emperor. They were able, instead, to take a middle course by sending in 1595 the large subsidy referred to in chapter vii (p. 109). Valued at 45,000 r. in Moscow, this was appraised by Prague merchants at more than 400,000 r., exclusive of 3 forties of sables so rare as to be priceless. On display this amazing gift required twenty chambers in the emperor's palace to contain it, without the inclusion of the squirrel skins, which had to be left in the freight wagons outside. So great was the delight of the emperor with this gift that he was constrained to write "to his uncle the Spanish king, to his brother, to the Pope, to all his relatives, and to the frontier princes" telling them about it.[74] Because of the tremendous increase in value of Russian furs at Prague, the Russians were able to bestow a huge subsidy upon the Habsburgs at little more than a tenth of its value to themselves, plus the cost of freightage, which in this instance did not include customs tolls, since envoys and their suites were exempt from them. A subsidy of 400,000 r. in money would have bankrupted the Muscovite state, for its total annual income at that time was not much greater than that.

Furs helped to hold the Turkish power in check on other occasions. The Crimean Tatars, whose khan was a vassal of the Turkish sultan, and the Russian cossacks of the Dnepr and Don rivers periodically raided each other's territory, causing much devastation. Moscow, faced with the necessity of restoring order within Russia after the Troublous Times and occupied with the war in the west against Poland, could not afford to become involved in a conflict in the south with the Crimean khanate or the Ottoman empire. Hence, to pacify the khan after serious cossack raids and to induce him to restrain his own warriors, the tsar made gifts of furs and other goods to him and his chieftains.[75] In June,

[74] *Pamiatniki diplomaticheskikh snoshenii drevnei Rossii s derzhavami inostrannymi*, II, 292–293.

[75] Ogloblin, IV, 61, 64, 86, 89, 93; Zabelin, pp. 1–4; I. D. Miloslavskii, "Stateinyi spisok o posol'stve Il'i Danilovicha Miloslavskago i d'iaka Leonteia Lazorevskago v Tsar'grad v 7150 godua," *Vremennik imperatorskago moskovskago obshchevstva istorii i drevnostei rossiiskikh*, Vol. VIII (1850), pt. 2, pp. 32, 37, 39, 56, 96, 126; *P.S.Z.*, II, 894.

1614, at an audience with the tsar, Crimean envoys were each presented with gifts which included neckpieces of beaver or squirrel fur, caps of fox fur, and other articles made of furs. The following month Prince Volkonskii carried with him as gifts to Khan Djanbek-Girei, to the heir-apparent, to the wife of the khan, and to his chieftains sables and fur garments worth several thousand rubles.[76] In 1627 one shipment of 1,070 rubles' worth of sables and another of 4,327 rubles' worth were sent to the khan.[77]

While seeking to preserve peace with the vassal state, the Crimean khanate, Moscow did not omit friendly overtures to the imperial state, the Ottoman empire. With equal liberality it bestowed gifts of sables upon the Porte itself. In 1615 the tsar and his father, the patriarch Filaret, sent to Constantinople with the Russian envoys 120 sables worth 450 r. for the sultan, 80 sables worth 170 r. for the vizir, 280 sables worth 290 r. for various pashas, and 200 sables worth 165 r. "for distribution for the sake of the sovereign's affairs."[78] Donations such as these, but in larger proportions, were made again in 1624 when Russian ambassadors journeyed to Constantinople. Besides furs for Orthodox dignitaries, the Russian ambassadors carried with them 1,950 sables worth 2,667 r. for distribution as follows: 210 sables worth 1,122 r. and three live sables to the sultan, 120 sables worth 190 r. to the vizir, 200 sables worth 255 r. to the pashas under the vizir, a forty of sables worth 35 r. to each of the pashas of Kaffa and Azov, 240 sables worth 300 r. "for the sake of the sovereign's affairs," 360 sables worth 230 r. for ransoming prisoners, and 760 sables worth 500 r. for purchases.[79] Four years later sables were taken to Constantinople in even larger proportions and distributed to the same individuals.[80] In fact, the Turkish officials soon came to expect, and even demanded, gifts of sables from Russian envoys.[81]

The Muscovite policy of remaining at peace with the Porte and its Crimean vassal was put, however, to a severe test when in 1637 Russian cossacks seized Azov, holding it for more than four years against the attacks of the Turks and Crimean Tatars. This seizure of Azov almost precipitated war between Turkey and Russia because of the protection normally accorded the cossacks by Moscow

[76] *R.I.B.*, IX, 318–327, 349–379.
[77] Butsinskii, *op. cit.*, p. 50 n.; Ogloblin, IV, 165.
[78] Zabelin, p. 43.
[79] *Ibid.*, pp. 378–380.
[80] *Ibid.*, pp. 510–513.
[81] Kapterev, p. 286.

and the suspicion that Moscow secretly supported them. Moscow averted a war perilous to it by denying aid in 1642 to the besieged cossacks and by showering the Turkish dignitaries with sable and fox furs. The Russian ambassadors, Miloslavskii and Lazarev, who went to Constantinople in 1643, took with them 8,000 rubles' worth of furs for the sultan and 2,000 rubles' worth more for the vizir and pashas. With the aid of these gifts, or bribes, amicable relations were restored between the two powers.[82]

Some of the furs received by the tsar were neither sold nor given as gifts, but were employed in the household of the tsar. The Sable Treasury and Treasury Court sent a certain number of them to the household, mainly for the royal wardrobe. Two Workmen's Chambers (*Masterskiia Palaty*), one for the tsar and tsarevich, the other for the tsaritsa and her daughters, made the furs into coats, caps, and other articles of apparel, as well as blankets for the bedchamber and sledge travel.[83] Occasionally, also, furs were made into yokes for the horses ridden by the tsar.[84] Another use to which furs were put was the wrapping of gold in them for storage in iron chests.[85] Curious to us today, this use is suggestive of the abundance of furs possessed by the tsar.

Furs as a Medium of Exchange

The uses to which the state frequently put its furs gave to them the character of a medium of exchange. In the purchase of goods with furs, in the payment of services with furs, in the giving of gifts of furs, in the payment of subsidies and bribes in furs—in all these expenditures the furs were not paid to the recipients with the thought that they personally would use all of them. Nor were they paid to the recipients as fur merchants. Rather, the furs were used in these ways because it was known that they could be readily disposed of for other goods, being themselves easily transported and not perishable.[86] Several of the uses to which the tsar put his furs were paralleled by similar uses of them among his subjects;

---

[82] Sergei Zhigarev, *Russkaia politika v vostochnom voprose,* pp. 88–89; Ogloblin, IV, 93; Miloslavskii, pp. 39, 45, 56, 96, 121.

[83] Viktorov, I, 188, 189, 197, 212, 214, 301, 311, 314, 315.

[84] *R.I.B.*, IX, 217.

[85] Viktorov, I, 247; A. A. Vvedenskii, "Sluzhashchie i rabotnye liudi u Stroganovykh v XVI–XVII v.," *Trud v Rossii,* I (1924), 58.

[86] Cf. Kapterev, p. 457; also Ogloblin, IV, 93, where it is recorded that in 1656 the Sable Treasury was sent to the tsar while he was on the Lithuanian campaign.

they paid them out for services and presented them as gifts.[87] In other words, furs were still used as money in Russia in the seventeenth century, recalling the Russia of Kiev and Novgorod, which had so used them. Indeed, the continuance of their use as money into the seventeenth century is one of the characteristics of Russia's economy which mark it as backward in comparison with Western Europe, where by that time the use of gold and silver currency was well established and virtually exclusive.

This use of furs as money is understandable in view of the fact that Russia produced almost no gold and silver itself, and the influx of these precious metals from the new world was late in reaching Russia. Yet the role of furs as a medium of exchange in the seventeenth century was neither as distinctive nor as widespread as in Old Russia. The Russia of Ivan the Terrible and of the first Romanovs was moving farther and farther from the natural economy of Novgorod and approaching the money economy of Peter the Great and his successors. Although necessarily the line between furs as a commodity of exchange and furs as a medium of exchange cannot be drawn precisely in an economy where much trade was still transacted through barter, furs seem to have circulated more as a commodity in the Russian markets of the seventeenth century than as money. The old fur money of Novgorod, the kuny, had long since disappeared. Silver and copper coins had replaced them, and the growing use of metal coins eliminated to an increasing extent the need of passing fur pelts from hand to hand in the market places. This change is reflected in the less frequent appearance of sables and other furs in the expenditure lists of the state in the late seventeenth century.[88] Significant, too, is the fact that furs were not valued in terms of themselves, as in the days of Novgorod, but in terms of the metallic currency units of the day, the ruble, altyn, denga, and others. The true role of furs as money thus becomes evident: in the absence of enough precious metals for an exclusively metallic currency, the Russians continued to utilize furs as a medium of exchange, but definitely as a secondary, a supplementary, medium. Moreover, furs were not the only commodity to serve in this capacity; other goods were likewise used.

The markedly supplementary role of furs as currency in Euro-

[87] Olearius, pp. 83, 89; C. H. Carlisle, *La Relation de trois ambassades*, p. 37.
[88] *D.A.I.*, VI, 97–111.

pean Russia was not so noticeable in Siberia during the seventeenth century; here they circulated more extensively as money. And this is not surprising. Siberia was a new country, young economically. The amount of money sent into Siberia was not large; goods rather than money were in demand.[89] Furs were abundant and always wanted by the visiting merchants, so that it was both natural and inevitable that they should be used as a medium of exchange, just as in the California gold rush gold dust and nuggets passed from hand to hand in place of minted coins. For currency purposes the belly-strips were especially utilizable. Serving men and private enterprisers used furs to purchase supplies, and the fees collected by the state, such as the boat fees at Berezov and the court and customs fees elsewhere, were sometimes paid in furs.[90] Nevertheless, even in Siberia furs were valued in money terms, except sometimes when dealing with the natives, and towards the end of the century an increase in the money in circulation is noticeable in the greater number of customs payments made in currency.[91]

The fact that furs were generally acceptable in Russia in place of money enabled the state to dispose of its furs in several ways that were not strictly commercial. Because of this fact and because the tsar possessed more furs than other goods acceptable as money, the Sable Treasury acquired a particular significance. When its supply of precious metals was insufficient, the state could fall back upon its store of furs as an almost equally liquid form of wealth. The Sable Treasury thus became a sort of supplementary "mint," the Russian equivalent of the "gold fund" of the mercantilist countries of the West.[92] That is the essential fact revealed by an examination of the state's disposal of its furs, a fact which becomes even more evident when we study its sale of furs in the export markets.

Reasons for the State's Participation in the Fur Trade

Before leaving the fur trade of the state to consider the private fur trade, we will gain a clearer understanding of both branches if we pause to inquire into the reasons for the unique character of the Russian fur trade. Only in Russia do we find—at least during the modern period—the state participating in and dominating

[89] Cf. below, p. 153.
[90] *D.A.I.*, IV, 23, 211, VI, 359, XI, 31, 33; Ogloblin, IV, 158.
[91] Ogloblin, II, 38–39.
[92] I. M. Kulisher, *Istoriia russkogo narodnogo khoziaistva*, II, 238.

the fur trade. Elsewhere it was conducted through private initiative and private capital. The explanation of this peculiarity of the Russian trade lies in the historical development of Russia and in its geographical situation.

The Russia of Kiev was a commercial state, a collection of principalities whose rulers were both princes and merchants, military leaders who also carried on trade, acquiring their wares by raid and the levying of tribute. The tradition arose that the prince was a businessman as well as a ruler, and it continued long after Kievan Russia fell. It was still strong in Russia during the sixteenth and seventeenth centuries, a period when in Western Europe the national monarch left business largely to his subjects and devoted himself to the task of governing. The age-old tradition that the conquered peoples owed tribute to their conquerors also continued in Russia through the sixteenth and seventeenth centuries. In the meantime, after the fall of Kiev a new Russia was formed. This Russia was created by transforming an agglomeration of petty feudal principalities into the Muscovite state. The grand princes of Moscow enlarged their feudal holdings by annexing through conquest, purchase, and inheritance almost all the Russian centers on the Volga and thus established the Muscovite Russian state. In the course of this process the concept developed that the state was the patrimony (votchina) of the grand prince, and although the grand princes became "tsars" and fashioned an absolute state by the beginning of the seventeenth century, the original feudal concept that the prince's holdings were his personal property continued to be accepted without real opposition.[93] Hence, the Muscovite state was looked upon as the personal property of the tsar, his to do with as he saw fit; his subjects were his retainers, his servants, his slaves; he was the master, the "father." As the legal owner of the land of the state he was entitled to a tenth of its first fruits, he could do whatever he wished with its resources and the products it yielded; he could trade them to foreigners, he could reserve them entirely to himself.[94] Thus, Russian tradition established the tsar himself as the preëminent entrepreneur in the country.

Historical tradition sanctioned the participation and preëminence of the tsar in the commerce of Russia; historical accident

[93] Mel'gunov, pp. 169–170.
[94] *Ibid.*, p. 172.

encouraged them. During the feudal period of the thirteenth to fifteenth centuries the Russian principalities were subject to the rule of the Tatar Golden Horde on the lower Volga. The Horde ruled the Russian principalities simply as tributaries which were sources of revenue and soldiers. The heavy exactions of the Horde and the numerous raids and incursions to which the Tatars subjected Russia made a widespread and healthy economic development impossible, with the result that, whereas in Europe in this period there developed an active and aggressive commercial class, possessing an ever-growing capital wealth, in Russia such a class failed to take form. Had a strong commercial class been allowed to develop, it might have attacked and sought to break down the patrimonial concept of the state and have developed trade on its own account and with its own capital. It might, for instance, have undertaken itself to exploit Siberia in place of the state, as Canada was exploited by the Hudson's Bay Company and Alaska later by the Russian-American Company. Instead, the initiative and momentum which the Muscovite princes acquired in consolidating the Russian people and throwing off the Tatar yoke was carried over by them from the political to the economic sphere. First as grand princes of Moscow, then as tsars of all the Russias they dominated the Russian commercial world; they developed trade and commerce and expanded it as part of their patrimonal economy, making use of the gosts and the gostinyia merchants as their agents. In this fashion trade developed in Russia at the top rather than from the bottom.

The Russian tsar, like the other European monarchs who emerged from a feudal society, continually found his needs outrunning his financial resources, and for that reason was compelled to make use of all available sources of income. In a state like Muscovite Russia, which was considered the patrimony of the sovereign, commercial enterprise provided an important means for raising revenue. The modern belief in the financial and other advantages to be derived by the monarch of a country from permitting his subjects to trade freely was a notion quite foreign to the tsars and far in advance of the economic development of Russia.[95] On the contrary, pressed by financial need, the tsar not only resorted to the obvious and direct method of increasing his revenue by engaging in trade, but also set up monopolies. The most profitable

[95] *Ibid.*, p. 181.

traffics, the commodities most in demand were quickly seized upon and reserved to the state. The silk trade, the liquor traffic, the sale of caviar, the export grain trade were a few of the state's monopolies, of which there were a good number.[96] Some were temporary, to meet certain financial emergencies; others were of long duration, until they ceased to be profitable. The fur trade belonged to the latter category; not until 1762 was the state's monopoly of it officially terminated, long after it had ceased to be really profitable to the state.[97]

Historical circumstances, several of which are peculiar to Russia, thus explain both the domination of the fur trade by the state and the means of the state's participation in it. In the economic sphere, the tradition of the tsar as the first businessman of Russia, the absence of a strong commercial class, and the state's need of revenue determined that the fur trade, made so profitable by the growing foreign demand for Russian furs and the opening of new resources in Siberia, should be dominated by the state. In the political sphere, the tradition of imposing tribute upon conquered peoples and the patrimonial concept of the Muscovite state determined how the state should acquire its furs: tribute collected from its newly conquered Siberian subjects and a tenth of the first fruits taken from Siberia by its Russian subjects.

Yet, however much historical factors sanctioned the participation of the state in the fur trade, it is highly doubtful whether the state could have played such a part in it, had it not been for the geographical contiguity of the Muscovite state to Siberia. If the Russians had had to cross an ocean, as did the French, the Dutch, and the English, the state undoubtedly would never have ventured into the Siberian fur trade but would have left the dangers and risks to the private initiative of its subjects. One may justifiably assume this because, when the Russian fur trade later crossed the North Pacific into the northwestern part of North America, that is exactly what the state did—it left the development of the fur resources of the Aleutian Islands and Alaska to a privately initiated corporation, the Russian-American Company. As in so many other major historical developments, so here, geographical position played a definitive role.

---

[96] Olearius, p. 88.

[97] William Coxe, *Account of the Russian Discoveries between Asia and America*, pp. 209–210; A. K. Korsak, *Istoriko-statisticheskoe obozrenie torgovykh snoshenii Rossii s Kitaem*, p. 41.

CHAPTER IX

THE PRIVATE TRADE IN FURS

In spite of the slow development of a strong commercial class in Russia and the competition from the state faced by private trade, the private enterprisers carried on a flourishing trade in furs. Handicapped though they were by the sale of furs by the state and by their exclusion from certain markets, still they managed to circumvent many of the state's restrictions on their trade and found for themselves a large field in which to do a lucrative business. Indeed, the weak Russian commercial class strengthened itself measurably in the seventeenth century through its participation in the fur trade. Its activities became as much a part of the fur trade as did those of the state.

The pioneering of the fur enterprisers in Siberia, as well as their other activities, and the attempts of the state to control them have already been related. Therefore, we turn to the organization and conduct of the private traffic in furs. The organization and conduct of this traffic may best be described by showing (1) what men engaged in it, (2) how these men acquired their furs, (3) what trade routes they followed and (4) in which centers they traded furs, (5) the trade cycle between Russia and Siberia, and (6) the size of the private fur trade.

Participants

The private fur trade in Russia and Siberia was carried on by individual enterprisers. The joint-stock trading company, which made its appearance in Western Europe in the course of the sixteenth and seventeenth centuries, did not arise in Russia until the eighteenth century; hence corporative combinations of private capital were not a factor in the exploitation of Siberia's furs,[1] and there was never any tendency towards a private monopoly of the fur trade. On the contrary, the trade remained open to anyone possessed of a moiety of capital and sufficient initiative; thus enterprisers of little or moderate capital were as active in it as were those of large resources.

---

[1] A. S. Lappo-Danilevskii, *Russkiia promyshlennyia i torgovyia kompanii v pervoi polovine XVIII stoletiia,* p. 6; A. V. Semenov, *Izuchenie istoricheskikh svedenii o rossiiskoi vneshnei torgovle i promyshlennosti s poloviny XVII-go stoletiia po 1858 god,* I, 73 ff.

Many persons participated in the fur trade, private enterprisers—traders and promyshlenniks—state employees, and hired workers, or pokruchenniks. Although these three types of participants might serve as a basis of classification, a more clarifying scheme is one based on the extent to which the various enterprisers participated in the transfer of furs from their source in Siberia to the domestic and export markets in Russia. On this basis three groups may be distinguished.

The first group comprises those enterprisers who resided and operated wholly within Siberia, usually within a particular part of that country. These men acquired furs at the source by hunting or by trade with the natives and brought them to local trade centers for sale, or they bought furs in the smaller trade centers and sold them in the larger ones in Siberia. To this group belong those enterprisers who were promyshlenniks in the narrower sense, men who confined their business to the hunting and trapping of animals and the sale of their pelts in the town or settlement out of which they operated. In this group, too, were middlemen traders, who exchanged goods with the natives, promyshlenniks, or other traders for furs and then disposed of the furs in the trade centers of Siberia.[2] Many of these local enterprisers were traders and promyshlenniks by profession. Others were peasants who farmed in the warm months and hunted in the winter; and many were, as we already know, the serving men in state service, into whose hands many of the Siberian furs fell.[3] Naturally, the largest number of these enterprisers were men of small capital, otherwise they would not have limited their business to a particular region in Siberia. There were exceptions, of course, notably Iarofei Khabarov, who, though a Siberian rather than a Russian enterpriser, was a large-scale operator.[4] Although many of the local enterprisers possessed capital sufficient to finance only their own individual activities, some were able to employ pokruchenniks and even agents to assist them.[5] In the early years of the occupation of Siberia these enterprisers were immigrants, chiefly from the north of Russia, but in

[2] K. V. Bazilevich, "Krupnoe torgovoe predpriiatie v moskovskom gosudarstve v pervoi polovine XVII veka," *Izvestiia akademii nauk,* Otdelenie obshchestvennykh nauk, ser. 7 (1932), No. 9, p. 806; *idem,* "Tamozhennye knigi kak istochnik ekonomicheskoi istorii Rossii," *Problemy istochnikovedeniia,* I, 115.

[3] *Idem,* "Krupnoe torgovoe predpriiatie," p. 806.

[4] Cf. *D.A.I.,* III, 102, which refers to one Ivan Kvashin, a promyshlennik who operated on a considerable scale along the upper Olekma and Shilka rivers.

[5] *D.A.I.,* II, 160, 263, III, 277, 279, 347.

the course of time an indigenous Russian population arose, many of whom made their living from the fur trade. One further element may be considered as belonging in this first group, namely, the Siberian natives. Their importance in the trade as hunters was no less than that of the promyshlenniks.

The second group of fur enterprisers was composed of men who may be called traveling or visiting enterprisers (*proezzhye torgovye i promyshlennye liudi*). These, for the most part, lived in Russian towns and traveled themselves to Siberia to acquire their furs. Either they were professional traders, of rank below that of gostinaia or sukonnaia sotnia, from Moscow and such northern towns as Ustiug, Kholmogory, Solvychegodsk, and, less often, from Volga towns like Iaroslavl, Nizhnii Novgorod, and Kazan; or they were peasants and artisans who had branched out from their villatic agricultural trade and their crafts into the Siberian fur trade.[6] A few lived in Siberia—for instance, Christianized natives—and made their headquarters there rather than in Russia.[7] In addition to trading, these enterprisers often participated in hunting expeditions and even organized their own hunting parties. Their individual capital was small, although a few of them operated with capital of five hundred, a thousand, or fifteen hundred rubles, large amounts for those days (1,000 r. then were the equivalent of 12,000 to 15,000 prewar rubles),[8] and even employed agents of their own. But most of them worked with resources of less than a hundred rubles and many with less than forty rubles. Correspondingly, the average number of furs which they individually brought out of Siberia was not large, as many as could be carried on one or two horses. Four hundred and thirty-six men brought 848 forties of sables through Mangazeia in 1630, and in June and July of 1641 two hundred and forty-seven men brought 28,000 rubles' worth of furs through this town, an average of less than 80 pelts for the first group and an average value of little more than 100 r. for the other. Of the Russian enterprisers who operated in Siberia these traveling traders constituted much the majority.[9] In this group may be included the veovodas and other state officials in Siberia who carried furs back with them to Russia.

[6] Ogloblin, II, 43, III, 150, 153; *D.A.I.*, IV, 276; P. N. Butsinskii, *Mangazeia i mangazeiskii uezd*, p. 51; Bazilevich, "Tamozhennye knigi," pp. 125, 126.

[7] S. V. Bakhrushin, "Sibirskie sluzhilye tatary v XVII v.," *Istoricheskie zapiski*, I (1937), 63–64.

[8] V. O. Kliuchevskii, *Opyty i issledovaniia*, pp. 160, 164, 171.

[9] Butsinskii, *op. cit.*, pp. 27, 50–51; Ogloblin, II, 23, 34; Bazilevich, "Krup-

The third group consisted of merchant-capitalists—their numbers were not great—who conducted large-scale trade and who themselves rarely went to Siberia.[10] These men possessed the largest capital resources found in the Russian business world and developed extensive business organizations of the family type, beyond which the late-developing Russian capitalism did not evolve in the seventeenth century. Most of them either were members of the gostinaia or sukonnaia sotnia or were the tsar's gosts; some had risen from a small beginning as peasant-traders or artisans, or were the sons of merchants who so began.[11] Since the export trade rested in their hands, they constituted the strongest group in the fur trade, though without ever becoming the dominant group. Their investments in single trading expeditions to Siberia reached amounts as high as four or five thousand rubles or more, though a thousand rubles, more or less, appears as the most common amount invested in a single expedition.[12] Indicative of the dimensions of their operations is the fact that the shipment of furs of one of these merchant-capitalists to Arkhangelsk in 1647 constituted nearly half the number of furs purchased that year in Ustiug, a major fur center. Where the lesser merchants measured their fur shipments in a few dozens of forties, these merchant-capitalists measured them in one or two hundreds of forties.[13] For the conduct of their business activities in Siberia, which included the organization of hunting expeditions as well as trade, they employed agents and pokruchenniks, numbering from a dozen or so to as many as a hundred. Many of these merchants owned their own shops and storehouses in Russian and Siberian towns, and even their own blockhouses in the Siberian forests.[14] Like the traveling merchants,

noe torgovoe predpriiatie," pp. 801–803; *idem*, "Torgovlia velikogo Ustiuga v seredine XVII veka," *Uchenye zapiski instituta istorii rossiiskoi assotsiatsii nauchno-issledovatel'skikh institutov obshchestvennyk nauk*, IV (1929), 100–101; *D.A.I.*, III, 102, IV, 19.

[10] But cf. *R.I.B.*, II, 1062, and Ogloblin, III, 154.

[11] Bazilevich, "Krupnoe torgovoe predpriiatie," p. 784; *idem*, "Tamozhennye knigi," pp. 125, 126.

[12] Butsinskii, *op. cit.*, p. 51; S. V. Bakhrushin, "Agenty russkikh torgovykh liudei XVII veka," *Uchenye zapiski instituta istorii rossiiskoi assotsiatsii nauchno-issledovatel'skikh institutov obshchestvennykh nauk*, IV (1929), 75, 76, 77.

[13] Bazilevich, "Torgovlia velikogo Ustiuga," pp. 100, 101.

[14] *D.A.I.*, III, 43, IV, 88, 89, VIII, 4, 5; Bakhrushin, "Agenty russkikh torgovykh liudei," p. 88; Bakhrushin, "Torgi gostia Nikitina v Sibiri i Kitae," *Sbornik statei: Pamiati Aleksandra Nikolaevicha Savina, 1873–1923*, Trudy instituta istorii rossiiskoi assotsiatsii nauchno-issledovatel'skikh institutov obshchestvennykh nauk, I (1926), 373; Bazilevich, "Krupnoe torgovoe pred-

most of them resided in Moscow and the towns of northern Russia, but a small number of them were inhabitants of the Volga towns.[15] Besides this class of professional merchants, another kind of big capitalist engaged occasionally in the fur trade. This was the great landowner, usually a member of the titled nobility or a relative of the tsar, who employed his bonded peasants to carry on his trading operations in Siberia and Russia. A few church officials and monasteries also utilized their bonded peasants to engage in the fur trade.[16]

If it was the enterprisers who supplied the required initiative and capital for the exploitation of the Siberian fur resources, it was the employee who made any sort of extensive operations possible. Assistants and employees were needed both to acquire the pelts and to transport them from Siberia to Russia. As a lower order of employees there stood the hired workers or pokruchenniks, a group worth more study than has been accorded them. In the fur trade their participation seems to have been chiefly as hunters, whose compensation was a specified share of whatever they caught.[17] Ordinarily men without capital, they were provided by their employers with food supplies and hunting equipment during the time of their employment. Many pokruchenniks were drawn from a migrant class of men called *guliashchie liudi*. They were free men, often peasants originally, who migrated about the country in search of employment or some means of livelihood.[18] Some pokruchenniks also were promyshlenniks of small means, or erstwhile promyshlenniks who had suffered economic disaster.[19] In addition to these, there was another type of employee, who, however, played only a minor role in the fur trade. This was the shop clerk (*lavochnyi sidelets*), who tended the shops maintained in Siberia by some of the wealthy merchant-capitalists.[20]

---

priiatie," p. 792; G. N. Potanin, "Privoz i vyvoz tovarov goroda Tomska v polovine XVII stoletiia," *Vestnik imperatorskago russkago geograficheskago obshchestva*, Vol. XXVII (1859), pt. 2, pp. 134, 139; N. I. Kostomarov, *Ocherki torgovli moskovskago gosudarstva v XVI i XVII vv.*, p. 303.

[15] See above, n. 6; *R.I.B.*, II, 1062; Potanin, *op. cit.*, p. 134.

[16] Bazilevich, "Tamozhennye knigi," pp. 125–126; Ogloblin, II, 31, III, 153; Butsinkii, *op. cit.*, p. 50.

[17] *D.A.I.*, II, 160, 263, III, 102, 277, 279, 347, IV, 19, 88, 89, VIII, 5, 6; G. Vernadskii, "Gosudarevy sluzhilye i promyshlennye liudi vostochnoi Sibiri XVII veka," *Zh.M.N.P.*, n.s., LVI (1915), 339–340.

[18] G. V. Lantzeff, *Siberia in the Seventeenth Century*, p. 141 n. 123.

[19] Ogloblin, II, 50, 104.

[20] Bakhrushin, "Agenty russkikh torgovykh liudei," pp. 82–83; *idem*, "Torgi gostia Nikitina," pp. 368, 373, 376.

A superior order of employees comprised men who functioned as agents. More is known about them than about the other employees. They were entrusted with important business assignments and given considerable freedom of action and responsibility, which they sometimes abused.[21] They moved about Russia and Siberia, buying and selling furs and other goods and organizing hunting expeditions. These agents were of several kinds, varying according to their juridical status and their relations with the employers. Merchants who operated at all extensively turned first to the close members of their families, to a brother, son, grandson, or nephew, for their agents, since the family tie assured greater faithfulness. It was usually from these men that the successor to the family business came. A second type commonly employed was the poor or orphaned relation. He was not, however, a free man like the first type; he was legally dependent upon the head of the family, and his remuneration was limited to his keep. The largest group of agents was probably the *prikázchiks,*[22] free and independent businessmen who entered into a contractual relation with their employers. Some prikazchiks served simply as hired employees for a stated salary and a stated period of time. Others worked on a commission basis, receiving a third to a half of the profits from the transactions they conducted. Still others pooled their own capital with capital provided by their employers, enjoyed for the duration of the venture whatever special privileges the employers enjoyed, and shared the profits equally, a relation which did not necessarily preclude the prikazchik from carrying on simultaneously business operations of his own.[23] Most of the prikazchiks in the Siberian trade were men from the towns of northern Russia, who made their headquarters in one of them, but a few prikazchiks remained in Siberia for a number of years, maintaining their headquarters in one of the towns there.[24] A fourth type of agent was the individual who voluntarily entered into a client-patron relationship with his employer. He received his keep and a small salary, or occasionally part of the profits from his operations. Agents of this sort came chiefly from the class of lesser merchants and promyshlenniks and

---

[21] Bazilevich, "Krupnoe torgovoe predpriiatie," p. 805; Ogloblin, III, 151; *A.A.E.*, IV, 441.

[22] Although *prikazchik* is a word of several uses in Russian, its extension to agents standing in a juridically dependent relation to their employers is incorrect (Bakhrushin, "Agenty russkikh torgovykh liudei, pp. 74, 81).

[23] Bazilevich, "Torgovlia velikogo Ustiuga," p. 10.

[24] Bakhrushin, "Torgi gostia Nikitina," p. 372.

from the peasant class. A fifth kind was the employee who became bound more or less involuntarily to his employer or master. He might be a Siberian native, purchased while a boy, an indebted merchant or promyshlennik paying off an obligation or the son of such a person, or again an enserfed peasant who became separated from agriculture and engaged wholly in trade. The bondage of such men often lasted many years, but it did not prevent them from trading on their own account in addition to carrying on the business of their masters. The nature of their remuneration, if any, is not clearly understood.[25]

Acquisition of Furs

Two methods were employed to obtain Siberian furs for sale in Russia. The first method was that of trade. Goods procured in Russia were exchanged for furs from the natives, local traders, promyshlenniks, and serving men in Siberia. This was perhaps the more widely used method. Both Russian and foreign imported goods were employed for this purpose, and since very few even of the necessities and minimum comforts of life were produced in Siberia, the goods taken there for exchange consisted of articles and materials of clothing, food supplies and drink, articles for domestic use, metal wares, firearms, hunting equipment, and the like. Grain, coarse cloth, linen, hides, soap, ready-made clothing, axes, ironwork of various sorts, honey, wine, and wax were the more common Russian goods carried to Siberia, whereas woolens, both English and Lithuanian—and later from Hamburg—textiles including silks, unworked metals, copper, pewter, and iron, spices and sweets, "head" sugar, and paper were the foreign goods most often sent there.[26]

The big merchant-capitalist obtained such goods through his business organization, the activities of which frequently extended to several of the Russian trade centers. For instance, the merchant brothers Bosov, whose headquarters were at Ustiug, sent their agents to Arkhangelsk and Iaroslavl, as well as to Vologda, Mos-

[25] *Idem,* "Agenty russkikh torgovykh liudei," pp. 72–87; Bazilevich, "Krupnoe torgovoe predpriiatie," pp. 801–805; *idem,* "Tamozhennye knigi," p. 126; I. S. Makarov, "Volostnye torzhki v sol'vychegodskom uezde v pervoi polovine XVII v.," *Istoricheskie zapiski,* I (1937), 203–204, 207–210.

[26] Kostomarov, p. 302; Potanin, *op. cit.,* pp. 129–131, 136–138, 140–141; Butsinskii, *op. cit.,* pp. 40–41; *idem, Zaselenie Sibiri,* pp. 180–181; Bazilevich, "Krupnoe torgovoe predpriiatie," pp. 794–795; Ogloblin, II, 23, 32, 121–123; Samuel Purchas, *His Pilgrimes,* XIII, 254–255; *A.A.E.,* II, 257; *A.I.,* II, 28.

cow, Nizhnii Novgorod, Kazan, and Viatka on trading operations, in the course of which they acquired the goods that were sent to Siberia.[27] The smaller enterpriser had, of course, to depend upon a more limited scale of operations, purchasing his goods in the town where he maintained his headquarters and perhaps in one or two other towns. The trade in Siberia was almost entirely barter, furs for goods. Money, especially in the earlier years, was scarce, and for the natives it possessed little value, whereas the Russian inhabitants needed goods rather than money.[28] The natives gradually lost their economic separateness and entered into trade relations with the Russians. Among them beads and other ornaments, metalwork of copper, pewter, and iron, and foreign textiles were especially in demand. The Russians willingly took such Russian goods as coarse textiles, ready-made clothing, boots, and hunting equipment, and foreign goods like English and Dutch textiles and articles of luxury.[29]

The second method by which the Russian enterprisers obtained their furs in Siberia was the direct one of hunting and trapping the animals. For this purpose, they either organized hunting expeditions of their own or participated in one organized by someone else. These expeditions were organized in Siberia, frequently by the big merchants' agents, who, upon reaching a Siberian trade center, hired pokruchenniks to hunt for them as a means of acquiring furs in addition to their trade.[30] Such hunting parties, which were generally known as vatagas, and in the second half of the seventeenth century sometimes as *arteli,* represented coöperative ventures on the part of some or all of their members.[31]

Two kinds of them can be distinguished. The first was strictly a hunting party, and was made up of independent enterprisers, or of pokruchenniks, or of both. Independent enterprisers, that is traders, promyshlenniks, and agents, participated on the basis of shares, or *uzhiny,* determined according to the capital (in supplies and equipment) which each invested in the expedition, and

[27] Bazilevich, "Krupnoe torgovoe predpriiatie," pp. 789, 794–795.

[28] Kostomarov, p. 303. The need of goods rather than money is sharply illustrated by the circumstances which led the state to forbid in 1662 the purchasing of furs with copper money. See above, p. 77.

[29] Bazilevich, "Krupnoe torgovoe predpriiatie," pp. 806–807; Makarov, p. 204.

[30] Bazilevich, "Krupnoe torgovoe predpriiatie," p. 792; Bazilevich, "Tamozhennye knigi," p. 115; N. N. Ogloblin, "Semen Dezhnev (1638–1671 gg.)," *Zh.M.N.P.*, CCLXXII (1890), 253–254, 265; *D.A.I.*, VII, 150.

[31] *D.A.I.*, VIII, 6.

in proportion to his share each man received a part of the catch.[32] Such participants were sometimes called *uzhínniks.*[33] Pokruchenniks usually participated in these expeditions as the hired workers either of a member of the party, or of an outside enterpriser not a member of the party, or of the organizer, who might or might not himself join the expedition. Illustrative of the membership of these hunting parties were two parties organized at Iakutsk in June and July, 1642, by Leontii Tolstoükhov, an agent of the Bosov brothers and an independent enterpriser in his own right. One was made up of seventeen pokruchenniks hired by him and furnished with 650 rubles' worth of supplies and equipment; the other was composed of two of his agents and two pokruchenniks and was supplied with 151 rubles' worth of provisions and equipment. Both were sent down the Lena to hunt. In the same July another Bosov agent, Fedor Vorypaev, organized a hunting party made up of two of his nephews, one of his own pokruchenniks as leader or peredovshchiki,[34] with another pokruchennik, eight more pokruchenniks, and four uzhinniks, with whom went supplies and equipment valued at 525 r.[35] In 1645, one Grishka Grigoriev from Kholmogory uezd went sable hunting along the Olekma River with five pokruchenniks and one uzhinnik.[36] The size of these vatagas varied, from small groups of three, four, or five men to large ones of thirty, forty, or fifty men.[37] The assembling of large groups appears to have occurred oftener in Eastern than in Western Siberia.

Although organized primarily for hunting, these expeditions are known also to have carried on trade with the natives, the men exchanging for furs their extra supplies and such easily transported goods as beads and trinkets. This trade was transacted either at the blockhouses of the promyshlenniks or in the villages of the natives. With the Samoeds, Tungus, and the natives of northeastern

[32] *D.A.I.*, III, 214; Ogloblin, II, 34, 104–105; Vladimir Dal', *Tolkovyi slovar' zhivogo velikorusskago iazyka,* IV, 968.

[33] Bazilevich, "Krupnoe torgovoe predpriiatie," p. 792; *D.A.I.*, III, 102. The documents refer often to "promyshlennik so-and-so and *tovarishchi.*" Vernadskii (*op. cit.*, p. 340), is unable to place the status of the tovarishchi, but the natural supposition is that they were either uzhinniks working with the promyshlennik named or members of a vataga or section of a vataga of which the latter was the leader.

[34] See below, p. 156.

[35] Bazilevich, "Krupnoe torgovoe predpriiatie," p. 792.

[36] *D.A.I.*, II, 102.

[37] *D.A.I.*, VIII, 4; *R.I.B.*, II, 851; Ogloblin, II, 32, 104–105; S. P. Krasheninnikov, *A History of Kamtschatka, and the Kurilski Islands,* p. 111.

Siberia, who distrusted the Russians as much as the Russians distrusted them, it often took the primitive form of "dumb" trade, in which the seller threw his wares into a clearing where they were claimed by the buyer, who, approaching cautiously, took them, left his own in return, and departed hastily.[38]

The second kind of hunting expedition did not differ greatly from the first. What set it apart from the first, however, was its character of a raiding party; to obtain its furs it engaged in activities besides that of hunting and trading. It explored new lands, conquered the natives, and exacted tribute for the state and for the party's members.[39] The organization of these expeditions and the part they played in the conquest of Siberia have already been described in an earlier chapter. The men who joined these expeditions, besides the serving men sent by the Siberian authorities, were the same as those participating in the purely hunting expeditions, that is, traders, promyshlenniks, agents, and pokruchenniks.[40]

Detailed information is lacking about the organization of a hunting expedition and the conduct of a Siberian sable hunt in the seventeenth century. A complete description, however, has been left by Krasheninnikov of the sable hunt as conducted in the upper Vitim country in the early or middle eighteenth century,[41] and this description seems, from what scattered information we possess, to apply in general to sable hunting during the seventeenth century.

Sables were hunted usually in the winter months because it was then that their pelts were at their best.[42] In the summer, in addition to their customary fare of small animals and birds, they ate a kind of berry which caused them to itch and therefore to rub against trees, with damage to their pelts.[43] Also, the young, brought forth in late March or early April, did not acquire coats with the desired length of hair until the following winter. Such young sables as were caught in the summer or fall, called *nedosoboli,*[44] brought a very low price.

Hunting parties set out for the hunting grounds at various times

---

[38] Bazilevich, "Krupnoe torgovoe predpriiatie," p. 792 n. 1; Vernadskii, *op. cit.*, p. 341 n. 1; S. V. Bakhrushin, "Iasak v Sibiri v XVII veke," *Sibirskie ogni,* 1927, No. 3 (May–June), pp. 120–121.

[39] Vernadskii, *op. cit.*, pp. 342–343.

[40] *D.A.I.*, IV, 19; cf. Ogloblin, I, 319.

[41] Krasheninnikov, pp. 109–115.

[42] Cf. *D.A.I.*, III, 214; Ogloblin, I, 319.

[43] Cf. Ogloblin, II, 18.

[44] Cf. above, p. 51 n. 11.

of year, depending upon the length of time required to reach them. Usually it was in the summer. Those who hunted along the upper Vitim left in late August, whereas those who went to the lower Lena or Indigirka and Kolyma rivers left much earlier, in June and July. But from Tomsk, parties departed as late as January.[45] An expedition carried with it large supplies of equipment and provisions, which included flour, salt, fishing nets, sable nets, axes, boots, cooking vessels, and many other articles.[46] The Vitim hunters traveled in small boats, which carried three or four men and supplies; larger boats were used as well. Olekma hunters sailed in boats that carried ten or eleven men and supplies.[47]

Upon arriving at the hunting grounds, the party erected a blockhouse, if none was already there, and here they lived until the rivers froze over, meanwhile acquiring a winter's supply of fish.[48] At this time the company chose a leader or peredovshchik from the most experienced men, delegating complete authority to him.[49] He divided the company into small groups, sometimes called *chunitsy*, and appointed a leader to each except his own.[50] This division was unalterable, for, although there might be only eight or ten in the whole party, they never all hunted in the same place. The company chief also assigned the place where each group was to hunt.

Arriving at its assigned place, each group built a small hut. In the vicinity of the hut the hunters prepared trap-pits, holes dug in the ground and surrounded at a distance of four feet by sharp stakes six to seven feet high.[51] The holes were covered with boards to keep the snow out. Through the stakes to the pit was a narrow entrance over which a board was so nicely suspended that the slightest contact with it by a sable turned it, and, turning, it threw the animal into the pit. The traps were baited with fish or meat.[52]

---

[45] Bazilevich, "Krupnoe torgovoe predpriiatie," p. 792; *D.A.I.*, III, 276, 280; Ogloblin, I, 319.

[46] Bazilevich, "Krupnoe torgovoe predpriiatie," p. 792 n. 1; Vernadskii, *loc. cit.* Each member of the Vitim hunting parties carried 1,000 pounds of rye flour, 35 pounds of wheat flour, 35 pounds of salt, 10 pounds of groats, and to every two men there were a net, dog, 250 pounds of dog food, a bed, and two cooking vessels. The expedition of seventeen pokruchenniks organized by Tolstoükhov was provided, among other things, with 15,000 pounds of rye flour, 70 pounds of vessels, 50 small bells, 1,400 feet of fishing net, 50 hunting axes, 20 elkskin boots, 20 sable nets, 30 mittens, 20 cups, 5 crowbars, and 20 cooking pans.

[47] *D.A.I.*, VIII, 6.

[48] *D.A.I.*, III, 173, 347; Vernadskii, *op. cit.*, p. 339.

[49] Cf. *D.A.I.*, VIII, 6.

[50] *D.A.I.*, III, 173; Dal', IV, 1377.

[51] Cf. Ogloblin, III, 214.

[52] *Ibid.*, II, 18.

The hunters stayed at one hut until they had made a sufficient number of traps—each hunter was supposed to make twenty in one day—and then moved on to another location, where a new hut and more traps were built. When about ten of such stops had been made, the group leader divided the party in half and sent one half back to bring up the supplies left in the several huts, while he went on with the remaining men to build more huts and traps. The first half, returning to the huts already built, inspected the traps, picked up any sables found in them, reset the traps, and then skinned the animals and smoked the pelts. If they feared being robbed by the natives, they hollowed out stakes and put the pelts in them, sealing the ends with snow, which froze, and buried the stakes in the snow near the hut. Here they were picked up by the whole group on its return from the hunt. When the first half rejoined the rest of the group, these others in turn went back to pick up provisions, while the leader took the first half and went on again.

If the hunters found few sables in their traps, they resorted to hunting them with nets and dogs,[53] although this method was possible only when there were fresh tracks in the snow. The sables lived either in holes in the ground or in nests which they built in the trees. Following the tracks to a hole, the hunter placed about it a net into which the sable had to step when emerging. Then the hunter sat near by and waited with his dog, sometimes a whole day or two. Each net had small bells tied to it which signaled the hunter when his prey emerged, whereupon he set his dog after the animal to make the kill. When the tracks led to a group of holes, the hunter resorted to smoking the sable out, a procedure not possible when there was only one hole, because the sable would suffocate rather than pass through the smoke. If the sable was traced to the foot of a tree, the hunter, if he could see it, attempted to shoot it, with a blunt arrow.[54] But if unable to see it, he cut the tree down, having placed his net at the point where the top would fall and where the sable would jump. Sometimes no sable appeared, and then the hunter searched the hollows of the tree, for after one escape from a net or trap, the sable was not easily deceived a second time.

Upon completing their hunting the groups returned to the blockhouse, where the group leaders reported the number of sables

[53] Cf. *D.A.I.*, III, 214; Jodocus Crull, *The Ancient and Present State of Muscovy*, I, 59; J. P. Kilburger, "Kurzer Unterricht von dem russischen Handel," *Buschings Magazin*, III (1769), 328; Ogloblin, II, 18.

[54] Paul of Aleppo, *The Travels of Macarius, Patriarch of Antioch*, II, 7.

caught, as well as any wrong-doing among the members, for which punishment was meted out. The whole company then set out for home as soon as the rivers were free of ice. After paying the tithe to the state, the sables were sold and the proceeds, money or goods or both, were divided in accordance with whatever arrangement the company had previously agreed upon.

Trade Routes

The routes which the fur traffic followed in the sixteenth and seventeenth centuries were mainly water routes, since in both Russia and Siberia the many rivers afforded the easiest means of communication. Along them the fur traders passed between the hunting grounds and trade centers of Siberia and the markets of Russia. In Siberia, virtually all routes carried fur traffic, since the fur trade was the original and greatest economic activity there; in Russia, the fur trade was concentrated in the north, thus the routes in Russia of the fur trade were situated in that half of the Muscovite state north of the upper Volga River. These routes were many, too many to consider their courses in detail; some of those details are shown on the map accompanying this study.[55] Our interest, rather, is in their general course and their more important features.

Study of the map reveals that the routes of the fur trade in Russia and Siberia during the seventeenth century formed a neat and well-defined pattern. In Russia there were four focal points, each of which was connected with the other three by series of rivers and portages. Two of these points were the western termini of the fur-trade routes; the one was Arkhangelsk in the north, the chief export center to Western Europe, the other was Moscow, the center of the state's fur trade and an export center in its own right. The other two points were the western approaches to the Ural Mountains, the Pechora River in the north and the Kama River to the south, from the eastern tributaries of which the crossing of the Urals into Siberia was made. From Arkhangelsh to the Pechora there were two routes, one by sea along the Arctic coast to the mouth of the Pechora, the other by rivers and portages across the northern littoral (*Pomoriia*) to Ust-Tsilma on the Pechora.[56] Be-

[55] A more extended description of the trade routes is found in R. J. Kerner, *The Urge to the Sea*, pp. 29–30, 66–88, with the accompanying maps, nos. 4, 12–16, which are excellent and in great detail.

[56] S. V. Bakhrushin, *Ocherki po istorii kolonizatsii Sibiri v XVI i XVII vv.*,

tween Arkhangelsk and the Kama the route followed the Dvina and Vychegda rivers and the tributaries of the latter. Moscow and the Pechora were connected by a route which went overland from Moscow to Vologda, thence by the Sukhona, Vychegda, Vym, and tributary rivers to the Pechora at Ust-Izhma.[57] Between Moscow and the Kama there were two routes also, of equal distance, a northern one through Vologda and along the Vychegda and its tributaries to the Kama, the other by way of the Volga River system to the confluence of the Kama with it.[58] Arkhangelsk and Moscow were joined by the Vologda-Sukhona-Dvina route, and the Pechora and Kama rivers were accessible to each other over the Visherka River and its tributaries.[59]

Joining the trade routes in Russia with those in Siberia were seven routes. One of them was an ocean route; two of them passed from the Pechora to the Ob Gulf; the other four originated at the Kama and converged on the Tobol River, a tributary of the Irtysh. The ocean route, the northernmost and the prolongation of the sea route from Arkhangelsk, went from Pustozersk at the mouth of the Pechora through the Iugorskii Straits to Ial-mal Peninsula, which it crossed to the Ob Gulf.[60] Of the two northern land crossings the more northerly left the Pechora by the Usa River, crossed the Urals over the Kamen[61] portage near the northernmost point of the Ural chain, and passed down the Sob River to Sob customs barrier on the lower part of the Ob Gulf;[62] the other left the Pechora farther up its course, at the Shchugor River, crossed the Urals by either of two portages, and passed down the tributaries of the Sosva River and that river itself to Berezov on the southern end of the Ob Gulf.[63] The northernmost of the crossings from the Kama went from Cherdyn across the Urals to the Losva River, thence via the

pp. 62, 80–81; *R.I.B.*, II, 1062, 1076, 1080, 1088–1092; A. A. Titov, *Sibir' v XVII v.*, pp. 50–51. *Ibid.*, pp. 9–22 and 30–36 have been translated into English in Kerner, *op. cit.*, pp. 165–175.

[57] Bakhrushin, *Ocherki*, pp. 61, 103; Ogloblin, IV, 137; Titov, p. 51.

[58] Bakhrushin, *Ocherki*, pp. 89, 103; Kostomarov, p. 303; Titov, p. 61; *D.A.I.*, II, 170; G. F. Müller, "Nachrichten von der Handlung in Sibirien," *Sammlung russischer Geschichte*, III, 417–418; Purchas, XIII, 180; cf. S. F. Platonov, *Ocherki po istorii smuty v moskovskom gosudarstve XVI–XVII vv.*, pp. 18, 26.

[59] Bakhrushin, *Ocherki*, p. 89; Platonov, *op. cit.*, p. 12.

[60] Bakhrushin, *Ocherki*, pp. 81–82; Purchas, XIII, 217–220, 228–229.

[61] *Kamen* means "stone" or "rock" and was the customary designation of the Urals at that time, as well as of many other mountain ranges in Siberia.

[62] Bakhrushin, *Ocherki*, p. 62; *R.I.B.*, II, 162, 1076; Butsinskii, *Zaselenie Sibiri*, p. 176.

[63] Bakhrushin, *Ocherki*, p. 63; *R.I.B.*, II, 1068.

Tura to the Tobol River.[64] South of it was the Solikamsk-Verkhoturie overland route, which went directly from the Kama to the upper Tura River, a tributary of the Tobol.[65] Farther south was the Chusovaia River route, which on the Siberian side entered the Tura below Verkhoturie.[66] Southernmost of the crossings was the overland route via Ufa across the Ufa steppes to Tiumen on the lower Tura.[67]

In Siberia two major routes, continuations of the Pechora and Kama crossings, extended east and west across the continent, bending towards each other at the Lena River to focus on Iakutsk, situated on the middle Lena, which was long the foremost administrative and commercial center in Eastern Siberia. The northern route went from the mouth of the Ob Gulf through Taz Gulf to Mangazeia, thence to Turukhansk on the lower Enisei, up the Lower Tunguska River, and down the Viliui to the Lena.[68] The southern route proceeded along the Tobol and Irtysh rivers to the middle Ob, eastward along the Ob to the Vakh or Ket rivers, from either of which the Enisei was reached by means of portages.[69] From the Enisei, specifically, from Eniseisk, the southern route continued eastward by ascending the Upper Tunguska or Angara River, from the upper part of which the route divided, one branch going to the Lena by way of the Ilim River and the Lena portage,[70] the other entering the upper Amur basin from Lake Baikal.[71] From Iakutsk the trade routes spread fanwise farther into Eastern Siberia. The Iana, Indigirka, Kolyma, and other rivers in northeastern Siberia were reached either overland from Iakutsk or by the Lena River and the Arctic Ocean.[72] Due east was the Sea of Okhotsk, the route to which passed along the Aldan and Maia rivers, reaching the coast by means of portages.[73] The Amur basin

[64] Bakhrushin, *Ocherki*, pp. 88–89.

[65] *Ibid.*, pp. 90, 102–103; N. Ianitskii, "Torgovlia pushnym tovarom v XVII v.," *Kievskiia universitetskiia izvestiia*, LII (No. 9, 1912), 4, citing *Permskaia starina*, I, 42.

[66] Bakhrushin, *Ocherki*, pp. 90–91, 101; Titov, p. 11; *Sibirskiia letopisi*, p. 11.

[67] Bakhrushin, *Ocherki*, p. 107; Titov, pp. 14, 44.

[68] Bakhrushin, *Ocherki*, pp. 114, 127; *R.I.B.*, II, 96; Titov, pp. 21, 37, 51.

[69] Bakhrushin, *Ocherki*, pp. 110–112; Titov, pp. 30, 46–47, 81–82; N. Spafarii, *Puteshestvie chrez Sibir'*, Zapiski imperatorskago russkago geograficheskago obshchestva po otdeleniiu etnografii, X (No. 1, 1882), 67–83, 84–85.

[70] Bakhrushin, *Ocherki*, pp. 124–127; *D.A.I.*, II, 238–239, 242–245, III, 38–39, VIII, 325; Spafarii, *op. cit.*, pp. 87–101; Titov, pp. 32, 46–47, 52.

[71] Bakhrushin, *Ocherki*, pp. 136–138; *D.A.I.*, III, 344, 391–392, 395–396; Titov, pp. 31, 47, 106; Spafarii, *op. cit.*, pp. 87, 118, 123–129, 134–140.

[72] Bakhrushin, *Ocherki*, pp. 128–130; *D.A.I.*, III, 276, 277, 279, 280–281, VI, 406–407; Titov, pp. 32–33, 52–53.

[73] Bakhrushin, *Ocherki*, pp. 139–140; *D.A.I.*, III, 55–56, 333, VI, 404, 406.

to the south was approached by two routes, the Aldan and Zeia rivers for one and the Olekma River and Tugir portage for the other.[74] Communication between the two major east-west routes was maintained in a north and south direction by means of three of the four great river systems in Siberia, by the Ob-Irtysh, the Enisei, and the Lena.[75] Communication between the two was possible also by way of the Chichui portage, which joined the upper Lena with the upper reaches of the Lower Tunguska.[76]

Of the routes just sketched six in particular stand out. The first is the Pechora route along its southern or Vychegda branch. Despite the fact that this route was usable only during the months of June, July, and August, when the Kamen portage was open, most of the furs taken out of Siberia were transported over it. Not only did traders and promyshlenniks who traveled its Siberian extension, the route eastward through Mangazeia and Turukhansk, make use of it, but traders returning to Russia over the southern route followed the Ob River on down to either Berezov or the Sob barrier and thence across the Urals to the Pechora River instead of continuing the southern route by way of the Irtysh and Verkhoturie. Nine hundred and nineteen men registered at the Sob-Obdorsk barriers in 1639 (Obdorsk lay just across the bay from Sob barrier), and 745 men in 1640. The 638 outgoing travelers who registered in 1641 at Sob barrier as against the 125 incoming travelers indicate how preponderantly this route served as an exit from Siberia. It was also used by the state to transport its sable treasuries from Berezov, Surgut, Narym, Ketsk, Tomsk, Eniseisk, Krasnoiarsk, and Iakutsk.[77] Its use chiefly as the way of exit from Siberia arose from the fact that its marshes and rapid mountain rivers made the transporting of the heavy and large goods imported into Siberia difficult; but for transporting the light furs on the return journey the Pechora route was both possible and preferable, since, with the exception of two relatively short stretches, travel was downstream to the mouth of the Vychegda River and therefore faster.[78] This route from Siberia continued in active use throughout the seven-

[74] Bakhrushin, *Ocherki*, pp. 134–135; *D.A.I.*, III, 51–55, 103–104, 260, 352, IV, 94, 178, VI, 153, 405; Titov, p. 33; Spafarii, *op. cit.*, pp. 133, 164, 165.

[75] Bakhrushin, *Ocherki*, p. 116; Titov, pp. 17, 19–20, 34–37, 44, 50–51; *D.A.I.* VI, 405; *R.I.B.*, II, 1050.

[76] Bakhrushin, *Ocherki*, p. 128; *D.A.I.*, II, 239, 249, 252, VI, 403, VII, 51–52.

[77] But cf. *D.A.I.*, VIII, 325, and Potanin, *op. cit.*, p. 139, which show that the Iakutsk and Tomsk sable treasuries were sent also via Tobolsk and Verkhoturie.

[78] *R.I.B.*, II, 1068–1069.

teenth century, but was ordered closed in 1704 by Peter the Great in favor of the Verkhoturie route.[79]

The second outstanding route was the Vychegda-Solikamsk-Verkhoturie route. In distinction from the Pechora route this was the chief way of entrance into Siberia for traders and promyshlenniks, as well as being the official route along which the state conducted the advance into Siberia. Sixteen hundred and fifty men passed through Verkhoturie in 1636 on their way to hunt and trade in Siberia, and 870 men in 1637. However, towards the end of the century an increasing number of persons used this way also for the return trip to Russia, though their numbers by no means equaled the number of eastbound travelers.[80]

The third and fourth important routes were the two trans-Siberian routes. Their importance derived from being the trunk lines along which was maintained communication between the ever-eastward-advancing centers of the fur trade in Siberia and the Russian markets. Over the northern route, the older of the two, the Russian enterprisers pushed through its principal point, Mangazeia, into the fur regions of the lower Enisei and lower Lena, 500 to 1,000 men passing through Mangazeia yearly in each direction.[81] But after the establishment of Iakutsk Mangazeia could not compete with it for control of the lower Lena country and northeastern Siberia, and although Iakutsk could be reached over the northern route, this route possessed the disadvantage of a dangerous and uncertain passage through the Ob Gulf and Taz Gulf. Iakutsk was more easily reached by the southern route. With the decline in fur resources around Mangazeia and in the lower Enisei basin the northern route lost much of its importance after the middle of the century. Indeed, the state abandoned the Sob-Mangazeia sea route in the 'sixties because it was too dangerous, and thereafter its employees traveled to Mangazeia via the Einsei.[82] The southern route, on the other hand, remained important not only throughout the century, but well into modern times. It had the advantage of being the natural extension of the Kama route and with it became the state's official route across Siberia. It also passed through more habitable country and was the most direct route not only to Iakutsk, but to the Amur Valley as well.[83]

---

[79] Bakhrushin, *Ocherki*, pp. 61, 63, 68, 76, 78–80; Titov, p. 20.
[80] Bakhrushin, *Ocherki*, pp. 105–106; Platonov, *op. cit.*, p. 13.
[81] Bakhrushin, *Ocherki*, p. 120; Butsinskii, *Mangazeia*, p. 51.
[82] Bakhrushin, *Ocherki*, pp. 114–115, 122–123, 127.
[83] *Ibid.*, p. 110; *D.A.I.*, II, 170.

The other two outstanding routes were the Ob-Irtysh River from Tobolsk to its mouth and the Vologda-Sukhona-Dvina route between Moscow and Arkhangelsk. The fact that the Pechora and Kama routes tended to be one-way made the Ob-Irtysh important as the connecting link for those entering Siberia at Verkhoturie and destined for Mangazeia and for those returning along the southern route and desiring to pass into Russia via the Pechora. Until the 'sixties the Ob-Irtysh was the official route to Mangazeia.[84] The Vologda-Sukhona-Dvina route gained its importance from the fact that most of Russia's trade with Western Europe moved over it.

Several of the less important routes deserve brief notice. The sea passage from Arkhangelsk to Mangazeia was considerably traveled until its closure, despite the dangers from ice and the long delays caused by adverse weather. As many as 160 or 170 men a year went to Mangazeia by this way.[85] The northern branch of the Pechora route was traveled chiefly by enterprisers from the towns situated along it, though sometimes men returning from Siberia preferred it to the Vychegda branch because it passed through fewer uninhabited regions.[86] The Cherdyn crossing of the Urals was the first official route into Siberia, until the building of the Solikamsk-Verkhoturie route in 1596 and 1597; thereafter it was used chiefly by Permians.[87] In the second half of the seventeenth century the Ufa route, long traversed by caravans between Kazan and Central Asia, and a variant route through Kungus were traveled increasingly by traders and promyshlenniks from towns all along the Volga, despite Moscow's prohibition against its use. This travel, in turn, increased the importance of the Volga route to Siberia. The importance of both these routes attached to the fur trade in the Volga towns rather than to that between Siberia and northern Russia.[88] In northeastern Siberia the sea route, stormy and dangerous, and the overland route through wild and desolate country seem to have been equally used.[89] Of the two routes from Iakutsk to the Amur the Olekma was the more traveled, whereas traffic to and from the Amur appears to have passed equally from Iakutsk and from Lake Baikal.[90]

[84] Bakhrushin, *Ocherki*, pp. 62, 76, 120.

[85] *Ibid.*, pp. 80, 83–84; *R.I.B.*, II, 1051, 1062, 1070, 1072, 1084, 1087–1088, 1092; Purchas, XIII, 204, 208, 226.

[86] Bakhrushin, *Ocherki*, p. 63.

[87] *Ibid.*, pp. 89–90; *R.I.B.*, II, 142–144.

[88] *A.I.*, V, 90, 304, 455; *D.A.I.*, VIII, 287; Bakhrushin, *Ocherki*, pp. 107–109.

[89] *D.A.I.*, III, 276, 277, 280, V, 336; Bakhrushin, *Ocherki*, pp. 128–131.

[90] *D.A.I.*, IV, 85–86, VIII, 59–60; Bakhrushin, *Ocherki*, p. 134.

Several routes gained use because they made it possible for traders and promyshlenniks to avoid vexatious customs delays and fees. This was one of the attractions which offset the dangers of the ocean route from Arkhangelsk to Mangazeia. It was the advantage of the Berezov route across the Urals until a customs barrier was erected above Berezov on the Sosva River. Thereafter this route was particularly suited to travelers between the northern maritime towns in Russia and Surgut and Tobolsk.[91] The advantage of customs evasion obtained in connection with the Ufa and Chusovaia routes, on which barriers were not erected until the middle of the century, and even then a choice of several roads across the Ufa steppes allowed the continuance of such evasion.[92] For enterprisers operating on the Stony Tunguska River and the lower Enisei the Vakh River afforded both a shorter route from the Ob to the Enisei and the absence of customs barriers along it.[93] Lastly, the Chichuisk crossing long attracted travelers because it permitted them to go from the Olekma to Turukhansk without any customs stops.[94]

Trade Centers

The private trade in furs concentrated itself in the towns of northern Russia. The opening in the middle of the sixteenth century of the White Sea route to Europe, to which most of Russia's furs went, brought a shift of the center of gravity of the private fur trade from Moscow and Novgorod to the towns of the north, where it remained throughout the seventeenth century. Furs were traded in other parts of Russia, in the towns of the Volga basin and at points along the southern and western frontiers of Russia—sometimes in considerable numbers—but most Siberian furs passed directly to the northern trade centers, from which they were sent to Arkhangelsk and abroad or distributed to the various trade centers of central and western Russia.

The foremost internal centers of the private fur trade in the seventeenth century were Ustiug and Solvychegodsk. Both these towns, first Ustiug and then Solvychegodsk, overtook and passed Moscow and Kholmogory as the foremost centers of the private trade. When Russia's trade with the West shifted from Moscow and Novgorod to the mouth of the Dvina and when the Russians

[91] *R.I.B.*, II, 1071, 1073; Bakhrushin, *Ocherki*, pp. 74, 77.

[92] *A.I.*, IV, 284, V, 90; *D.A.I.*, VIII, 259; Bakhrushin, *Ocherki*, pp. 101, 108–109; Kostomarov, p. 303.

[93] Bukhrushin, *Ocherki*, pp. 112–114; Titov, p. 36.

[94] Bakhrushin, *Ocherki* p. 128; *D.A.I.*, VIII, 59–60.

SIBERIA
NOVAIA ZEMLIA
KARA SEA
BAY OF MEZEN
Mezen
Lampozhnia
Pustozersk
Ust-Tsilma
Ust-Izhma
Izhma R.
Pechora
Usa
Rogovyi gorodok
Sob
Obdorsk
IUGORSKII STRAITS
IAL-MAL PEN.
OB GULF
TAZ GULF
MANGAZEIA
Taz
Enisei R.
Turukhansk
Lower Tunguska R.
Stony Tunguska R.
Upper Tunguska R.
Eniseisk
Kheta
Khatanga
Kotuikan
Moiero
Olenek
Zhigansk
Lena R.
Lana R.
Viliui R.
IAKUTSK
Olekma R.
Vitim R.
Chona
Chichuisk
Lena Portage
Ilimsk
Bratsk
Makovsk
Ket R.
Ketsk
Narym
Sym R.
Tym R.
Vakh R.
Ob R.
Surgut
Berezov
Sygva R.
Sosva R.
Shchuga R.
Konda R.
Vishera R.
Vishera
Koma R.
Cherdyn
Losva
Solikamsk
Pelym R.
Pelym
Lozva
Verkhoturie
Tavda R.
Turinsk
Tura
Tagil R.
Chusovaia R.
Irbit
Perm
Tiumen
TOBOLSK
Tobol
Irtysh R.
Tara
Tomsk
VYCHEGODSK
Iarensk
Vym R.
Mezen
Pera R.

opened the southern route into Siberia, Ustiug became the chief beneficiary of the greatly intensified traffic in furs which followed. The shift to Ustiug, noticeable as early as the 1570's, became inevitable with the loss of Narva in 1581 and was completed by the second quarter of the seventeenth century.[95]

Ustiug and Solvychegodsk both derived their importance mainly from the Siberian trade, and many of their merchants devoted themselves exclusively to it. Most of the furs brought out of Siberia came to these towns, to which were added a modest number of inferior pelts from Perm, Solikamsk, the northern maritime towns, and the Viatka River towns.[96] In both towns a large number of furs were sold in wholesale lots to merchants and traders who came to them from all over Russia and who exchanged for furs goods, some of which were then sent to Siberia. But the larger number of furs were not sold in Ustiug and Solvychegodsk; instead they were held there in storage and later sent to other fur markets in Russia. Both towns were also centers for a residual local fur trade.[97] Their eminence as the great entrepôts of the Siberian fur trade they owed to their geographical position near the junction of the heavily traveled Vychegda route to Siberia with the Sukhona-Dvina route; on the latter they stood midway between Arkhangelsk and Moscow. They naturally became the focal points for the trade between Siberia and these two other major trade centers.[98] During the first half of the seventeenth century Ustiug was a much bigger center than Solvychegodsk. In 1634 it stood seventh among Russian towns in economic importance, whereas Solvychegodsk ranked eighteenth. After the middle of the century, however, Solvychegodsk assumed first place among domestic fur centers, Ustiug's fur trade dropping off as other lesser centers of the trade arose.[99]

---

[95] Bazilevich, "Torgovlia velikogo Ustiuga," p. 89; A. A. Vvedenski, *Torgovyi dom, XVI–XVII vekov*, p. 92; cf. Makarov, p. 201, and E. D. Stashevskii, "Piatina 142-go goda i torgovo-promyshlennye tsentry moskovskago gosudarstva," *Zh.M.N.P.*, n.s., Vol. XXXIX (1912), May, pp. 99, 102.

[96] Bazilevich, "Torgovlia velikogo Ustiuga," pp. 90, 92, 94.

[97] Platonov, *op. cit.*, pp. 13–14; Bakhrushin, *Ocherki*, pp. 68, 189, cf. p. 79; Bazilevich, "Tamozhennye knigi," p. 124; *idem*, "Torgovlia velikogo Ustiuga," pp. 92, 95; Stashevskii, p. 102.

[98] Johann de Rodes, "Bedenken über den russischen Handel im Jahre 1653," *Beiträge zur Kenntniss Russlands und seiner Geschichte*, p. 256; Stashevskii, *loc. cit.;* Bazilevich, "Krupnoe torgovoe predpriiatie," pp. 789–793; Bazilevich, "Tamozhennye knigi," p. 114; Müller, *op. cit.*, pp. 417, 420.

[99] Stashevskii, pp. 99, 102; Bazilevich, "Torgovlia velikogo Ustiuga," pp. 91, 92. It should be noted that the sable trade at Ustiug was very uneven. From 1642 to 1647 the annual turnover fluctuated between 16,974 skins (20,550 r.) and 5,531 (6,000 r.). Bazilevich, "Torgovlia velikago Ustiuga," p. 91.

Furs which entered the north from Siberia and which did not go to Ustiug or Solvychegodsk went to the maritime towns, particularly to Kholmogory. These towns, Kholmogory, Pinega, Mezen, the Lampozhnia markets, Pustozersk, and its Pechora suburbs, Ust-Tsilma and Ust-Izhma, were among the principal centers of the fur trade during the sixteenth century, for they were located on the northern branch of the Pechora route, which was virtually the sole channel for Siberian furs until the opening of the Kama route.[100] They continued to be active centers of the fur trade up to 1620; thereafter they occupied a less prominent place in the trade.

Numerous Samoeds from Russian and Siberian Iugra, as many as two or three thousand, visited Pustozersk each winter with sables and other furs which they had trapped or traded from the Mangazeia Samoeds. Some of them also traveled the six hundred-odd miles farther west to Mezen and the Lampozhnia fairs with their pelts.[101] At the same time many traders and promyshlenniks from these towns journeyed to Siberia for furs, some by sea or the Sob barrier to Mangazeia, others by way of Berezov to Tobolsk, Surgut, and other Ob towns.[102] Each year flotillas of as many as twenty-five or thirty *kóchas,* flat-bottomed sailboats built with a deck and carrying a maximum of ten men and around twelve thousand pounds, assembled at Kholmogory and set out for Mangazeia by sea.[103] Some time prior to 1607 traders from Pustozersk began gathering at a trade station near the Kamen portage, a place called Rogovyi *gorodok,* where they engaged in a brisk trade with the Samoeds, quite free of customs supervision. This station was in use as late as 1615.[104] Meanwhile, traders from Kholmogory and other Russian towns came to the maritime centers and bought furs, most of which they carried to Kholmogory for sale to the foreigners in the summer.[105] But the year 1620 brought the closing of the sea route to the Ob Gulf, and with the loss of their unique advantage

[100] Kostomarov, p. 272; V. O. Kliuchevskii, *Skazanii inostrantsev o moskovskom gosudarstve,* p. 256; Heinrich von Staden, *Aufzeichnungen über den moskauer Staat,* p. 213; Bakhrushin, *Ocherki,* p. 62; Richard Hakluyt, *The Principal Navigations,* I, 286.

[101] Purchas, XIII, 193, 213, 224, 227, 236, 237; Joseph von Hamel, *England and Russia,* pp. 120–122; Bakhrushin, *Ocherki,* pp. 72–73, 74.

[102] *A.I.,* II, 27–28; *R.I.B.,* II, 1071, 1073, 1083, 1085, 1087; Butsinskii, *Mangazeia,* p. 42; Bakhrushin, *Ocherki,* pp. 72, 74, 84; Hakluyt, *loc. cit.*

[103] *R.I.B.,* II, 1051, 1062, 1088, 1092; Purchas, XIII, 202, 207, 226; Bakhrushin, *Ocherki,* p. 80.

[104] *R.I.B.,* II, 166–167; Purchas, XIII, 227; Bakhrushin, *Ocherki,* 71–72, 73.

[105] Purchas, XIII, 213; Bakhrushin, *Ocherki,* p. 62.

these towns lost much of their importance in the fur trade.[106] Thereafter, deprived of its sea trade with Mangazeia and displaced by Arkhangelsk as the site of the trade with the foreigners, Kholmogory could not compete with Ustiug and Solvychegodsk, which benefited far more than it did by the unrestricted access to Siberia made possible through the opening of the southern Kama route. The great fur center of the sixteenth century became a secondary entrepôt in the fur trade of the seventeenth century. Mezen and Lampozhnia, after 1600, merged into one town, the fairs of the latter being transferred to Okladnikov suburb near old Mezen, and there a new Mezen arose.[107] Pustozersk and its outlying suburbs, Ust-Tsilma and Ust-Izhma, grew but little after 1620. They functioned as frontier stations where furs could be bought from visiting Samoeds or from residents who brought them from Siberia.[108]

Several other centers existed in the north. One was the annual market in March at Blagoveshchensk monastery on the Vaga River, to which many merchants from various towns came and carried on an active exchange of goods. Large numbers of furs were sent there from Ustiug and Solvychegodsk, usually far more than could be sold. The attraction of this market appears to have been the fact that it opened several months before the one at Arkhangelsk. It was particularly important for those traders who wished to obtain goods, especially goods of peasant manufacture, for trade in Siberia, and for promyshlenniks in need of hunting equipment and supplies.[109] Another center was Kargopol, near Lake Lakh, west of the Dvina. Furs were traded here, but how great the trade in them was and whether furs of Siberian or local origin predominated are not clearly indicated by the sources.[110] Two others were Cherdyn and Solikamsk. They were frontier stations on the Kama route, where a small number of furs were bought and sold.[111] Trade in Siberian furs also arose in the seventeenth century at Turinsk settlement on the Vym River and at Iarensk and Tuglima on the Vychegda River.[112]

[106] Cf. Butsinskii, *Mangazeia*, p. 40.
[107] Platonov, *op. cit.*, p. 10; Von Hamel, pp. 316–317.
[108] Bakhrushin, *Ocherki*, pp. 69, 71–72, 73, 75; *D.A.I.*, III, 83, 86, IV, 341–344.
[109] Bazilevich, "Torgovlia velikogo Ustiuga," pp. 95, 96; *idem*, "Krupnoe torgovoe predpriiatie," pp. 790, 793, 795.
[110] *Sobranie gosudarstvennykh gramot i dogovorov*, II, 139; Butsinskii, *Mangazeia*, p. 42.
[111] Stashevskii, p. 104.
[112] Bazilevich, "Torgovlia velikogo Ustiuga," p. 91.

The furs which entered the north went in greatest part to satisfy the foreign demand; a much smaller number of them were sold to the inhabitants of the north. The rest were sent to the great trade centers of central Russia for sale. Such centers were Totma, Vologda, and Iaroslavl on the route between Ustiug and Moscow; Nizhnii Novgorod, Markariev, and Kazan on the upper Volga; Viatka, Perm, and, of course, Moscow. Many of the furs, perhaps most of them, which were traded in these towns came from Ustiug and Solvychegdosk, but these towns also received furs directly from Siberia, for we find their merchants and promyshlenniks operating in Siberia along with those from the northern towns, albeit in fewer numbers.[113] Totma, the first large town on the road south from Ustiug, provided a market for the sale of a considerable number of furs during the second and third quarters of the seventeenth century.[114] Vologda was the great transit center between the interior of Russia and Arkhangelsk; all fur traders from the north passed through it on their way south. It served both as a secondary entrepôt for Siberian furs, many of its merchants bringing them from Ustiug and Solvychegodsk, and as the principal market for pelts acquired in Russia (Russian pelts were inferior to Siberian pelts and therefore not in demand abroad); and it functioned also as a major center for purchasing goods for the Siberian trade.[115] Iaroslavl was an even greater transit point and entrepôt than Vologda, for it stood at the crossing of the north-south route from the White Sea with the east-west route of the upper Volga. Many furs were bought and sold here. For the Siberian trade it was highly important as a place to buy Russian goods, especially leather and peasant goods. No large shipment went to Siberia without Iaroslavl goods.[116]

The foremost of the Volga trade centers were Kazan and Nizhnii Novgorod, which ranked in 1634 as the second and fourth wealth-

---

[113] *A.I.*, III, 327; Ogloblin, II, 49, 52, 104, III, 152; Butsinskii, *Mangazeia*, p. 42; Bazilevich, "Torgovlia velikogo Ustiuga," p. 97; Bakhrushin, "Agenty russkikh torgovykh liudei," p. 75.

[114] Kostomarov, p. 281; *D.A.I.*, III, 105–106.

[115] Bazilevich, "Tamozhennye knigi," p. 123; *idem*, "Krupnoe torgovoe predpriiatie," pp. 790, 793; De Rodes, pp. 241, 256; Von Staden, pp. 142–143; Kostomarov, pp. 282–283; Platonov, *op. cit.*, p. 27; Kliuchevskii, *Skazaniia inostrantsev*, p. 255; Stashevskii, p. 102.

[116] Bazilevich, "Tamozhennye knigi," pp. 118, 123; *idem*, "Krupnoe torgovoe predpriiatie," pp. 789, 790, 793, 795–796; *idem*, "Torgovlia velikogo Ustiuga," p. 96; G. D. Khilkov, *Sbornik kniazia Khilkova*, p. 182; Stashevskii, p. 100; Kostomarov, p. 284; Platonov, *op. cit.*, pp. 28–29.

iest towns in the Muscovite state.[117] They were the transit and storage points for goods to and from eastern Russia, Siberia, and Astrakhan at the mouth of the Volga. They afforded markets for furs sent from Ustiug and Solvychegodsk on the one hand, and were entrepôts for the furs entering Russia over the Volga route on the other. The country around Kazan still yielded in the seventeenth century a number of medium-quality furs other than sables and some fine martens, so Kazan continued to serve as the site of a local fur trade of some dimensions. Most of the Asiatic goods sent to Siberia were acquired in Kazan and Nizhnii Novgorod.[118]

Not far down the Volga from Nizhnii Novgorod, at Makariev, stood the monastery of St. Makarii Zheltovodskii, which held from the tsar the privilege of holding an annual fair in July. This fair was visited by merchants from all parts of Russia and from Siberia. Furs were included among the goods traded. One year the tsar's merchants bought ten thousand rubles' worth of furs there.[119] At Viatka and Perm the trade in furs was a moderate one. Fur traders visited them in fewer numbers and less regularly than the other Volga towns. Nevertheless, traders from these towns were among those who traveled to Siberia for furs, and Perm and Viatka goods are mentioned in the Siberian customs books.[120]

Although Moscow yielded in the seventeenth century to Ustiug as the foremost center of the private fur trade, it retained importance for the private trade, since it continued to be the first town in Russia commercially as well as politically. Many traders and promyshlenniks came from Siberia directly to Moscow to dispose of their furs. The serving men who accompanied the sable treasuries from Siberia usually sold their furs in Moscow; and merchants at Ustiug and Solvychegodsk usually sent shipments of furs to the capital. Goods, both Russian and foreign (from the east), were purchased here for the Siberian trade. Most of the big fur merchants kept offices in Moscow, for Russian capital tended to concentrate itself there and the tsar often called them for the performance of various services. However, the fact that Moscow was

---

[117] Stashevskii, p. 99.

[118] Bazilevich, "Torgovlia velikogo Ustiuga," pp. 94, 99; *idem*, "Krupnoe torgovoe predpriiatie," pp. 790, 793, 796–797; De Rodes, p. 251; Giles Fletcher, *Russia at the Close of the Sixteenth Century*, p. 9; Kostomarov, p. 295; Stashevskii, pp. 100–101; Kliuchevskii, *Skazaniia inostrantsev*, p. 295.

[119] Kostomarov, pp. 295–296; Ogloblin, II, 52, IV, 75.

[120] Bazilevich, "Tamozhennye knigi," p. 119; *idem*, "Krupnoe torgovoe predpriiatie," pp. 790, 796, 797; Butsinskii, *Mangazeia*, p. 42; *R.I.B.*, II, 142–144; Ogloblin, II, 49; Purchas, XIII, 207; Stashevskii, p. 101.

the center of the tsar's fur trade placed those who would trade there on a large scale at a disadvantage not found in other towns.[121]

Since Siberia was given over primarily to the fur trade, in nearly every kind of settlement—blockhouse, suburb, ostrog, and town—trade in furs was carried on at some time or other.[122] The towns and ostrogs built by the state were, naturally, the more important centers, and of them more were to be found in Western Siberia than in other parts of Siberia because it was older and more settled. Outstanding trade centers, however, were few, even late in the seventeenth century, there being not more one or two in each major section of the century. It is to these few principally that we give our attention.

Two of the outstanding trade centers were in Western Siberia, namely Mangazeia and Tobolsk. Of the two, Mangazeia enjoyed much the more spectacular, but a short-lived, prosperity, for it was in all respects a boom town, which arose with the advance of the Russians into northern Siberia and declined when the fur resources gave out. It gained importance first as the center for the rich area around the Taz Gulf and river, and then, when the supply of fur-bearing animals in that area was depleted, Mangazeia retained its importance because of its position as the point of entry into the rich hinterland constituted by the lower Enisei, the Lower Tunguska, and the Viliui rivers.[123] Mangazeia had the reputation of yielding the finest sables in Siberia.[124] The men, five hundred to a thousand of them, who traveled yearly over the northern route passed through it, and most of them wintered in the town or made it their temporary headquarters. Traders from Russia came here to buy furs, and promyshlenniks from the forest to sell them.[125] So great was the traffic through Mangazeia that the state collected annually for its tithe furs worth ten, twelve, fifteen, and even seventeen thousand rubles.[126] Such receipts meant that through Mangazeia alone private enterprisers took out more furs than did the state out of all Siberia. But, dependent upon an increasingly distant hinterland, the town was doomed when a new center was

[121] Bazilevich, "Krupnoe torgovoe predpriiatie," pp. 793, 797; De Rodes, p. 256; Stashevskii, pp. 99–100; Kostomarov, p. 284; Bakhrushin, "Agenty russkikh torgovykh liudei," p. 75; Bakhrushin, "Torgi gostia Nikitina," p. 374.

[122] *D.A.I.*, III, 40, 336, IV, 49–50, 208, 210; Ogloblin, I, 104, II, 43–44.

[123] Butsinskii, *Mangazeia*, p. 51; Bakhrushin, *Ocherki*, p. 120.

[124] Purchas, XIII, 220, 227.

[125] Butsinskii, *Mangazeia*, pp. 16–17; Purchas, XIII, 249–250; Bazilevich, "Krupnoe torgovoe predpriiatie," p. 792.

[126] Butsinskii, *Mangazeia*, p. 49.

created in that hinterland. In 1646 the tithe receipts dropped to five thousand rubles, and from then on Mangazeia, though still important, ceased to be a leading center of the fur trade. Tobolsk, on the other hand, was not a boom town. It experienced a steady and healthy growth which made it the most important town in Siberia during the seventeenth century.[127] Its rise was due to its position as the chief administrative center of Siberia and to its location on the southern route at the juncture of the Tobol and Irtysh rivers. In its earlier years many fine pelts—sables, squirrels, black foxes, wolverines, and beavers—were sold there, but in later years it was only the cheaper kinds of martens, beavers, and foxes which were available.[128] As the center of gravity of the trade advanced to the east, Tobolsk acquired increasing significance as a general trade center.[129]

A third major trade center was Eniseisk, together with the adjacent Makovskii ostrog or Makovsk. Eniseisk was the place from which most of the promyshlenniks and traders who went into the regions of the Stony Tunguska and Angara rivers and Lake Baikal operated. Many townsmen, promyshlenniks, and migrants were to be found in the town. Here many hunting expeditions were organized; here many traders from Russia came to purchase the furs acquired by such expeditions.[130] Makovsk, which lay but a short distance west of Eniseisk, acquired importance from the fact that the portage from the Ket river to the Enisei began there. It became for those arriving late in the fall a suitable wintering point, from which they could transport their goods to Eniseisk at their convenience. About a third of a mile from the ostrog a settlement of traders arose where shops, storehouses, and boat-building facilities were maintained, especially by the big merchants.[131]

Two other places complete the list of outstanding centers. These were the Lena portage and Iakutsk. At the Lena portage, which was the vital link between the Lena and Angara river systems, an active center of the fur trade developed. Here many trading and hunting expeditions to the east were organized. Here the natives and the Russian inhabitants of the region came to dispose of their furs and to buy Russian and foreign goods. Storehouses and shops

[127] Kostomarov, p. 304.

[128] Purchas, XIII, 232; Bazilevich, "Tamozhennye knigi," p. 115.

[129] Kostomarov, *loc. cit.;* Purchas, *loc. cit.*, Ianitskii, p. 6.

[130] Bazilevich, "Tamozhennye knigi," p. 115; Spafarii, *op. cit.*, p. 87; Bakhrushin, "Torgi gostia Nikitina," p. 372.

[131] Bakhrushin, *Ocherki*, p. 111; Spafarii, *op. cit.*, p. 84.

were erected near the portage and boat-building facilities at its eastern end. Furthermore, a number of enterprisers made it their terminal point where they transacted their trade and returned to Russia without continuing on to Iakutsk.[132] The greater center, however, was Iakutsk. Its central geographical situation in Eastern Siberia made it a natural gathering place for enterprisers of all sorts, whereas the sparseness of settlement in that part of Siberia left it almost the only settlement of any size there. Persons bound for northeastern Siberia and for the Sea of Okhotsk passed through Iakutsk, as did many of those going to the Amur. After great inroads had been made into the fur supply in Western Siberia, Eastern Siberia, especially along the Lena, Vitim, Indigirka, and Kolyma rivers, became the place where, after the middle of the seventeenth century, the best sables could be found. For this reason large-scale enterprisers who operated throughout Siberia organized hunting expeditions only in Eastern Siberia and confined their activities in Western Siberia to trade. Many traveling enterprisers were willing to undergo the long journey and the greater hardships of life on the far-eastern frontier for the sake of the greater profits from the best sables. Thus Iakutsk became a flourishing center where expeditions to the "best sable places" were organized and where the finest sables could be bought.[133] Little is known of the value of the furs taken by private enterprisers through Iakutsk, but it must have been as great or greater than through Mangazeia.[134]

Of the lesser trade centers in Siberia several may be mentioned briefly. Verkhoturie, Berezov, and the Sob-Obdorsk barriers stand out less as fur centers than as the points of ingress and egress from Siberia, although at Berezov and the Sob barrier an exceptionally brisk trade in furs was carried on in the earlier years.[135] During the first decade or two of the conquest Tiumen rivaled Tobolsk as a trade center. It continued active through the seventeenth century, acquiring importance from the fact that the road to Irbit and Ufa branched off there.[136] Irbit, situated about one hundred and sixty

[132] Bakhrushin, *Ocherki*, pp. 125–126; *idem*, "Torgi gostia Nikitina," pp. 372–373; *D.A.I.*, II, 154, 158, 160, 253; Kostomarov, p. 305.

[133] Bazilevich, "Tamozhennye knigi," p. 115; *idem*, "Krupnoe torgovoe predpriiatie," p. 792; Spafarii, *op. cit.*, pp. 134, 137; Ianitskii, p. 6; Ogloblin, II, 18.

[134] See below, pp. 179–180.

[135] Bakhrushin, *Ocherki*, pp. 76–79, 104, 107; Bazilevich, "Tamozhennye knigi," p. 115; Butsinskii, *Zaselenie Sibiri*, pp. 176–180; Potanin, *op. cit.*, pp. 125, 133; Ianitskii, *loc. cit.*; Kostomarov, p. 304.

[136] Bazilevich, "Tamozhennye knigi," p. 115; Ianitskii, p. 5; *A.I.*, V, 305; Titov, pp. 27, 42–43.

miles southeast of Verkhoturie, within whose jurisdiction it lay, became the site of an active market, which grew rapidly and remained important down to recent times. Held by right of a charter granted by the tsar in 1643, the Irbit market, by the end of the century, became a principal place for the purchase of grain and all goods in general that entered Siberia, and in exchange for them furs were often given. Many traders and promyshlenniks were attracted there by the lax enforcement of the customs regulations.[137] In Eastern Siberia Irkutsk developed late in the century into a center of significance, as did Nerchinsk, the growth of which was due to the export trade to China.[138] Tomsk, Surgut, Narym, Tara, and Kuznetsk in Western Siberia, Krasnoiarsk, Bratsk, Barguzin, Verkholensk, Zhigansk, and Okhotsk in Eastern Siberia were the remaining centers of lesser importance.[139]

Trade Movements

The cycle by which furs were acquired in Siberia, brought to Russia, and there sold was one requiring from two to six years to complete. The initial and final phases of the cycle occurred in Russia. The one overlapping the other, they occupied altogether about a year's time. The intermediate phase took place in Siberia and required variously from one to four or five years. One who invested capital in the Siberian fur trade, therefore, frequently waited a long time before realizing upon his investment. Although the following description of the cycle applies particularly to the activities of the merchant-capitalists, it is representative of the fur trade as a whole. It was often the boats of the capitalists which gave the smaller enterprisers means of transport, it was their capital which made possible many hunting expeditions, and it was their large-scale operations which most influenced market conditions.

The beginning of the cycle in Russia took place during the winter months. In the fall, after the close of the Arkhangelsk market, enterprisers assembled their goods preparatory to departure for Siberia. Some merchants sent as many as forty, fifty, sixty, some-

[137] Kostomarov, *loc. cit.; A.I.*, V, 125–126; Ogloblin, II, 28, 59; Kh. Trusevich, *Posol'skiia i torgovyia snosheniia Rossii s Kitaem*, p. 70; Müller "Nachrichten von der Handlung in Sibirien," *Sammlung russischer Geschichte*, III, 430; Bakhrushin, "Torgi gostia Nikitina," p. 373.

[138] Ianitskii, p. 6; cf. Trusevich, p. 73.

[139] Bazilevich, "Tamozhennye knigi," p. 115; *idem*, "Krupnoe torgovoe predpriiatie," p. 790; Potanin, *op. cit.*, pp. 125–141; *D.A.I.*, III, 40, IV, 208–211.

times seventy horses or cartloads to Siberia with goods.[140] Departures were timed so as to reach Verkhoturie for the opening of the navigation season there, which occurred late in March or early in April.[141] Winter travel to Verkhoturie over the snow was rapid, and the 1200-mile journey from Moscow to this Ural town required only three to five weeks.[142] Similarly, those who entered Siberia at Sob customs barrier or Berezov sought to reach there in time for an early departure eastward.[143]

At Verkhoturie, as at Sob and Kirtas barriers, each man declared his goods and paid customs on them, for Siberia was considered by Moscow as separate from Russia for customs purposes.[144] Supplies were replenished, sometimes pokruchenniks hired, and at Verkhoturie the transfer to boats was made. The river boats commonly used were called *doshchaníks.* They were flat-bottomed, up to fifty feet in length, and equipped with both oars and sails. The largest of them carried fifty men with provisions and goods.[145] For sailing to Mangazeia, *kochas,* decked boats quite similar to doshchaniks, were used. The change from river to ocean boats was made at Sob and Obdorsk barriers.[146] Since a majority of enterprisers did not own their own boats, they arranged to travel with those who did, though occasionally a group would arrange to rent state boats from the Siberian authorities.[147] For the sake of protection and mutual assistance it was customary for groups of boats to travel together as caravans.[148] From Verkhoturie enterprisers descended the Tura and Tobol rivers to Tobolsk, whence they proceeded to their several destinations.

The length of time necessary to complete the Siberian phase of the cycle depended chiefly upon the distance traveled, but somewhat also upon whether or not hunting as well as trade was undertaken. Distances in Siberia were great, and travel was slow, for, although the Siberian rivers afforded natural highways, they were not always the most direct routes, and travel upstream and across

---

140 Bazilevich, "Krupnoe torgovoe predpriiatie," p. 789; *idem,* "Torgovlia velikogo Ustiuga," p. 100; Bakhrushin, "Torgi gostia Nikitina," p. 371; Makarov, pp. 203–204.

141 Bakhrushin, *Ocherki,* pp. 104, 106.

142 *Ibid.,* p. 104; Titov, p. 11; Müller, *op. cit.,* p. 417.

143 Cf. *R.I.B.,* II, 1068–1069, and Bakhrushin, *Ocherki,* pp. 76, 79.

144 *A.A.E.,* IV, 441–442.

145 Kostomarov, p. 304; J. F. Baddeley, *Russia, Mongolia, China,* II, 346 n. 4; *D.A.I.,* VIII, 7; Ogloblin, II, 24.

146 Bakhrushin, *Ocherki,* pp. 76, 116–117.

147 Ogloblin, II, 32–33, 34, 104–105.

148 Bakhrushin, *Ocherki,* pp. 76, 114–115; Potanin, *op. cit.,* p. 129.

portages often took much time. Overland travel was in many instances faster and more direct, especially in winter on the snow, but such travel was feasible only for short journeys, since no extensive post system existed and the cost to an individual, or even to a group, of long journeys by horse and cart or sledge was prohibitive. Inasmuch as travel in Siberia went oftenest by rivers, it was governed by their navigable seasons, which for most of them was half a year or less, during the warmer months. This in turn meant that long journeys had to be broken by several months of partial or entire inactivity at wintering points, a circumstance adding greatly to the time of travel.

The time spent in travel on the rivers varied with conditions, with the weather, with the season—high spring or low autumn waters—with impediments to navigation such as rapids, cascades, adverse winds, or floating ice. However, the time normally taken in travel between given points remained within fairly definite limits. Travelers entering Siberia at Verkhoturie reached Tobolsk, four hundred miles down the river, in two weeks or less; the return trip they made in two and a half to four weeks.[149] From Tobolsk, those going to Tara took two to four weeks, to Sob or Obdorsk barrier a little over two weeks.[150] Much longer was the journey eastward from Tobolsk to Makovsk and Eniseisk (1,300 miles), which required from three to four months, and the trip from Tobolsk to Tomsk, which consumed two and a half months' time.[151] The voyage to Mangazeia, because of the unreliable winds in the Ob and Taz gulfs, varied greatly. Leaving Tobolsk in mid-July, with favoring winds one might reach Mangazeia in late September, but with adverse winds not until November or even January.[152] From Mangazeia to Eniseisk, a distance of six hundred miles, was a two months' trip, and from Mangazeia to Iakutsk via the Lower Tunguska and Viliui rivers a four or four and a half months' trip.[153] To travel from Eniseisk to the Amur took five months or more, the distance from Eniseisk to Nerchinsk being about sixteen hundred miles.[154] The journey from Eniseisk to Ilimsk required two and a

[149] Titov, pp. 9–10, 12, 13–14; Müller, *op. cit.*, p. 417.

[150] Titov, pp. 14, 15, 19–20, 44, 50–51; Spafarii, *op. cit.*, p. 168.

[151] Titov, pp. 16–17, 30, 46–47, 81; Bakhrushin, *Ocherki*, pp. 111–112; Trusevich, p. 72.

[152] Bakhrushin, *Ocherki*, pp. 116, 118–120; Butsinskii, *Mangazeia*, p. 29.

[153] Titov, pp. 21, 35, 37, 51; *R.I.B.*, II, 963, 1050; Müller, p. 453.

[154] Titov, pp. 30–31, 47–48, 82, 106; Spafarii, *op. cit.*, pp. 101, 112, 115–119, 122, 123, 127, 138–140; *D.A.I.*, III, 344; Müller, *op. cit.*, pp. 452–453, 459, 466.

half to three and a half months; the crossing of the Lena portage was a matter of a few days, and the descent of the Lena to Iakutsk of two weeks or more.[155] From Iakutsk, one could reach the Kolyma River (980 miles) in three or three and a half months.[156] Less is known of the time required for the return trips to Russia. It would appear, however, not to differ greatly from the time spent in eastward travel. What was upstream travel eastward became downstream westward.[157] Returning over the Pechora route, traders and promyshlenniks passed from Sob barrier to Solvychegodsk, a distance of two thousand miles, in three months.[158]

Besides the time spent in travel itself, additional time was taken by customs stops, the organization of travel groups and boat caravans, and, of course, the acquisition of furs. Those who limited themselves to trade could, with conditions favorable, finish their trade and begin the return journey within the same season that they arrived at their destination. However, many traders passed several months in trade at a given point, and many of them traded in more than one town or ostrog. Those who joined hunting expeditions had to allow for the intervening winter hunting season between the times of arrival and departure. Under these circumstances, the trip from Russia to the towns of Western Siberia required two navigation seasons and an intervening winter, though if haste were necessary, the journey to the nearer towns, those on the lower Ob and Irtysh and its tributaries, and back might be made in one navigation season. Thus, for instance, boat caravans formed at Tobolsk and Berezov and made the ten weeks' voyage to Tomsk, arriving there in September or October. There the members of the caravan remained over the winter, exchanging goods for furs, and departed early the following summer.[159] Traders going to Mangazeia for trade followed a similar schedule.[160] From the southern towns of Western Siberia, even from as far as Tomsk,

[155] *D.A.I.*, II, 173, 238, 243–245, 248, III, 38–39, 239; *R.I.B.*, II, 969. From Ilimsk to Iakutsk was a distance of 1,200 miles (Müller, *op. cit.*, p. 470).

[156] *D.A.I.*, III, 276–278, 279–281, III, 51–55, 102–103, 333, IV, 404, VI, 404–407; Titov, pp. 32–33; Spafarii, *op. cit.*, p. 165; Müller, *op. cit.*, pp. 472–473.

[157] Cf. Titov, pp. 20, 35, 37, 44, 51; cf. *D.A.I.*, II, 248, with VI, 403; cf. Bakhrushin, "Torgi gostia Nikitina," p. 372.

[158] Titov, pp. 50–51; Bakhrushin, *Ocherki*, p. 63. Some notion of the cost of a commercial journey from Moscow to Siberia may be drawn from the experience of gost Gavril Romanovich Nikitin. To send an expedition from Moscow to Ilimsk and maintain it there for a season cost him 978 r. (Bakhrushin, "Torgi gostia Nikitina," p. 383).

[159] Potanin, *op. cit.*, pp. 125, 129, 133, 136, 139; *R.I.B.*, II, 1068.

[160] Cf. Bakhrushin, *Ocherki*, pp. 118–120, and Butsinskii, *Mangazeia*, p. 50.

the return journey was made occasionally in the winter by horse.[161] The round trip to Makovsk and Eniseisk required as a minimum two navigation seasons and a winter, for most of the summer was spent in reaching these posts. Some traders were known to have taken as long as a year and a half to get there from Russia.[162] Trips to Iakutsk and back were, on an average, three to four years in duration, since the Lena could not be reached from Russia within one navigation season. For example, the Bosov agent, Vorypaev, left Ustiug in January, 1640, and returned from Iakutsk in August, 1643. Winter stops were customarily made at Makovsk-Eniseisk or the Lena portage on the southern route, and Mangazeia and Chona portage on the northern route.[163] But if at Iakutsk one joined a hunting party into the hinterland, one prolonged one's absence from Russia another year.

After the return of enterprisers to Russia, to Ustiug or Solvychegodsk, ten months or a year usually passed before the turnover of capital invested in a Siberian venture could be completed. Because enterprisers arrived back in Russia late in August, and from September on into December—occasional overland travelers from Western Siberia were as late as March—which was too late for the furs to be sent to the market at Arkhangelsk, some of the furs were sold in Ustiug and Solvychegodsk and others were sent to the various trade centers of Russia, preliminary to the big market at Arkhangelsk.[164] One of the first centers to which the furs were sent was the market at Blagoveshchensk on the Vaga in March, for which traders departed in February. Because too many furs were brought there for all of them to be sold, shipments were dispatched subsequently to Vologda, Iaroslavl, Moscow, the Volga towns, and others, although occasionally furs were sent to these towns prior to the Blagoveshchensk market. Then, in June and July, the furs unsold at these centers and those arriving late from Siberia were shipped to Arkhangelsk for the foreign market. There was, however, no assurance that all one's furs could be sold even at this market, so sometimes it was necessary to return to one of the domes-

[161] Bazilevich, "Krupnoe torgovoe predpriiatie," p. 789; Makarov, p. 203; cf. Titov, pp. 14, 19, 44.

[162] Bakhrushin, *Ocherki*, p. 111; N. G. Spafarii, "Pis'mo Nikolaia Spafariia k boiarinu Artemonu Sergeevichu Matveevu," *Russkii arkhiv*, 1881, No. 1, p. 56; Baddeley, II, 259.

[163] Bakhrushin, *Ocherki*, pp. 111, 120, 126; *R.I.B.*, II, 962; Bazilevich, "Krupnoe torgovoe predpriiatie," p. 791.

[164] *Sbornik imperatorskago russkago istoricheskago obshchestva*, CXVI, 23; Bazilevich, "Torgovlia velikogo Ustiuga," p. 90.

tic centers and there try to dispose of the remaining ones.[165] With the sale of the last from a given shipment of furs from Siberia the trade cycle was completed. Yet, while one cycle was being completed, another was being started; when selling furs in the domestic markets and at Arkhangelsk, merchants and traders purchased Russian and foreign goods preparatory to the dispatch of another expedition to Siberia in the following winter.[166]

Trading operations as extensive as these demanded considerable capital and a business organization of at least moderate proportions; hence, it was chiefly the merchant-capitalists who traded on this scale. Smaller traders, unless acting as agents for the big merchants, were restricted to operations of more limited dimensions. However, it is quite possible that they either made arrangements to travel with the caravans of the big merchants or joined together and commissioned one of their number to carry the goods of several of them to distant centers for sale, each member of the group sharing the expenses of the commissioned member.

The cycle followed by the fur trade did not hold rigidly to the course described, for the possible variations were many, more than can be noted here. But the pattern remained the same. Each spring a host of enterprisers crossed the Urals and distributed itself through the length and breadth of Siberia to hunt and to buy furs, and each fall another host of them recrossed the Urals bringing back furs acquired during several months' or several years' activity in Siberia. During the winter and following summer the returned traders sold their furs in the domestic centers of Russia and to the foreigners at Arkhangelsk, thereby completing one cycle and leaving them free to begin another. Through the repetition of this cycle year in and year out they exploited the fur resources of Siberia.

Extent of the Private Fur Trade

The desire to determine the extent of the private traffic in furs launches the investigator into a subject about which he encounters an even greater scarcity of information than in the investigation of the fur revenue of the state. How large a number of furs was taken out of Siberia by private enterprisers, what their value was, and what profits these enterprisers made from the fur trade are

[165] Bazilevich, "Krupnoe torgovoe predpriiatie," pp. 792–794; De Rodes, p. 256.

[166] Bazilevich, "Krupnoe torgovoe predpriiatie," pp. 794–798; Bakhrushin, "Torgi gostia Nikitina," p. 371.

questions which must remain all but unanswered by the data extant outside the archives. The most that can be said is that the volume and value of furs acquired in Siberia by private enterprisers and sold in Russia exceeded the number and value of those obtained by the state. This conclusion is based on the few figures we possess about the tithe collected by the state. The figures available apply mostly to Mangazeia. They are:[167]

Year	Value in rubles
1626	14,062
1627	15,492
1628	15,354
1631	12,952
1635	10,749
1636	17,265
1637	13,729
1638	11,443
1641	11,812
1642	12,594
1646	5,113

These figures mean that, with the exception of the year 1646, which seems to mark the beginning of the decline of Mangazeia, private enterprisers, after paying the tithe, carried away annually during these years furs to the value of not less than 96,740 r. and as high as 154,385 r.[168] The state's total fur income we have estimated at 45,000 r. in 1625, increasing to 100,000 r. in 1645.[169] Thus through Mangazeia alone traders and promyshlenniks carried out of Siberia more furs than the state obtained from all of Siberia then under its dominion.

What few other figures we have tell the same story. At Iakutsk, which supplanted Mangazeia as the great fur center of Siberia, the state collected in 1641 sables to the number of 7,997, worth 9,700 r. for its tithe.[170] Accordingly, private enterprisers must have carried away during the year slightly less than 72,000 sables worth 87,300 r. That these tithe receipts were no more than average for Iakutsk, and were perhaps below average, is suggested by the fact

[167] Butsinskii, *Mangazeia*, p. 49.

[168] For instance, between July 12 and September 1, 1635, the Mangazeian authorities collected a goods (*pozhivotnoe*) tax of one denga per ruble, which amounted to 565 r. This means that goods and furs to the value of 113,000 r. (200 d. = 1 r.) passed through Mangazeia during this one month and a half (Butsinskii, *Mangazeia*, p. 52).

[169] See above, pp. 113–114.

[170] S. V. Bakhrushin, "Istoricheskie sud'by Iakutii," *Iakutiia: sbornik statei*, p. 311.

that the year before the furs collected from all sources there totaled 27,000 r. in value.[171] If we recall that the highest annual fur revenue collected at Mangazeia was under 25,000 r. (7,143 r. iasak, 17,729 r. tithe), that in 1640 the area under the jurisdiction of Iakutsk (established only eight years before) was no bigger than that administered by Mangazeia, and that the Iakutsk iasak rate was only a little higher than the Mangazeia rate, we are warranted in concluding that the tithe receipts at Iakutsk for 1640 amounted to at least 15,000 r. and maybe more.[172] This figure points to a private trade through Iakutsk alone that was greater than the 81,648 r. in fur receipts of the state for all Siberia that year.[173] Some three decades later, in 1674, the state collected at Eniseisk furs valued at 6,221 r. as its tithe, which means that 56,000 rubles' worth of furs, or half the estimated contemporary fur income of the state, were taken by private enterprisers through this town, which ranked below Iakutsk in importance.[174] The only figures for Siberia as a whole, and the only other available figures of any significance, are those given by the financial survey of 1702 for the years 1698 and 1699. In those years approximately 16,800 and 42,200 pelts respectively were collected as tithe.[175] These figures indicate that 151,000 and 379,900 pelts were taken out of Siberia by private enterprisers. The iasak for those years was 105,837 and 109,900 skins.

Illustrative of the volume of trade carried on by Russian traders in Siberia, but insufficient for determining the size of the fur traffic there, are these amounts of goods taken into Siberia: 62,393 rubles' worth of goods entered through Verkhoturie in 1636 and 62,214 in 1637, but only 25,056 in 1692. At Sob barrier goods worth 16,494 r. and 9,301 r. entered in 1639 and 1640 respectively.[176] However, a natural tendency of traders to undervalue their goods when declaring them at customs suggests that the value of the goods represented by these figures was actually higher.[177]

Lacking exact information about the volume of the private trade in furs in Siberia, we must resort, if we desire some notion of that

[171] P. N. Miliukov, "Gosudarstvennoe khoziaistvo Rossii v sviazi s reformoi Petra velikago," *Zh.M.N.P.*, CCLXXI (1890), 346 n. 1.

[172] Butsinskii, *Mangazeia*, pp. 25, 49; N. V. Volens, "Ocherk khoziaistvennogo stroia Iakutii," *Iakutiia: sbornik statei*, p. 679; *D.A.I.*, VI, 404–408. A great fluctuation in fur receipts from one year to the next was not abnormal.

[173] See above, p. 111.

[174] *D.A.I.*, VI, 355–359.

[175] See above, p. 116.

[176] Bakhrushin, *Ocherki*, pp. 79, 105–106.

[177] Ogloblin, II, 31–32.

volume, to approximation on the basis of the conclusions established in connection with the fur income of the state. For this purpose, the figures relating to the returns during the best years of the fur trade, that is, the middle of the seventeenth century, are most suitable. At that time the fur income of the state reached 125,000 r., of which an estimated maximum of 30 per cent was derived from the tithe. Such figures mean that the private enterprisers obtained 375,000 rubles' worth of furs in Siberia, and took out of Siberia, after paying the tithe, furs worth 337,000 r., Siberian value. Because 30 per cent appears to be the upper limit of the tithe, the figures 300,000 to 325,000 r. Siberian value seem a safer approximation of the value of furs taken out of Siberia by private enterprisers in an average good year during the height of the fur trade.

Great as the private fur trade was, greater even than the state's fur trade, still the tsar remained unquestionably the first fur merchant of Russia. We know little of the annual turnover or profits of individual merchants, but we know enough to assert that not even the biggest merchant-capitalist could approach the annual volume of trade carried on by the tsar. The greatest shipment of furs from Siberia of which we have record is one of 6,767 sables, valued at not less than 10,000 r., received in 1650 by the Bosov brothers at Ustiug. This shipment was exceptional, for ordinarily the number of furs which they received annually was lower, as the following figures for sable pelts and belly-strips show.[178]

Year	Fur shipments
1637	6,702 pelts
	3,584 strips
1638	4,940 pelts
	4,020 strips
1639	3,180 pelts
1640	342 pelts
	5,260 strips
1643	4,626 pelts
1651	1,488 pelts
1653	1,715 pelts
1654	1,410 pelts

On the other hand, the value of the goods which this firm sent yearly to Siberia seems to have fluctuated between 200 r. and 5,000 r. In 1646, they sent money and nineteen horses with goods to

[178] Bazilevich, "Krupnoe torgovoe predpriiatie," p. 790.

the extent of 3,000 r., and the following year nineteen horses with goods valued at 2,066 r. In some years they sent thirty and forty horses loaded with goods, and in the months December, 1639, and January, 1640, they attained their maximum shipment, carried by seventy-one horses. On the basis of the figures for the year 1646–1647, the goods carried by the seventy-one horses must have been worth from 7,000 to 8,000 r., maybe as much as 10,000 r.[179] Since one of the Bosov brothers was a gost and the other a member of the gostinaia sotnia, their business may be considered typical of the big merchants.[180] That being so, one may conclude that the average annual fur business of the big merchants was not more than 5,000 r. and that a 10,000-ruble turnover of furs in one year was exceptional, a conclusion corroborated by the fact that the largest amount of capital taken through Mangazeia at one time by a single individual was 5,500 r. in money.[181] Thus the preponderance of the tsar in the fur trade is evident.

Although it is difficult to measure the size of the private fur trade statistically, the great scope of the trade is attested by its personnel and geographical extent. As participants the fur trade attracted men from many walks of life, so many that they represented a cross section of Russian society. Principally professional merchants, but also large landowners, monastic officials, high churchmen, voevodas, and other Siberian officials invested large sums in the fur trade, giving it a stable capital structure, while petty traders, promyshlenniks, peasants, artisans, serving men, and itinerants supplied the numerical strength, giving body to the trade. Geographically the fur trade spread over a vast area, which embraced all Siberia and half Russia. Siberia was given over primarily to it, as was northern Russia, and to it central Russia devoted an important part of its economic energy. Between the Siberian fur centers and the Russian markets ranged a far-flung network of routes, over which fifteen hundred to two thousand or more enterprisers passed yearly, bringing thousands of pelts from far forests to the centers of commerce. These facts argue graphically, if not exactly, the extent of the private fur trade.

---

[179] *Ibid.*, p. 789.

[180] *Ibid.*, p. 785. The assumption that the business of the Bosov brothers was typical of the merchant-capitalists in capital invested and scale of operations is supported by the data given in Bakhrushin, "Torgi gostia Nikitina," pp. 371–383, 387.

[181] Butsinskii, *Mangazeia*, p. 51; cf. Bazilevich, "Torgovlia velikogo Ustiuga," p. 91.

If the fur trade had had to depend solely upon the demand for furs in Russia itself, it would never have reached the proportions it did, for the domestic consumption of furs alone was not sufficient. Rather, it was the foreign demand which gave the fur trade its great vitality and scope. We turn, therefore, to the export fur traffic, the description of which will enable us to comprehend the full significance of the Russian fur trade.

CHAPTER X

THE EXPORT OF FURS TO EUROPE

THE EXPORT TRADE was the keystone of the Russian fur trade. Most of Russia's furs were sent abroad in response to the increased demand for them which had manifested itself in the sixteenth century and which continued through most of the seventeenth century. Thus, in order fully to determine the scope and importance of the fur trade in the economic life of Russia, which is the basic objective of this study, it is essential to ascertain the points to which Russia's furs were exported and the place of these fur exports in relation to Russian foreign trade as a whole. We begin by first noting the centers in which the export traffic in furs was conducted.

Russian Centers of the Export Trade

Except to Persia and China, Russian merchants ordinarily did not go abroad in the pursuit of commerce—if one excludes border trade—for only the gosts and guild merchants might legally do so.[1] Consequently, the export of Russian furs was in the hands of foreign merchants, and these furs reached the foreign markets chiefly through the European and Asiatic merchants who frequented the Russian trade centers. Almost all these centers lay along the western and southern periphery of the Muscovite state, reaching northward to Arkhangelsk on the White Sea and eastward to distant Nerchinsk near the Amur River.

The greatest of the Russian fur export centers was Arkhangelsk, the one really Russian seaport and the point through which the great bulk of Russia's export traffic passed during the seventeenth century. It was built in 1585 upon request by Dutch merchants for harborage at the mouth of the Dvina safe from Norwegian corsairs in the White Sea, and was soon made the sole point in the north for trade between Russians and foreigners, except those foreigners exempted by the tsar.[2] Its real development did not begin, however,

[1] N. I. Kostomarov, *Ocherki torgovli moskovskago gosudarstva*, p. 319; Jacob Reitenfels, *Skazaniia svetleishemu gertsogu toskanskomu Koz'me tret'mu o Moskovii*, p. 133.

[2] V. A. Kordt, *Ocherk snoshenii moskovskago gosudarstva s respublikoiu soedinennykh Niderlandov do 1631 g.*, pp. li–lvii; *D.A.I.*, III, 85.

until after 1613. Then, the Troublous Times having come to an end, that growth was rapid and steady down to the beginning of the eighteenth century.[3] The importance of Arkhangelsk arose almost entirely from the summer trade there with the merchants who came from the West.[4] Ice closed the port eight or nine months out of the year and its permanent population was small. Late in June and early in July of each year the ships of the foreign merchants appeared at the mouth of the Dvina—the voyage from Holland and England required from four to six weeks[5]—and thereupon followed several weeks of commercial activity, which reached its peak in late July and early August. By late August most of the ships had departed, lest they become icebound.[6] At first only some ten or a dozen ships came annually, but in the early seventeenth century their numbers had risen to thirty and forty a year, and by the end of the century as many as a hundred arrived in a year.[7] The trade at Arkhangelsk was entirely wholesale, since retail selling by foreigners was forbidden, and was conducted either on board ship or in the official market place, where numerous shops and storehouses were erected by the state and rented to the merchants, both foreign and Russian.[8]

Of the volume of furs which passed through Arkhangelsk little is known specifically, but one may be certain that the volume was large and that it surpassed the fur exports of any other center, for it was to Arkhangelsk that most of the furs which came from Siberia to Ustiug and Solvychegodsk were sent.[9] Exact information about fur exports from Arkhangelsk is known only for the year 1653. These exports were as follows:[10]

---

[3] A. Iziumov, "Razmery russkoi torgovli XVII veka cherez Arkhangel'sk v sviazi s neobsledovannymi arkhivnymi istochnikami," *Izvestiia arkhangel'skago obshchestva izucheniia russkago severa*, 1912, No. 6, pp. 254–258.

[4] S. F. Platonov, *Ocherki po istorii smuty v moskovskom gosudarstve XVI–XVII vv.*, pp. 11–12; Iziumov, *loc. cit.*

[5] Kordt, p. cclxii.

[6] Kostomarov, p. 273; Mildred Wretts-Smith, "The English in Russia during the Second Half of the Sixteenth Century," *Transactions of the Royal Historical Society*, ser. 4, III (1920), 77 n. 4.

[7] I. I. Liubimenko, "Torgovyia snosheniia Rossii s Angliei pri pervykh Romanovykh," *Zh.M.N.P.*, n.s., Vol. LXVI (1916), p. 28; Kostomarov, *loc. cit.*; J. P. Kilburger, "Kurzer Unterricht von dem russischen Handel," *Buschings Magazin*, III (1769), 322.

[8] *D.A.I.*, III, 192, V, 195; Liubimenko, *loc. cit.*; Kostomarov, pp. 275–276.

[9] K. V. Bazilevich, "Tamozhennye knigi kak istochnik ekonomicheskoi istorii Rossii," *Problemy istochnikovedeniia*, I (1933), 114.

[10] Johann de Rodes, "Bedenken über den russischen Handel im Jahre 1653," *Beiträge zur Kenntniss Russlands und seiner Geschichte*, p. 254.

Exports	Value in rubles
579 forties (23,160 pelts) of sables	57,900
360 forties (14,400 pelts) of martens	6,480
287 forties (11,480 pelts) of minks	4,592
288 forties (11,520 pelts) of ermines	864
355,950 squirrel pelts	5,688
15,970 fox pelts	11,978
28,795 pelts of various kinds of cats	3,600
18,748 sable tails and strips	4,687
15,500 sable ends	775
598 sable edges	1,495
Total	98,059

During the last quarter of the sixteenth century and the first decade of the seventeenth a substantial trade in furs was carried on along the Murmansk coast of the Kola Peninsula. All foreign vessels had to pass along this coast, and undoubtedly a few of them made it, rather than Arkhangelsk, their destination, although no outstanding center of trade arose there, unless it was the Pechenga monastery. After 1613, however, the Murmansk coast seems to have lost whatever importance it had possessed in the trade with Europe.[11]

Next to Arkhangelsk, Novgorod was at this time the most important export center of the fur trade. Long the principal point of contact with the West and especially flourishing while Ivan held Livonia and the port of Narva on the Gulf of Finland, it did not yield its preëminence to Arkhangelsk until the seventeenth century.[12] Notwithstanding the separation of Novgorod from the Baltic by Swedish territory, the Novgorodans had access, with certain limitations (sometimes quite vexatious), to several ports such as Narva, Reval, and Riga, where they were permitted to maintain staples.[13] Foreign merchants, German, Dutch, and Scandinavian, continued to visit Novgorod in the seventeenth century, and a few of them lived there.[14] A number of furs were included among the

[11] A. V. Tishchenko, "K istorii Koly i Pechengi v XVI veke," *Zh.M.N.P.*, n.s., Vol. XLVI (1913), pt. 2, pp. 109–112; *Torgovaia kniga, Zapiski otdeleniia russkoi i slavianskoi arkheologii russkago arkheologicheskago obshchestva*, I (1851), 132–133; Samuel Purchas, *His Pilgrimes*, XIII, 224–225.

[12] Cf. De Rodes, p. 256.

[13] Adam Olearius, *The Voyages and Travels of the Ambassadors Sent by Frederick, Duke of Holstein*, p. 34; Richard Hakluyt, *The Principal Navigations*, I, 209, II, 166–167; A. P. Lassen, "Commerce in the Baltic from 1500 to 1700," p. 79; Kostomarov, p. 288.

[14] Kostomarov, p. 289; V. O. Kliuchevskii, *Skazaniia inostrantsev o moskovskom gosudarstve*, p. 273; *P.S.Z.*, I, 267.

exports from Novgorod.[15] Thus, in 1673 there were sent from this town:[16] 2 forties of sables; 2 forties of martens; 141 forties of minks (5,640 pelts); 1,719 forties of squirrels (68,760 pelts); 753 forties of cats (30,120 pelts); 111 forties of foxes (4,440 pelts); 3 sable paws; 29 [squirrel] paws; 5 cat paws; 43 rabbit paws; 38 fox paws. Novgorod obtained its furs chiefly from Kholmogory, Ustiug, and Solvychegodsk by way of Vologda and Iaroslavl, though some it received from the Dvina region by way of Kargopol and Belozero and from Moscow.[17]

Pskov, not far from Novgorod, was a fur export center of some importance, though much less important than Novgorod.[18] Many of the foreign merchants who traded at Novgorod traded also at Pskov; indeed, its commercial experience differed little from that of Novgorod, with which it was closely affiliated.

Arkhangelsk and Novgorod were the two main export points for furs. Over the seventeenth century as a whole none of the other centers could equal them; nevertheless, these others are worthy of attention. South of Novgorod near the western frontier is the town of Briansk. Prior to the middle of the seventeenth century it possessed little commercial importance, since the recurrent conflicts between Russia and Poland stifled the economic development of that region. After the peace of Andrusovo in 1667, however, more peaceful conditions prevailed, and trade began to develop here. The Swine Market at Briansk grew rapidly and by the end of the century reached a point where it ranked close to the markets at Arkhangelsk and Makariev in importance. Many furs were sold here by both private merchants and the tsar's treasury merchants to Polish, Lithuanian, and, probably, German merchants.[19]

Another center was Astrakhan at the mouth of the Volga River, which as a general export center ranked next to Arkhangelsk

[15] Ogloblin, IV, 56, 66, 155, 167.

[16] Kilburger, p. 266.

[17] A. K. Il'inskii, "Gorodskoe naselenie novgorodskoi oblasti v XVI i XVII veke," *Zh.M.N.P.*, CLXXXV (1876), 251, 252–253, 262; K. V. Bazilevich, "Krupnoe torgovoe predpriiatie v moskovskom gosudarstve v pervoi polovine XVII veka," *Izvestiia akademii nauk*, Otdelenie obshchestvennykh nauk, ser. 7, No. 9 (1932), p. 805; Hakluyt, I, 298.

[18] Kliuchevskii, *op. cit.*, p. 296; De Rodes, p. 256; cf. Ogloblin, IV, 167.

[19] Kostomarov, pp. 308–309; Ogloblin, IV, 66, 84, 88, 93, 164; B. G. Kurts, "Iz istorii torgovykh snoshenii Rossii s Kitaem v XVII st.," *Novyi vostok*, XXIII–XXIV, 331; S. V. Bakhrushin, "Torgi gostia Nikitina v Sibiri i Kitae," *Sbornik statei: Pamiati Aleksandra Nikolaevicha Savina, 1873–1923*, Trudy instituta istorii rossiiskoi assotsiatsii nauchno-issledovatel'skikh institutov obshchestvennykh nauk, I (1926), 369, 374.

and Novgorod in the seventeenth century, being the center of the trade between Russia and Asia. An exceptionally cosmopolitan town, it was visited by merchants from Persia, India, and the Ottoman empire, and by merchants from Russia and Siberia.[20] But it was the sale of furs there by the state and the export of them to Persia, not the private fur traffic, that gave Astrakhan importance as a fur-export center.[21]

The remaining fur markets on the periphery of Russia were situated along the southern frontier of Siberia. There were, in the seventeenth century, six towns in particular from which furs passed into the Asiatic countries adjoining Siberia. These were Tara and Tomsk in Western Siberia, and Selenginsk, Nerchinsk, Albazin, and Irkutsk in Eastern Siberia. Tara and Tomsk were points of export to Central Asia and, occasionally, to China. They were visited chiefly by a group of merchants known as Bukharans, by Tatars, and by a few Kalmyks. In the earlier years of the seventeenth century Siberian merchants traveled to Tomsk and then to Lake Iamish on the road to Sungaria where they met caravans from the latter place and carried on an exchange of goods.[22] Selenginsk, Nerchinsk, Albazin, and Irkutsk were centers of export to Mongolia and China. With the exception of Nerchinsk during the decade of the 'nineties, none of them equaled Tomsk and Tara, for they were not established until after the middle of the century. Selenginsk was the site of a border traffic in furs with the Mongols, but its small population limited the growth of trade there.[23] Nerchinsk was the most important of the four. To it Mongols and Chinese came to trade, and from it Russians journeyed five or six days up the Argun River to Lake Dalai, where they traded with the Chinese. After the treaty with China in 1689, Nerchinsk became the point from which both state and private caravans departed for Pekin and to which they returned. During this period it was

[20] Grigorii Kotoshikhin, *O Rossii v tsarstvovanie Aleksiia Mikhailovicha*, p. 165; A. Malinovskii, "Izvestie ob otpravleniiakh v Indiiu rossiiskikh poslannikov, gontsov i kupchin tovarami i o priezdakh v Rossiiu indeitsev, s 1469 po 1751 god," *Trudy i letopisi obshchestva istorii i drevnostei rossiiskikh*, VII (1837), 140, 160.

[21] Kostomarov, pp. 299–301; Ogloblin, III, 342, IV, 61, 159.

[22] G. N. Potanin, "Privoz i vyvoz tovarov goroda Tomska v polovine XVII stoletiia," *Vestnik imperatorskago russkago geograficheskago obshchestva*, Vol. XXVII (1859), pt. 2, p. 143; G. D. Khilkov, *Sbornik kniazia Khilkova*, p. 527; Ogloblin, IV, 12; Purchas, XIII, 232, 253; Bakhrushin, *op. cit.*, p. 373; cf. A. A. Titov, *Sibir' v XVII v.*, pp. 35–36.

[23] J. F. Baddeley, *Russia, Mongolia, China*, II, 256–257, 269, 421.

the most important export point in Siberia.[24] Albazin, during the few decades of its occupation by the Russians, was the scene of a modest trade with the Chinese in furs and other goods.[25] In the last decade of the seventeenth century Irkutsk acquired importance for the Siberian-Chinese trade as a frontier outpost, where many private merchants outfitted themselves for the journey across Mongolia and to which they returned.[26]

The most important export center in Siberia throughout most of the seventeenth century was situated not on the frontier but well within Siberia. This was Tobolsk. Most of Siberia's foreign trade focused here; it attracted more merchants from Central Asia than did either Tara or Tomsk, and furs from all over Siberia flowed to it.[27]

In Russia itself there were a few trade centers in the interior from which furs were carried away by foreign merchants. There was only one, however, in which furs in any quantity were bought by foreigners. That was Moscow, and it functioned as an export center primarily because the fur trade of the state centered there. Anxious to acquire Oriental luxuries and finery, the tsar permitted and encouraged merchants from the Near and Middle East to come to Moscow, where they exchanged their goods at the Treasury Court or Sable Treasury for sables and other furs. Merchants attached to the suites of visiting envoys and the members themselves of these suites also carried abroad furs purchased of the tsar.[28] Besides Moscow, foreign merchants occasionally visited Kazan, Nizhnii Novgorod, Iaroslavl, and Viazma in order to purchase furs.[29]

From the foregoing dozen or more export centers large numbers of pelts passed into both Europe and Asia; and few indeed were the countries of either continent which did not become familiar with Russian furs. However, although Russian furs reached nearly

---

[24] *Ibid.*, pp. 278–279; *A.I.*, V, 519.

[25] Baddeley, II, 227, 228–229; Kh. Trusevich, *Posol'skiia i torgovyia snosheniia Rossii s Kitaem (do XIX v.)*, p. 159.

[26] Bakhrushin, *op. cit.*, pp. 376–377.

[27] Kostomarov, p. 304; Purchas, XIII, 232; Ogloblin, II, 24, 37, 81, 156, IV, 18; Khilkov, *loc. cit.;* Samuel Collins, "Nyneshnee sostoianie Rossii, izlozhennoe v pis'me k drugu zhivushchemu v Londone," *Chteniia*, 1846, No. 1, pt. 3, p. 23.

[28] Kotoshikhin, p. 165; Malinovskii, pp. 140–141, 144, 153, 160; De Rodes, pp. 251–252; Ogloblin, III, 156; Paul of Aleppo, *The Travels of Macarius, Patriarch of Antioch*, II, 21; *P.S.Z.*, I, 457.

[29] A. G. Viktorov, *Opisanie zapisnykh knig i bumag, starinnykh dvortsovykh prikazov, 1584–1725 g.*, I, 88; Kotoshikhin, *loc. cit.*

every country in Europe and Asia, our interest is primarily in those with whose merchants Russia engaged directly in trade. By examining the fur trade with each of these countries and the extent of furs as an export to each, we may best judge the extent and importance of the export fur trade as a whole. The remainder of this chapter will be devoted to the European trade—trade with Holland, Germany, and England in particular. It was this trade which held special importance for the private merchants.

The Trade with Holland

Foremost among the Europeans who traded in Russia were the Dutch. In point of capital invested, ships sent to Russia, and number of merchants trading there they stood first. Commercial relations between the Dutch and Russians began in the Baltic, first through Riga, Reval, and Dorpat, then at Novgorod itself.[30] The Russian occupation of the port of Narva (1559–1581) greatly facilitated direct trade with foreigners and thus Russia's commerce with the Low Countries increased in that period.[31] But this promising trade was checked when Ivan IV lost Narva to the Swedes in 1581, and although thereafter the Dutch continued to trade with Russia at Novgorod and the Baltic ports, they turned to the unencumbered White Sea route for the development of their trade with the Muscovites.[32] They had first appeared at the mouth of the Northern Dvina in 1578;[33] then, with the establishment of Arkhangelsk in 1585, they built a factory there and set about expanding their trade. By the beginning of the seventeenth century they had displaced the English as the leading foreign traders on the Dvina, and after the Troublous Times they became the outstanding European merchants in Russia, a position they held throughout the century.[34]

The leading merchants of Europe, the Dutch possessed far

---

[30] Kliuchevskii, *op. cit.*, pp. 273, 293; Hakluyt, I, 298.

[31] I. I. Liubimenko, "The Struggle of the Dutch with the English for the Russian Market in the Seventeenth Century," *Transactions of the Royal Historical Society*, ser. 4, VII (1924), 29; Kordt, pp. xv, xviii; Heinrich Storch, *Historisch-statistische Gemälde des russischen Reichs am Ende des XVIII Jahrhunderts*, IV, 280.

[32] Kostomarov, p. 253; *A.A.E.*, III, 264; Hakluyt, *loc. cit.;* J. R., "The Trade's Increase," *Harleian Miscellany*, IV, 215.

[33] Kordt, p. xxxiii.

[34] W. R. Scott, *The Constitutions and Finance of English, Scottish and Irish Joint-Stock Companies to 1720*, II, 48; Liubimenko, "The Struggle of the Dutch with the English," pp. 39–40, 49, 51; J. R., "The Trade's Increase," p. 213.

greater financial resources than the merchants of any of the other countries trading with Russia, and they offered a greater variety of, as well as cheaper, goods.[35] At first they sent fewer than ten ships a year to Arkhangelsk, but by 1613 the number of these ships had risen to thirty annually. For the whole seventeenth century it remained on an average between thirty and forty, though in 1630 one hundred Dutch ships (supposedly), and in 1635 and 1658 more than fifty, came to Arkhangelsk.[36] The Dutch did not gain as advantageous privileges in Russia as did the English, but they enjoyed half exemption from customs tolls, and individual merchants obtained the privilege held by the English of extending their trading activities from Arkhangelsk into the interior.[37] In 1649 they lost their customs exemption, as did all foreign merchants similarly privileged, and were required to pay full customs duties thereafter. However, they were no longer confronted with the competition offered by the complete exemption of the English.[38] On the Dutch side, trade with Russia was open to all who wished to venture it, privileged monopolies being contrary to the policy of the States General in Holland. Ordinarily, the Russian trade was carried on by individual merchants, but it was not unusual for two or three to pool their resources in joint enterprises.[39]

Furs were one of the most important commodities taken out of Russia by the Dutch. The evidence shows that from the time of their establishment at Arkhangelsk, if not earlier, to the end of the seventeenth century they carried on an extensive and flourishing trade in Russian furs. Even before the Dutch had penetrated the White Sea to Arkhangelsk, while they were still pushing eastward along the Murmansk coast, the Stroganovs sent several shipments of furs and other goods to Amsterdam and Dordrecht in charge of their Dutch employee, Oliver Brunel.[40] Once established in the north, the Dutch bought all kinds of furs and bought them in large

[35] Liubimenko, "Torgovyia snosheniia Rossii s Angliei," p. 183; *idem*, "The Struggle of the Dutch with the English," p. 49.

[36] I. M. Kulisher, *Russische Wirtschaftsgeschichte*, p. 438; Walter Raleigh, "Observations Touching Trade and Commerce," p. 16; G. V. Forsten, *Akty i pis'ma k istorii baltiiskago voprosa v XVI i XVII stoletiiakh*, I, 307 n.; Kordt, pp. cclxxxv–cclxxxvi; Liubimenko, "The Struggle of the Dutch with the English," p. 48; cf. Kilburger, pp. 290, 292, 296, 300.

[37] Kostomarov, p. 252; Kordt, pp. cclxix, cclxxii–cclxxiii; Liubimenko, "The Struggle of the Dutch with the English," p. 37.

[38] Kostomarov, p. 253.

[39] Kordt, pp. cclxxx–cclxxxi.

[40] *Ibid.*, pp. xxxiii–xlv; S. F. Platonov, *Proshloe russkogo severa*, pp. 66, 78; Ernst Baasch, *Holländische Wirtschaftsgeschichte*, p. 344.

quantities. According to the "Trade Book," which covers the years 1585–1610, they were purchasers of such inexpensive kinds of furs as squirrels, wildcat, and rabbit, medium-priced furs like ermines, minks, weasels, and wolves, and the expensive sables, martens, foxes, and beavers. Wildcat skins and squirrels they contracted for in lots of as many as 100,000, wolves in 5,000 lots, martens in 4,000 lots, rabbits in lots of 1,000, and minks, ermines, weasels, and arctic foxes in lots of 100 to 500. The Book does not mention the number of sable pelts contracted for.[41] Even without this specific data one would conclude that the Dutch bought large numbers of Russian furs, for they carried all kinds of them to many parts of Europe, to France, Portugal, Spain, and Italy, countries not in direct commercial contact with Russia, and even to England and Germany.[42] For instance, in 1646 the Dutch shipped into France furs, leather, and Russian hides to the amount of 675,000 louis.[43] Further evidence of large Dutch purchases of furs is the episode in which the Amsterdam house of Bontemantel advanced so much money in Russia in 1640 that in the following year scarcely any furs came on the open market.[44] We know, moreover, that the Dutch merchants participating in the Russian trade placed a high value on the fur traffic. There is the incident of a Iaroslavl merchant, Anton Laptaev, who took a cargo of sables, foxes, and squirrels to Amsterdam by way of Riga. Arriving at Amsterdam, he was unable to sell them because the merchants there agreed not to buy them. Returning to Russia with some of these same merchants, he sold his furs to them at Arkhangelsk for a very good price. They explained their conduct on the ground that, if the Russians started trading in Holland, the Dutch would lose a very profitable trade.[45]

Beyond the fact that furs were a major export of the Russians in the trade with the Dutch the question arises whether or not they were the first export in value. The variety and large numbers of furs which the Dutch purchased and the extensive market which they supplied suggest that furs were indeed first; in fact, one

[41] *Torgovaia kniga*, I, 132–133; D. S. van Zuiden, "Nieuwe bijdrage tot de kennis van de Hollandsch-Russische relaties in de 16e-18e eeuw.," *Economisch-historisch jaarboek tot de economische geschiedenis van Nederland,* II (1916), 264.

[42] *Torgovaia kniga, loc. cit.;* Forsten, I, 307 n. 1; Gerhard Fischer, *Aus Zwei Jahrhunderten leipziger Handelsgeschichte, 1470–1650,* p. 356; France, Commission des Archives Diplomatiques, *Recueil des instructions données aux ambassadeurs et ministres de France: Russie,* I, 22.

[43] Baasch, p. 319.

[44] *Ibid.*, p. 341.

[45] *A.A.E.*, IV, 19.

investigator of the Russian sources on Dutch-Russian trade ranks them as the most important.[46] But he fails to give his authority for this statement, and the evidence otherwise available does not permit a conclusion one way or the other. Of this, however, we may be sure, that is, that the Dutch were the largest purchasers of furs of any single national group of merchants trading in Russia. That conclusion the evidence warrants.[47]

As an indication of the importance of the fur trade for Russia we list the kinds of goods which the Dutch brought into Russia, in exchange for many of which they acquired furs. The following list, though detailed, is more representative than complete: iron and such iron goods as padlocks, knives, needles; brooches; various sorts of copper, copper basins, bells; tin, pewter vessels, lead; wrought and coined gold and silver; brass foil; various paints; rice; writing paper; wines of many kinds, brandy; a great variety of drugs; sugar, syrups, sweetmeats, peaches, prunes, saffron, incense; herring, whale fins; pearls, turquoise, glass beads, mirrors; various kinds of linen, wool, and silk goods; bottles, glass bowls; playing cards; horsecloths; Nürnberg manufactures, and so on.[48] Many of these goods the Dutch obtained in France.[49]

The Trade with Germany

The closest rivals of the Dutch in Russia were the Germans and the English. Of the two, the Germans probably carried on the greater trade over the period 1550–1700, for they traded with the Russians not only at Arkhangelsk, but also through the Baltic and overland through Poland-Lithuania. Their Baltic trade was the oldest, the Baltic having been the scene of the flourishing Novgorod-Hansa trade. At the middle of the sixteenth century this trade had declined considerably as a consequence of the eviction of the Hansa from Novgorod in 1494, but it revived in part when Narva came under Russian control. Lübeck predominated in this Russian-German trade through the Baltic and was the chief beneficiary of the Narva trade, though merchants from Danzig and Hamburg also participated in it.[50] In 1603, after Narva fell to Sweden, Lübeck

[46] Kordt, p. cclxxxiv.
[47] Cf. *Torgovaia kniga, loc. cit.*
[48] Kordt, pp. cclxxxii–cclxxxiii; Van Zuiden, *op. cit.*, p. 264; Jacques Savary, *Le Parfait Négociant*, II, 273–274.
[49] France, Commission des Archives Diplomatiques, *Recueil des instructions: Russie*, I, 26–27; Savary, *loc. cit.*
[50] *R.I.B.*, Vol. XV, pt. 1, p. 136; Lassen, p. 235.

received from the tsar the right to trade freely in Novgorod, Pskov, and Moscow, besides other privileges, privileges which were renewed in 1636 and 1651. How much trade the Lübeck merchants conducted as a result of their privileges is not known, but they continued throughout the century to regard their Baltic trade with Russia as important.[51] German trade with Russia through the White Sea began in 1604 when a few vessels from Hamburg appeared at Arkhangelsk.[52] Subsequently, merchants from Bremen appeared there, and a few from Lübeck, but among the Germans it was the Hamburg merchants who most used this route.[53] They sent approximately ten vessels a year to the Dvina. At least ten Hamburg and four Bremen ships are known to have come to Arkhangelsk in 1673, and at least thirteen Hamburg vessels in 1707.[54] Like the Dutch, some Hamburg and Bremen merchants were allowed to trade in the interior of Russia.[55]

The overland trade between Germany and Russia, which was very likely as great or nearly as great as the German trade at Arkhangelsk, began to develop after the closing of the Hanseatic factory at Novgorod. At the middle of the sixteenth century it was quite active and continued so throughout that and the seventeenth centuries. It was, until the later seventeenth century, largely indirect trade, passing through the hands of the Polish and Lithuanian merchants as intermediaries. Towards the end of that century, however, the Polish-Lithuanian merchantry declined, and the Germans, as well as a few Russians, who were then beginning to trade outside their own country, took over more and more of the transit trade across Poland.[56] Several routes joined Germany and Poland, on the one hand, and Russia and Poland, on the other. The main route from Poland to Germany was the *Hohe Landstrasse,* which entered Germany at Breslau and passed through Oberlausitz to

[51] Lassen, pp. 84–86, 235; Storch, IV, 227–228; Kostomarov, pp. 254–255; *P.S.Z.*, I, 266–268.

[52] Heinrich von Staden, *Aufzeichnungen über den moskauer Staat,* p. 143 n. 8.

[53] Kilburger, pp. 247–248, 322. Late in the seventeenth century German merchants from Brandenburg sought to engage in the trade at Arkhangelsk (*P.S.Z.*, II, 972–973).

[54] Kilburger, pp. 290, 292; *Sbornik imperatorskago russkago istoricheskago obshchestva,* XXXIX, 411.

[55] Storch, IV, 430; Liubimenko, "The Struggle of the Dutch with the English," p. 43.

[56] P. J. Marperger, *Schlesischer Kauffmann,* p. 282; Hugo Rachel, "Polnische Handels- und Zollverhältnisse im 16. bis 18. Jahrhundert," *Jahrbuch für Gesetzgebung, Verwaltung und Volkswirtschaft im deutschen Reich,* n.s., Vol. XXXIII (1909), pt. 2, p. 59.

Leipzig.[57] Others passed from Breslau and Posen in western Poland to Madgeburg, Frankfurt an der Oder, Danzig, and Lübeck.[58] From Poland to Russia, routes passed from Posen, Warsaw, Lublin, and Krakow to the western Russian towns along the frontier, chiefly Novgorod, Pskov, and Smolensk.

Furs stood high among the Russian goods exported to Germany. Whether they stood first, as they did when Novgorod was a Hanseatic factory, cannot be said, since evidence is lacking to support a contention either way. But of the continued importance of furs as a Russian export commodity to Germany there can be no doubt. In each of the more important German cities maintaining commercial connections with Russia in the sixteenth and seventeenth centuries there was an active trade in furs, most of them coming from Russia. Danzig, according to a Spanish visitor to the city in 1574, imported a "great quantity" of sables, martens, and other furs from Russia. In fact, this man lists no other goods as imports from Russia.[59] A magistrate's ordinance in the year 1603 reveals Lübeck as an active wholesale center of the fur trade. Squirrel skins were sold in lots of 50, 250, and up to 1,000, and martens and ermines in 25-piece lots.[60] The "Trade Book" states that otters and beavers, which were contracted for in lots of 5,000, and wolverines, contracted for in lots of 8,000, went to Germany. Since the "Trade Book" refers to the White Sea trade, we may assume that these were furs taken by Hamburg merchants.[61] Kilburger, writing of Russian trade about 1673, asserts that the Hamburg merchants of that time bought up all the mink pelts available in Russia and sold them throughout Germany to be made into women's caps, with the result that no mink fur was worn in Russia.[62] In Breslau, situated on the *Hohe Landstrasse*, there arose a big trade in furs in the second half of the seventeenth century.[63] According to a contemporary merchant, who describes the Breslau trade of the late seventeenth and early eighteenth centuries, the fur traffic there was in the hands

[57] H. F. Heller, "Die Handelswege Inner-Deutschlands im 16., 17. und 18. Jahrhundert und ihre Beziehungen zu Leipzig," *Neues Archiv für sächsische Geschichte und Alterthumskunde*, V (1884), 13–14.

[58] *Ibid.*, pp. 20, 44; Rachel, pp. 44, 59; G. Fischer, p. 348.

[59] Forsten, I, 163.

[60] Heinrich Lomer, *Der Rauchwarenhandel*, pp. 11–12.

[61] *Torgovaia kniga, loc. cit.*

[62] Kilburger, p. 225.

[63] Rachel, *loc. cit.*; G. Fischer, *loc. cit.*; E. von Ranke, "Kölns binnendeutscher Verkehr im 16. und 17. Jahrhundert," *Hansische Geschichtsblätter*, XXIX (1924), 72; Johannes Falke, *Die Geschichte des deutschen Handels*, II, 49.

of the Russians, Poles, and Polish Jews, who sold furs of many kinds in the markets of this Silesian town—sables, martens, foxes, wolverines, lynxes, beavers, otters, minks, wolves, ermines, and squirrels—and maintained splendid warehouses for their storage. They obtained many of these furs from Russia, especially the sables, foxes, and martens. A large number of them were bought by Poles and the local landed gentry, but the larger number were sent to other towns, particularly to Leipzig.[64] This town was the most important of the German fur centers, and because the export of Russian furs to Germany converged on it, it merits special attention.

Prior to the sixteenth century, Leipzig had been a growing, but not outstanding, Saxon town. In that century, however, it developed into one of the most important commercial centers in central Germany, and, continuing an unabated growth, became preëminent there in the following century. It owed its rise mainly to its central location on most of the trade routes across Germany, especially on the *Hohe Landstrasse,* to the sanction of its three fairs and restrictions against competing towns obtained from the emperor in 1497 and 1507, and to the migration there of many merchants and artisans as settlers.[65] Its fairs, which were the basis of its economic life, attracted large numbers of merchants from all parts of Europe, and some from the Near East, so that in time this Saxon town became the great meeting place of the trade between the Slavic East and the Latin and Teutonic West.[66]

As a part of its development Leipzig established itself not only as the center of the German, but also of the European fur trade. Many fur traders and furriers were among those who settled in Leipzig.[67] Indeed, the furriers at Leipzig, who conducted a big business making the furs into articles of wear for sale at the fairs, were the largest purchasers of the furs brought to Leipzig.[68] Pelts of many kinds were sold there, chiefly sables, martens, minks, ermines, and otters.[69] Meanwhile, the fairs, frequented by mer-

[64] Marperger, pp. 282–283.

[65] Ernst Kroker, *Handelsgeschichte der Stadt Leipzig,* pp. 75–76; Friedrich Rauers, "Zur Geschichte der alten Handelsstrassen in Deutschland," *Petermanns Mitteilungen,* Vol. LII (1906), pt. 3, p. 54; Ernst Hasse, *Geschichte der leipziger Messen,* pp. 18–21; Gheron Netta, *Die Handelsbeziehungen zwischen Leipzig und Ost- und Südosteuropa bis zum Verfall der Warenmessen,* p. 30; G. Fischer, pp. 13 ff., 163 ff.

[66] Netta, pp. 35, 39; Hasse, pp. 458–459; G. Fischer, pp. 353–354.

[67] G. Fischer, pp. 355–445 *passim.*

[68] *Ibid.,* p. 348; J. H. Heiderich, *Das leipziger Kürschnergewerbe,* pp. 9–12.

[69] Heiderich, *loc. cit.;* G. Fischer, p. 352.

chants from all parts of Europe, made Leipzig the European center of the fur trade, a distinction which it had attained by the middle of the sixteenth century. When the reopening of the Hanseatic factory at Novgorod was under consideration at the meeting of the Hansetag at Lübeck in 1554, the Riga representatives explained that the fur trade could not be redirected to Novgorod because it was already in the hands of the Leipziger.[70] This position as the foremost fur center of Europe Leipzig has retained down to modern times.[71]

Most of the furs sold at Leipzig—and the best of them—came from Russia. Large numbers of sables and martens, animals then found but rarely outside of Russia, were disposed of here, while Russian squirrels gave to its fur traffic much of its bulk.[72] Some of the furs were brought directly from Russia. There is record of several Leipzig merchants who traveled to Moscow to buy furs and other Russian goods, and probably other Leipziger traveled to Russia as Lübecker because of the privileges the latter enjoyed there.[73] In the late seventeenth century, also, a few Russian merchants brought furs directly to Leipzig.[74] But the majority of Russian furs came through the channels of intermediaries, by way of the previously mentioned fur centers in Germany, Danzig, Lübeck, Hamburg, and Breslau, also from Cologne and the Polish towns Posen and Warsaw. Leipzig merchants, or their agents, visited these towns to buy furs, and, in turn, the merchants of these towns brought their furs to the Leipzig fairs.[75] During fair time at Leipzig nearly all the Breslau fur dealers were to be found there.[76] The Jewish merchants from Posen were also regular visitors from 1675 on.[77] Thus it was to Leipzig that most of the furs exported from Russia to Germany came. At the same time, it was to Russia as the source of most of its furs that Leipzig owed its importance as the center of the European fur trade. These circumstances and the European scope of the Leipzig fur market warrant the conclusion that furs were one of the principal Russian exports to Germany.

The goods which the Germans brought to Russia were much the

[70] Lassen, p. 75, citing *Kölner Inventar*, Anhang No. 16, pp. 372–373.
[71] Heiderich, p. 1.
[72] *Ibid.*, pp. 9–12.
[73] Von Staden, pp. 55, 204, 205; G. Fischer, pp. 417–419; Kroker, pp. 93–94.
[74] Netta, pp. 39, 40.
[75] *Ibid.*, p. 35; G. Fischer, pp. 348, 353–365; Hasse, p. 459; Von Ranke, p. 67.
[76] Von Ranke, p. 72.
[77] Marcus Breger, *Zur Handelsgeschichte der Juden in Polen während des 17. Jahrhunderts*, p. 21.

same as those shipped there by the Dutch. Woolen and cotton textiles and goods, fine linen and silk goods made in Europe, muslin, hardware, needles and pins, cutlery, and gold- and silverware, paper—these were some of the more important ones.[78]

The Trade with England

England's commerce with Russia in the sixteenth and seventeenth centuries passed, for the most part, through Arkhangelsk. To be sure, English ships touched at Narva, Reval, and Riga and carried away Russian goods, but the number of such ships appears to have been small and the furs carried away by them few.[79] English trade with Russia began in 1553 when Chancellor discovered the White Sea route. His discovery led to the formation in 1555 of a joint-stock company, variously named but known usually as the Muscovy Company, which obtained from Queen Mary and from her successors a monopoly of the Russian trade.[80] From the Russian tsars it acquired various privileges, the most important of which were a monopoly of the White Sea route—which it enjoyed until the Dutch appeared there—full exemption from customs tolls, and the right to trade and to maintain factories within Russia. The last three privileges it retained until 1649.[81]

By virtue of the monopoly grant to the Muscovy Company from the English crown the company's activities constituted practically the whole of English-Russian commerce down to 1669, when the company's existence was terminated. Its fortunes fluctuated widely in the course of its more than a century of existence. The years up to 1581 seem to have been the most prosperous; in some of them the company sent as many as seventeen ships to the Dvina in one year.[82] Thereafter its fortunes declined. The Dutch began to cut into its trade seriously and company agents in Russia carried on trade of their own on the side, embezzling much of its capital, so that by the end of the sixteenth century it was sending but two or three ships a year to Arkhangelsk. The Muscovy Company was

[78] Kilburger, pp. 292–295; Netta, p. 79.

[79] Anthony Jenkinson, *Early Voyages and Travels to Russia and Persia,* I, cviii, II, 218; N. R. Deardorff, *English Trade in the Baltic during the Reign of Elizabeth,* p. 230; Scott, II, 41–42; J. R., "The Trade's Increase," p. 215.

[80] Scott, II, 37–38; Hakluyt, I, 318–329.

[81] Liubimenko, "Torgovyia snosheniia Rossii s Angliei," pp. 14–16, 18–27; Kostomarov, pp. 242–251; Hakluyt, I, 313–318.

[82] Scott, II, 46–47; Liubimenko, "Torgovyia snosheniia Rossii s Angliei," p. 142; J. R., "The Trade's Increase," p. 213; Wretts-Smith, p. 77 n. 1.

reorganized in 1607 and received fresh capital, which carried it tolerably until 1620, when its trade became almost nonexistent. Another reorganization took place, and there followed a period of prosperity,[83] but after 1635 the financial difficulties which so often dogged the company again caused it trouble. In addition, in 1649 the tsar dispossessed it of its privileges and expelled it from Russia, ostensibly on account of the regicide of Charles I but chiefly because of the opposition of the Russian merchants to its privileged position.[84] In 1654 it was allowed to return, provided it paid full customs and traded only at Arkhangelsk; and it did resume a small-scale trade on that basis. But, although that trade later increased, the company's heyday had passed, for without its privileges it was unable to compete with the Dutch, who had surpassed the English in spite of the latter's greater advantages. Unable to regain its privileges, the company wound up its affairs in 1669 and was replaced by a regulated company.[85] Only at the end of the century did English trade in Russia manage to regain its former prosperity.[86]

As an export from Russia furs occupied a less prominent place in the trade with England than they did in the trade with Holland and with Germany. They yielded first place to naval stores—hemp, flax, ropes, sperm oil, tallow, wax—which were in great demand for England's rapidly growing marine. These articles the Muscovy Company made the basis of its exports from Russia.[87] But, next to ship's stores, furs were the most important staple brought from Russia by the company's ships. The abundance of furs in Russia and their relatively low cost constituted one of the inducements for organizing the company, and Chancellor, returning in 1556 from his second trip to Russia, brought back "waxe, trane oyl, tallow, furres, felts, yarnes, and such like to the summe of 20000. li. sterling."[88] In 1557 the company sent a skinner to Russia to supervise the purchase of furs.[89] It did not buy indiscriminately. That same

[83] Scott, II, 48–57, 64; Jenkinson, I, cix.

[84] Liubimenko, "Torgovyia snosheniia Rossii s Angliei," p. 15; *P.S.Z.*, I, 167–169.

[85] Scott, II, 65–67.

[86] *Sbornik imperatorskago istoricheskago obshchestva,* XXXIX, 36, 411; Liubimenko, "Torgovyia snosheniia Rossii s Angliei," p. 16.

[87] Hakluyt, I, 383, 400; Jenkinson, II, 225; Deardorff, pp. 221–223; Scott, I, 50; Great Britain, Historical Manuscripts Commission, *Calendar of the Manuscripts of the Most Hon. the Marquis of Salisbury,* V, 462–463.

[88] William Camden, *The History of the . . . Princess Elizabeth,* p. 103; Hakluyt, I, 297–298, 357.

[89] Hakluyt, I, 383.

year it instructed its agents to send "plentie" only of those furs "which bee most vendible, as good marterns . . . and mynkes," provided they were reasonable in price. "As for sables and other rich furres, they bee not every mans money: therefore you may send the fewer."[90] In 1560 the company officials complained of the poor quality of many of the pelts sent them and informed their agents of the proclamation issued that year "that no furs shall be worn here, but such as the like is growing here within this our realme," which prompted them to order no "great provision of any rich furres except principall sables and lettes [martens]."[91]

The difficulty experienced by the company in getting good pelts arose in part from the diminution of the supply of fur-bearing animals at this time in Russia. But mainly it was due to illicit traffic in furs on the part of its employees in Russia, as well as by the sailors on its ships, who not only bought the best furs on the Dvina, but stole from their timbers the fine ones belonging to the company and substituted their own poor ones.[92] By 1584, however, stringent measures virtually eliminated the illicit trade of the sailors. Meanwhile, up to the early 'eighties the company succeeded in carrying on a good trade in furs—if we can trust the statement of a contemporary French observer—a trade devoted chiefly to the less expensive kinds of furs, such as "wolverings," minks, squirrels, coarse sables, "bever bellies, bever backs, bever wool," and wolfskins.[93] But with the decline in the company's fortunes after 1581 the purchase of furs fell off. The "Trade Book" lists the English as important purchasers only of beavers and wolverines, and the chief agent of the company in Russia fails to include furs among the principal exports for the year 1596.[94]

In general, furs continued in the seventeenth century as the second most important export of the Muscovy Company from Russia. Yet during the Troublous Times, when all but maritime Russia was sadly disrupted by conflict, the company attempted to support its enterprise by turning to fur trade in the Pechora, along with whale fishing in the Arctic.[95] In the year 1611-1612 three com-

[90] *Ibid.*

[91] *Ibid.*, p. 400.

[92] Jenkinson, II, 206–207, 213; Wretts-Smith, p. 78 n. 1.

[93] A. A. Chumikov, "Materialy dlia istorii russkoi torgovli," *Chteniia*, 1875, No. 4, pt. 5, p. 160; Wretts-Smith, p. 77 n. 3.

[94] *Torgovaia kniga, loc. cit.;* Great Britain, Historical MSS Commission, *Calendar of the Manuscripts of the Most Hon. the Marquis of Salisbury, loc. cit.*

[95] Scott, II, 53; Purchas, XIII, 223.

pany factors wintered at Pustozersk, seeking to establish contacts by which they might persuade the Pechora and Perm traders to sell their furs at Pustozersk rather than at Kholmogory and Arkhangelsk.[96] During the winter of 1614–1615 one company agent carried on trade at Pustozersk, journeying also to Rogovyi *gorodok* for barter with the Samoeds, while another wintered at Ust-Tsilma, whence he brought sable, wolverine, wolf, ermine, squirrel, and other skins.[97] The number of furs they obtained is not reported, but three river boats were required to carry them to the company ship at the mouth of the Pechora; light and compact, furs could be carried in substantial quantities in such boats.[98] This Pechora venture does not appear to have been pursued further, however.

From 1615 to 1663 there is practically no information regarding fur exports to England, beyond the fact that there were such exports.[99] But for the years 1663 and 1669 we have records of the furs received from Russia at the port of London, through which four-fifths of England's trade passed. In 1663, there were imported from Russia 500 beaver skins, 2,900 seal [?] skins, 400 ermine pelts, 2,000 hundreds of catskins, 10 hundreds of squirrel skins, and 15,000 sable tips, the total value of which was £3,507. Together these represented the second largest item of imports, the first being potashes to the value of £9,648. Total imports from Russia that year were valued at £17,765. In 1669, the last year of the Muscovy Company's existence, fur imports were relatively unimportant: 1,295 seal skins and 62 hundreds of squirrel skins, together valued at £222, were all the furs received in a total of goods worth £9,239, in which several other commodities were imported in greater amounts.[100] For the remainder of the century it is doubtful that English purchases of Russian furs increased, since the English were beginning their penetration into the Hudson's Bay country at that time. Like the Dutch, the English reëxported some of their Russian furs to other countries, especially to the Levant.[101]

The goods which the Muscovy Company sold in Russia consisted predominantly of English woolen cloth. Of total exports to Russia

[96] Purchas, XIII, 207, 220–221, 231, 245.
[97] *Ibid.*, pp. 258–260.
[98] *Ibid.*, p. 260.
[99] Paul of Aleppo, II, 23.
[100] These figures were taken from photographs of the original records and are made available through the courtesy of Dr. L. A. Harper of the University of California.
[101] Paul of Aleppo, *loc. cit.*

in 1663, valued at £24,000, cloth accounted for £19,000. In 1669, cloth made up half the exports, which totaled £40,000. The next most important commodities were lead and tin. The rest of the company's exports to Russia were composed of small quantities of the sort of goods taken there by the Dutch and Germans.[102]

The Trade with Other Countries

Trade with Holland, Germany, and England formed the great part of Russia's European commerce. The smaller part was carried on with the neighboring states, Poland-Lithuania, Sweden, Norway, and Denmark. Most of this trade took place with Poland-Lithuania and Sweden, Russia's immediate neighbors to the west. Trade with Poland was for a long time limited largely to the towns on the Russian-Polish frontier and was handicapped by the repeated warfare between the two states. Nevertheless, it was not an insignificant trade, and after 1678 greater freedom was granted the merchants of each country to trade in the other.[103] The trade with Sweden followed a similar course. Much of it was transacted in the western towns, in Tikhvinsk, Kargopol, Novgorod, and Pskov, and in the ports of Narva, Reval, and Riga. In 1661, by the treaty of Kardin, the Russians received the right to trade in Stockholm, Kolyvan, Vyborg, and other towns under Swedish dominion theretofore not open to Russian merchants. In return, the Swedes were allowed to trade in several Russian towns previously closed to them.[104] Trade with Denmark and Norway was of minor consequence. The Danes, not a strong people commercially, sent a few ships to the Baltic ports visited by the Russians, and occasionally they appeared at Pskov, Novgorod, and Arkhangelsk.[105] The Norwegians carried on a small trade with the Russians at Vardö and along the Murmansk coast, and probably they sent a few ships now and then to Arkhangelsk.

The extent of the export of furs to these countries can only be surmised. A number of furs must have been shipped to Poland, for many of the Russian furs bought and sold in Germany came

[102] Liubimenko, "Torgovyia snosheniia Rossii s Angliei," pp. 152–157; Wretts-Smith, p. 78 n. 3; J. R., "The Trade's Increase," p. 214; Bazilevich, "Krupnoe torgovoe predpriiatie," pp. 793, 794.

[103] Kostomarov, p. 308; *P.S.Z.*, II, 173, 781.

[104] *D.A.I.*, IV, 270–271; E. E. Zamyslovskii, "Snosheniia Rossii s Shvetsiei i Daniei v tsarstvovanie Fedora Alekseevicha," *Russkii vestnik*, 1889, No. 1, pp. 9–11.

[105] Khilkov, pp. 248–249.

there by way of Poland. Posen, one of the most important of Polish towns, is known to have been a thriving fur center, the source of many of the furs that came to Leipzig, Danzig, and Lübeck. The Jews, who predominated in the Posen fur trade, did a big business in fox, bear, otter, sable, marten, and beaver pelts.[106] To be sure, Poland itself yielded some furs in the seventeenth century, but, with the supply of fur-bearing animals in European Russia greatly depleted, there is no reason to believe that Poland's supply was not also exhausted. Most of the furs found in Polish markets must have come from Siberia through Russia.[107] The places from which the Poles procured furs were chiefly Novgorod, Pskov, and the Swine Market at Briansk. With respect to the Scandinavian countries little can be said beyond the fact that Russian furs were shipped to them.[108] Presumably the Swedes included Russian furs among their purchases at Reval, Novgorod, Pskov, and Kargopol, and it is to be expected that the Russians, when they began visiting Swedish ports, carried furs as part of their goods. The Danes, small as their trade with Russia was, must have taken away with them a fairly large proportion of furs, since they appear to have done much of their trading at Novgorod and Arkhangelsk.[109] Inasmuch as trade between Russia and Norway occurred chiefly in Lapland and on the Kola Peninsula, long-established fur regions, furs would seem to have been a staple in their trade. Suggestive is the record of an attempt by Norwegians to establish connections at Pustozersk for the purpose of fur trade.[110]

The principal goods taken to Russia by the Polish and Lithuanian merchants were commodities acquired from the West rather than those produced in Poland, since Polish goods were the same as those produced in Russia.[111] The chief Swedish commodities imported into Russia were copper and iron.[112] It is not clear what the Danes and Norwegians sold the Russians. One would assume that it was fish and goods from the West.

Notwithstanding that France, Italy, Spain, and Portugal were important consumers of Russian furs, there is no trustworthy evi-

[106] Breger, pp. 11, 20–21; cf. Marperger, p. 282.

[107] Lewes Roberts, *The Merchants Mappe of Commerce,* p. 176; Tishchenko, p. 109 n. 6.

[108] Augustin von Mayerberg, *Puteshestvie v Moskoviiu barona Avgustina Maierberga i Goratsiia Vil'gel'ma Kal'vuchchi,* p. 32.

[109] *Torgovaia kniga,* p. 133.

[110] S. V. Bakhrushin, *Ocherki po istorii kolonizatsii Sibiri,* p. 72.

[111] Reitenfels, p. 187; Roberts, p. 164.

[112] Zamyslovskii, pp. 9–10.

dence of direct trade between these countries and Russia. Only for the French is there record of a vessel having visited Russia: one came to Arkhangelsk in 1586.[113] The French on several occasions in the late sixteenth and the seventeenth centuries entered into negotiations looking to the establishment of direct trade with Russia, a trade in which furs promised to be the most important export. But the only result was the granting of privileges to whatever French company might be formed—privileges which were never used—and to the end of the seventeenth century the exchange of goods between France and Russia remained securely in the hands of the Dutch.[114] Boris Godunov made an abortive attempt in 1603 to establish trade with Tuscany, an attempt which appears to have been unique as far as Italy was concerned.[115] De la Neville, who visited Moscow in 1689, mentions Italians as residents in the Foreign Suburb of Moscow, but whether they were traders or artisans he does not say.[116] Beyond a proposal to harry Dutch commerce in the North Sea and Arctic Ocean, Spain seems to have given no attention to the Russian trade.[117] Portugal, likewise, carried on no direct trade with Russia. The exchange of Italian, Spanish, and Portuguese goods for Russian commodities, like that of French goods, took place almost entirely through the Dutch, the English carrying a small part of the trade.

The State's Export Trade with Europe

The export of furs to the countries of Europe was a traffic in which the private enterprisers played, and were allowed to play, the greater part. It was open to all who wished to participate in it and was subject to no restrictions not common to trade in general.[118] This does not mean, however, that the state exported few furs to Europe; on the contrary, its fur exports there were considerable. However, in comparison with its position in the export fur

[113] France, Commission des Archives Diplomatiques, *Recueil des instructions: Russie*, I, 11.

[114] *Ibid.*, pp. 13–16, 22–23, 27–31, 54, 56–59, 62, 72–73; Forsten, I, 193, 297–298, 300–301; P. I. Potemkin, "Stateinoi spisok posol'stva stol'nika i namestnika borovskago, Petra Ivanovicha Potemkina, v Frantsiiu v 7175 (1667) gode," *Drevniaia rossiiskaia vivliofika*, IV, 518; *Sbornik imperatorskago istoricheskago obshchestva*, XXXIV, ii–iii, v; cf. J. B. Colbert, *Lettres, instructions et mémoires de Colbert*, Vol. II, pt. 2, pp. 605, 609, 800–802; *P.S.Z.*, II, 278–279.

[115] Forsten, I, 214.

[116] De la Neville, "Zapiski de-la Nevilla o Moskovii," *Russkaia starina*, LXXII (1891), 275.

[117] Forsten, I, 302–307.

[118] De Rodes, p. 251.

traffic to Asia, its participation in the European fur trade was not so conspicuous.

The export of furs to Europe by the state was well established by the middle of the sixteenth century, and with the growth of Russia's commerce with the West that export developed. Under the last Rurikovich tsars it had taken place chiefly at Moscow, though Ivan IV succeeded in sending a few treasury merchants abroad to trade in foreign markets.[119] When the fur resources of Siberia were opened to the state, its export of furs to Europe naturally increased. It expanded its commercial operations so that by 1608, at least, it was sending treasury caravans with furs to Arkhangelsk, which, along with treasury caravans to Novgorod, Pskov, and later the Swine Market at Briansk, became the principal means of exporting furs to Europe.[120] Upon those occasions when the tsar sent his envoys to European courts, treasury merchants with furs accompanied them, and in a few rare instances the Romanov tsars sent treasury merchants independently into Western markets to trade. Russia's lack of a merchant marine, however, and the opposition of foreign merchants to encroachments upon their carrying trade long effectively blocked commercial operations abroad by Russian merchants.[121]

The state did a big export business with Europe in furs—big enough, in fact, to make it the greatest individual exporter of furs from Russia, but its prominence did not extend beyond that. It did not try to monopolize in any way the export of furs to the European countries, except in so far as its efforts to secure all the best furs that came out of Siberia gave it a monopoly position in that traffic; and since it failed to get all such furs, not even that kind of monopoly obtained. The size of the state's fur exports to Europe can only be guessed at. In the middle of the seventeenth century it was sending ten to twenty thousand rubles' worth of furs to Arkhangelsk each year.[122] The furs it shipped to Novgorod, Pskov, and Briansk, which was then beginning its commercial development, and the furs sold at Moscow may be estimated roughly as equal to those sent to Arkhangelsk. Yet it must also be borne in

[119] Kordt, p. xvii n. 2; *R.I.B.*, XVI, 91.

[120] A. A. Kizevetter, *Russkii sever*, pp. 48, 56; Kurts, p. 331; Viktorov, I, 87, 88.

[121] *A.A.E.*, IV, 19; Khilkov, p. 254; Ogloblin, IV, 56.

[122] Kizevetter, p. 56; Kurts, *loc. cit.;* Ogloblin, III, 341, IV, 56, 84, 88, 93, 94, 167.

mind that often a shipment of furs was not sold out.[123] The state's fur exports after 1650 probably continued at the same level as at the middle of the century, dropping off towards the end of the century as its fur revenue decreased, trade with China began, and competition from Canadian furs began to be felt. During the sixteenth century and the early seventeenth its exports were lower. Comparing the fur exports of the state with other commodities which it exported to Europe, we find furs exceeded by caviar and silk, which were state monopolies, and undoubtedly equaled, if not exceeded, by grain, flax, hemp, and hides, a fact which points to Europe as the market mainly of the private Russian exporters of furs.[124]

The goods acquired by the state were much the same as those obtained by private merchants, though naturally the tsar gave particular attention to military supplies and equipment. Also he was a big buyer of luxury goods from the West—fine fabrics, French and German wines, jewelry, precious stones, gold, silver, and glasswork—which he needed to maintain the dignity and splendor of court befitting an exalted monarch.[125]

Holland, Germany, England, Poland-Lithuania, Sweden, Denmark, and Norway—those were the countries in Europe with whose merchants Russia carried on trade during the sixteenth and seventeenth centuries. The Dutch, Germans, and English accounted for much the greater part of the furs exported from Russia. With the Dutch and the Germans, furs ranked at the top, or very near it, among the goods which they purchased in Russia. With the English, furs stood as the second most important commodity brought by them from Russia. Less is known about the fur exports to the other four countries. In Poland-Lithuania there is good reason to suppose that furs were a primary Russian export. With respect to the Scandinavian countries the data permit no more positive assertion than that furs were exported to them in appreciable quantities. In exchange for furs the Russian merchants acquired many necessary and useful commodities, which were produced either not at all in Russia or in small quantities, especially woolen cloth, make-up silk, linen, and cotton goods, a variety of manufactured wares and hardware, spices, and the iron, copper, lead, and tin needed for domestic manufactures.

[123] Ogloblin, IV, 56, 84, 88.
[124] De Rodes, pp. 249–250, 253–254.
[125] *D.A.I.*, III, 206–207, VI, 89–92; Khilkov, p. 181.

Importance of the European Export Trade

How great the export of furs to Europe by private enterprisers was can only be roughly estimated. Calculations in the preceding chapter set the value of the furs taken out of Siberia by private enterprisers during an average good year at the round figure of 300,000 to 325,000 rubles in terms of Siberian prices.[126] Probably about four-fifths of Russia's furs were exported. If so, on the basis of the higher prices of furs in the export centers, the value of those exported to Europe would seem to have approached an average 300,000 r. annually, though great fluctuations occurred in the fur yield from year to year, as the figures for the fur receipts of the state from Siberia have shown us. That the figure 300,000 r. is near the truth is suggested by the export of 98,000 rubles' worth of furs from Arkhangelsk in 1653; for the handling of one-third of the fur exports through that port seems a fair measure of its importance as the leading export center. But these calculations are admittedly guesswork and are advanced here merely to give some sort of measure of the extent of Russia's fur traffic with Europe.

For the most part the importance of the European export trade is evident. The function of the European market as the foundation of the Russian fur trade, and the direct connection between the highly stimulated fur traffic and Russian expansion into Siberia have been iterated and elaborated upon in the course of this study. What has not been stressed, however, is the significance of the Europe-based fur trade as the most important single factor in the creation of a comparatively strong and numerically increasing Russian commercial class during the seventeenth century. As we saw earlier, such a class did not develop in Russia at the time that it did in Western Europe, and even late in the sixteenth century the commercial element in Russia had not taken substantial form as an independent class or shown signs of economic power.[127] But the facts that the fur trade was open to all who would risk its perils, that the state did not and could not interfere seriously in private participation in the trade, and that large profits accrued to successful traders enabled the few established big merchants in the seventeenth century to increase their power and resulted in the appearance of new merchants and a greater number of them.

[126] See above, p. 181.

[127] A. S. Lappo-Danilevskii, *Russkiia promyshlennyia i torgovyia kompanii v pervoi polovine XVIII stoletiia,* pp. 9–10.

Most of the big merchants of Russia in this century were engaged in the Siberian-European fur trade; most of the big commercial fortunes were derived from it; and, as we previously noted, men from all ranks in Russia engaged in this trade, many of the big merchants having risen from small beginnings.[128] Thus, in addition to the benefits of commercial exchange, which furs made possible, the fur trade possessed this special significance of contributing to the emergence of a middle class and to the rise of a commercial capitalism in Russia.

The middle of the seventeenth century witnessed the apogee of the Russian fur trade. It was then that expansion in Siberia reached its peak and furs were brought to Russia in the greatest abundance. But the fur trade could not remain at that height; soon unfavorable market conditions appeared, created by that same abundance of furs. Hitherto, the demand had usually exceeded the supply, but now the reverse situation began oftener to occur, and in this new situation the state was the most influential factor. Its fur receipts, greatly increased by conquests in Eastern Siberia, accumulated in large amounts in the Sable Treasury; the treasury's efforts to dispose of them depressed the market price and threatened the private traders with serious losses. This situation arose as early as 1649, as a letter of the gost Vasilii Fedotov to his agent at Iakutsk testifies. Fedotov instructed his agent not to pay high prices for sables because they had become very cheap in the Russian markets, the treasury having an excess of them.[129] A decade or so later, the Serb, Juraj Križanić, then resident in Tobolsk, pointed to the same condition: the penetration always farther to the east in pursuit of furs had brought such a quantity of them into the treasury that they were greatly depreciated in value.[130] Normally, as the pristine abundance of fur-bearing animals was reduced, this situation would have corrected itself, but a new factor appeared, the competition in the European markets of beavers and foxes from North America. In fact, some of these beaver and fox pelts were imported into Russia itself. This was not a new experience in the Russian fur trade—the Dutch had imported beavers into Russia as early as 1621—but in the second

[128] *Ibid.*, p. 11; Bazilevich, "Krupnoe torgovoe predpriiatie," pp. 784, 801–802, 806–807; *idem*, "Tamozhennye knigi," pp. 125–126; Bakhrushin, "Torgi gostia Nikitina," pp. 359–375; see above, p. 149.

[129] Bazilevich, "Krupnoe torgovoe predpriiatie," p. 794.

[130] J. Križanić, *Russkoe gosudarstvo v polovine XVII veka*, chap. (*razdel*) 51, p. 122 (in Supplement to No. 5, *Russki Beseda*, 1859); Kurts, p. 334.

half of the seventeenth century the imports of them, as well as of some other furs, assumed more significant proportions.[131] Russia was losing the dominance of the European fur market which it had enjoyed for so long. The star of the Russian fur trade was setting in Europe; the star of the Canadian fur trade was beginning to rise. Nevertheless, to the end of the seventeenth century the Russian fur trade continued to be active and to serve as the principal source of Europe's furs. Throughout the eighteenth century, too, many Russian furs went to Europe, especially to Leipzig. But the center of gravity of the Russian fur trade shifted then from the West to the East; the Russians discovered in Asia a new market as great as the one they were losing in Europe. The expansion eastward, which had created the plethora of furs, ended by supplying its own remedy—by bringing the Russians into contact with the Chinese, and for the eighteenth century the history of the Russian fur trade is to be written in terms of the trade with China. But that is another story, which is outside the province of this study.

[131] Kordt, p. cclxxxiii; Kilburger, pp. 276, 288, 298; Savary, II, 174; Colbert, Vol. II, pt. 2, p. 801.

CHAPTER XI

THE EXPORT OF FURS TO ASIA

IN CONTRAST TO the export of furs to Europe, Russia's export fur traffic to Asia was dominated by the state. Whereas in the European trade the state was content to export its furs on the same basis as did the private merchants, in the Asiatic trade it manifested those efforts at monopoly which marked its activities in Siberia: it sought to reserve, if not all, certainly the best part of the fur traffic to itself. This difference is explained not so much by the fur trade as by the silk trade. Silk during the late sixteenth and the seventeenth centuries was probably the most important single import from Asia into Europe. In view of the proximity of Russia to the countries in Asia which were then the chief sources of silk, the tsar sought to benefit from this advantage, and consequently he made the silk trade in Russia a monopoly of the state. To secure himself in this monopoly he made the traffic in those goods which were in great demand in these Asiatic countries also state monopolies, and sables and other fine furs were such goods.[1] However, the monopoly of the export of furs to Asia was not merely a means to an end, but an end in itself as well; there were definite advantages for the tsar in monopolizing the traffic in fine furs.

THE STATE'S EXPORT MONOPOLY

The state's monopoly of the export trade in furs with Asia did not arise at any specific time, nor was it a complete and flat denial of all private participation in it. Only at the end of the seventeenth century did it approach that extreme and then only with respect to certain kinds of furs. Rather, the monopoly of the state tended to follow the development of Russian trade with Asia and usually applied only to the better furs, since those commanded the best market. When there appeared a new market for furs which promised large returns, the state asserted its political authority and took over the most lucrative part of that market, though in some instances it was slower to take action than in others. The silk monopoly, with which the fur monopoly became associated, did

[1] Johann de Rodes, "Bedenken über den russischen Handel im Jahre 1653," *Beiträge zur Kenntniss Russlands und seiner Geschichte*, p. 247; J. P. Kilburger, "Kurzer Unterricht von dem russischen Handel," *Buschings Magazin*, III (1769), 311; *A.A.E.*, IV, 303.

not arise until the second quarter of the seventeenth century, hence the incentive for the state's extending its restrictions against private competition was not intensified until then. Thus, not until the middle of that century did the monopoly of fur exports assume widespread proportions, and not until the end of the century and the beginning of the next did it reach its maximum extent. In short, this monopoly evolved without much planning or forethought.

A partial monopoly of the sale of furs to Asiatic merchants had already appeared in the sixteenth century as the result of certain restrictions upon the trade of foreign merchants who came to Moscow. Foreign merchants were required, upon arriving in Moscow, first to present themselves at the tsar's treasury. Here the officials selected from their goods those desired for the treasury and reimbursed them with money or goods, often furs, or both.[2] Only after this procedure had been gone through, might foreign merchants do business with private merchants in Moscow. En route to Moscow, foreign merchants—at least Asiatic merchants—were not to engage in trade.[3] If their destination was a town other than Moscow, they were to present themselves first to the customs officials of that town, where the same procedure was followed as at the treasury in Moscow.[4] In this fashion the state reserved to itself first selection of the goods brought to Russia by the merchants from Asia and made possible the purchase by the state, without private competition, of as much silk as it saw fit. At the same time it put itself in the position to be the first to sell its furs and other goods to these merchants.

These requirements, which applied to all foreign merchants who came to Moscow, the state supplemented in the seventeenth century with restrictions applying to particular merchants. Thus, in 1677, it ordered that Moscow merchants should not sell to Persian merchants sables costing 100 r. or more a forty; in 1681, it stipulated that promyshlenniks and traders who came to Moscow with furs from Siberia were not to sell them to foreign or Greek merchants without permission of the state.[5] Since it was the fine furs

[2] G. Kotoshikhin, *O Rossii v tsarstvovanie Aleksiia Mikhailovicha*, p. 165; N. I. Veselovskii, *Pamiatniki diplomaticheskikh i torgovykh snoshenii moskovskoi Rusi s Persiei*, I, 194–197, 202, 211, 212, 305, II, 58, III, 11–12, 36; Jacob Reitenfels, *Skazaniia svetleishemu gertsogu toskanskomu Koz'me tret'mu o Moskovii*, p. 133; Richard Hakluyt, *The Principal Navigations*, II, 87; *D.A.I.*, VII, 122, 124–125.

[3] Veselovskii, III, 262.

[4] *Ibid.*, pp. 70–71; *A.I.*, IV, 39.

[5] *A.A.E.*, IV, 303; *P.S.Z.*, II, 89–90, 325.

which were most sought by the Persian and Greek traders—the most important of the Asiatic merchants to come to Moscow—these regulations meant that the state would allow only a residual trade to private merchants.

At the same time, Asiatic merchants traded also in other towns than Moscow, in Astrakhan particularly and in the towns along the Volga. With respect to these towns we do not find in the available documents restrictions definitely limiting the sale of furs to foreign merchants. Yet the state had, by the beginning of the seventeenth century, specified certain goods as prohibited goods, which the Russians were not to sell to foreigners. What, precisely, were prohibited goods is not stated fully.[6] We know that living sables, foxes, ermines, and squirrels were included among them, since the tsar frequently presented them as gifts to Asiatic potentates and did not wish them cheapened through private traffic.[7] We have seen too that certain furs were prohibited goods in Moscow. These circumstances incline us to the belief that, when the state undertook seriously to make the silk trade a monopoly, it imposed in Astrakhan and the other Volga cities the same sort of restrictions upon the sale of furs to merchants from Asia that it did in Moscow.

Besides trading with Asiatic merchants who came to Russia, the state often sent caravans with furs and other goods to Persia and, occasionally, to Khiva and Bukhara. In the sixteenth century it was the policy of the state to exclude private merchants altogether from these expeditions. In the seventeenth century it permitted a few chosen ones to accompany them, but it forbade these merchants to traffic in prohibited goods.[8] The treasury merchants, on the other hand, who were private merchants in the service of the state, were excepted and allowed to trade in certain prohibited goods as a form of compensation for their service. Thus, Rodion Pushkin, who took a small shipment of furs and other treasury goods to Persia in 1616, was allowed to take 11 forties of sables, 4 forties of weasels, cloth, ivory, and mirrors of his own; also, the gosts Syroezhin and Tushkanov, who went in 1652 with a diplomatic-commercial expedition destined for India, were permitted to take 2,500 rubles' worth of furs and other goods of their own.[9] Private expeditions abroad were

[6] *A.I.*, III, 212, 259, IV, 16–17, 39.
[7] Veselovskii, I, 311, 341, III, 157, 655–656.
[8] *Ibid.*, I, 341, III, 235, 356.
[9] *Ibid.*, III, 156–157, 168–169; V. A. Ulianitskii, "Snosheniia Rossii s sredneiu Azieiu i Indieiu v XVI–XVII vv.," *Chteniia*, 1888, No. 3, pt. 2, p. 24.

generally forbidden to Russian merchants, but to what extent the state specifically prohibited the journeying of private caravans to Persia and the khanates of Central Asia is not known.[10]

In Siberia, the state attempted restriction of the export of furs to Asia by private merchants, both Russian and Asiatic, to a much greater degree than it did in Russia. This resulted ultimately in a complete monopoly of the trade in sables and black foxes, which commanded the best market. But it was only at the end of the seventeenth century that the state attempted such a far-reaching monopoly. In the beginning, it depended mainly upon the restrictive measures applied to the Siberian trade in general to limit private export of furs. For a long time the only regulation specifically restricting private fur exports was that which required the natives not to sell furs to foreigners.[11] Then, in 1664, the voevoda of Tobolsk was ordered not to allow the sale there of sables, beavers, foxes, and other good furs to foreign merchants. A privileged group of foreign merchants, known as Bukharans, might buy such furs but might not export them from Siberia; they had to exchange them for other Siberian or Russian goods.[12]

Not until the last decade of the seventeenth century did the state undertake on a grand scale to restrict the export of furs by private individuals. It took this step because of its desire to secure its position in the newly established trade with China, which promised to be extremely profitable. At this time the state's trade was suffering more than the private trade from the decreasing supply of sables. The voevodas of Eastern Siberia more than ever kept for themselves the best furs coming into the local treasuries, sending the mediocre and poor ones to Moscow, a form of graft which they tried to conceal by overvaluing the inferior pelts and complaining of the scarcity of good ones. In the meantime, the good pelts thus illegally obtained they sent with agents of their own to China. The authorities at Moscow felt obliged therefore to clamp down on this illegal and damaging competition.[13] In 1693 the state decreed that sables costing more than 40 r. and black foxes were not to be exported by private individuals to China or any other country. It also specified that traders going to China must obtain a passport from the local

[10] Cf. *A.I.*, IV, 70.

[11] See above p. 74 n. 21.

[12] *D.A.I.*, IV, 355, 361. The order was repeated in 1697 and 1698. See nn. 15 and 16 below.

[13] *P.S.Z.*, III, 282–283, 357, 359.

authorities in Siberia.[14] Then, four years later, it decreed a monopoly of all sables and black foxes, requiring that all such skins should be taken into the treasury either as iasak or tithe, or by purchase.[15] In the following year, it ordered that henceforth private traders might go to China only with the biennial treasury caravans, and finally, in 1706, it excluded private traders altogether from the export trade to China.[16]

These decrees of the state from 1697 to 1706 concerning the China trade mark the extreme point of its efforts to establish a monopoly of Asiatic exports. However, the pattern of evolution of the state's monopoly was in general the same, wherever the trade with Asia was concerned. The monopoly began as a partial one, the state reserving to itself the right of dealing first with the merchants who came into Russia from Asiatic countries. The monopoly was then broadened to exclude Russian merchants from the sale of the better furs to Asiatic merchants, and, finally, to exclude Russian merchants from any trade in sables, as well as in black foxes. Also, the state forbade Russian merchants to leave Russia or confined their foreign travel to its own commercial caravans periodically sent abroad, thus making the export monopoly virtually complete.

We turn now to examine the export of furs to the several countries in Asia with whose merchants Russia traded, namely, Persia, the Ottoman empire, the khanates of Central Asia, India, and China. Our interest is to ascertain the character of the state's trade with each country and the relative importance of furs as an export commodity.

The Trade with Persia

Russia's greatest trade with an Asiatic country was with Persia. Direct trade between the two countries began soon after Ivan IV conquered Astrakhan in 1555. During the remainder of the sixteenth and throughout the seventeenth centuries it grew steadily, being considerably facilitated by the friendly political relations between the Russian tsar and the Persian shah. In this trade the state participated very extensively, trafficking with the Persians chiefly at Moscow and Astrakhan and also sending treasury caravans with goods to Persia. From the outset of Russian-Persian com-

---

[14] *P.S.Z.*, III, 164–165.

[15] *P.S.Z.*, III, 282–283, 358–359, 405–406. The prohibition was reaffirmed the following year (*P.S.Z.*, III, 498, 501–502, 505, 507).

[16] *P.S.Z.*, III, 502–503, IV, 336.

mercial relations many Persian merchants—some of them agents of the shah; others, private enterprisers—visited Moscow and there carried on an exchange of goods with the tsar's treasury.[17] By the second half of the seventeenth century these Persian merchants constituted the largest group of Asiatic traders in Moscow.[18] On its side, the tsar's treasury began early to send its merchants to Persia. During the reigns of Ivan IV, Fedor Ivanovich, and Boris Godunov such trade abroad took place almost entirely as an adjunct to the diplomatic missions sent to the court of the shah. After the Troublous Times, however, the treasury began to send purely commercial expeditions to Persia, as well as trade caravans to Astrakhan, where many Persian and other foreign merchants congregated each year. At the middle of the seventeenth century the treasury's trade with Persia had reached the point where a caravan with goods went annually either to Persia or Astrakhan, and during the reign of Aleksei Mikhailovich (1645–1676) the Persian trade of the state rose greatly in volume.[19]

The position of furs in the trade with Persia is clearly that of the most important commodity exported there by the state, though whether the state exported furs there in quantities sufficient to make them first of all Russian exports to Persia cannot be said. But we may be sure that even on that basis they still ranked among the highest. The kind and quantity of goods which Persian merchants bought in Russia are illustrated by those which one Khosrov Alei, a merchant of the shah, carried away in 1594. He took with him 27½ forties of sables, 180 red foxes, 70 arctic foxes, 5 black foxes, 20 martens, 7 garments (*portishchi*) of sable bellies, 7 of weasels, 14 coats of sable, 3 of squirrel, 1 of marten, 100 waistcoats (*iufti*) of sable bellies, 7 blankets of red foxes, and 3 of weasels, 120 suits of armor, 600 pounds of tin, 2,400 pounds of lead, 1,200 pounds of birch [bark ?], 80 pounds of pure wax, 160 pounds of beaver-gland extract (*struia*), 200 knives, 200 hides, 2 chests of glass, 28

[17] Veselovskii, I, 45, 153, 191, 202, 213, 279, 297, 305, II, 58, 398, III, 1, 11–12, 17, 25, 60, 259, 262, 640.

[18] Heinrich Storch, *Historisch-statistische Gemälde des russischen Reichs am Ende des XVIII Jahrhunderts*, IV, 433.

[19] Veselovskii, II, 55, III, 156–157, 168–169, 361, 547; Ogloblin, III, 341–343, IV, 159, 164; A. G. Viktorov, *Opisanie zapisnykh knig i bumag starinnykh dvortsovykh prikazov, 1584–1725 gg.*, I, 95, 96; *R.I.B.*, XXIII, 1413, cf. pp. 1481–1482, 1531–1532, 1563–1564; F. A. Kotov, "O khodu v persitskoe tsarstvo i iz Persidu v Turetskuiu zemliu i v Indiiu, i v Urmuz, gde korabli prikhodiat," *Vremennik imperatorskago moskovskago obshchestva istorii i drevnostei rossiiskikh*, Vol. XV (1852), pt. 2, p. 1.

walrus tusks, and writing paper.[20] The value of these goods is not given, but furs, especially sables, foxes, and martens, customarily carried a much higher price per unit than did the other goods, so that here they appear to stand highest on the basis of value.[21] The 20 sable garments, 100 fine red foxes, 50 weasels, 200 common foxes, 100 squirrel coats, 50 fox coats, and 5 marten coats which another Persian merchant carried away from the tsar's treasury in the same year constituted about the same proportion of furs to other goods as did the furs taken in the transaction of Khosrov Alei.[22] Records of other goods received by Persians show a similar proportion of furs to other commodities.[23]

In 1618 a treasury caravan went to Persia with 1,000 rubles' worth of sables and cloth, and in 1627 a treasury agent was given 40 forties of sables to use in buying raw silk from Persian merchants.[24] The only instance of anything like complete records of trade with Persia is the treasury caravan to Persia in the years 1663–1665. The treasury merchants in charge of this caravan took with them sables and sable bellies appraised at 32,800 r., cloth (mostly English) appraised at 23,949 r., copper appraised at 3,000 r., and 14,000 r. in money, a total of 76,749 r. Of this amount, 71,454 rubles' worth was disposed of in Persia at prices which brought a profit of 5,196 r., or 7 per cent.[25] With the money thus obtained the merchants bought Persian goods to the extent of 73,586 r., used 1,507 r. for caravan expenses, and brought the rest back to Moscow.[26] There is no record of the amounts which the sale of the Persian goods yielded, hence a picture of the complete turnover of capital is not possible. However, in view of the expenses involved in making the trip to Persia and the relatively small profit on the sale of Russian goods in Persia, this expedition would appear not to have made very much profit. These figures do indicate, nevertheless, a large volume of business with Persia at this time. In fact, Persia was the principal market for the furs which the state exported.

The principal commodity which the state received in exchange for furs was, as we have already indicated, silk, in both the raw

[20] Veselovskii, I, 311.
[21] Cf. De Rodes, p. 247, and *A.A.E.*, IV, 303.
[22] Veselovskii, I, 213.
[23] *Ibid.*, II, 58, III, 168–169, 243.
[24] *Ibid.*, III, 547; Ogloblin, IV, 165.
[25] *R.I.B.*, XXIII, 1413–1425, 1449.
[26] *R.I.B.*, XXIII, 1478, 1481–1482.

and fabricated forms. Persia was at this time the principal source of the world's silk, which accounts for the frequent and, in later years at least, large treasury expeditions to Persia. Besides silk the treasury merchants bought quantities of cotton stuffs and cotton goods, also Morocco leather, paper, and a few precious stones.[27]

The Greek Merchants

The next largest trade of the tsar's treasury was that which it maintained with the Greek merchants from the Ottoman empire. Most of them came from Moldavia and Greece, but their trading operations extended throughout the Ottoman empire and into Persia.[28] In contrast to the active role played by the treasury in the trade with Persia, the role of the treasury in the Greek trade was a passive one: the Greek merchants came to Moscow and there carried on an exchange of goods with it. No treasury caravans were sent even to the southwestern frontier towns, let alone to the Ottoman empire itself.

Little is known of the trade with the Greek merchants prior to the middle of the seventeenth century. At that time, according to Kotoshikhin, from fifty to a hundred of them visited Moscow each year. Many of them had been engaged in this trade a long time, a circumstance which points to long-standing commercial relations between Russia and the Ottoman empire.[29] But there is good reason to suppose that the number was even greater. The numerous Orthodox clergymen of all ranks who came to Moscow seeking the tsar's charity invariably brought with them so-called relatives (*plemianiki*), who were usually none other than merchants. In their capacity as "relatives" these merchants enjoyed transportation of themselves and their goods between Putivl and Moscow and support while in Moscow, all at the expense of the treasury, as well as exemptions from the prevailing customs dues and fees. They were thereby enabled to buy goods cheaply, particularly furs, and to sell them abroad at a tremendous profit, which they had to divide with their cleric-patron.[30] The trade of the Greeks at Moscow flour-

[27] Veselovskii, I, 129, 194–197, 213, 305, III, 12–13, 17, 36, 171, 546, 640–641.

[28] De Rodes, pp. 251–252; Kilburger, p. 313.

[29] Kotoshikhin, p. 165; N. F. Kapterev, *Kharakter otnoshenii Rossii k pravoslavnomu vostoku v XVI i XVII stoletiiakh,* p. 268.

[30] Kapterev, pp. 113, 188, 252, 264; Paul of Aleppo, *The Travels of Macarius, Patriarch of Antioch,* II, 289. Some of the Greek hierarch immigrants who settled in Russia made use of their privileged position to engage either directly or through "relatives" in an export trade in furs (Kapterev, p. 153).

ished until the beginning of the last quarter of the century. At that time the appearance of several abuses, such as secret trade, prompted the tsar to ban most of the Greek merchants from Moscow and to confine their trade to Putivl, the town of entry on the southwestern frontier.[31]

The Greek merchants not only carried away large numbers of sables and other furs from the tsar's treasury in Moscow, but they took almost exclusively furs, excepting money.[32] This is the assertion both of the Swedish resident in Moscow, De Rodes, and of the Russian, Kotoshikhin, and it is confirmed by the few figures available to us.[33] These figures refer to the decade of the 1670's and show that the Department of Ambassadors paid out to the Greek merchants sables as follows:

Inclusive dates	Value in rubles
March 7 to June 20, 1672	1,044
March 12 to July 15, 1673	1,138
September 6, 1673, to August 1, 1674	1,363
October 6, 1674, to July 4, 1675	23,190

Money is the only other means recorded here for the payment of the Greeks for their goods. The goods which they brought to Moscow were mainly gold, silver, vessels, plates, cups, silk textiles, gold brocade, precious stones, jewelry, saddles, reins, bits, and some others. Silk was less prominent in this trade, but because gold, silver, and precious stones were greatly desired by the tsar, he reserved the trade with the Greeks to himself.[34]

The Trade with Central Asia

The trade which arose between Russia and the khanates of Central Asia was of secondary importance in comparison with the trade with Persia and the Greek merchants.[35] Yet it was an active trade and important locally, at least for Siberia. It began soon after the Russian conquest of Astrakhan. Merchants from Khiva, Bukhara, Samarkand, Tashkent, and other towns in Central Asia began trading at Astrakhan, which quickly developed into the center of trade with these merchants. Subsequently they extended their

[31] *P.S.Z.*, II, 75, 104; N. I. Kostomarov, *Ocherki torgovli moskovskago gosudarstva*, pp. 258–259; Kapterev, p. 268.

[32] Ogloblin, III, 89; *D.A.I.*, VI, 92–93, VII, 122.

[33] De Rodes, p. 251; Kotoshikhin, *loc. cit.; D.A.I.*, VII, 124–125.

[34] Kotoshikhin, *loc. cit.;* De Rodes, pp. 251–253; *D.A.I.*, VII, 124–125; *A.A.E.*, IV, 291; Kapterev, p. 164.

[35] Ulianitskii, p. 41.

activities to the towns on the upper Volga and to Moscow itself.[36] Meanwhile a particular group of these merchants, who passed under the name of "Bukharans," undertook trade with the Russians in Siberia soon after the latter appeared there. The importance for the Russians of the Bukharans' trade is attested by a petition to the tsar in 1597 to send Bukharans to Tobolsk for trade and by the willingness of subsequent tsars to let them trade in the Volga cities and northern towns.[37] These Bukharans, who, despite their name, probably included in their numbers merchants from places other than Bukhara, formed a sort of freemasonry of Central Asian merchants and carried their trade as far south as India and as far east as China. Several of them maintained their headquarters and permanent residence at Tobolsk.[38]

The trade between Russia and Central Asia remained almost entirely in the hands of the merchants from the several Asiatic khanates. On several occasions in the sixteenth and seventeenth centuries the state sent expeditions to Khiva and Bukhara to gain from their rulers the same rights of trade there for Russians as their subjects enjoyed in Russia, and also to seek commercial connections with India. In neither objective, however, did the Muscovite envoys succeed.[39] However, the state's role was not wholly an inactive one; it sent caravans of goods to Astrakhan, as we have seen, and with the just-mentioned missions to Bukhara and Khiva went the tsar's treasury merchants and his goods.

The kind of data about fur exports available for the trade with Persia is lacking for the trade with Central Asia. Hence the prominence of furs in this trade cannot be proved as conclusively. Yet, in the one instance of a record of the goods sent with an expedition to Central Asia—to Bukhara in 1646—furs and some ivory, together worth 1,000 r., made up the shipment. There are several other indications that furs were a major item among the goods sold by the tsar's treasury to the merchants from Central Asia.[40] First, the rulers of the khanates of Central Asia frequently re-

[36] *Ibid.*, pp. 5–6, 8; Ogloblin, III, 156; Veselovskii, II, 177, 258, III, 642; Kostomarov, p. 259.

[37] *Sobranie gosudarstvennykh gramot i dogovorov*, II, 129; *P.S.Z.*, II, 816–817; Samuel Purchas, *His Pilgrimes*, XIII, 232, 253; Ulianitskii, pp. 12–13.

[38] Ogloblin, III, 156; Gaston Cahen, *Histoire des relations de la Russie avec la Chine sous Pierre le Grand (1689–1730)*, p. 71; Kh. Trusevich, *Posol'skiia i torgovyia snosheniia Rossii s Kitaem (do XIX v.)*, pp. 12–13, 159; G. D. Khilkov, *Sbornik kniazia Khilkova*, p. 527.

[39] Ulianitskii, pp. 9–10, 19, 20, 37–38, 46, 56; Khilkov, pp. 446–460.

[40] Ulianitskii, pp. 20–21.

quested the tsar to send them sables.[41] Second, the Bukharan envoy to Russia in 1671, Mulafor, stated that the Russian goods in greatest demand in Bukhara were good sables, black foxes, ermines, woolen cloth, and walrus ivory.[42] Third, whenever and wherever furs were procurable, the Bukharans bought them extensively, as is shown by their trade in Siberia prior to the state's prohibition of the sale of furs to foreigners there (1664).[43] Fourth, there was a great similarity between the trade with Central Asia and that with Persia. Beyond this, however, the available evidence does not go. Subsequently, though, we shall see that there is sound reason to assume that furs were the chief article of export to Central Asia by the Bukharans in Siberia.

The goods which the Central Asian merchants brought into Russia were silk, raw and fabricated, various cotton, linen, and coarse woolen textiles and garments made of them, sheepskin coats, saltpeter, rhubarb (highly valued as an antiscorbutic), a few precious stones, and some goods from India.[44]

The Trade with India

The trade of the state with merchants from India developed late in the second half of the seventeenth century, and was not extensive. As in the trade with the Greeks, the treasury played a passive role, but not from choice. On three occasions, in 1646, in 1652, and in 1675, the tsar's treasury officials organized expeditions to India for the purpose of opening direct trade with that country. But the first two got no farther than Bukhara and Persia, and the third, though it reached Kabul in Afghanistan, a state vassal to the Indian mogul, had its request for permanent commercial intercourse refused.[45] Not until the period 1695–1701 did a Russian expedition (sent by the treasury) successfully trade in India.[46]

[41] *Ibid.*, pp. 12 n. 1, 14; Veselovskii, II, 166.

[42] Khilkov, p. 528.

[43] Ogloblin, I, 319, IV, 29; Purchas, *loc. cit.;* Veselovskii, I, 268; V. O. Kliuchevskii, *Skazaniia inostrantsev o moskovskom gosudarstve*, p. 272.

[44] Ulianitskii, pp. 14, 43; Khilkov, p. 527; Purchas, XIII, 232; Ogloblin, II, 24–25; G. N. Potanin, "Privoz i vyvoz tovarov goroda Tomska v polovine XVII stoletiia," *Vestnik imperatorskago russkago obshchestva*, Vol. XXVII (1859), pt. 2, pp. 133, 138, 143.

[45] A. F. Malinovskii, "Izvestie ob otpravleniiakh v Indiiu rossiiskikh poslannikov, gontsov i kupchin tovarami i o priezdakh v Rossiiu indeitsev, s 1469 po 1751 god," *Trudy i letopisi obshchestva istorii i drevnostei rossiskikh*, VII (1837), 125–130, 142–144, 153–157; Ulianitskii, pp. 24, 31–32, 34–35, 36–37, 53–54.

[46] Malinovskii, pp. 160–165.

Thus it was through the Indian merchants (or foreign merchants representing Indian rulers) who came to Astrakhan, the Volga towns, and Moscow that the treasury carried on its trade with India. Desirous of developing the treasury's trade with India, Tsar Aleksei Mikhailovich showed the Indian merchants particular consideration. The first of them to appear in Russia arrived in Moscow in 1645. Two years later a party of twenty-five came to Astrakhan, and one of their number went on to Moscow to gain permission for Indian merchants to trade regularly in Russia. Thereafter the Indian traders were frequent, if not numerous, visitors to Russia. However, after the death of Aleksei, their protector, their trade was restricted to Astrakhan as was the trade of most Orient merchants.[47]

Furs were the principal commodity sold to the Indian merchants by the treasury; they were also the staple commodity stocked by the abortive treasury expeditions. The Indian merchant who came to Moscow in 1647 told the treasury officials that, if permitted to trade in Russia, his fellow-merchants were ready to buy sables that were not too expensive, linen coats, copper, and other goods.[48] Thus, in 1663, when three Armenian merchants, who represented the mogul of India, came to Moscow with a large amount of goods, the tsar's officials paid for them to the extent of 10,472 r. in sables, cloth, and other goods.[49] When the treasury officials were organizing the expedition of 1675, an Indian merchant in Moscow informed them that sables worth from 10 to 30 r. a pair, red cloth, walrus tusks, Russian leather, and mirrors were in great demand in India. Thus the officials sent 174 sables worth 500 r. and 300 rubles' worth of other goods with the expedition.[50] The expedition of 1646 went with more than 5,000 r. in goods and that of 1695 with about 18,000 r. in goods, but the amount of sables and other furs included is not stated.[51] The goods which the treasury acquired from the Indian merchants were chiefly cotton, silk, and linen textiles and goods, Morocco leather, paints, sugar, and precious stones.[52] It was the hope of tapping a new source of silk and silk goods, as well as of precious stones, gold, and silver, that had led Aleksei to make special efforts to develop trade with India.

[47] *Ibid.*, pp. 140–141, 160; Ulianitskii, pp. 32, 34, 44, 56.
[48] Ulianitskii, p. 33.
[49] Malinovskii, pp. 144–146.
[50] *Ibid.*, pp. 153–154.
[51] *Ibid.*, pp. 137, 165; Ulianitskii, p. 24.
[52] Malinovskii, pp. 141–142, 165; Ulianitskii, pp. 33, 34.

The Trade with China

Trade between China and Russia did not become established on anything like a regular basis until the last decade of the seventeenth century, and it was not until the eighteenth century that a permanent basis for this trade was evolved. Thus in some respects trade with China falls outside the time limit set for this study. Nevertheless, the first attempts of the Russians to establish commercial relations with the Chinese extend over the second half of the seventeenth century, and even then the almost exclusive role of furs in the Chinese trade was evident. Moreover, this trade holds special interest for us because China subsequently became the great market for Russia's furs and because the trade with China is the one instance for which we have an adequately documented history of the attempt of the state to monopolize the export of furs.

Direct trade between Russia and China first occurred in 1656, after which there followed on the part of the Russians an irregular exploratory trade which did not attain a regular basis until 1689. To establish friendly political relations and to arrange for reciprocal rights of trade Moscow sent, between 1654 and 1676, three missions to Pekin: the first, 1654–1658, under Fedor Baikov, a merchant; the second, 1658–1662, under Ivan Perfiliev, a boiar-son from Tara, and Setkul Ablin, a Tobolsk Bukharan; and the third, 1675–1676, under Nikolai Spafarii, a noted and learned Moldavian Greek.[53] As was the custom, treasury merchants with goods from the tsar's treasury accompanied the envoys, and a few private merchants were permitted to go along.[54] However, none of the three missions succeeded in attaining the desired objectives. A fourth one, however, a strictly commercial venture by the state, was eminently successful. The Siberian Department sent Setkul Ablin, experienced in Asiatic trade, to Pekin in the years 1668–1672 with furs and other goods. He was joined in Siberia by many private Russian merchants and in Kalmuk territory by some two hundred Bukharans. Ablin sold the treasury's goods in Pekin and returned with Chinese goods which yielded the state a handsome profit.[55]

In the meantime, the Russians in Siberia began trading, inde-

---

[53] N. N. Bantysh-Kamenskii, *Diplomaticheskoe sobranie del mezhdu rossiiskim i kitaiskim gosudarstvami s 1619 po 1792-i god*, pp. 8–13; J. F. Baddeley, *Russia, Mongolia, China*, II, 25–53, 132–147, 207; Trusevich, pp. 18–21, 24–27.

[54] Ogloblin, III, 340.

[55] Bantysh-Kamenskii, pp. 13–14; B. G. Kurts, "Iz istorii torgovykh snoshenii Rossii s Kitaem v XVII st.," *Novyi vostok*, XXIII–XXIV, 333–334.

pendently of Moscow, with the Chinese both along the border and at Pekin. In the year 1670 about fifty Chinese merchants appeared at Nerchinsk, and therewith began at this Russian outpost, and also at Lake Dalai, a not inconsiderable trade between the Russians and Chinese.[56] A small trade also arose at near-by Albazin, which lasted for the few decades of Russian authority there.[57] In the year 1674–1675 the first Russian caravan of purely private organization went to Pekin. Comprised of forty-three men and headed by the Eniseisk boiar-son, Ivan Porshennikov, and a gost's agent, Gavril Romanovich Nikitin, it left Russian territory at Selenginsk and went by way of Urga to Pekin, where it remained seven weeks, its members being allowed to trade freely, though business at the time there was bad.[58] But from the time of this caravan and Spafarii's mission until the Treaty of Nerchinsk in 1689 no more expeditions went to Pekin. Chinese hostility because of the Amur controversy stood in the way.[59]

It was only after the dispute between Russia and China over the Amur had been settled that Moscow was able to gain formal permission for Russians to trade in China. By the fifth article of the Treaty of Nerchinsk each state accorded the subjects of the other the right to trade in its territory.[60] Immediately, private traders began to visit Pekin. In 1690 a diplomatic messenger to Pekin from Nerchinsk was accompanied by 80 or 90 men bringing with them sixty cartloads of furs.[61] In 1691 a caravan of 77 or 130 Russians came to Pekin purportedly for trade, and another in 1693 of 150 men.[62] It was not, however, until 1692 that Moscow saw fit to renew the treasury's trade with China. In that year it sent the merchant Isbrand Ides with a caravan to Pekin to trade and to study commercial conditions there. Many private traders attached themselves to his caravan, with the result that it numbered 175 men when it left Nerchinsk. Arriving back in Moscow in 1695, Ides advised the

[56] Trusevich, pp. 21, 22, 159; Baddeley, II, 196, 229.

[57] Baddeley, II, 227.

[58] *Ibid.*, pp. 256–257; Bantysh-Kamenskii, pp. 23–24; S. V. Bakhrushin, "Torgi gostia Nikitina v Sibiri i Kitae," *Sbornik statei: Pamiati Aleksandra Nikolaevicha Savina, 1873–1923*, Trudy instituta istorii rossiiskoi assotsiatsii nauchno-issledovatel'skikh institutov obshchestvennykh nauk, I (1926), 359–360, 375.

[59] Kurts, p. 334.

[60] Bantysh-Kamenskii, pp. 339–340.

[61] Cahen, pp. 76–77; J. B. du Halde, *Description géographique, historique, logique, politique, et physique de l'empire de la Chine et de la Tartarie chinoise*, IV, 280.

[62] Cahen, pp. 77–79, 80–81; Kurts, p. 336; Du Halde, IV, 343.

annual dispatch of treasury caravans with from 20,000 to 30,000 rubles' worth of furs and the exclusion of private traders from the Pekin trade.[63] To the annual caravans the state agreed—though by 1696 it had changed its decision in favor of biennial caravans—and in 1697 the treasury's first strictly commercial expedition set out for China, in charge of the guild merchant, Spiridon Liangusov. The state did not, however, exclude private traders, insisting instead that they go only with the treasury caravans, with the result that Liangusov's expedition was increased to 478 men when it left Nerchinsk. It reached Pekin late in 1698, and in 1701 Liangusov returned to Moscow.[64] Before this caravan had returned from Pekin, the Nerchinsk voevoda dispatched on his own authority a private one of 166 men.[65] Meanwhile, at Moscow the second treasury caravan was organized and placed under the merchant Bokov. With a personnel of 278 men, including many private merchants, it reached Pekin late in 1700 and returned to Moscow in 1703.[66] It was followed by other caravans, but their journeys fall outside our period.

Furs constituted an extraordinarily large share of the goods exported by the Russians to China; indeed, they played a far larger part in the Chinese trade than in that of any other country whose trade with Russia we have examined.[67] A rough estimate marks furs as comprising 80 to 90 per cent of the goods taken to Pekin or sold to the Chinese on the frontier. The explanation of this circumstance is readily seen: the long and expensive journey from Russia to China made the profitable sale of Russian or European goods in China infeasible.[68] On the other hand, Siberia, particularly Eastern Siberia, which produced little else than furs and where good furs were comparatively cheap, was much closer to China. With its cold climate in the north and with a large and wealthy luxury-loving class China offered an excellent market for furs. Cheap furs

[63] Cahen, pp. 81–87; Kurts, pp. 335–336.

[64] Cahen, pp. 57, 94–100; Trusevich, pp. 90, 96; Kurts, p. 337; *P.S.Z.*, III, 502.

[65] Kurts, *loc. cit.* Bakhrushin ("Torgi gostia Nikitina," pp. 376–377, 387), mentions briefly an expedition organized at Irkutsk by agents of Gavril Romanovich Nikitin, now a gost. It appears to have gone to Pekin via Mongolia in 1695–1696 and to have brought back Chinese goods which reached Moscow in 1698, where they were valued at 32,140 r. Whether Nikitin's expedition was an independent one or was part of the private caravan authorized by the Nerchinsk voevoda is not clear.

[66] Kurts, pp. 337–338; Cahen, p. 100.

[67] Kurts, p. 339; Trusevich, p. 83; Cahen, p. 25.

[68] Kurts, *loc. cit.*

which could not meet the cost of transport to Russia and costly furs with a limited market there could readily be sold in China.[69] Russian visitors to Pekin in the early 'seventies reported that good ermines sold at 2 r. apiece and that sables obtainable in Siberia for 1 r. sold in Pekin for 3 lans (about 4.2 r.) apiece.[70] Oddly, the demand in China for ermines and arctic foxes exceeded that for sables.[71] Squirrels were in the greatest demand; they were inexpensive and the Chinese furriers were exceptionally skillful at dyeing the cheap furs to look like the more expensive sorts.[72] However, all varieties of pelts sold very well there.[73] The natural procedure, therefore, was for the Russian merchants to exchange Russian and European goods in Siberia for furs, or to buy furs there and then take them to Pekin. There they acquired in exchange the Chinese goods—silk, gems, gold and silver, ivory, porcelain, and tea—so highly valued in Russia. For Siberian merchants there was little other choice.[74]

A more complete body of data exists about the size of the trade with China than about that of any other country with which Russia traded in the sixteenth and seventeenth centuries. For nearly all the expeditions which went to Pekin the amount of capital invested —furs, a few other goods, and money—and the value of the goods brought back are known. Baikov was first sent to Siberia, supposedly with 50,000 r. in money and goods to be exchanged there for goods from China; but that amount is extraordinarily large for that time, and 5,000 r. is the more likely figure. At any rate, he returned from Pekin with Chinese goods worth 1,669 r. (505 r. or 886 r., according to other sources).[75] Perfiliev and Ablin, according to two investigators, took with them 750 r. in money and goods and brought back Chinese goods valued at 1,057 r. (a third investigator gives the amounts 1,420 r. and 1,696 r. respectively).[76] The most successful of the expeditions prior to 1689, the second one made by Ablin, took 4,500 rubles' worth of goods and returned with Chinese

[69] L. D. le Comte, *Nouveaux mémoires sur l'état présent de la Chine*, I, 243–245; William Coxe, *Account of the Russian Discoveries between Asia and America*, p. 240. Trusevich (p. 89 n. 11), states that China had a population of 57,000,000 in 1640 and of 80,000,000 in 1680.

[70] Baddeley, II, 201, 368, 432.

[71] *Ibid.*, p. 147.

[72] A. K. Korsak, *Istoriko-statisticheskoe obozrenie torgovykh snoshenii Rossii s Kitaem*, p. 45; Bakhrushin, *op. cit.*, p. 374.

[73] Baddeley, II, 147, 202; Cahen, *loc. cit.; D.A.I.*, V, 293.

[74] Trusevich, pp. 97–103, 169–181; Bakhrushin, *op. cit.*, pp. 377–378; *P.S.Z.*, III, 504, 506.

[75] Bantysh-Kamenskii, pp. 8, 11; Trusevich, p. 19; Kurts, p. 333.

[76] Bantysh-Kamenskii, p. 13; Kurts, p. 335; Trusevich, p. 20.

goods appraised at 18,700 r., a profit of "14,212 r."[77] The treasury merchants with Spafarii carried sables worth 1,500 r. and 1,600 r. in money, but they had little chance to sell in Pekin because the entourage was confined to its compound and few Chinese traders were admitted.[78] Except for Ablin's second expedition the trade of these expeditions was small.

After 1689, however, the trade with China assumed really substantial proportions. The capital invested in Ides's expedition totaled 21,400 r., of which 3,000 r. belonged to Ides, 4,400 r. to the state, and 14,000 r. to private traders. The treasury merchants brought back as the state's share goods worth 12,000 r. and the private traders goods worth 38,000 r.[79] Liangusov's caravan was the first in which the state's investment exceeded that of the private merchants. The state sent goods worth 31,300 r. and received in exchange Chinese goods valued at 65,000 r., a profit of "24,054 r. 10 k. 3 d." [*sic*].[80] Bokov's caravan left Nerchinsk with goods totaling 81,500 r. Of this amount 4,300 r. is specified as belonging to Bokov, 10,500 r. to the serving men and other state employees with the expedition, and 32,000 r. to the treasury; the remaining 34,400 r. must have been invested by private enterprisers. The treasury sold its goods for 76,000 r., a profit of 45,300 r. What the others sold their goods for is not stated.[81]

Effectiveness of the State's Monopoly

The state's experience in Siberia in acquiring its furs showed that it was one thing to decree a monopoly and quite another to put it into effect. This being so, one naturally inquires, what success did the state have in enforcing its monopoly of the export of furs to Asia? The answer is, sometimes considerable success, at other times, virtually none at all. Susceptibility to bribery, abuse of official authority, and connivance with private enterprisers in evading the tsar's decrees were vices generally found throughout Muscovite

[77] Kurts, p. 334; Trusevich, p. 159; A. V. Semenov, *Izuchenie istoricheskikh svedenii o rossiiskoi vneshnei torgovle i promyshlennosti s poloviny XVII-go stoletiia*, III, 196.

[78] Trusevich, pp. 24, 159; Baddeley, II, 361, 365–366, 369, 372–374, 379, 411.

[79] Kurts, pp. 335–336.

[80] *Ibid.*, p. 337.

[81] *Ibid.*, p. 338. For all three treasury expeditions sent in the 'nineties to Pekin, Trusevich (pp. 95, 139, 160), and Semenov (III, 197) give amounts which are much larger than those given by Kurts. But the source of Semenov's figures is not given; Trusevich copies in part from Semenov, and his figures are not everywhere reliable. Therefore, Kurts' figures have been accepted as the most likely to be correct.

officialdom. Hence, the success with which the state could enforce its monopoly depended chiefly upon the opportunities existing at each export point for contravening that monopoly. The point is most clearly and emphatically illustrated by the trade with China.

Moscow undertook in the last decade of the seventeenth century, as we saw earlier, to take over the best part of the export of furs to China. With what success? Evasion of its monopoly regulations proved easy. It was impossible to patrol the border. The voevodas and customs officials themselves sent their agents to Pekin to trade.[82] To the Chinese, all Russian passports looked alike, whether the legitimate ones issued only at Moscow, the illegal ones given out by the Nerchinsk voevodas, or those forged outright. Moscow tried in 1706 to better the Pekin market for furs, where prices had been depressed by illegal competition, by excluding private traders altogether from the Chinese trade, but its efforts availed no more than before. The Russian envoy and commercial agent of the tsar, Sava Vladislavich, when he went to Pekin in the years 1725–1727, was amazed to learn that the Chinese records showed some fifty Russian caravans to Pekin, whereas the Russian official records showed only four political and ten commercial expeditions to the Chinese capital.[83] The predicament is obvious: it was impossible for the state to enforce a monopoly of so lucrative a fur market as China when the source of furs was closer than Moscow to the market; Eastern Siberia is nearer China than Moscow.

If the state could not enforce its monopoly in relation to exports to China, then it is very likely that it failed to do so for the export of furs from Western Siberia to Central Asia, though we have no specific evidence to prove it. Furs were in demand in Central Asia, and they were cheaper in Siberia than in Moscow, to which place the state tried to confine the sale of furs to Central Asian merchants. Siberia, moreover, was closer than Moscow to Central Asia. The Bukharans had traded extensively in furs before the state's prohibition of the sale of furs to foreigners; with a corrupt administration in Siberia, the Bakharans undoubtedly found ways of evading the prohibition. All these considerations point to a bootleg trade in furs with Central Asia, though not on so great a scale as with China. It is also these considerations which dispose us to the conclusion that furs were the principal export to Central Asia from Siberia.[84]

[82] Cf. *P.S.Z.*, III, 282, 359.

[83] Cahen, pp. 66–70, 94, lxix–lxx.

[84] See above, p. 220.

In European Russia, however, conditions were more favorable for successful enforcement of the prior or exclusive sale of furs to the merchants from Asia. Astrakhan was situated in a region which produced few fur-bearing animals except some common species, and Siberian traders and promyshlenniks, with their attention focused on the European market at Arkhangelsk, made no serious attempts to develop trade at Astrakhan.[85] Hence, one may conclude that the state was able to control the sale of furs there to the merchants from Persia, Central Asia, and India, and to keep its caravans to Persia free of private competition. The upper Volga towns, Kazan, Nizhnii Novgorod, and Iaroslavl, were centers of the fur trade in their own right; consequently a certain amount of trade in furs with Asiatic merchants was undoubtedly carried on by private merchants in these towns. Yet many of the merchants who came to these towns from Asia were commercial agents of Asiatic rulers, and their destination was Moscow. They were customarily provided with food, lodging, and transportation by the treasury, so that evasion of the interdict against their engaging in trade en route to Moscow was difficult and probably involved more risk than it was worth.[86] The same may be said with respect to Moscow. Some evasion no doubt occurred,[87] especially in connection with the prohibition against the sale of fine furs; but evasion was more difficult with the treasury so close at hand. The Greek merchants entered Russia from the southwest rather than through Astrakhan and the Volga towns, but the country through which they passed on their way to Moscow was without a fur trade of any consequence; hence it would seem that the state was able to enforce its monopoly of the sale of furs to them with little difficulty. A statement by the tsar in 1676 affirms that the trade with the Greeks had been, up to a few years before, without serious abuses.[88] Thus it may be concluded that the monopoly of the export of furs to Asiatic countries was effective in so far as the sale of furs occurred in European Russia, but was flagrantly violated in Siberia.

This account of the state's export trade with Asia completes the description of the fur trade of the state. Therefore, we pause here

[85] S. V. Bakhrushin, *Ocherki po istorii kolonizatsii Sibiri,* p. 109, and n. 2; cf. Veselovskii, II, 166.

[86] Veselovskii, I, 300, 308, III, 25, 48, 244, 259–260, 552.

[87] Cf. Kapterev, p. 268.

[88] *A.A.E.*, IV, 291.

to summarize that trade. The participation of the state, a characteristic peculiar to the Russian fur trade, was one of the outstanding instances of the tsar's role as the first merchant in Russia. Although the state bought some of its furs, it depended upon its political authority and organization to acquire the great part of them, levying tribute in furs on the natives of Siberia and collecting a tenth of all furs taken in Siberia by private enterprisers. In the acquisition of furs in Siberia and in the sale of furs to Asia it sought to create for itself a monopoly of the best furs. In this it was not wholly successful, for its restrictions against competing private enterprisers were widely disregarded, both by the private enterprisers themselves and by its own employees, who were commissioned with the task of enforcing these restrictions. Nevertheless, despite the inroads into its trade, the state stood out as the fur trade's most important participant. The furs which it received from Siberia constituted a highly valued source of its income, the importance of which is to be measured not so much in the actual value of the yearly receipts, but in what it enabled the state to do. Lacking adequate resources of gold and silver, the state was able to turn to furs not only to acquire those same precious metals, but to use furs in the place of them for purposes of diplomacy, for rewarding services, and for acquiring many goods which it could not obtain within its dominions. By means of its furs the state was able to buy from the foreigners much of its military equipment and supplies and the trappings and luxuries necessary for the dignity and splendor of court to which the tsars aspired. And lastly, they enabled the state to engage in the highly profitable silk trade, which in turn also enabled the tsar to acquire from the West many necessary and valuable goods.

CHAPTER XII

THE IMPORTANCE OF THE RUSSIAN FUR TRADE

As we come to the end of this account of the Russian fur trade, it is to the point to ask, What did the fur trade represent for Russia? In the first place, it represented one of the oldest, if not the oldest, means of livelihood for the Russian people. From the days of the Varangians, who founded the Kievan Russian state, and even from before that time, down to the end of the seventeenth century (beyond which this study does not go), the Russian people actively and extensively engaged in the trade in furs. In the second place, along with agriculture, the trade in furs was the most important single economic pursuit in Russia until the end of the seventeenth century. During the years of dominance of Kiev and Novgorod over the Russian people furs stood as the principal commodity produced by them and was their main article of export. Furs probably occupied as many, if not more, men in their acquisition and sale than did any other commodity. The leading merchants of both cities were those engaged in the fur trade. Only in the period of Muscovite dominance did furs yield first place to agriculture as the principal economic pursuit of the Russians, and that change occurred not because the fur trade diminished, but because Muscovite Russia developed an agrarian economy whereas Kiev and Novgorod had not done so. The fur trade continued to be tremendously important. That fact can best be seen, first, by examining the importance of the export traffic in furs, and then by noting certain significant aspects resulting from that traffic.

The Importance of the Fur Export Trade

If the importance of the export traffic in furs is to be measured in terms of monetary value, an estimate of from 400,000 to 500,000 rubles may be advanced as the value of the annual fur exports from Russia at the height of the trade, that is, in the middle of the seventeenth century.[1] Yet these figures really tell us very little;

[1] This rough estimate of the value and extent of all fur exports in the best years of the trade is reached by adding to the estimate of private exports made in chap. x (p. 207) a similarly calculated estimate of the state's fur exports. In the best years, the middle of the seventeenth century, the state received from Siberia furs worth around 100,000 r. or more in Siberian prices. Assum-

without some notion of the value of all exports annually from Russia in the period 1550–1700—which is not to be had—they are almost meaningless, except to indicate that the trade was large. The importance of the export fur trade must be determined by other means.

The "other means" is a quick review of such other commodities as were exported from Russia in large amounts: leather, wax, honey, tallow, flax, hemp, grain, caviar, and silk. Russian leather came into great demand in both Europe and Asia in the sixteenth and seventeenth centuries; in 1653 it accounted for one-third of the goods shipped from Arkhangelsk. Yet, because the cattle raised in Russia were inferior, the Russian leather merchants bought most of their hides from Poland, the Ukraine, and Podolia.[2] Wax, honey, and tallow were long standard Russian exports along with furs, but by the middle of the seventeenth century they were being consumed chiefly at home and were not exported in significant quantities to Asia.[3] Flax was sent abroad in great amounts, especially to England, Holland, and Germany, to be made into sails and linen goods, but it seems to have had little importance in the trade with Asia. Hemp became a leading export with the appearance in Russia of the Dutch and English, who needed it for ropes

---

ing that, as in the private trade, four-fifths of the state's furs were exported—though in view of the many domestic uses to which the state put its furs, that estimate may be too high—and allowing for prices higher by 20 per cent or more in the export centers, we reach a figure of 100,000 r. or more, which, added to the 300,000 r. or more of private exports, gives us the amount of 400,000 r., with 500,000 r. as a possible maximum under especially favorable market conditions.

If these calculations are close to the actual facts, we must qualify Fletcher's assertion with reference to fur exports in the late sixteenth century (*Russia at the Close of the Sixteenth Century*, p. 9). According to him, in some years furs were transported to Asia and Europe to the value of between 400,000 and 500,000 rubles. But the value of the ruble was then much higher than in the seventeenth century and the Russian supply of fur-bearing animals was nearing exhaustion, whereas the Russians had only begun to exploit the Siberian supply. This figure, therefore, even as a maximum, seems too high. An amount half as large as that appears more consistent with the facts as we understand them. Either Fletcher was misinformed, or his figure refers to the value of fur exports in terms of their prices in European markets. The 1595 subsidy to the Holy Roman Emperor was valued by Prague furriers at more than 400,000 r. (*Pamiatniki diplomaticheskikh snoshenii drevnei Rossii s derzhavami inostrannymi*, II, 292).

[2] Johann de Rodes, "Bedenken über den russischen Handel im Jahre 1653," *Beiträge zur Kenntniss Russlands und seiner Geschichte*, pp. 254, 256–257; M. N. Pokrovskii, *History of Russia*, pp. 257–258.

[3] Pokrovskii, *op. cit.*, p. 266; De Rodes, p. 258; Adam Olearius, *The Voyages and Travels of the Ambassadors Sent by Frederick, Duke of Holstein*, p. 49.

and ship rigging.[4] But in countries without a merchant marine hemp was much less in demand. This was also true of timber. The export of grain began in the seventeenth century to show some promise of its later role as a Russian export, yet prior to 1630 it did not figure as an export; though in individual years it was sold in large volume to foreign buyers, it was an irregular export and controlled by the state.[5] Caviar was a distinctly Russian export, yet it was exceeded by many other commodities and found its market mainly in Catholic countries.[6] Silk was a highly profitable export to Europe, but it did not assume importance as a Russian export until well into the seventeenth century, and, as we know, it was a traffic reserved to the state. Moreover, silk was not indigenous to Russia. Except for leather, each of the foregoing commodities was essentially a European export of Russia. Aside from leather, the important goods exported to Asia were cloth and the metals copper, lead, and pewter. But most of the cloth came originally from Europe, and so did the metals.[7]

The importance of the export trade in furs becomes clearer. During the period 1550–1700 no other commodity was exported from Russia in as large amounts to as many countries. The only commodity which approached furs in value and diversity of its foreign markets was leather, and much of it was first acquired abroad. On this basis, therefore, it may be asserted that furs were Russia's greatest export in the sixteenth and seventeenth centuries.

Other Significant Aspects

This primacy of furs among Russian exports gives the fur trade much importance. That importance increases when we view it in connection with certain other considerations. The export fur traffic gains particular significance when it is recalled that for Russia foreign trade was vital. Commercial intercourse with more advanced countries was essential if Russia was to overcome its backwardness; there were many commodities necessary for Russia's advance which were not found or made in Russia and which had to be imported. Hence, as the chief Russian export, furs embodied

[4] See above, p. 199 n. 87.

[5] I. I. Liubimenko, "The Struggle of the Dutch with the English for the Russian Market in the Seventeenth Century," *Transactions of the Royal Historical Society*, ser. 4, Vol. VII (1924), pp. 41–42; Pokrovskii, *op. cit.*, pp. 261–264.

[6] Pokrovskii, *op. cit.*, p. 265.

[7] N. I. Veselovskii, *Pamiatniki diplomaticheskikh i torgovykh snoshenii moskokskoi Rusi s Persiei*, I, 213, 311; *A.A.E.*, IV, 303.

more than any other commodity all that foreign trade meant to Russia.

Another significant aspect of the export traffic in furs is the function of furs as a medium of international exchange. Furs provided the state with an asset to offset its poverty in precious metals. Even late in the seventeenth century the state was still using furs as a form of negotiable wealth in place of gold and silver. Many of the goods which Russia exported to Asia along with furs were imported from Europe, and the silk which Russia sold to Europe came from Asia. In this manner Russia served as a middleman between Occident and Orient. But it required more than geographical location for Russia to act in that capacity; it required the help of native products with which to acquire the goods of one customer to be sold to the other. As a commodity in demand in both Europe and Asia and as one found in abundance in Russia, furs were preëminently suited to this purpose. Thus, in a sense broader than the economy of the tsar's government, furs were the Russian equivalent of the mercantilist "gold fund."

A third significant aspect, finally, is the immensely leavening influence which the fur trade exerted within Russia itself. It provided, on the one hand, the means for the development of an independent commercial class of demonstrable financial power. It served, on the other, as the most important single force behind the expansion of the Russian people into Siberia. Moreover, not only did it motivate that expansion, but it also paid the costs of it and gave to Russia an empire which promises to be the geographic and economic base of the Russia to come. Perhaps this leavening influence may not be regarded as directly connected with the export trade, but it must be remembered that it was the export market which gave the fur trade substance. Had the fur trade been based on the domestic market instead of the European market, the rise of a strong commercial class and the expansion of the Russians into Siberia would have come later and taken longer than they did.

Lest we end with a distorted perspective of the place of the fur trade in the economic pattern of Russia, we should remind ourselves that the economic life of the country directed itself into many other channels. Nor did the Russian fur traffic of this period, from the standpoint of the trade of Europe of its day, cut a large figure; furs were mainly a luxury good rather than a necessity, and the Russian trade in general was a small part of the commerce of Europe.[8] Nevertheless, the fact still stands that without its fur trade Russia would have found it even more difficult than it did to overcome the backwardness in which Mongol-Tatar rule left it. And if the history of Russian commerce were to be written in terms of any one commodity, it would have to be written, down to the end of the seventeenth century, in terms of the fur trade.

[8] Liubimenko, *op. cit.*, pp. 47–48; Ernst Baasch, *Holländische Wirtschaftsgeschichte*, p. 161.

BIBLIOGRAPHY

BIBLIOGRAPHY

THIS BIBLIOGRAPHY includes, with two or three minor exceptions, all the titles cited in the text of the present study, as well as a few more which are pertinent, but which the writer did not have occasion specifically to cite. In order to avoid confusion and to free the footnotes in the text, already long enough, from all but the minimum of essential information about the authorities cited, the full description of each title has been reserved to this bibliography. Hence, only the edition used in this study, if more than one exists, is listed. The writer has sought to make this bibliography as complete as possible for the subject, but it has not always been possible to gain access to the growing amount of material published by present-day Russian scholars on the economic life of seventeenth-century Russia. Primarily, therefore, this is a complete working bibliography; and if it is not a complete topical bibliography, certainly it approximates one. We preface it with a short discussion of the most important works used in this study, under these headings: bibliographical aids, sources, contemporary accounts, and monographs. The parenthetical number after each title mentioned in the bibliographical essay refers to its numbered position in the bibliography.

Bibliographical Aids

There are several bibliographical guides which possess varying degrees of usefulness for this study of the Russian fur trade. Such general Russian bibliographies as Ikonnikov's (1) and Mezhov's (4 and 5), though classic works in themselves, contribute little. The only general Russian bibliography in Western languages, Kerner, *Slavic Europe* (2), is of more value, since it lists the many contemporary accounts by foreigners who visited Russia. Topical bibliographies are of greater value. The most extensive of these is Mezhov, *Sibirskaia bibliografiia* (14), which serves for Siberian history as his Russian bibliographies do for Russian history. It was published, however, nearly four decades ago. For material published since then one should consult Kerner, *Northeastern Asia: A Selected Bibliography* (12). Very useful because it contains a select list of titles which bear directly on the field of Russian eastward expansion, of which this study is a part, is the short bibliographical essay by Kerner, "Russian Expansion to America:

Its Bibliographical Foundations" (13). What Professor Kerner does for the fur trade in Siberia and its background, Fritz Epstein, the editor of Von Staden's account of sixteenth-century Russia (83), does for the fur trade in Russia. His copious bibliographical footnotes proved exceptionally valuable. Adelung's (8) specialized bibliography of all the accounts left by travelers to Russia prior to 1700 is excellent within its limited scope. One who wishes to orient himself in the historical literature about Siberia should read Bakhrushin's essay in his *Ocherki po istorii kolonizatsii Sibiri v XVI i XVII vv.* (90).

Archival research on the Russia fur trade has been out of the question for the present study. However, for such research Ogloblin, *Obozrenie stolbtsov i knig sibirskago prikaza (1592–1768 gg.)* (35) is indispensable. It is a thoroughgoing catalogue of the documents in the archives of the Siberian Department, as well as of many documents about Siberia in other Russian archives. Bazilevich, "Tamozhennye knigi kak istochnik ekonomicheskoi istorii Rossii" (181), Ikonnikov, *Opyt russkoi istoriografii* (1), and Viktorov, *Opisanie zapisnykh knig i bumag starinnykh dvortsovykh prikazov, 1584–1725 g.* (57) are archival guides which serve as valuable supplements to Ogloblin.

Sources

There does not exist any important collection of documentary material that applies exclusively even to Russian trade in general, let alone to the fur trade in particular. To reconstruct the Russian fur trade one must draw from various source collections. Those most extensively used in this study are the standard ones, namely, *Akty istoricheskie* (39), *Dopolneniia k aktam istoricheskim* (40), *Akty arkheograficheskoi ekspeditsii* (16), *Russkaia istoricheskaia biblioteka* (43), *Polnoe sobranie zakonov* (46), and *Sobranie gosudarstvennykh gramot i dogovorov* (48).

The first three of these collections are of like character and cover the same period of time, for, with the exception of the first volume of each, the documents they contain fall within our general period, 1550–1700. Many of these documents refer to Siberia. They consist of orders and instructions sent by the officials of the tsar at Moscow to the voevodas in Siberia, of the reports of these voevodas to Moscow and of their orders and instructions, in turn, to the serving men under them, and of the reports of these serving men to the voevodas and, sometimes, to Moscow. These orders, instructions, and reports contain a great deal of information about the fur trade in Siberia, mostly about the state's trade, since they are official documents, but in them one finds also a fair amount of material concerning the private traders and their activities. These collections, in spite of the fact that they contain more documents about Russia than about Siberia, include, unfortunately, few that throw light on the fur trade in Russia. There are several documents which concern trade in Russia in general, but almost none that refers to the fur trade in particular.

The *Polnoe sobranie zakonov* and the *Sobranie gosudarstvennykh gramot i dogovorov* contain documents similar to those in the three first-named collections, but the collection of laws begins only with 1649, and the collection of charters and treaties contains relatively few documents that concern the fur trade. The *Russkaia istoricheskaia biblioteka* has a wider variety of documentary material, arranged, not in chronological order as in the other collections, but according to subject and kind of material. In Volumes II, VIII, and XV are found sections with "acts" relating to the history of Siberia, like those in the preceding collections, though they are limited chiefly to Western Siberia and to the first half of the seventeenth century. But Volume VIII contains also the valuable financial survey of Siberia for the years 1698 and 1699, the only document of its kind yet published, and "Acts relating to Foreigners," which for our purposes are useful in showing the payment of furs to the Europeans employed in Russia by the tsar. Volume IX contains the "Income-Disbursement Books of the Treasury Court for 1613–1614."

Besides these large collections there are several small ones which contain material bearing on the fur trade. Gnevushev, *Akty vremeni pravleniia tsaria Vasiliia Shuiskago* (22), Kuleshov, *Nakazy sibirskim voevodam v XVII v.* (28), Kuznetsov-Krasnoiarskii, *Istoricheskie akty XVII stoletiia* (29), Okun', "K istorii Buriatii v XVII v." (36), and Trotskii, *Kolonial'naia politika moskovskogo gosudarstva v Iakutii XVII v.* (52) are each collections, of one-volume compass or less, containing the same sort of material about Siberia as is found in the *Akty istoricheskie, Dopolneniia k aktam istoricheskim,* and the rest. The Russian edition of Müller's *Opisanie sibirskago tsarstva* (31) has a number of documents concerning the early years of the Russian occupation of Siberia which have been lost and are found nowhere else.

Torgovaia kniga (51), edited by Sakharov, Viktorov's archival guide (57), Zabelin, *Dopolneniia k dvortsovym razriadam* (58), Veselovskii, *Pamiatniki diplomaticheskikh i torgovykh snoshenii moskovskoi Rusi s Persiei* (56), and Khilkov, *Sbornik kniazia Khilkova* (27) comprise the remaining sources of importance for this study. The *Torgovaia kniga* is virtually the only body of data of any extent and detail about the trade in furs and other goods on the Dvina with the merchants from Europe. Viktorov includes extensive excerpts from the documents which he catalogues, and this guide, together with Zabelin's compilation, provides a great number of representative entries from the "Income-Disbursement Books of the Treasury Court" for the years 1613 to 1630. These two works throw much light on the manner in which the state disposed of its furs. Veselovskii's collection of documents from the archives of the Department of Ambassadors includes most of the official records of Russian-Persian relations from 1588 to 1621. These records make possible a picture of the export of furs by the state that is clearer for Persia than for any other country except China. Khilkov's collection comprises a miscellany of documents.

There remains one other source of importance to be noted. That is the archival guide compiled by Ogloblin and mentioned above. Ogloblin has quoted and summarized liberally the material in the documents which he classifies, so that this work assumes great value as a source, as well as a guide. It covers all phases of the fur trade in Siberia, both state and private, and provides us with as much data about the trade of the state in Moscow and the several export centers as does any one source. Yet it is a tantalizing work to use, for it often gives only a taste of richer material to be found in the archives of the Siberian Department, material not yet published which should go far towards clearing up many questions that are either wholly or partly unanswered for want of this material. Despite its summary character, the work, intended first as guide to the Siberian archives and second as a source book, is a masterpiece of its kind.

Contemporary Accounts

Considering the comparative obscurity of Russia in the acquaintance of Europeans during the sixteenth and seventeenth centuries, there exists an unexpectedly large literature written by foreigners who visited Russia and observed its life and customs. With the eyes of the outsider many of these foreigners saw Russian life in a broad perspective and noticed things which the Russians took for granted. Their accounts usually make some reference to the fur trade, the extent of which rarely failed to impress them. Although only a few of these contemporary accounts by foreigners give us detailed descriptions of the fur trade and although their information is not always accurate, together they help to fix the importance and scope of the export trade in furs, and thus to fill a very noticeable gap in the material of the standard documentary collections. For the present study the most useful of these accounts are those by Giles Fletcher (63), Sigismund von Herberstein (65), Johann Kilburger (69), Johann de Rodes (81), and Heinrich von Staden (83). The information contained in these and the many other contemporary accounts of foreigners has been assembled in an able monograph by Kliuchevskii, called *Skazaniia inostrantsev o moskovskom gosudarstve* (126).

Almost unique in Russian historical literature of the seventeenth century is the contemporary account of Kotoshikhin (d. 1667) (70), who was a junior official in the Department of Ambassadors. His account gives us important information about the trade of the tsar's treasury and about the government's finances, information some of which is not found elsewhere.

Monographs

There is an extensive literature of secondary works, in both book and periodical form, from which much important material has been drawn. It is a literature, however, which, with two exceptions, has concerned itself with the fur trade only as secondary or incidental to other subjects, usually to the history of Siberia or to Russian trade in the sixteenth and seventeenth centuries. This circumstance means, therefore, that the present study breaks virgin soil, with all the advantages and disadvantages of such pioneering. The writer has found only two works which deal in any detail with the Russian fur trade. One is by Ianitskii, "Torgovlia pushnym tovarom v XVII v." (191). It is a short account, a student seminar paper, which sketches the main features of the Russian fur trade in the seventeenth century. The other is a German inaugural dissertation by Klein, *Der sibirische Pelzhandel* (123). Though a longer treatment, it devotes scarcely more than a dozen pages to the fur trade prior to the eighteenth century.

The most useful and reliable of the secondary works are those based on archival investigation, and of these there are several. Bakhrushin, one of the foremost present-day historians of Siberia, has written four studies of much value for this present dissertation. His *Ocherki po istorii kolonizatsii Sibiri v XVI i XVII vv.* (90) gives a detailed description of the routes over which the fur trade passed, a description sufficiently broad to include many other data about the fur trade duplicated nowhere else. His "Iasak v Sibiri v XVII v." (174), traces the development of iasak as a political institution in Siberia under the Russians, as does Ogorodnikov's "Russkaia gosudarstvennaia vlast' i sibirskie inorodtsy v XVI–XVIII v.v." (213), along somewhat different lines. This short monograph by Bakhrushin, together with Ogorodnikov's, supplements the standard source collections and, taken with these collections, makes the discussion of the acquisition of furs by the state through tribute one of the most complete and best-documented parts of this present study. Bakhrushin's other two monographs are "Torgi gostia Nikitina v Sibiri i Kitae" (178) and "Agenty russkikh torgovykh liudei XVII veka" (173). The former describes the activities of an important business house of the late seventeenth century which carried on extensive commercial operations in Russia, Siberia, and China. The latter discusses the status and functions of the several types of agents employed by the Russian businessmen of the seventeenth century.

Equally important are the three monographs by Butsinskii, *K istorii Sibiri* (97), *Mangazeia i mangazeiskii uezd* (98), and *Zaselenie Sibiri* (99). Together they constitute a detailed history of Western Siberia from the beginning of the Russian occupation of Siberia to the middle of the seventeenth century. They have much that concerns the fur trade, perhaps more about the state's trade than the private trade, but still much of value for either subject, since they are based almost entirely on documents in the archives of the Siberian Department.

The pioneer histories of Siberia are *Opisanie sibirskago tsarstva* (31) and "Sibirskaia istoriia" (210) by G. F. Müller, who pioneered Siberian historiography in the eighteenth century. They give a good deal of information about the earlier years of the Russian conquest of Siberia for the sake of its furs.

Another important monograph is Potanin's "Privoz i vyvoz tovarov goroda Tomska v polovine XVII stoletiia" (223). It is a short article, but as yet the only published thing of its kind for

Siberia. A detailed analysis of the customs books of Tomsk for the years 1652 and 1653, it sheds light on the movement of goods in an important Siberian town, showing clearly the decided preponderance of furs as the chief native commodity of Siberia.

Miliukov has written a capital study of government finances in Russia during the reign of Peter the Great (206). Fortunately for us, he prefaces the main part of his study with a discussion of the state's finances in the seventeenth century and provides us with four or five items of information about the fur income of the state and its total income. These items, few though they are, are the only data as yet available on this subject.

A contemporary Russian scholar, Bazilevich, has written three short monographs, which were indispensable for this present study. The first, "Krupnoe torgovoe predpriiatie v moskovskom gosudarstve v pervoi polovine XVII veka" (180), describes in detail the business of a big merchant family of Ustiug, whose trade was based on furs from Siberia. The second, "Tamozhennye knigi kak istochnik ekonomicheskoi istorii Rossii" (181), describes the customs books of seventeenth-century Russia and Siberia as source material and in the course of the description provides us with much useful information about the private trade found nowhere outside of the archives. The third, "Torgovlia velikogo Ustiuga v seredine XVII veka" (182), traces the rise and recession of Ustiug during the seventeenth century as a major center where private merchants bought and sold furs and made their headquarters. These short articles, together with Bakhrushin's two articles on the private trade mentioned above (173 and 178), form the basis of that part of this present work which deals with the organization and conduct of the private fur trade. The five together represent the beginning of an investigation of the activities and organization of the Russian commercial class in the seventeenth century, a field of research to which, until recently, scholars have given scant attention.

The contemporary American scholar, Professor Robert J. Kerner, has initiated in *The Urge to the Sea* (121) a comprehensive program of research in the expansion of Russia. Those parts of his monograph which deal with the strategy, mechanics, and routes of expansion in Siberia are pertinent to this present study.

Besides the foregoing monographs a few others deserve short notice, for one reason or another. Kostomarov, in his *Ocherki torgovli moskovskago gosudarstva v XVI i XVII vv.* (129), has written a comprehensive and detailed account of Russian trade in the sixteenth and seventeenth centuries. This study makes the investigation of the traffic of particular commodities much easier, for it is a synthesis of the published documentary material available on the subject at the time Kostomarov wrote it (1862). For the economic history of Russia prior to the sixteenth century one must depend upon Mel'gunov, *Ocherki po istorii russkoi torgovli IX–XVIII v.v.* (143) and Nikitskii, *Istoriia ekonomicheskago byta velikago Novgoroda* (146). Vernadskii, "Gosudarevy sluzhilye i promyshlennye liudi vostochnoi Sibiri XVII veka" (239), presents a short but solid study of the status and activities of the serving men and promyshlenniks in Siberia, showing definitely that the two superficially distinct types differed very little fundamentally. Ogorodnikov, *Zavoevanie russkimi Sibiri* (147) is the best of the shorter accounts of the conquest of Siberia.

The works described in this brief essay are a small part of those listed in the following bibliography, but they are far the most important. Without them, investigation of the Russian fur trade in the sixteenth and seventeenth centuries would be impossible.

The titles in this bibliography have been classified according to (1) bibliographical aids, (2) sources, (3) contemporary accounts, (4) secondary works, and (5) periodical and other articles. To the titles of all Russian works and articles a literal English translation has been added. The titles of the two most frequently cited periodicals have been shortened to the same form used in the text, namely: *Chteniia v imperatorskom obshchestve istorii i drevnostei rossiiskikh pri moskovskom universitete* (Publications of the Imperial Society of Russian History and Antiquity at the University of Moscow), 185 vols. (Moscow, 1861–1916) to *Chteniia* (186); and *Zhurnal ministerstva narodnago prosveshcheniia* (Journal of the Ministry of Public Enlightenment), 362 vols. (St. Petersburg, 1834–1905; n.s. 70 vols., St. Petersburg, 1906–1917) to *Zh.M.N.P.* (247).

BIBLIOGRAPHICAL AIDS

General Bibliographies

1. Ikonnikov, Vladimir S. *Opyt russkoi istoriografii* (An essay in Russian historiography). 2 vols. in 4. Kiev, 1891–1908.

2. Kerner, Robert J. *Slavic Europe: A Selected Bibliography in the Western European Languages, Comprising History, Languages, and Literatures.* Harvard Bibliographies, library series, Vol. I. Cambridge, Mass., 1918.

3. *Knizhnaia letopis'* (Book chronicle). Vols. I——. Rossiiskaia tsentral'naia palata pri gosudarstvennom izdatel'stve. Moscow, 1907——.

4. Mezhov, Vladimir I. *Russkaia istoricheskaia bibliografiia: ukazatel' knig i statei po russkoi i vseobshchei istorii i vspomogatel'nym naukam za 1800–1854 vkl.* (Russian historical bibliography: guide to books and articles on Russian and general history and to the auxiliary sciences for 1800–1854 inclusive).

5. ———. *Russkaia istoricheskaia bibliografiia za 1865–1876 gg.* (Russian historical bibliography for 1865–1876). 8 vols. in 4. St. Petersburg, 1882–1890.

6. Ulianov, N. A., and Ulianova, V. N. *Ukazatel' zhurnal'noi literatury, alfavitnyi, predmetnyi, sistematicheskii, 1896–1905 gg.* (Guide to periodical literature, alphabetic, topical, systematic, 1896–1905). 2d ed., Moscow, 1913.

7. *Zhurnal'naia letopis'* (Periodical chronicle). Vols. I——. Tsentral'naia knizhnaia palata. Moscow, 1926——.

Topical Bibliographies

8. Adelung, Friedrich von. *Kritiko-literaturnoe obozrenie puteshestvennikov po Rossii do 1700 goda i ikh sochinenii ...* (Critical literary survey of travelers to Russia up to 1700 and their works). Translated from the German by Aleksandr Klevanov. In *Chteniia*, 1848, No. 9, pp. 1–104; 1863, No. 1 (January–March), pp. 105–174; 1863, No. 2 (April–June), pp. 185–305; 1863, No. 3 (July–September), pp. 1–86; 1863, No. 4 (October–December), pp. 87–168; 1864, No. 1 (January–March), pp. 169–264, i–v, i–iv.

Reprinted in one volume with the same title as above, Moscow, 1864. The *Chteniia* printing was used for this study.

Bazilevich, K. V. "Tamozhennye knigi kak istochnik ekonomicheskoi istorii Rossii." See no. 181.

9. Belov, Aleksei M. *Materialy k ukazateliu literatury o Sibiri na evropeiskikh iazykakh s 1917 po 1930 g.* (Material for a guide to the literature about Siberia in European languages from 1917 to 1930). Leningrad, 1931.

10. Chernevskii, P. O. *Ukazatel' materialov dlia istorii torgovli, promyshlennosti i finansov, v predelakh rossiiskoi imperii. Ot drevneishikh vremen do kontsa XVIII stoletiia* (Guide to the material for the history of trade, industry, and finance, within the limits of the Russian empire. From earliest times to the end of the eighteenth century). St. Petersburg, 1883.

EPSTEIN, FRITZ. See no. 83.

11. HENNING, GEORG. "Die Reiseberichte über Siberien von Herberstein bis Ides," *Mitteilungen des Vereins für Erdkunde zu Leipzig*, 1905, pp. 245–394. Leipzig, 1906.

12. KERNER, ROBERT J. *Northeastern Asia: A Selected Bibliography. Contributions to the Bibliography of the Relations of China, Russia, and Japan, with Special Reference to Korea, Manchuria, Mongolia, and Eastern Siberia, in Oriental and European Languages.* 2 vols. Berkeley, 1939.

13. ———. "Russian Expansion to America: Its Bibliographical Foundations," *The Papers of the Bibliographical Society of America*, XXV (1931), 111–129.

14. MEZHOV, VLADIMIR I. *Sibirskaia bibliografiia. Ukazatel' knig i statei o Sibiri na russkom iazyke i odnekh tol'ko knig na inostrannykh iazykakh za ves' period knigopechataniia* (Siberian bibliography. Guide to both books and articles about Siberia in Russian and to books only in foreign languages for the whole period of book publishing). 3 vols. in 2. St. Petersburg, 1903.

OGLOBLIN, NIKOLAI N. *Obozrenie stolbtsov i knig sibirskago prikaza (1592–1768 gg.).* See no. 35.

15. SLOVTSOV, IVAN I. *Materialy dlia bibliografii tobol'skoi gubernii. 1600–1889 gg.* I. "Puteshestviia i uchenye trudy" (Material for a bibliography of Tobolsk guberniia, 1600–1889. I. "Travels and scholarly works"). Tobolsk, 1890.

VIKTOROV, ALEKSEI G. *Opisanie zapisnykh knig i bumag starinnykh dvortsovykh prikazov, 1584–1725 g.* See no. 57.

SOURCES

16. Akademiia nauk, St. Petersburg. *Akty, sobrannye v bibliotekakh i arkhivakh rossiiskoi imperii, arkheograficheskoiu ekspeditsieiu imperatorskoi akademii nauk* (Acts collected in the libraries and archives of the Russian empire by the archeographic expedition of the imperial academy of sciences). 4 vols. St. Petersburg, 1836; index, St. Petersburg, 1838. (*A.A.E.*).

Akty arkheograficheskoi ekspeditsii. See no. 16.

Akty istoricheskie. See no. 39.

17. *Chronicle of Novgorod, 1016–1417, The.* Translated from the Russian by Robert Michell and Nevill Forbes. Royal Historical Society Publications. Camden 3d ser., Vol. XXV. London, 1914.

18. CHUMIKOV, A. A. "Materialy dlia istorii russkoi torgovli" (Material for the history of Russian trade), *Chteniia*, 1875, No. 4 (October–December), pt. 5, pp. 160–164.

19. COLBERT, JEAN B. *Lettres, instructions et mémoires de Colbert.* Pierre Clément, ed. 8 vols. in 10. Paris, 1861–1873.

Dopolneniia k aktam istoricheskim. See no. 40.

20. FORSTEN, GEORGII V., comp. *Akty i pis'ma k istorii baltiiskago voprosa v XVI i XVII stoletiiakh* (Acts and letters relating to the history of the Baltic question in the sixteenth and seventeenth centuries). 2 vols.

Zapiski istoriko-filologicheskago fakul'teta imperatorskago s.-peterburgskago universiteta, Vols. XXI and XXXI. St. Petersburg, 1889–1893.

21. France. Commission des Archives Diplomatiques. *Recueil des instructions données aux ambassadeurs et ministres de France depuis les traités de Westphalie jusqu'à la révolution française: Russie.* Alfred Rambaud, ed. 2 vols. Paris, 1890.

22. GNEVUSHEV, ANDREI M., comp. *Akty vremeni pravleniia tsaria Vasiliia Shuiskago (1606 g. 19 maia—17 iiulia 1610 g.)* (Acts of the time of the rule of Tsar Vasilii Shuiskii, May 19, 1606—July 17, 1610). In *Chteniia* (1915), No. 2, pt. 1, pp. i–xix + 1–422.
Reprinted in one volume, Moscow, 1914. The *Chteniia* printing was used for this study.

23. GOLOVIN, PETR P. "Instruktsiia pis'mianomu golove Poiarkovu" (Instructions to chief clerk Poiarkov), *Chteniia,* 1861, No. 1 (January–March), pt. 5, pp. 1–14.

24. Great Britain. Historical Manuscripts Commission. *Calendar of the Manuscripts of the Most Hon. the Marquis of Salisbury ... Preserved at Hatfield House, Hertfordshire.* 16 vols. in 12. London, 1883–1933.

25. Imperatorskoe russkoe istoricheskoe obshchestvo. *Sbornik ...* (Collection). 148 vols. St. Petersburg, 1867–1916.
Volumes XXXIV, XXXV, XXXIX, and CXVI used.

26. "Istoricheskie akty o podvigakh Erofeia Khabarova na Amure v 1649–1651 gg." (Historical acts concerning the exploits of Erofei Khabarov on the Amur in 1649–1651), *Zhurnal dlia chteniia vospitannikam voenno-uchebnykh zavedenii,* 1840, No. 105. St. Petersburg.

27. KHILKOV, GRIGORII D., comp. *Sbornik kniazia Khilkova* (Collection of Prince Khilkov). St. Petersburg, 1879.

Kölner inventar. See no. 55.

28. KULESHOV, VLADIMIR A., comp. *Nakazy sibirskim voevodam v XVII veke. Istoricheskii ocherk* (Instructions to Siberian voevodas in the seventeenth century. A historical outline). Tashkent, 1888.

29. KUZNETSOV-KRASNOIARSKII, INNOKENTII P., comp. *Istoricheskie akty XVII stoletiia (1633–1699). Materialy dlia istorii Sibiri* (Historical acts of the seventeenth century [1633–1699]. Material for the history of Siberia). 2 vols. Tomsk, 1890–1897.

30. MILOSLAVSKII, IL'IA D. "Stateinyi spisok o posol'stve Il'i Danilovicha Miloslavskago i d'iaka Leonteia Lazorevskago v Tsar'grad' v 7150 [1642] godu" (Journal of the embassy of Ilia Danilovich Miloslavskii and diak Leontei Lazorevskii to Constantinople in 1642), *Vremennik imperatorskago moskovskago obshchestva istorii i drevnostei rossiiskikh,* Vol. VIII (1850), pt. 2, pp. 1–136.

31. MÜLLER, GERHARD F. *Opisanie sibirskago tsarstva i veskh proizshedskikh v nem del ot nachala, a osoblivo ot pokoreniia ego rossiiskoi derzhave po sii vremena* (Description of the Siberian kingdom and all events occurring there from the beginning, especially from its subjugation to the Russian power, up to these times). 2d ed. St. Petersburg, 1787.

32. "Nakaz Narymskago ostroga voevode Vasil'iu Ivanovu 1622 goda, o

iasachnom i denezhnom sbore i kazennom khlebopashestve" (Instruction to voevoda Vasilii Ivanov in 1622 about the collection of iasak and money, and about state agriculture), *Vremennik imperatorskago moskovskago obshchestva istorii i drevnostei rossiiskikh,* Vol. XVII (1853), pt. 3, pp. 4–8.

33. NOVIKOV, NIKOLAI, comp. *Drevniaia rossiiskaia vivliofika, soderzhashchaia v sebe sobranie drevnostei rossiiskikh, do istorii, geografii i genealogii rossiiskiia kasaiushchikhsia* (Ancient Russian library, which contains a collection of Russian antiquities concerning history, geography, and genealogy). 20 vols. 2d ed., Moscow, 1788–1791.

34. ———. *Dopolnenie . . .* (Supplement). 11 vols. St. Petersburg, 1786–1801.

35. OGLOBLIN, NIKOLAI N. *Obozrenie stolbtsov i knig sibirskago prikaza (1592–1768 gg.)* (Survey of the rolls and books of the Siberian Department [1592–1768]). 4 vols. Moscow, 1895–1900.

36. OKUN', S. "K istorii Buriatii v XVII v." (Contribution to a history of the Buriats in the seventeenth century), *Krasnyi arkhiv,* Vol. LXXVI (1936), No. 3, pp. 156–191. Moscow.

Polnoe sobranie russkikh letopisei. See no. 42.

Polnoe sobranie zakonov. See no. 46.

37. POTANIN, G. N. "Materialy dlia istorii Sibiri" (Material for the history of Siberia), *Chteniia,* 1866, No. 4 (October–December), pp. 1–128; 1867, No. 1 (January–March), pp. 129–230; 1867, No. 2 (April–June), pp. 231–324.

38. POTEMKIN, PETR I. "Stateinoi spisok posol'stva stol'nika i namestnika borovskago, Petra Ivanovicha Potemkina, v Frantsiiu, v 7175 (1667) gode" (Journal of the embassy of chamberlain and lord of Borovsk, Peter Ivanovich Potemkin to France in 1667), *Drevniaia rossiiskaia vivliofika,* IV, 457–564.

39. Russia. Arkheograficheskaia kommissiia. *Akty istoricheskie* (Historical acts). 5 vols. St. Petersburg, 1841–1842; Index, 1843. (*A.I.*)

40. ———. *Dopolneniia k aktam istoricheskim* (Supplements to the historical acts). 12 vols. St. Petersburg, 1846–1872; Index, 1875. (*D.A.I.*)

41. ———. *Pamiatniki sibirskoi istorii XVIII v.* (Memorials of Siberian history of the eighteenth century). 2 vols. St. Petersburg, 1882–1885.

42. ———. *Polnoe sobranie russkikh letopisei* (Complete collection of Russian chronicles). 24 vols. in 11. St. Petersburg, 1841–1914.

43. ———. *Russkaia istoricheskaia biblioteka* (Russian historical library). 39 vols. St. Petersburg, 1875–1927. (*R.I.B.*)

44. ———. *Sibirskiia letopisi* (Siberian chronicles). St. Petersburg, 1907.

45. ———. Sobstvennaia ego imperatorskago velichestva kantseliariia. *Pamiatniki diplomaticheskikh snoshenii drevnei Rossii s derzhavami inostrannymi* (Memorials of diplomatic relations of Old Russia with foreign powers). 10 vols. St. Petersburg, 1851–1871.

46. ———. *Polnoe sobranie zakonov rossiiskoi imperii s 1649 goda* (Complete collection of laws of the Russian empire from 1649). [Series 1.] 44 vols. St. Petersburg, 1830. (*P.S.Z.*)

47. *Russian Primary Chronicle, The,* translated and edited by Samuel H. Cross. Harvard Studies and Notes in Philology and Literature, XII, 75–320. Cambridge, Mass., 1930.

Sbornik imperatorskago russkago istoricheskago obshchestva. See no. 25.

48. *Sobranie gosudarstvennykh gramot i dogovorov, khraniashchikhsia v gosudarstvennoi kollegii inostrannykh del* (Collection of state charters and treaties preserved in the state college of foreign affairs). Aleksei F. Malinovskii and others, eds. 5 vols. Moscow, 1813–1894.

49. SPAFARII, NIKOLAI G. "Pis'mo Nikolaia Spafariia k boiarinu Artemonu Sergeevichu Matveevu Iiul 1675" (Letter of Nikolai Spafarii to boiarin Artemy Sergeevich Matveev, July, 1675), Iu. V. Arsen'ev, ed., *Russkii arkhiv*, 1881, No. 1, pp. 52–57.

50. ———. *Puteshestvie chrez Sibir' ot Tobol'ska do Nerchinska i granits Kitaia russkago poslannika Nikolaia Spafariia v 1675 godu* (Journey across Siberia from Tobolsk to Nerchinsk and the borders of China of Russian ambassador Nikolai Spafarii in 1675), with introduction and notes by Iu. V. Arsen'ev, Zapiski imperatorskago russkago geograficheskago obshchestva po otdeleniiu etnografii, Vol. X. St. Petersburg, 1882.

51. *Torgovaia kniga* (Trade book), Ivan Sakharov, ed., Zapiski otdeleniia russkoi i slavianskoi arkheologii russkago arkheologicheskago obshchestva, I (1851), 106–139. St. Petersburg.

Incomplete versions in: Pavel A. Mukhanov, comp., *Sbornik Mukhanova* (Mukhanov's collection), 2d ed., Supplement, pp. 355–372, St. Petersburg, 1866; and *Vremennik imperatorskago moskovskago obshchestva istorii i drevnostei rossiiskikh*, VIII (1850), 1–22. Moscow.

52. TROTSKII, I. M., comp. *Kolonial'naia politika moskovskogo gosudarstva v. Iakutii XVII v.* (Colonial policy of the Muscovite state in Iakutiia in the seventeenth century). *Materialy po istorii narodov SSSR*, Vol. V = *Trudy istoriko-arkheograficheskago instituta akademii nauk SSSR*, Vol. XIV. Leningrad, 1936.

53. VAN ZUIDEN, D. S. *Bijdrage tot de kennis der Hollandsch-Russische relaties in de 16e–18e eeuw.* Amsterdam, 1911.

54. ———. "Nieuwe bijdrage tot de kennis van de Hollandsch-Russische relaties in de 16e–18e eeuw.," *Economisch-historisch jaarboek tot de economische geschiedenis van Nederland*, II (1916), 258–295.

55. Verein für hansische Geschichte. *Inventare hansischer Archive des sechszehnten Jahrhunderts.* 3 vols. Leipzig and Munich, 1896–1913.

56. VESELOVSKII, NIKOLAI I., comp. *Pamiatniki diplomaticheskikh i torgovykh snoshenii moskovskoi Rusi s Persiei* (Memorials of diplomatic and commercial relations of Muscovite Russia with Persia). 3 vols. Trudy vostochnago otdelniia imperatorskago russkago arkheologicheskago obshchestva, Vols. XX–XXII. St. Petersburg, 1890–1898.

57. VIKTOROV, ALEKSEI G., ed. *Opisanie zapisnykh knig i bumag starinnykh dvortsovykh prikazov, 1584–1725 g.* (Description of the record books and papers of the old court departments, 1584–1725). 2 vols. Moscow, 1877–1883.

VVEDENSKII, ANDREI A., *Torgovyi dom, XVI–XVII vekov.* See no. 168.

58. ZABELIN, IVAN E., comp. *Dopolneniia k dvortsovym razriadam po porucheniiu grafa Dmitriia Nikolaevicha Bludova sobrannyia iz knig i stolbtsov prezhdebyvshikh dvortsovykh prikazov arkhiv oruzheinoi pa-*

laty (Supplements to the court orders according to the commission of count Dmitrii Nikolaevich Bludov collected from the books and rolls belonging to the court departments of the archives of the Armory palace). In *Chteniia,* 1882, No. 1 (January–March), pt. 2, pp. 1–288, No. 3 (July–September), pt. 1, pp. 289–640.

Reprinted in one volume, Moscow, 1882. The *Chteniia* printing was used for this study.

CONTEMPORARY ACCOUNTS

59. BARBARO, GIOSOFAT, and CONTARINI, AMBROGIO. *Travels to Tana and Persia....* Translated from the Italian by William Thomas ... and S. A. Roy; edited by Lord Stanley. Hakluyt Society Works, Vol. XLIX. London, 1873.

60. CARLISLE, CHARLES H. *La Relation de trois ambassades de monseigneur le comte de Carlisle ... vers leurs sérénissimes majestés Alexey Michaelovitz, czar et grand duc de Moscovie; Charles, roi de Suéde, et Frederic III, roi de Danemark et Norwège.* Prince Augustin Galitzin, ed. Rev. ed., Paris, 1857.

61. COLLINS, SAMUEL. "Nyneshnee sostoianie Rossii, izlozhennoe v pis'me k drugu zhivushchemy v Londone" (The present state of Russia, written in a letter to a friend living in London), *Chteniia,* 1846, No. 1 (January–March), pt. 3, pp. 1–47.

62. DU HALDE, JEAN B. *Description géographique, historique, logique, politique, et physique de l'empire de la Chine et de la Tartarie chinoise.* 4 vols. 2d ed., The Hague, 1736.

63. FLETCHER, GILES, and HORSEY, SIR JEROME. *Russia at the Close of the Sixteenth Century. Comprising the Treatise* "Of the Russe Common Wealth" *by Dr. Giles Fletcher; and the Travels of Sir Jerome Horsey, Knt.* Edward A. Bond, ed. Hakluyt Society Works, Vol. XX. London, 1856.

64. HAKLUYT, RICHARD, comp. *The Principal Navigations, Voyages, Traffiques and Discoveries of the English Nation.* 10 vols. London, Toronto, and New York, 1927.

65. HERBERSTEIN, SIGISMUND VON, AND OTHERS. *Notes upon Russia: Being a Translation of the Earliest Account of That Country, Entitled Rerum Moscovitarum Commentarii, by the Baron Sigismund von Herberstein.* Translated and edited by R. H. Major. 2 vols. Hakluyt Society Works, Vols. X and XII. London, 1851–1852.

66. *Historiae ruthenicae scriptores exteri saeculi XVI.* Wojciech Starczewski, ed. Vol. I. Berlin and St. Petersburg, 1841.

Contains: Pt. II, Paulus Jovius Novocomena, "De legatione Basilii magnis principis Moscoviae ad Clementem VII. pontificem maximum liber," pp. 3–13; Pt. VI, "Anglorum navigatio ad Moscovitas," pp. 3–13.

67. IOVIUS, PAULUS. "The History, Written in the Latin tongue by Paulus Iouius, Byshop of Nuceria in Italie, of the Legation or Ambassade of Great Basilius Prince of Moscouia, to Pope Clement the VII. of That Name: in Which is Conteyned the description of Moscouia with the Regions Confinyng about the same, euen vnto the Great and Rych Empire of Cathay." Hakluyt Society Works, XII (1852), 228–256.

68. Jenkinson, Anthony, and Others. *Early Voyages and Travels to Russia and Persia. With Account of the First Intercourse of the English with Russia and Central Asia, by Way of the Caspian Sea.* E. Delmar Morgan and C. H. Coote, eds. 2 vols. Hakluyt Society Works, Vols. LXXII–LXXIII. London, 1886.

69. Kilburger, Johann P. "Kurzer Unterricht von dem russischen Handel, wie selbiger mit aus- und eingehenden Waaren 1674 durch ganz Russland getrieben worden," *Buschings Magazin für neue Historie und Geographie,* III (1769), 246–386. Hamburg.

70. Kotoshikhin, Grigorii. *O Rossii v tsarstvovanie Alekseiia Mikhailovicha* (Russia in the reign of Aleksei Mikhailovich). 3d ed., St. Petersburg, 1884.

71. Križanić, Juraj. *Russkoe gosudarstvo v polovine XVII veka. Rukopis' vremen tsaria Alekseia Mikhailovicha* (The Russian state in the middle of the seventeenth century. A manuscript of the time of tsar Aleksei Mikhailovich). 6 pts. in 1 vol. Moscow, 1859–1860.

72. Le Comte, Louis D. *Nouveaux mémoires sur l'état présent de la Chine.* 2 vols. 2d ed., Paris, 1697.

73. Marperger, Paul J. *Paul Jacob Marpergers . . . Schlesischer Kauffmann oder: ausführliche Beschreibung der schlesischen Commercien und deren jetzigen Zustandes.* Breslau and Leipzig, 1714.

74. Mayerberg, Augustin von. *Puteshestvie v Moskoviiu barona Avgustina Maierberga, chlena imperatorskago pridvornago soveta, i Goratsiia Vil'gel'ma Kal'vuchchi, kavalera i chlena pravitel'stvennago soveta nizhnei Avstrii, poslov avgusteishago rimskago imperatora Leopol'da k tsariu i velikomu kniaziu Alekseiu Mikhailovicha, v 1661 godu* (Journey to Muscovy of baron Augustin Mayerberg, member of the imperial privy council and Horace William Calvucci, cavalier and member of the administrative council of Lower Austria, ambassadors of the august Roman emperor Leopold to the tsar and grand prince Aleksei Mikhailovich, in 1661). Translated from the German by A. N. Shemiakin. In *Chteniia,* 1873, No. 3 (July–September), pt. 4, pp. 1–104, No. 4 (October–December), pt. 4, pp. 105–168; 1874, No. 1 (January–March), pt. 4, pp. 169–216.

Reprinted in one volume, Moscow, 1873. The *Chteniia* printing was used for this study.

75. Neville, De la (pseud.?). "Zapiski de-la Nevilla o Moskovii" (Memoirs of De la Neville about Muscovy), *Russkaia starina,* LXXI (September, 1891), 419–450, LXXII (November, 1891), 241–281.

76. Olearius, Adam. *The Voyages and Travels of the Ambassadors Sent by Frederick, Duke of Holstein, to the Great Duke of Muscovy, and the King of Persia, Begun in the Year 1633 and Finished in 1639.* Translated from the German by John Davies. London, 1662.

77. Paul, Archdeacon of Aleppo. *The Travels of Macarius, Patriarch of Antioch.* Translated from the Arabic by F. C. Belfour. 2 vols. London, 1829–1836.

78. Purchas, Samuel, comp. *Hakluyt Posthumus or Purchas His Pilgrimes, Contayning a History of the World in Sea Voyages and Lande Travells*

by Englishmen and Others. 20 vols. Glasgow and New York, 1906.

Volumes XI–XIII refer to Russia and Siberia.

79. REITENFELS, JACOB. *Skazaniia svetleishemu gertsogu toskanskomu Koz'me tret'mu o Moskovii. Paduia, 1680 g.* (Accounts for the most serene duke of Tuscany, Cosmo III, about Muscovy. Padua, 1680). In *Chteniia*, 1905, No. 3 (July–September), pt. 2, pp. 1–128; 1906, No. 3 (July–September), pt. 3, pp. 129–228.

Reprinted in Moscow, 1905. The *Chteniia* printing was used for this study.

80. ROBERTS, LEWES. *The Merchants Mappe of Commerce.* London, 1638.

81. RODES, JOHANN DE. "Bedenken über den russischen Handel im Jahre 1653," *Beiträge zur Kenntniss Russlands und seiner Geschichte*, pp. 241–276. G. Ewers and M. von Engelhardt, eds. Sammlung russischer Geschichte, Vol. X. Dorpat, 1816–1818.

82. SAVARY, JACQUES. *Le Parfait Négociant ou instruction générale pour ce qui regarde le commerce des marchandises de France, et des pays étrangers.* 2 vols. 5th ed. rev., Lyon, 1700–1701.

83. STADEN, HEINRICH VON. *Aufzeichnungen über den moskauer Staat.* Fritz Epstein, ed. Hamburgische Universität. Abhandlungen aus dem Gebiet der Auslandskunde, Vol. XXXIV. Hamburg, 1930.

84. STRALENBERG, PHILIP J. *An Historico-Geographical Description of the North and Eastern Parts of Europe and Asia; but More Especially of Russia, Siberia, and Great Tartary, etc.* Translated from the German. London, 1736.

85. TITOV, ANDREI A. *Sibir' v XVII v. Sbornik starinnykh russkikh statei o Sibiri i prilezhashchikh k nei zemliakh* (Siberia in the seventeenth century. A collection of Old Russian articles about Siberia and the lands bordering it). Moscow, 1890.

SECONDARY WORKS

86. ANDRIEVICH, VLADIMIR K. *Istoriia Sibiri* (History of Siberia). 5 vols. in 2. St. Petersburg, 1889.

87. BAASCH, ERNST. *Holländische Wirtschaftsgeschichte.* Handbuch der Wirtschaftsgeschichte. Georg Brodnitz, ed. Jena, 1927.

88. BADDELEY, JOHN F. *Russia, Mongolia, China. . . .* 2 vols. London and New York, 1919.

89. BAKHRUSHIN, SERGEI V. *Kazaki na Amure* (Cossacks on the Amur). Leningrad, 1925.

90. ———. *Ocherki po istorii kolonizatsii Sibiri v XVI i XVII vv.* (Outline of the history of the colonization of Siberia in the sixteenth and seventeenth centuries). Moscow, 1927.

91. ———. *Pokruta na sobolinykh promyslakh XVII veka* (Contracts in the sable trade in the seventeenth century). N.p., n.d.

92. BANTYSH-KAMENSKII, NIKOLAI N. *Diplomaticheskoe sobranie del mezhdu rossiiskim i kitaiskim gosudarstvami s 1619 po 1792-i god* (Collection relating to diplomatic relations between the Russian and Chinese states from 1619 to 1792). V. M. Florinskii, ed. Kazan, 1882.

93. BEREZHKOV, MIKHAIL N. *O torgovle Rusi s Gansoi do kontsa XV veka*

(The trade of Russia with the Hanse up to the end of the fifteenth century). Zapiski istoriko-filologicheskago fakul'teta imperatorskago s.-peterburgskago universiteta, Vol. III. St. Petersburg, 1879.

94. BERKH, VASILII N. *Tsarstvovanie tsaria Mikhaila Fedorovicha i vzgliad na mezhdutsarstve* (The reign of Tsar Mikhail Fedorovich and a review of the interregnum). St. Petersburg, 1832.

95. BRASS, EMIL. *Aus dem Reiche der Pelze.* 2 vols. in 1. Berlin, 1911.

96. BREGER, MARCUS. *Zur Handelsgeschichte der Juden in Polen während des 17. Jahrhunderts, mit besonderer Berücksichtigung der Judenschaft Posens.* Inaugural dissertation. Breslau, 1932.

97. BUTSINSKII, PETR N. *K istorii Sibiri: Surgut, Narym i Ketsk do 1645 g.* (A contribution to the history of Siberia: Surgut, Narym, and Ketsk to 1645). Kharkov, 1893.

98. ———. *Mangazeia i mangazeiskii uezd (1601–1645 gg.)* (Mangazeia and the Mangazeia uezd, 1601–1645). Kharkov, 1893.

99. ———. *Zaselenie Sibiri i byt pervykh eia nasel'nikov* (The settlement of Siberia and the life of its first settlers). Kharkov, 1889.

100. CAHEN, GASTON. *Histoire des relations de la Russie avec la Chine sous Pierre le Grand (1689–1730).* Paris, 1912.

101. CAMDEN, WILLIAM. *The History of the Most Renowned and Victorious Princess Elizabeth, Late Queen of England.* 4th ed. rev., London, 1688.

102. CHULKOV, M. *Istoricheskoe opisanie rossiiskoi kommertsii pri vsekh portakh i granitsakh ot drevnikh vremen do nyne nastoiashchego* (Historical description of Russian commerce at all ports and along all boundaries from ancient times to the present). 21 vols. St. Petersburg and Moscow, 1781–1788.

103. COXE, WILLIAM. *Account of the Russian Discoveries between Asia and America; to Which Are Added, the Conquest of Siberia, and the History of the Transactions and Commerce between Russia and China.* 2d ed. rev., London, 1780.

104. CRULL, JODOCUS. *The Ancient and Present State of Muscovy, Containing a Geographical, Historical and Political Account of All the Nations and Territories under the Jurisdiction of the Present Czar. . . .* 2 vols. London, 1698.

105. DAL', VLADIMIR. *Tolkovyi slovar' zhivogo velikorusskago iazyka* (Dictionary of the living great Russian language). J. A. Baudouin de Courtenay, ed. 4 vols. 4th ed. rev., St. Petersburg and Moscow, 1912.

106. DEARDORFF, NEVA R. *English Trade in the Baltic during the Reign of Elizabeth,* Studies in the History of English Commerce in the Tudor Period, pp. 213–332. New York, 1912.

107. D'IAKONOV, MIKHAIL A. *Ocherki obshchestvennago i gosudarstvennago stroia drevnei Rusi* (Outlines of the social and political structure of Old Russia). 4th ed. rev., St. Petersburg, 1912.

108. FALKE, JOHANNES. *Die Geschichte des deutschen Handels.* 2 vols. in 1. Leipzig, 1859.

109. FIRSOV, N. A. *Polozhenie inorodtsev severo-vostochnoi Rossii v moskovskom gosudarstve* (Position of the natives of northeastern Russia in the Muscovite state). Kazan, 1866.

110. FIRSOV, NIKOLAI N. *Chteniia po istorii Sibiri* . . . (Readings on the history of Siberia). 2 vols. in 1. Moscow, 1920–1921.

111. FISCHER, GERHARD. *Aus zwei Jahrhunderten leipziger Handelsgeschichte 1470–1650 (die kaufmännisch Einwanderung und ihre Auswirkungen).* Leipzig, 1929.

112. FISCHER, JOHANN E. *Sibirische Geschichte.* . . . 2 vols. St. Petersburg, 1768.

113. GOETZ, LEOPOLD K. *Deutsch-russische Handelsgeschichte des Mittelalters.* Lübeck, 1922.

114. GOLDER, FRANK A. *Russian Expansion on the Pacific, 1641–1850.* Cleveland, 1914.

115. HAMEL, JOSEPH VON. *England and Russia, Comprising the Voyages of John Tradescant the Elder, Sir Hugh Willoughby, Richard Chancellor, Nelson, and Others to the White Sea, etc.* Translated from the German by John S. Leigh. London, 1854.

116. HASSE, ERNST. *Geschichte der leipziger Messen.* Fürstlich Jablonowski'-schen Gesellschaft: Preisschriften, XXV. Leipzig, 1885.

117. HEIDERICH, JEAN H. *Das leipziger Kürschnergewerbe.* Heidelberg, 1897.

118. KAPTEREV, NIKOLAI F. *Kharakter otnoshenii Rossii k pravoslavnomu vostoku v XVI i XVII stoletiiakh* (Character of Russia's relations with the orthodox East in the sixteenth and seventeenth centuries). 2d ed. Sergiev Posad, 1914.

119. KARAMZIN, NIKOLAI M. *Istoriia gosudarstva rossiiskago* (History of the Russian State). 12 vols. 2d ed., St. Petersburg, 1818–1829.

120. KASHIN, V. N. *Torgovlia i torgovyi kapital v moskovskom gosudarstve* (Trade and commercial capital in the Muscovite state). Pamiatniki sotsial'no-ekonomicheskoi istorii Rossii. A. I. Zaozerskii and V. N. Kashin, eds. Leningrad, 1925 [1926?].

121. KERNER, ROBERT J. *The Urge to the Sea: The Course of Russian History.* Berkeley, 1942.

122. KIZEVETTER, ALEKSANDR A. *Russkii sever* (The Russian North). Vologda, 1919.

123. KLEIN, JOSEPH. *Der sibirische Pelzhandel und seine Bedeutung für die Eroberung Sibiriens.* Inaugural dissertation. Bonn, 1906.

124. KLIUCHEVSKII, VASILII O. *History of Russia.* Translated by C. J. Hogarth. 5 vols. London and New York, 1911–1931.

125. ———. *Opyty i issledovaniia* (Essays and researches). Petrograd, 1918.
Contains: "Khoziaistvennaia deiatel'nost' solovetskogo monastyria v belomorskom krae," pp. 1–31; "Russkii rubl'," pp. 107–183.

126. ———. *Skazaniia inostrantsev o moskovskom gosudarstve* (Foreign accounts about the Muscovite state). New ed., Petrograd, 1918.

127. KORDT, VEN'IAMIN A. *Ocherk snoshenii moskovskago gosudarstva s respublikoiu soedinennykh Niderlandov do 1631 g.* (Outline of the relations of the Muscovite state with the republic of the united Netherlands to 1631). In *Sbornik imperatorskago istoricheskago obshchestva,* CXVI, iii–cccxlvii. St. Petersburg, 1902.

128. KORSAK, ALEKSANDR K. *Istoriko-statisticheskoe obozrenie torgovykh snoshenii Rossii s Kitaem* (Historical-statistical survey of trade relations of Russia with China). Kazan, 1857.

129. KOSTOMAROV, NIKOLAI I. *Ocherki torgovli moskovskago gosudarstva v XVI i XVII vv.* (Outlines of the trade of the Muscovite state in the sixteenth and seventeenth centuries). Sobranie sochinenii N. I. Kostomarova; istoricheskiia monografii i izsledovaniia, Bk. VIII, vol. XX. St. Petersburg, 1905.

130. KRASHENINNIKOV, STEPAN P. *A History of Kamtschakta, and the Kurilski Islands, with the Countries Adjacent.* Translated from the Russian by James Grieve. London and Glocester, 1764.

131. KROKER, ERNST. *Handelsgeschichte der Stadt Leipzig; die Entwicklung des leipziger Handels und der leipziger Messen, von der Gründung der Stadt bis auf die Gegenwart.* Leipzig, 1925.

132. KULISHER, IOSIF M. *Istoriia russkogo narodnogo khoziaistva* (History of Russia's national economy). 2 vols. Moscow, 1925.

133. ———. *Istoriia russkoi torgovli do XIX-go veka vkliuchitel'no* (History of Russian trade through the nineteenth century). Petrograd, 1923.

134. ———. *Russische Wirtschaftsgeschichte.* Handbuch der Wirtschaftsgeschichte. Georg Brodnitz, ed. Jena, 1925.

135. KURTS, B. G. *Russko-kitaiskie snosheniia v XVI, XVII i XVIII stoletiiakh* (Russo-Chinese relations in the sixteenth, seventeenth, and eighteenth centuries). Vseukrainskaia nauchnaia assotsiatsiia vostokovedeniia. Kharkov, 1929.

136. LANTZEFF, GEORGE V. *Siberia in the Seventeenth Century: A Study in Colonial Administration.* Univ. Calif. Publ. Hist., Vol. 30. Berkeley, 1943.

137. LAPPO-DANILEVSKII, ALEKSANDR S. *Organizatsiia priamogo oblozhenie v moskovskom gosudarstve so vremen smuty do epokhi preobrazovanii* (The organization of direct taxation in the Muscovite state from the Troublous Times to the epoch of reforms). Zapiski istoriko-filologicheskago fakul'teta imperatorskago s.-peterburgskago universiteta, Vol. XXIII. St. Petersburg, 1890.

138. ———. *Russkiia promyshlennyia i torgovyia kompanii v pervoi polovine XVIII stoletiia* (Russian industrial and trading companies in the first half of the eighteenth century). St. Petersburg, 1899.

139. LASSEN, ANDREW P. "Commerce in the Baltic from 1500 to 1700, with Special Reference to the Decline of the Hanseatic league." Unpublished doctoral dissertation. Berkeley, 1934.

140. LIKHACHEV, NIKOLAI P. *Razriadnye d'iaki XVI veka. Opyt istoricheskago izsledovaniia. . . .* (Ranking diaks of the sixteenth century. An essay in historical investigation). St. Petersburg, 1888.

141. LODYZHENSKII, KONSTANTIN. *Istoriia russkago tamozhennago tarifa* (History of the Russian customs tariff). St. Petersburg, 1886.

142. LOMER, HEINRICH. *Der Rauchwarenhandel. Geschichte, Betriebsweise und Warenkunde.* Leipzig, 1864.

143. MEL'GUNOV, PETR P. *Ocherki po istorii russkoi torgovli IX–XVIII v.v.* (Outline of the history of Russian trade from the ninth to the eighteenth centuries). Posthumous ed., Moscow, 1905.

144. MILIUKIN, A. S. *Ocherki po istorii iuridicheskago polozheniia inostrannykh kuptsov v moskovskom gosudarstve* (Outline of the history of the juridi-

cal position of foreign merchants in the Muscovite state). Zapiski imperatorskago novo-rossiiskago universiteta iuridicheskago fakul'teta, Vol. VIII. Odessa, 1912.

MÜLLER, GERHARD F. *Opisanie sibirskago tsarstva.* See no. 31.

———. *Sammlung russischer Geschichte.* See no. 155.

145. NETTA, GHERON. *Die Handelsbeziehungen zwischen Leipzig und Ost- und Südosteuropa bis zum Verfall der Warenmessen.* Inaugural dissertation. Zurich, 1920.

146. NIKITSKII, ALEKSANDR I. *Istoriia ekonomicheskago byta velikago Novgoroda* (History of the economic life of Novgorod the Great). Moscow, 1893.

147. OGORODNIKOV, VLADIMIR I. *Zavoevanie russkimi Sibiri* (Conquest of Siberia by the Russians). Vol. II, pt. 1. *Ocherki istorii Sibiri do nachala XIX st.* Vladivostok, 1924.

148. ———. *Russkaia gosudarstvennaia vlast' i sibirskie inorodtsy v XVI–XVIII v.v.* (Russian administration and the Siberian natives from the sixteenth to eighteenth centuries). *Ibid.*, pt. 3. Irkutsk, 1920.

149. PIRENNE, HENRI. *Medieval Cities, Their Origins and the Revival of Trade.* Translated from the French by F. D. Halsey. Princeton, 1925.

150. PLATONOV, SERGEI F. *Boris Godunov.* Petrograd, 1921.

151. ———. *Ocherki po istorii smuty v moskovskom gosudarstve XVI–XVII v.v.* (Outlines of the history of the "Troubles" in the Muscovite state in the sixteenth and seventeenth centuries). Zapiski istoriko-filologicheskago fakul'teta imperatorskago s.-peterburgskago universiteta, Vol. LII. St. Petersburg, 1899.

152. ———. *Proshloe russkogo severa; ocherki po istorii kolonizatsii Pomor'ia* (The past of the Russian North; outline of the history of the colonization of the maritime country). Petrograd, 1923.

153. POKROVSKII, MIKHAIL N. *History of Russia, from the Earliest Times to the Rise of Commercial Capitalism.* Translated from Vol. I of the Russian edition and edited by J. D. Clarkson and M. R. M. Griffiths. New York, 1931.

154. ———. *Ocherk istorii russkoi kultury* (Outline of the history of Russian culture). 2 vols. 5th ed., Petrograd, 1923.

155. *Sammlung russischer Geschichte.* G. F. Müller, ed. 9 vols. St. Petersburg, 1732–1764; Vol. X, Dorpat, 1816–1818.

156. SCOTT, WILLIAM R. *The Constitutions and Finance of English, Scottish and Irish Joint-Stock Companies to 1720.* 3 vols. Cambridge, England, 1910.

157. SEMENOV, ALEKSEI V. *Izuchenie istoricheskikh svedenii o rossiiskoi vneshnei torgovle i promyshlennosti s poloviny XVII-go stoletiia po 1858 god* (Study of the historical knowledge about Russian foreign trade and industry from the middle of the seventeenth century to 1858). 3 vols. St. Petersburg, 1859.

158. SEREDONIN, SERGEI M. *Sochinenie Dzhil'sa Fletchera "Of the Russe Common Wealth" kak istoricheskii istochnik* (Giles Fletcher's work "Of the Russe Common Wealth" as an historical source). Zapiski istoriko-filologicheskago fakul'teta imperatorskago s.-peterburgskago universiteta, Vol. XVII. St. Petersburg, 1891.

159. SHATILOV, M. B. *Vakhovskie ostiaki* (Vakhov Ostiaks). Trudy tomskogo kraevogo muzeia, Vol. IV. Tomsk, 1931.
160. SHCHAPOV, A. P. *Sochineniia* (Works). 3 vols. St. Petersburg, 1906–1907.
161. SHCHEGLOV, IVAN V. *Khronologicheskii perechen' vazhneishikh dannykh iz istorii Sibiri, 1032–1882 gg.* (Chronological summary of the most important data from the history of Siberia, 1032–1882). Irkutsk, 1883.
162. SLOVTSOV, PETR A. *Istoricheskoe obozrenie Sibiri* (Historical survey of Siberia). 2 vols. in 1. St. Petersburg, 1886.
163. SOLOV'EV, SERGEI M. *Istoriia Rossii s drevneishikh vremen* (History of Russia from earliest times). 7 vols. St. Petersburg [1894?–1895?].
164. STORCH, HEINRICH. *Historisch-statistische Gemälde des russischen Reichs am Ende des XVIII Jahrhunderts.* 8 vols. St. Petersburg and Leipzig, 1799–1803.
165. SVIATLOVSKII, VLADIMIR V. *Primitivno-torgovoe gosudarstvo, kak forma byta* (The primitive commercial state as a type of culture). Zapiski istoriko-filologicheskago fakul'teta imperatorskago s.-peterburgskago universiteta, Vol. CXVIII. St. Petersburg, 1914.
166. TRUSEVICH, KH. *Posol'skiia i torgovyia snosheniia Rossii s Kitaem (do XIX v.)* (Ambassadorial and commercial relations of Russia with China [to the nineteenth century]). Moscow, 1882.
167. VINCENT, JOHN M. *Costume and Conduct in the Laws of Basel, Bern, and Zurich, 1370–1800.* Baltimore, 1935.
168. VVEDENSKII, ANDREI A. *Torgovyi dom, XVI–XVII vekov* (A commercial house of the sixteenth and seventeenth centuries). Leningrad, 1924.
169. WITSEN, NIKOLAUS. *Noord und oost Tartarye.* 2 vols. Amsterdam, 1692.
170. ZAMYSLOVSKII, EGOR E. *Gerberstein i ego istoriko-geograficheskiia izvestiia o Rossii . . . s prilozheniem materialov dlia istoriko-geograficheskago atlasa XVI v.* (Herberstein and his historical-geographical information about Russia . . . with added information for an historical-geographical atlas of the sixteenth century). Zapiski istoriko-filologicheskago fakul'teta imperatorskago s.-peterburgskago universiteta, Vol. XIII. St. Petersburg, 1884.
171. ZHIGAREV, SERGEI. *Russkaia politika v vostochnom voprose (eia istoriia v XVI–XIX vekakh, kriticheskaia otsenka i budushchiia zadachi)* (Russian policy in the Eastern question: its history from the sixteenth to the nineteenth century, a critical evaluation of it, and its future problems). 2 vols. Moscow, 1896.

ARTICLES

172. BAER, K. G. VON. "Uebersicht des Jagd-Erwerbes in Sibirien, besonders im Östlichen," *Beiträge zur Kenntniss des russischen Reichs und der angränzenden Länder Asiens*, VII (1845), 117–272. St. Petersburg.
173. BAKHRUSHIN, SERGEI V. "Agenty russkikh torgovykh liudei XVII veka" (The agents of the Russian merchants of the seventeenth century), *Uchenye zapiski instituta istorii rossiiskoi assotsiatsii nauchno-issledovatel'skikh institutov obshchestvennykh nauk*, IV (1929), 71–88. Moscow.
174. ———. "Iasak v Sibiri v XVII veke" (Iasak in Siberia in the seventeenth century), *Sibirskie ogni*, 1927, No. 3 (May–June), pp. 95–129.
175. ———. "Istoricheskie sud'by Iakutii" (The historical destiny of Iaku-

tiia), *Iakutiia: sbornik statei,* P. V. Vittenburg, ed., pp. 275–322. Leningrad, 1927.

176. ———. *Sibirskie slobodchiki v XVII v.* (Siberian slobodchiks of the seventeenth century), Trudy gosudarstvennogo kolonizatsionnogo nauchno-issledovatel'skogo instituta, II (1926), 127–138. Moscow.

177. ———. "Sibirskie sluzhilye tatary v XVII v." (Siberian serving Tatars in the seventeenth century), *Istoricheskie zapiski,* I (1937), 55–80.

178. ———. "Torgi gostia Nikitina v Sibiri i Kitae" (The trade of gost Nikitin in Siberia and China), *Sbornik statei: Pamiati Aleksandra Nikolaevicha Savina, 1873–1923.* Trudy instituta istorii rossiiskoi assotsiatsii nauchno-issledovatel'skikh institutov obshchestvennykh nauk, I (1926), 355–390. Moscow.

179. Bazilevich, K. V. "K voprosu ob izuchenii tamozhennykh knig XVII v." (On the question of the study of the customs books of the seventeenth century), *Problemy istochnikovedeniia,* II (1936), 71–90. Trudy istoriko-arkheograficheskogo instituta akademii nauk SSSR, Vol. XVII. Moscow and Leningrad.

180. ———. "Krupnoe torgovoe predpriiatie v moskovskom gosudarstve v pervoi polovine XVII veka" (A big commercial enterprise in the Muscovite state during the first half of the seventeenth century), *Izvestiia akademii nauk,* Otdelenie obshchestvennykh nauk, ser. 7, 1932, No. 9, pp. 783–811. Leningrad.

181. ———. "Tamozhennye knigi kak istochnik ekonomicheskoi istorii Rossii" (The customs books as a source of the economic history of Russia), *Problemy istochnikovedeniia,* I (1933), 110–129. Trudy istoriko-arkheograficheskogo instituta akademii nauk SSSR, Vol. IX. Moscow and Leningrad.

182. ———. "Torgovlia velikogo Ustiuga v seredine XVII veka" (The trade of Ustiug the Great at the middle of the seventeenth century), *Uchenye zapiski instituta istorii rossiiskoi assotsiatsii nauchno-issledovatel'skikh institutov obshchestvennykh nauk,* IV (1929), 89–102. Moscow.

183. Beazley, C. Raymond. "The Russian Expansion towards Asia and the Arctic in the Middle Ages (to 1500)," *American Historical Review,* XIII (1907–1908), 731–741.

184. Beliaev, I. D. "O geograficheskikh svedeniiakh v drevnei Rossii" (Geographical knowledge in old Russia), *Zapiski imperatorskago russkago geograficheskago obshchestva,* VI (1852), 1–264. St. Petersburg.

185. Bogoroditskii, D. "Ocherk torgovli Nizhniago-Novgoroda za XVI i XVII vv." (Outline of the trade of Nizhnii-Novgorod for the sixteenth and seventeenth centuries), *Kievskiia universitetskiia izvestiia,* LII (No. 7, July, 1912), 1–24.

186. *Chteniia v imperatorskom obshchestve istorii i drevnostei rossiiskikh pri moskovskom universitete* (Publications of the Imperial Society of Russian History and Antiquity at the University of Moscow). 185 vols. Moscow, 1861–1916. (Cited as *Chteniia.*)

187. Chulkov, N. P. "Erofei Pavlov Khabarov: dobytchik i pribyl'shchik XVII veka" (. . . freebooter and profiteer of the seventeenth century), *Russkii arkhiv,* 1898, Bk. 1, No. 2, pp. 177–190.

188. DOVNAR-ZAPOL'SKII, MITROFAN V. "Torgovlia i promyshlennost' Moskvy v XVI–XVII vv." (Trade and industry of Moscow from the sixteenth to seventeenth centuries), *Moskva v ee proshlom i nastoiashchem,* VI (No. 2, 1910), 5–67.

189. GROSBERG, O. "Das nördliche Eismeer und die wirtschaftliche Erschliessung Sibiriens," *Deutsche Monatsschrift für Russland,* II (1913), 983 ff.

190. HELLER, HERMANN F. "Die Handelswege Inner-Deutschlands im 16., 17. und 18. Jahrhundert und ihre Beziehungen zu Leipzig," *Neues archiv für sächsische Geschichte und Alterthumskunde,* V (1884), 1–72. Dresden.

191. IANITSKII, N. "Torgovlia pushnym tovarom v XVII v." (The trade in furs in the seventeenth century), *Kievskiia universitetskiia izvestiia,* LII (No. 9, September, 1912), 1–33.

192. IL'INSKII, A. K. "Gorodskoe naselenie novgorodskoi oblasti v XVI i XVII veke" (Urban settlement of Novgorod province in the sixteenth and seventeenth centuries), *Zh.M.N.P.,* CLXXXV (1876) June, 210–278.

193. IZIUMOV, A. "Razmery russkoi torgovli XVII veka cherez Arkhangel'sk v sviazi s neobsledovannymi arkhivnymi istochnikama" (Size of Russian trade of the seventeenth century through Arkhangelsk in connection with unworked archival sources), *Izvestiia arkhangel'skago obshchestva izucheniia russkago severa,* 1912, No. 6 (March 15), pp. 250–258.

194. J. R. [or KYLL?]. "The Trade's Increase," *Harleian Miscellany,* IV, 212–231. London, 1809.

195. KRASNOPEROV, I. M. "Ocherk promyshlennosti i torgovli smolenskago kniazhestva s drevneishikh vremen do XV veka" (Outline of the industry and trade of Smolensk principality from earliest times to the fifteenth century), *Istoricheskoe obozrenie: Sbornik istoricheskago obshchestva pri imperatorskom s.-peterburgskom universitete,* VII (1894), 64–111. St. Petersburg.

196. KURTS, B. G. "Iz istorii torgovykh snoshenii Rossii s Kitaem v XVII st." (From the history of the commercial relations of Russia with China in the seventeenth century), *Novyi vostok,* XXIII–XXIV, 331–340. Moscow.

197. KUSKE, BRUNO. "Die weltwirtschaftlichen Anfänge Sibiriens und sein Nachbargebiet vom 16. bis 18. Jahrhundert," *Jahrbuch für Gesetzgebung, Verwaltung und Volkswirtschaft im deutschen Reiche,* n.s., Vol. XLVI (1922), pt. 1, pp. 201–250, pt. 2, pp. 85–116 [391–422]. Leipzig.

198. LAPPO-DANILEVSKII, A. S. "Inozemtsy v Rossii v tsarstvovanie Mikhaila Fedorovicha" (Foreigners in Russia in the reign of Mikhail Fedorovich), *Zh.M.N.P.,* CCXLI (1885) September, 66–106.

199. LIUBIMENKO, INNA I. "Letters Illustrating the Relations of England and Russia in the Seventeenth Century," *English Historical Review,* XXXII, (No. 125, January, 1917), 92–103.

200. ———. "Les Marchands anglais en Russie au XVIIe siècle," *Revue historique,* CXLI (No. 1, September–October, 1922), 1–39.

201. ———. "A Project for the Acquisition of Russia by James I," *English Historical Review,* XXIX (No. 114, April, 1914), 246–256.

202. ———. "The Struggle of the Dutch with the English for the Russian Market in the Seventeenth Century," *Transactions of the Royal Historical Society,* ser. 4, Vol. VII (1924), pp. 27–51.

203. ———. "Torgovyia snosheniia Rossii s Angliei pri pervykh Romanovykh" (Commercial relations of Russia with England in the time of the first Romanovs), *Zh.M.N.P.*, n.s., LXVI (November–December, 1916), 1–32, 137–190.

204. Makarov, I. S. "Volostnye torzhki v sol'vychegodskom uezde v pervoi polovine XVII v." (Volost trade centers in Solvychegodsk uezd in the first half of the seventeenth century), *Istoricheskie zapiski*, I (1937), 193–219.

205. Malinovskii, Aleksei F. "Izvestie ob otpravleniiakh v Indiiu rossiiskikh poslannikov, gontsov i kupchin tovarami i o priezdakh v Rossiiu indeitsev, s 1469 po 1751 god" (Information concerning the dispatch of Russian envoys, messengers, and merchants with goods to India and the arrival of Indians in Russia, from 1409 to 1751), *Trudy i letopisi obshchestva istorii i drevnostei rossiiskikh, uchrezhdennago pri imperatorskom moskovskom universitete*, VII (1837), 121–207.

206. Miliukov, Pavel N. "Gosudarstvennoe khoziaistvo Rossii v sviazi s reformoi Petra velikago" (State economy of Russia in relation to the reforms of Peter the Great), *Zh.M.N.P.*, CCLXXI (1890), September, 1–107, October, 301–357; CCLXXII (November–December, 1890), 1–79; CCLXXIII (January–February, 1891), 1–47; CCLXXIV (March–April, 1891), 30–146; CCLXXVI (July–August, 1891), 289–393; CCLXXVII (September–October, 1891), 408–482; CCLXXIX (1892), January, 65–124, February, 261–347.

207. Müller, Gerhard F. "Nachrichten von der Handlung in Sibirien," *Sammlung russischer Geschichte*, III, 413–612.

208. ———. "Nachrichten von dreien im Gebiete der Stadt Casan, wohnhaften heidnischen Völkern, den Tscheremissen, Tschuwaschen, und Wotiacken," *ibid.*, pp. 305–412.

209. ———. "Nachrichten von Seereisen, und zur See gemachten Entdeckungen, die von Russland aus längst den Küsten des Eismeeres und auf dem Ostlichen Weltmeere gegen Japon und Amerika geschehen sind," *ibid.*, pp. 1–304

210. ———. "Sibirskaia istoriia" (Siberian history), *Ezhemesiachnyia sochineniia i izvestiia o uchenykh delakh akademii nauk*, XVIII (October, 1763), 354–368; XIX (1764), January, pp. 3–43, February, pp. 99–135, March, pp. 195–237, April, pp. 291–324, May, pp. 387–418, June, pp. 483–528.

211. Ogloblin, Nikolai N. "Semen Dezhnev (1638–1671 gg.)," *Zh.M.N.P.*, CCLXXII (November–December, 1890), 249–306.

212. Ogorodnikov, E. K. "Pribrezh'ia ledovitago i belago morei s ikh pritokami po knige bol'shago chertezha" (Coast of the Arctic and White seas with the tributaries, according to the book of the grand survey), *Zapiski imperatorskago russkago geograficheskago obshchestva po otdeleniiu etnografii*, VII (1877), 1–265.

213. Ogorodnikov, Vladimir I. "Russkaia gosudarstvennaia vlast' i sibirskie inorodtsy v XVI–XVIII v.v." (The Russian administration and the Siberian natives from the sixteenth to eighteenth century), *Sbornik trudov professorov i prepodavatelei gosudarstvennogo irkutskogo uni-*

versiteta, otdel 1, "Nauki gumanitarnye," I (1921), 69–113. Irkutsk. This is the next to last chapter of the larger work under the same title. See no. 148.

214. OKSENOV, A. V. "Politicheskiia otnosheniia moskovskago gosudarstva k iugorskoi zemle" (Political connections of the Muscovite state with Iugra), *Zh.M.N.P.*, CCLXXIII (January–February, 1891), 245–272.

215. ———. "Slukhi i vesti o Sibiri do Ermaka" (Reports and news of Siberia prior to Ermak), *Sibirskii sbornik (Prilozhenie k 'Vostochnomu obozreniiu'), 1886 g.*, IV, 107–117. St. Petersburg, 1887.

216. ———. "Snosheniia Novgoroda velikago s iugorskoi zemlei" (Relations of Novgorod the Great with Iugra), *Literaturnyi sbornik Vostochnago obozreniia*, pp. 425–445. St. Petersburg, 1885.

217. ———. "Starye puti iz predelov moskovskago gosudarstva v sibirskuiu zemliu" (Old routes from the frontier of the Muscovite state to Siberia), *Tomskiia gubernskiia vedomosti*, 1888, No. 12.

218. ———. "Torgovye snosheniia russkikh s obitateliami severo-zapadnoi Azii do epokhi Ermaka" (Commercial relations of the Russians with the inhabitants of northwestern Asia prior to the period of Ermak), *ibid.*, 1888, No. 10, pp. 7–9, No. 11, pp. 13–15.

219. POGODIN, M. "Drevniaia russkaia torgovlia" (Early Russian trade), *Zh.M.N.P.*, Vol. XLVIII (1845), pt. 2, pp. 81–132.

220. POKROVSKII, B. "Torgovlia" (Trade), *Entsiklopedicheskii slovar'*, LXVI, 541–588. St. Petersburg, 1901.

221. POPOV, V. A. "Dvizhenie narodonaseleniia v vologodskoi gubernii" (The movement of population in the Vologda district), *Zapiski imperatorskago russkago geograficheskago obshchestva po otdeleniiu statistiki*, II (1871), 61–282.

222. POTANIN, GRIGORII N. "O karavanoi torgovle s dzhungarskoi Bukhariev v XVIII v." (The caravan trade with the Sungarian Bukharans in the 18th century), *Chteniia*, 1868, No. 2 (April–June), *otdel* 5, pp. 21–113.

223. ———. "Privoz i vyvoz tovarov goroda Tomska v polovine XVII stoletiia" (The import and export of goods at Tomsk in the middle of the 17th century), *Vestnik imperatorskago russkago geograficheskago obshchestva*, Vol. XXVII (1859 [printed 1860]), pt. 2, pp. 125–144.

224. PYPIN, A. N. "Pervyia izvestiia o Sibiri i russkoe eia zaselenie" (First information about Siberia and its settlement by Russians), *Vestnik Evropy*, XXVI (No. 8, August, 1891), 742–789.

225. RACHEL, HUGO. "Polnische Handels- und Zollverhältnisse im 16. bis 18. Jahrhundert," *Jahrbuch für Gesetzgebung, Verwaltung und Volkswirtschaft im deutschen Reich*, n.s., Vol. XXXIII (1909), pt. 2, pp. 41–62 [469–490].

226. RALEIGH, SIR WALTER. "Observations Touching Trade and Commerce with the Hollander, and Other Nations," *A Select Collection of Scarce and Valuable Tracts on Commerce*, pp. 1–29. J. R. McColloch, ed. London, 1859.

227. RANKE, ERMENTRUDE VON. "Kölns binnendeutscher Verkehr im 16. und 17. Jahrhundert," *Hansische Geschichtsblätter*, Verein für hansische Geschichte, XXIX (1924), 64–77.

228. Rauers, Friedrich. "Zur Geschichte der alten Handelsstrassen in Deutschland," *Dr. A. Petermanns Mitteilungen aus Justus Pethes' geographische Anstalt,* Vol. LII (1906), pt. 3, pp. 49–59; map no. 6. Gotha.

229. Savel'ev, Pavel. "O torgovle volzhshikh bulgar v IX i X vekakh" (The trade of the Volga Bulgars in the ninth and tenth centuries), *Zh.M.N.P.*, Vol. XLIX (1846), pt. 2, pp. 31–50.

230. Seredonin, Sergei M. "Istoricheskii ocherk zavoevaniia aziatskoi Rossii" (Historical outline of the conquest of Asiatic Russia), *Aziatskaia Rossiia,* I, 1–38. St. Petersburg, 1914.

231. Solov'ev, Sergei M. "Moskovskie kuptsy v XVII v." (Muscovite merchants in the seventeenth century), *Sovremennik,* Vol. LXXI (1858), No. 10, pp. 427–440.

232. ———. "Russkaia promyshlennost' i torgovlia v XVI veka" (Russian industry and trade in the sixteenth century), *ibid.*, Vol. LXI (1857), No. 1, pt. 2, pp. 1–12.

233. Stashevskii, E. D. "Piatina 142-go goda i torgovo-promyshlennye tsentry moskovskago gosudarstva" (The one-fifth capital levy of 1634 and the commercial-industrial centers of the Muscovite state), *Zh.M.N.P.*, n.s., XXXVIII (1912) April, 248–319, XXXIX (1912) May, 79–113.

"The Trade's Increase," *Harleian Miscellany.* See No. 194.

234. Tishchenko, A. V. "K istorii Koly i Pechengi v XVI veke" (A contribution to the history of Kola and Pechenga in the sixteenth century), *Zh.M.N.P.*, n.s., XLVI (July–August, 1913), 99–113.

235. Tret'iakov, P. M. "Pervobytnaia okhota v severnoi Azii" (Primitive hunting in northern Asia), *Iz istorii rodovogo obshchestva na territorii SSSR,* pp. 220–262. Izvestiia gosudarstvennoi akademii istorii material'noi kul'tury, Vol. CVI. Moscow and Leningrad, 1935 [1934].

236. Tyzhnov, I. I. "Obzor inostrannykh izvestii o Sibiri 2-i poloviny XVI veka" (Sketch of the information of foreigners about Siberia in the second half of the sixteenth century), *Sibirskii sbornik (Prilozhenie k 'Vostochnomu obozreniiu'), 1887 g.*, pp. 101–147. St. Petersburg, 1887.

237. Ulianitskii, V. A. "Snosheniia Rossii s sredneiu Azieiu i Indieiu v XVI–XVII vv." (The relations of Russia with Central Asia and India in the sixteenth and seventeenth centuries), *Chteniia,* 1888, no. 3 (July–September), pt. 2, pp. 1–62.

238. Vernadskii, George. "The Expansion of Russia," *Transactions of the Connecticut Academy of Sciences,* XXXI (July, 1933), 393–425.

239. ———. "Gosudarevy sluzhilye i promyshlennye liudi vostochnoi Sibiri XVII veka" (The state serving men and enterprisers of Eastern Siberia in the seventeenth century), *Zh.M.N.P.*, n.s., LVI (March–April, 1915), 332–354.

240. ———. "Protiv solntsa" (Against the sun), *Russkaia mysl',* XXXV (No. 1, January, 1914), 56–79. St. Petersburg.

241. Volens, N. V. "Ocherk khoziaistvennogo stroia Iakutii" (Outline of the economic organization of Iakutiia), *Iakutiia: sbornik statei,* P. V. Vittenburg, ed., pp. 675–702. Leningrad, 1927.

242. Vvedenskii, Andrei A. "Anika Stroganov v svoem sol'vychechegodskom khoziaistve" (Anika Stroganov in his Solvychegodsk business), *Sbornik*

statei po russkoi istorii posviashchennykh S. F. Platonovu, pp. 90–113. Petrograd, 1922.

243. ———. "Sluzhashchie i rabotnye liudi u Stroganovykh v XVI–XVII v." (The serving men and working men of the Stroganovs in the sixteenth and seventeenth centuries), *Trud v Rossii*, I (1924), 54–71.

244. WRETTS-SMITH, MILDRED. "The English in Russia during the Second Half of the Sixteenth Century," *Transactions of the Royal Historical Society*, ser. 4, III (1920), 72–102.

245. ZAMYSLOVSKII, EGOR E. "Chertezhi sibirskikh zemel', XVI–XVII vekov" (Geographical survey of the Siberian lands, sixteenth and seventeenth centuries), *Zh.M.N.P.*, CCLXXV (May–June, 1891), 334–347.

246. ———. "Snosheniia Rossii s Shvetsiei i Daniei v tsarstvovanie Fedora Alekseevicha" (Russia's relations with Sweden and Denmark in the reign of Fedor Alekseevich), *Russkii vestnik*, 1889 (No. 1, January), pp. 1–36.

247. *Zhurnal ministerstva narodnago prosveshcheniia* (Journal of the Ministry of Public Enlightenment). 362 vols. St. Petersburg, 1834–1905. New series, 70 vols. St. Petersburg, 1906–1917. (Cited as *Zh.M.N.P.*).

INDEX

INDEX

www.ingramcontent.com/pod-product-compliance
Lightning Source LLC
LaVergne TN
LVHW020537100826
845148LV00010B/1512